Islam and the Abode of War

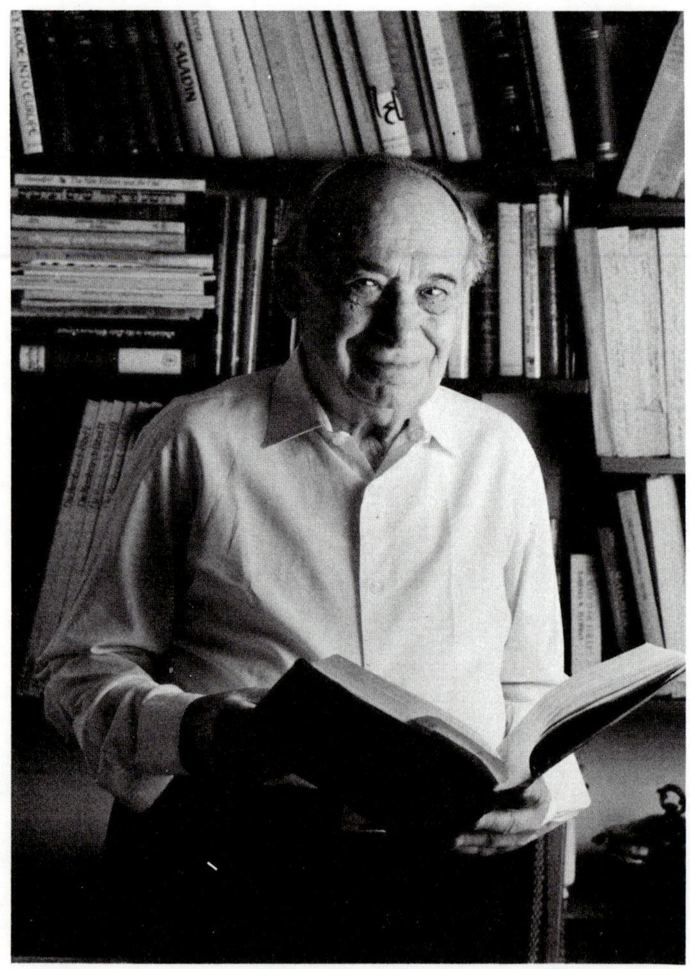

Professor David Ayalon

[illegible]

[illegible]
[illegible] Monks, Mongols [illegible]

[illegible]

[illegible]

[illegible]

[illegible]

[illegible]

[illegible]

[illegible]

[illegible]

[illegible]

[illegible]

[illegible]

[illegible]

Also in the Variorum Collected Studies Series:

DAVID AYALON
Outsiders in the Lands of Islam:
Mamlūks, Mongols and Eunuchs

GILLES VEINSTEIN
Etat et société dans l'Empire ottoman, XVIe–XVIIIe siècles

NEHEMIA LEVTZION
Islam in West Africa: Religion, Society and Politics to 1800

R.W. THOMSON
Studies in Armenian Literature and Christianity

AMNON SHILOAH
The Dimension of Music in Islamic and Jewish Culture

C.F. BECKINGHAM
Between Islam and Christendom: Travellers, Facts and
Legends in the Middle Ages and the Renaissance

DONALD P. LITTLE
History and Historiography of the Mamlūks

JEAN-CLAUDE GARCIN
Espaces, pouvoirs et idéologies de l'Egypte médiévale

GEORGE MAKDISI
Religion, Law and Learning in Classical Islam

WILFERD MADELUNG
Religious and Ethnic Movements in Medieval Islam

R.B. SERJEANT
Studies in Arabian History and Civilisation

GEORGES VAJDA
Etudes de théologie et de philosophie arabo–islamiques
à l'époque classique

FRANZ ROSENTHAL
Muslim Intellectual and Social History

J.D. LATHAM
From Muslim Spain to Barbary: Studies in the History
and Culture of the Muslim West

David Ayalon

Islam and the Abode of War

Military slaves and Islamic adversaries

VARIORUM
1994

Published by VARIORUM
Ashgate Publishing Limited
Gower House, Croft Road,
Aldershot, Hampshire GU11 3HR
Great Britain

Ashgate Publishing Company
Old Post Road,
Brookfield, Vermont 05036
USA

ISBN 0-86078-430-4

British Library CIP Data
Ayalon, David
Islam and the Abode of War: Military Slaves
and Islamic Adversaries. —
(Variorum Collected Studies Series; CS 456)
I. Title II. Series
909.097671

US Library of Congress CIP Data
Ayalon, David
Islam and the Abode of War: Military Slaves
and Islamic Adversaries / David Ayalon
p. cm. — (Collected Studies Series: CS456)
Includes index. ISBN 0-86078-430-4 (alk. paper)
1. Mamelukes. 2. Egypt—history—1250–1517. 3. Syria—
history—1260–1516. 4. Slavery—Middle East—history.
I. Title. II. Series: Collected Studies; CS456
DT96.A848 1994 94–6793
962'.02—dc20 CIP

The paper used in this publication meets the minimum requirements of the American National Standard for Information Sciences - Permanence of Paper for Printed Library Materials, ANSI Z39.48-1984. ∞ ™

Printed by Galliard (Printers) Ltd
Great Yarmouth, Norfolk, Great Britain

COLLECTED STUDIES SERIES CS456

CONTENTS

This volume contains **xii** + 298 pages

PREFACE

This volume of collected reprints is closely connected with the one previously published by Variorum (*Outsiders in the Lands of Islam*, 1988). Both deal with The Abode of Islam vis-à-vis The Abode of War. But whereas the earlier one is confined to the study of the role played by people from the second Abode who came over to the first and converted to Islam, the present volume deals also with the military struggle between the two Abodes.

A brief reference to each of the studies here included may be of use.

No. I, which was written for the twenty-sixth International Congress of Orientalists in New Delhi (1964) was not intended to be published, and was stencilled in a limited number of copies. However, it has been frequently cited by scholars, and I have been repeatedly asked to give it a wider circulation; this is one reason for its inclusion here. Another reason, and an even weightier one, is that it still has aspects which were not developed in subsequent studies of mine. Also important is the whole picture of the formation of the Mamlūk institution and its antecedents, as I saw them at that time. Particularly deserving of notice is the conclusion at which I had already then arrived, that the building of Sāmarrā, and its establishment as the Capital of Islam instead of Baghdad, was caused first and foremost by Caliph al-Muᶜtaṣim's formation of his Mamlūk regiment. A special study, upholding and strengthening that conclusion, is in preparation now.

No. II was published in the *Encyclopaedia of Islam*, second edition, in an abridged form. Here the full version is published for the first time. It gives a more comprehensive picture of Mamlūk military slavery in Egypt and Syria in the Mamlūk sultanate (1250–1517) than the abridged version.

No. III points at the very strong links connecting the Ayyūbid and the Mamlūk regimes, particularly their mamlūk elements, and these within the framework of the development of the Mamlūk institution in the Lands of Islam in general.

No. IV deals with the terms Baḥrī Mamlūks and Burjī Mamlūks as the respective designations of the earlier and later periods of the Mamlūk sultanate. It shows that these designations are wrong, and suggests instead the use of the 'Turkish-Kipchaki' and the 'Circassian' periods. It also points out that these incorrect designations are mainly the creation of Islamicists, with hardly any corroboration in the Mamlūk sources. In a rather unsystematic search for the earliest scholar using these misnomers, I went back as far as G. Weil's *Geschichte des Abbasiden Chalifats in Egypten* (Stuttgart, 1860), stating at the same time that there might have been European scholars who preceded Weil in that usage.

Now I learn, with gratitude, from Professor P.M. Holt, that a much earlier scholar, D'Herbelot, had already used them (*Bibliothèque Orientale*, Paris, 1697, pp. 174, 211, 545), and possibly also Pococke, in his *Historia Dynastiarum* (1663). Baḥrī and Burjī are the names of the two most famous regiments of the sultanate and nothing else. A detailed comparison between the two is made in the study, which also contains a follow up to my article 'The Circassians in the Mamluk Kingdom' (reprinted in my Variorum volume of 1977, No. IV), because the Burjī regiment was composed mainly of Circassians. Incidentally, my study of the ethnic composition of Mamlūk military society has never been published, except for its Circassian part. A summary of that unpublished part is made in No. II.

In Nos. V and VI I try to offer a partial explanation for the coming into being and persistence of two major elements of the Mamlūk socio–military system, without which that system would have quickly crumbled, namely: a) the unavoidable need for recruiting the Mamlūk at a tender age; and b) the non-hereditary character of Mamlūk aristocracy, which is contrary to human nature.

In No. VII the non-Mamlūk forces of the sultanate are studied. Two facets of that study are worthy of note: a) the sources of that period offer the historian a much better opportunity than any other Muslim medieval sources for reconstructing that kind of force; b) that reconstruction puts them vis-à-vis the Mamlūk military society, thus accentuating the special characteristics of that society.

No. VIII deals with the economic decline of the Mamlūk sultanate, from the third reign of al-Nāṣir Muḥammad b. Qalāun (1309–1340) onwards, covering internal as well as external factors. Some of the negative aspects of the Mamlūk system are discussed in this context. It was, however, a decline which embraced much wider areas than that of the sultanate. The causes of that wider decline have to be traced, as stressed in that article.

Nos. IX and X were originally written as one study which, because of its length, had to be split into two. The unusually rich and most reliable data furnished by Ibn Iyās (and supplemented by Ibn Ṭūlūn) about the first years of the Ottoman occupation of Egypt and Syria make it possible to follow closely the attitude of the Ottomans to the defeated Mamlūks and offer a quite convincing explanation for the reason which led them to spare those of Egypt and finish off those of Syria. This task can be carried out properly only through constant comparison and reference to Mamlūk society in the Mamlūk sultanate. In view of the paucity of source material after the chronicle of Ibn Iyās, the systematic study of the few years of Ottoman rule that it covers can serve as a better and safer start for the reconstruction of Mamlūk society in Ottoman Egypt in the years that followed.

No. XI is dedicated to proving the synonymy of the terms *khādim* and *khaṣī* (eunuch) in the early Muslim sources. This is a uniquely vital task, because otherwise the history of the eunuchs in Islam, whose importance is almost unparalleled, cannot be written. I started that proving 'campaign' in an earlier article, reprinted by Variorum in *Outsiders in the Lands of Islam* (1988, No. III), and have continued it in a long Appendix in a book on the eunuchs in Islam, which I have just finished (called *Eunuchs, Caliphs and Sultans – A Study in Power Relationships*). I consider a 'superoverkill' in connection with such a pivotal term as absolutely necessary.

No. XII points out the fact that of all the fronts in which the victorious Arab Muslim armies advanced from the Arab peninsula in the first decades of Islam's existence, the only one on which they were stopped (and stopped for centuries) was that of Nubia, in the Nile valley. The article tries to explain the causes of the Nubians' success, and its implications.

No. XIII contains in a nutshell my basic view that Islam, in its struggle against Christian (mainly Western) Europe was bound to be the loser. It had already ceased being a world sea power during the eleventh century, and only the Mamlūk military system (which has no parallel in any other civilization) postponed for centuries the same or similar results on land. That view is developed in greater detail in other studies of mine.

No. XIV is an attempt to widen the scope of the subject of my book *Gunpowder and Firearms in the Mamlūk Kingdom* (London, 1956, 1978), so that it would include an overview of the impact of that revolutionary weapon on the Muslim world as a whole. Its basic thesis is that that invention was ultimately bound greatly to increase Christian Europe's military superiority over Islam. The reason for this is that all Muslim states, including the mighty Ottoman Empire, lacked a wide industrial substructure, and so were faced with only two bad alternatives: either to produce firearms of inferior quality, or to buy obsolete or obsolescent weapons from their Christian–European adversaries.

What emerges from the four volumes of mine published by Variorum is the decisiveness of the slave institution in Muslim society, particularly its socio–military component, which played such a major role in the expansion and defence of Islam. A main factor shaping that society and its destiny is the close connection between women, eunuchs and mamlūks, what I call 'The Great Triangle'. This is a central theme in my book on the eunuchs in Islam, already mentioned in this introduction, and *the* central theme in an article called 'The Harem – A Major Source of Islam's Military Might', which is in press (a book in memory of Professor Joshua Prawer, to be published in Jerusalem).

*

* *

I am indebted to the following editorial boards, editors, and publishers for permitting me to reproduce the articles appearing in this volume, as follows: *The Encyclopaedia of Islam* (2nd edition), E.J. Brill, Leiden (II), *Revue des Etudes Islamiques*, Librairie Orientaliste P. Geuthner, Paris (III, V); *Tārīḫ*, Philadelphia (IV); Professor Aryeh Levin, *Jerusalem Studies in Arabic and Islam*, The Hebrew University, Jerusalem (VI, VIII, XII); Professor A. Noth, *Der Islam*, Walter de Gruyter, Berlin (VII); *Studia Islamica*, Editions Maisonneuve & Laroche, Paris and Professor A. Udovitch, Department of Near Eastern Studies, Princeton University, Princeton (IX): also Professor A. Udovitch, Princeton University (X, XIV); *Arabica*, E.J. Brill, Leiden (XI); Professor M. Sharon, The Hebrew University, Jerusalem, Israel (XIII).

As usual, the cooperation of Variorum deserves every praise. Dr John Smedley and Ruth Peters were extremely helpful in overcoming, with much understanding and unlimited forbearance, the difficulties encountered in the preparation of the present volume.

Many thanks are also due to Mrs Deborah Gerber for preparing the index under difficult conditions.

Finally, I have the great pleasure of thanking my wife, Professor Myriam (Mimi) Rosen-Ayalon, who, while I had been completely absorbed in another project, constantly urged me to find the time for working on this volume. Without that its appearance would have been postponed for a very long time.

DAVID AYALON

Jerusalem,
December 1993

PUBLISHER'S NOTE

The articles in this volume, as in all others in the Collected Studies Series, have not been given a new, continuous pagination. In order to avoid confusion, and to facilitate their use where these same studies have been referred to elsewhere, the original pagination has been maintained wherever possible.

Each article has been given a Roman number in order of appearance, as listed in the Contents. This number is repeated on each page and quoted in the index entries.

To Mimi

I

THE MILITARY REFORMS OF CALIPH AL-MU^cTAṢIM

Their Background and Consequences

This paper was written for the 26th International Congress of Orientalists in New Delhi (1964), and has never previously been published. It deals with only certain aspects of the background and consequences of al-Muᶜtaṣim's military reforms, and should be seen as a draft, with many of the conclusions being tentative. It was not intended for publication, and for that reason the scientific apparatus is abbreviated and reference to works on the Abbasid period, to which I am indebted, is only rarely made.

The decision to publish the paper now has been made in response to repeated requests by colleagues and others, and because it still contains aspects which have been insufficiently developed, or not developed at all, in later studies of mine. Also important is the whole picture of the formation of the Mamlūk institution and its antecedents, as I saw them at that time.

Note the Appendix and Addenda at the end of the paper.

The Mamlūk institution – with all its variants and offshoots – is one of the most important and most enduring socio-military institutions which Islam has known throughout its long and rich history. It constituted an integral part of the general Muslim slave institution,[1] and as such it started almost simultaneously with the birth of Islam, with its roots deep in *Jāhiliyya* practices. But as a central and decisive factor in Muslim history it dates only from the rule of the ᶜAbbāsid caliph al-Muᶜtaṣim (833-842), whose military reforms were considerably wider than the formation of his Mamlūk regiment.

The contemporary sources provide the reader with ample information on the motives which induced the ᶜAbbāsid caliphs to prefer the Mamlūks over all other military elements in their service, and about the process which led to the actual substitution of these elements by the Mamlūks and to the transfer of the capital from Baghdad to Sāmarrā. The best way for learning those motives and for following that process

1. The Mamlūk institution can be studied only within the framework of the general Muslim slave institution.

is through the study of the attitude of the ᶜAbbāsids to: a) the *Mawālī* (including the eunuchs); b) the *Abnā'* and Khurāsānis; c) the Arabs. In the following lines only some salient aspects of the subject will be dealt with.

a) *The* Mawālī

In order to appreciate the full extent of the intimate connections existing between the Mamlūks and the *Mawālī*, a well-known fact should be reiterated, namely, that a *Mawlā* is basically a freedman who owes allegiance and homage (*walā'*) solely to his master-manumittor. Among the *Mawālī* there was always an extremely great proportion of manumitted slaves. Furthermore, one of the most common names for the Turkish and other Mamlūks from the time of the reign of al-Muᶜtaṣim onwards, is *Mawālī*. And last but not least: whatever applies to the *Mawālī* in the sense of "clients", applies even more strongly to the *Mawālī* in the sense of manumitted slaves.

Though the Umayyads had already employed the *Mawālī* in their service on a great and growing scale, their meteoric rise to power took place only under the ᶜAbbāsids, a process which started at the very inception of that caliphate. Some shrewd remarks made by two of the earliest ᶜAbbāsid caliphs give us an insight into the causes which led this dynasty to rely so heavily on the *Mawālī*.

1) ᶜAbd al-Ṣamad b. ᶜAlī, a prominent member of the ᶜAbbāsid family, once said to caliph al-Mahdī (775–785): "O Commander of the Believers! we are a family (*ahl bayt*) whose hearts are imbued with the love of our *Mawālī* and with the desire to prefer them over others. You yourself went to such extremes, that you entrusted them with all your affairs, and made them your close intimates by day and by night. I am afraid that this will cause your Khurāsāni army and commanders a change of heart." To this al-Mahdī answered: "The *Mawālī* deserve such a treatment, for only they combine in them the following qualities. When I sit in a public audience, I may call a *Mawlā* and raise him and seat him by my side, so that his knee will rub my knee. As soon, however, as the audience is over, I may order him to groom my riding animal, and he will be content with this, and will not take offence. But if I demand the same thing from somebody else, he will say: 'I am the son of your supporter and intimate associate', or 'I am a veteran in your [ᶜAbbāsid] cause (*daᶜwa*)' or 'I am the son of those who were the first to join your [ᶜAbbāsid] cause'. And I shall not be able to move him from his [obstinate] stand (*lā adfaᶜuhu ᶜan dhālika*)" (Ṭabarī, III, p. 531, ll. 4–15).

2) The following episode is told about al-Mahdī's predecessor as caliph, his father, al-Manṣūr (754–775). A high-ranking Umayyad was captured and brought to al-Manṣūr. The caliph promised him that he would spare his life if he gave him true answers to several questions which he would ask him. One of the questions was why the Umayyads were defeated and their rule came to an end. The answer was: because of the disorganization of their information service.[2] Another question was: in whom did the Umayyads find loyalty and trustworthiness (*wafā'*). The answer was: in the *Mawālī*. Then comes the following comment of the transmitter of this story: al-Manṣūr wanted at first to employ the members of his own ᶜAbbāsid family (*ahl baytihi*) in his information service, but later he decided that this would humiliate them and he therefore employed his *Mawālī* instead of them (Ṭabarī, III, p. 414, ll. 15–21).

These two episodes, as well as many other kinds of evidence, demonstrate clearly how the *Mawālī* – because of their inferior status and their great dependence on the Muslim ruler, and because of their accepting readily, as a result of that inferiority, any kind of work offered to them, however menial or unrespectable – succeeded in infiltrating into state posts and positions of vital importance, and in coming so near the caliph's person that they ultimately became his most trusted confidants and advisors.

Among these people the eunuchs, who are frequently classified as *Mawālī*, deserve special mention. Since the eunuchs (*khadam*, sing, *khādim*) were much more cut off from the rest of society and were, therefore, much more dependent on their master than any other kind of *Mawālī*, they were particularly trusted by him. The establishment of the eunuchs in the caliphal court is attributed to as early a caliph as Muᶜāwiya, but under the Umayyads they play only an inferior role. Under the ᶜAbbāsids their great and growing power is felt almost from the very beginning of that dynasty's rule. In Hārūn al-Rashīd's reign (786–809) their influence becomes immense; most confidential missions are entrusted to them. Al-Rashīd's most trusted friends were said to have been his *Mawlā*, the commander Harthama b. Aᶜyan and his eunuch Masrūr al-Kabīr. It was mainly eunuchs who attended his deathbed. The carriers of the dispatches which broke the news of his death to his sons were solely eunuchs. It was a eunuch who was entrusted with carrying the caliphal symbols of office from Ṭūs, where

2. *fa-qāla lahu al-Manṣūr min ayna utiya Banū Umayya ḥattā intashara amruhum qālā min taḍyīᶜ al-ᶜakhbār*. I am not sure at all that my translation is correct, but I believe that this does not affect the conclusions to be derived from that episode.

al-Rashīd died, to Baghdad. Eunuchs as military commanders become a familiar phenomenon under the ᶜAbbāsids, especially in the Byzantine frontier.

Al-Amīn (808–813) was blamed for flooding his court with eunuchs. He might have well surpassed his father, but he undoubtedly learned from him and followed his example. In the reign of al-Ma'mūn (813–833) the evidence of eunuch presence and influence is abundant. Under al-Muᶜtaṣim, who was mainly occupied with the creation of his Mamlūk corps and with other military reforms, information about eunuchs decreases considerably, but this might be accidental. The eunuchs continued to play a prominent role in the ᶜAbbāsid court centuries after al-Muᶜtaṣim. They, as well as the *Mawālī*, are frequently mentioned together with the members of the ᶜAbbāsid family (*ahl-al-bayt*), the Hāshimites and the commanders (*quwwād*) as taking part in highly important councils, decisions and plots.

The rise of the *Mawālī* and of the eunuchs as a major force in the capital, and particularly in the court, together with the atmosphere which surrounded them, was an essential preliminary to the creation of a corps of Mamlūks and to its establishment as the backbone of the caliphal armies and as the élite of the capital's military society. The Mamlūks, themselves foreign upstarts without connections, completely dependent on their master, and frequently called *Mawālī*, fitted very well into the already existing pattern of a court dominated by freedmen, 'clients' and eunuchs. Here I shall refer only to the Mamlūks' relations with the eunuchs. Eunuchs, in increasing numbers, were entrusted with the supervision of the Mamlūks, especially the juniors and youngsters. This process reached a high peak in the days of caliph al-Muᶜtaḍid (892–902), whose famous Mamlūk regiment, *al-ghilmān al-ḥujariyya* was supervised by eunuchs (*al-khadam al-ustādhūn*) (Hilāl al-Ṣābī, *Wuzarā'*, pp. 12–13). Such relations between eunuchs and Mamlūks were undoubtedly an integral and a most substantial part of Mamlūk military societies, as may be seen from the functions which the eunuchs fulfilled in the Mamlūk sultanate of Egypt and Syria (1250–1517) (see my "*L'Esclavage du Mamelouk*" *passim*).

b) *The* Abnā' *(and Khurāsānīs)*

While the ᶜAbbāsid court became more and more conditioned accepting the Mamlūks, and accepting them as the élite of its military forces, the ᶜAbbāsid capital was by no means subject to the same process. For in Baghdad grew up a strong and proud military element, composed of free-born people, who would not accept the Mamlūks in their midst.

This was the main, if not the sole, reason for transferring the capital from Baghdad to Sāmarrā.

This statement of mine necessitates a rather detailed explanation, which will include, amongst other things, a comparison between the Khurāsānī overthrow of the Umayyads in the middle of the eighth century and the Khurāsānī overthrow of caliph Amīn in the early ninth century. The conclusions derived from that comparison are different in some essential points (though by no means wholly) from views expressed on the same subject both by older and more modern students of the ᶜAbbāsid period.

There were some very substantial differences between the Khurāsānī westward advance in the middle of the eighth century and that of the early ninth century. On the first occasion the Arab element was extremely strong, perhaps even predominant, particularly in the higher ranks. It is worth noting that the struggle which ended in Abū Muslim's domination of Khurāsān, took place, throughout most of its stages, between Arab tribal groups. Only in the very last stages of the struggle are non-Arabs mentioned as a specific group, and then as the last in the list (Ṭabarī, II, 1993, ll. 19–20; 1994, l. 8; 1998, ll. 102). It is very instructive that all the twelve *nuqabā'* of Abū Muslim were Arabs (Ṭabarī, II, 1988, ll. 5–15), a fact about which the Arabs prided themselves (Jāḥiz, *Manāqib*, pp. 12, l. 17–14, l, 8). The Umayyad armies, which were defeated by the Khurāsānī armies, were also composed mainly of Arabs. This is specially true of their crack units.

On the second occasion a very different picture emerges. The Arabs hardly appear as a group on the Khurāsānī side (with the exception of those who cooperated, to a certain extent, with the Khurāsānīs during the actual siege of Baghdad). The racial elements which are specifically mentioned on this side are Bukhārīs, Khawārizmīs and Atrāk (the last are mentioned several times). This proves that the people of Eastern Khurāsān, Transoxania and perhaps even beyond, were strongly represented in the armies of Ṭāhir, Ma'mūn's commander. This is significant, for the Turkish Mamlūks did not come alone to Baghdad in the days of al-Ma'mūn and al-Muᶜtaṣim, but together with their Transoxanian neighbours.

Whereas one has to work hard in order to discover traces of Arabs in Ma'mūn's armies, their presence in Amīn's armies is very evident, mainly outside the capital, but also inside it. Yet the role they play, though by no means small, is far inferior to that of another element, which bore the brunt of the struggle. I mean the people of Baghdad, and this statement is not confined to the dregs of the town's population, as so often stressed by the students of the struggle under discussion. It was the military and paramilitary elements of the Baghdad population which constituted the backbone of the forces resisting al-Ma'mūn's armies' advance both outside and inside the capital.[3] These were usually called *Ahl Baghdād* and sometimes even *jund Ahl Baghdād.* In the first big clash between the two rival forces, which was one of the most decisive throughout the whole struggle, Amīn's army, headed by the famous commander ᶜAlī b. ᶜĪsā b. Māhān, was composed of 50,000 horsemen and infantrymen of *Ahl Baghdād* who were registered in the Diwan (*faᶜaqada lahu ᶜalā khamsīn alf fāris wa-rājil min ahl Baghdād wa-dafaᶜa ilayhi dafātir al-jund* Ṭabarī, III, p. 817, ll 13–14). No mention whatsoever is made of any unit from any other place. The term *Ahl Baghdād* as a military fighting force is mentioned time and time again during the struggle, and it even persists for many years after the capture of the capital. That the "people of Baghdad" were considered as the force *par excellence* fighting Ṭāhir's armies, may be learnt from the following instance. We are told by al-Ṭabarī that, after Amīn was killed, "both armies: the army of Ṭāhir and the army of the people of Baghdad" regretted his death (*inna al-jundayn jund Ṭāhir wa-jund ahl Baghdād nadimū ᶜalā qatl Muḥammad*) (Ṭabarī, III, p. 224, ll 18–19). Thus *these* were the two really important armies facing each other in the Amīn–Ma'mūn trial of strength (see also immediately below on the role of the *Abnā'*).

The core and nucleus of that military body called *Ahl Baghdād* were the *Abnā'*. These are sometimes called *Abnā' al-Dawla*, *Abnā' al-Daᶜwa* or *Abnā' al-Shīᶜa* but their common name is just *Abnā'* – (sing. *Abnāwī* or *Banawī*). They were, in all probability, the descendants of the Khurāsānīs who brought the ᶜAbbāsids to the throne, and who included both Iranians and Arabs. They underwent a further Arabisation because of their new environment. We can establish their origin and mixed racial composition from various phrases scattered in the sources. In the Aghānī they are called on one occasion *Abnā' al-Shīᶜa al-Khurāsāniyya*, and on another occasion *Abnā' al-jund al-Khurāsāniyya* (XVIII, p. 61, ll, 9–11; p. 100, ll. 26–27). Al-Jāḥiẓ also speaks of their Khurāsānian origin, as we shall see below. Al-Khwārizmī says that "the Abnā' are the sons of the Dihqāns" (*al-Abnā' hum abnā' al-dahāqīn*) (*Mafātīḥ al-ᶜUlūm*, p. 119, ll. 7–8.), which points to their Iranian as well as their noble origin.[4] Aḥmad b. Abī Ṭāhir Ṭayfūr's evidence deserves special attention. He calls them *Abnā' Khurāsān al-muwalladūn* (*Kitāb Baghdād*, p. 143, l. 16),[5] which proves that they did not consist only of Iranians, but included Arab elements as well. There is, on the other hand, no

3. The criminals, vagabonds, etc. of the town joined the battle at a comparatively late stage, and only during the siege. See also below.

4. On their noble origin see also below.

proof that they were descendants of the ᶜAbbāsids. The fact that they were called *abnā' al-dawla* can not serve as such proof, for the word *dawla* is very elastic in its meaning, especially in the early ᶜAbbāsid period (see also F. Rosenthal, art. *Dawla* in EI[2,]I). Furthermore, I do not know of any member of the ᶜAbbāsid family who is said by the sources to have been one of the *Abnā'*.

Three additional facts, which as far as I know, have been overlooked by the students of the subject under discussion should be borne in mind.

1) The *Abnā'* are hardly mentioned *before* the struggle between Amīn and Ma'mūn. Therefore, the period of their formation and taking shape is completely obscure.

2) Never in their history were the *Abnā'* as active as during that struggle.

3) The *Abnā'* are stationed exclusively, or almost exclusively, in Baghdad. Practically all the information on them in the chronicles, either during the struggle or after it, is confined to that city. Furthermore, the conclusion based on that kind of information is fully substantiated by the clear testimony of al-Jāḥiẓ. In *Manāqib al-Atrāk* the *Banawī*, defending the superiority of the Abnā' over the other military elements which constitute the caliphal armies, says: "As for me, my origin (or my main trunk) is Khurāsān ... and my branch is Baghdad" (*anā aṣlī Khurāsān ... wa-farᶜī Baghdād*) (*Manāqib*, p. 15, ll. 2, 6). A little further the same *Banawī* says: "The whole of Baghdad is ours. It is quiet as long as we are quiet, and it stirs as long as we stir. The whole world is dependent on Baghdad and follows it. ... We were brought up by the caliphs and we are the neighbours of the viziers. We were born in the courts of our kings and under the wings of our caliphs. We adopted their manners and followed their example. We know nobody else but them and we are known only as their and nobody else's" (*Manāqib*, p. 16, ll. 13–15, ll. 17–19).

In the above cited passages from *Manāqib al-Atrāk* the purely Baghdadi character of the *Abnā'* is stressed time and again. It is stated in the clearest possible terms that they are Baghdadis and nothing else, that they are very proud of this fact, as well as of the fact that they grew

5. On the next page of the same source these are called simply *Abnā'* (p. 144, l. 9), which shows that no group or element other than the *Abnā'* is intended here. For the full translation of the passage see Appendix. The Arab ᶜAbdallāh b. Ḥumayd (the son of the famous Qaḥtaba aṭ-Ṭā'ī) was a well known commander of the *Abnā'* (Ṭabarī, III, p. 840, ll. 5–7).

under the auspices and patronage of the caliphs and enjoyed their special attention and privilege. All this could take place only in Baghdad.

The *Abnā'*'s pride in being of Khurāsānī origin on the one hand, and inhabitants of Baghdad on the other, and their desire to merge these two qualities into one, find their most striking expression in the following remark. "And it [i.e. Baghdad] is the Khurāsān of ᶜIraq" (*wa-hiya Khurāsān al-ᶜIrāq*) (*Manāqib*, p. 15, l. 18). Thus there is an unbroken continuity and full harmony between their past and their present. Though they live now in Baghdad, they still stay on Khurāsānī soil.

As we know practically nothing of the *Abnā'* before the reign of Amīn, any theory of how they came into being can not be proved with certainty. Still, the following theory seems to me to be plausible, in the present state of our knowledge.

When the ᶜAbbāsids built Baghdad they transferred into it, in all probability, their choicest and most trusted troops and followers, of whom the Khurāsānīs constituted a very substantial part.[6] The descendants of those Khurāsānīs also served as soldiers, and received preferential treatment from the caliphs. They were very numerous,[7] and formed a first class military body, as can be learnt from Jāḥiẓ's *Manāqib al-Atrāk*, from Ṭayfūr's *Kitāb Baghdād* (see Appendix), and, last but not least, from the part they played in the struggle between Amīn and Ma'mūn.

The central place which the *Abnā'* occupied in that struggle and their privileged status, are well illustrated by the following instances.

1) As stated before, ᶜAlī b. ᶜĪsā b. Māhān headed 50,000 soldiers of *Ahl Baghdād* in the first big clash between the armies of the two brothers. On the verge of total defeat, and shortly before being killed, ᶜAlī b. ᶜĪsā addressed his whole army in the following words: "Where are the owners of bracelets and crowns?[8] O community of the Abnā'" (*ayna aṣḥāb al-aswira wal-akālīl yā maᶜshar al-Abnā'*) (Ṭabarī, III, p. 824, ll. 14–15.)

2) Shortly after ᶜAlī b. ᶜĪsā's defeat and death, Amīn sent against Ṭāhir 20,000 soldiers of the *Abnāᶜ*, under the command of ᶜAbd al-Raḥmān b. Jabala al-Abnāwī (Ṭabarī, III, pp. 826, l. 17–827, l. 2). The series of battles between Ṭāhir and ᶜAbd al-Raḥmān b. Jabala, who headed a pure and very big *Abnāwī* force, were by far the fiercest

6. This does not mean that the Baghdadi garrison was composed solely of such kinds of troops.

7. For their numbers see below.

8. Amīn bestowed frequently crowns and bracelets upon soldiers who distinguished themselves in battle. Other ᶜAbbāsid caliphs also bestowed the same distinction, but much less frequently.

which had been fought out between the two sides outside Baghdad.[9] In one of the most critical stages of these battles ^cAbd al-Raḥmān addressed his army: "O community of the *Abnā'*! O sons of the Kings and holders (?) of swords! They [i.e. Ṭāhir's soldiers] are ^cAjam[10] and are not people of resistance and perseverance! Hold out against them! My father and mother are your ransoms!" (*Yā ma^cshar al-abnā' yā abnā' al-mulūk wa-alfāf al-suyūf innahum la-^cAjam wa-laysū bi-aṣḥāb muṭāwala wa-lā ṣabr fa-iṣbirū lahum fidākum abī wa-ummī*) (Ṭabarī, III, p. 829, ll. 4–5).

3) Ḥusayn b. ^cAlī b. ^cĪsā b. Māhān returned from the Jazīra (on the Jazira episode see below) with his heart set upon deposing caliph Amīn. On entering Baghdad he was received with great pomp and honour by *al-Abnā' wa-Ahl Baghdād* (Ṭabarī, III, p. 846, ll. 12–15). His speech to his audience, which was intended to make his plans public, opened with the words *Yā ma^cshar al-Abnā'* (*ibid*, pp. 846, l. 21–847, l. 1).

4) When Amīn, shortly before he was killed, saw that everything was lost, he ordered *all his army and commanders* to assemble in the square adjoining his palace (*wa-amara bi-iḥḍār kulli man kāna ma^cahu fī al-madīna min al-quwwād wal-jund fa-jumi^cū fī al-raḥba*) (Ṭabarī, III, p. 930, ll. 19–20). He opened his speech to the whole gathering with the words. "O community of the *Abnā'* and those who were first to adopt the right course"[11] (*Yā ma^cshar al-Abnā' wa-ahl al-sabq ilā al-hudā*) (Ṭabarī, III, p. 931, ll. 6–7).

5) When the position of the besieged became desperate, some of Amīn's commanders suggested to him that he should leave Baghdad with 700 of his most faithful *Abnā'* mounted on the 1000 thoroughbreds still left with the city's defenders. The aim of this planned retreat was to rally support from the Jazīra and Syria (Ṭabarī, III, pp. 911–912).[12]

---

9. The *Abnāwī* troops fighting under the command of ^cAbd al-Raḥmān seem to have possessed high military qualities. This can be deduced from the phrase: *wa-nadaba ma^cahu fursān al-Ahnā^c wa-ahl al-ba's wal-najda wal-ghanā' minhum* (Ṭabari, III, p. 827, ll. 3–4).

10. This is additional proof of the overwhelming predominance of the non-Arab Khurāsānis in Ma'mūn's armies, as contrasted with the Khurāsāni armies of Abū Muslim.

11. Here the intention is, in all probability, to those who were the first to join the ^cAbbasid cause. This also points to the connection between the *Abnā'* and the early followers of the ^cAbbasids.

12. It is worthwhile noting that the suggestion was made by commanders who did not belong to the *Abnā'*. When Ṭāhir learnt of the scheme he was greatly worried. He succeeded in crushing it with the help of his supporters in Amīn's court.

6) When Amīn's killers broke into the house in which he was kept by his captors, and advanced towards him with drawn swords, he expressed his despair of life by saying: *innā lillāh wa-innā ilayhi rājiᶜūn dhahabat wallāhi nafsī fī sabīl Allāh*, but he added forthwith: "Is there no stratagem! [by means of which I can be saved]. Is there no saviour! *Is there none of the Abnā'*?!" (*amā min ḥīla amā min mughīth amā min aḥad min al-Abnā'*) (Ṭabarī, III, pp. 922, l. 20–923, l.1.

The above instances prove beyond any possible doubt that the *Abnā'* were the mainstay of Amīn throughout the whole struggle, from the first clash and up to his very death (for additional instances see below). True, his relations with them were not always good. Certain elements of the *Abnā'* helped in bringing about his temporary deposition during the siege, whereas he himself showed some signs of favouring the Arabs at their expense (see below). But under the extreme strains and stresses of a terrible siege, such frictions and antagonisms could hardly be avoided even between the closest allies. In spite of all that, only the *Abnā'* could be trusted in smuggling the caliph out of the besieged city and in forming a nucleus and a rallying point for his supporters in his place of exile. Furthermore, it was the *Abnā'*, and nobody else, whom Amīn mentioned as his possible saviours in the very last moments of his life.

I have no intention of detracting from the part played by the mob of Baghdad, including criminals released from prison and other kinds of ruffians. These people (frequently called *ᶜurāt*, *ᶜuryān* or *ᶜayyārūn*), many of whom fought with most primitive arms against well equipped and well trained troops, performed military feats which are really astounding (Ṭabarī, III, pp. 868–899). Yet such elements, by their very nature, could constitute only an addition, however important, to the main forces defending the town. The considerable space which the sources allot to the description of the fighting of these elements and the unbounded admiration with which they accompany this description, can be easily explained by the fact that such an attitude and such a stand were completely unexpected from this quarter. On the other hand, there was nothing unusual in the fighting of the forces defending the town, and therefore their exploits were greatly overshadowed in the sources by those of the *ᶜurāt*.[13] It has already been shown above that the *Abnā'* con-

13. This does not imply that the *Abnā'* or others of Amīn's regular troops were prepared to fight for Amīn to the very end. Antagonisms and discord prevailed in Amīn's camp. Besides, money and bribery played an important part in *both* camps. Many regular soldiers deserted Amīn and went over to the enemy, especially towards the end of the siege. In spite of all that, it would be wrong to minimize the contribution of the regular and trained troops to the defence of Baghdad. Suffice it to mention here the havoc caused

stituted the mainstay of Amīn's power.[14] But they were by no means the only fighting element, outside the *ᶜurāt*, in Baghdad. They are definitely not identical with the *whole* body which comes under the title *Ahl Baghdād*, although they constituted its élite. The *Ahl al-Ḥarbiyya*, or simply Ḥaribbya (the people of the quarter bearing that name), the *Ahl al-Arbāḍ*, etc, who are frequently mentioned as a fighting body, were not composed solely of *Abnā'*.[15] There must have been in Baghdad strong military and paramilitary bodies outside the descendants of the early Khurāsānīs, as well as well-to-do civilians who could handle arms and were prepared to fight in defence of their city. Admittedly, the sources do not make it possible, quite often, to draw a clear line between the various fighting elements defending the ᶜAbbāsid capital.[16]

The resistance of Baghdad's defenders was broken and the city capitulated. Yet the power of the military and parahmilitary elements living in the capital, though weakened, was far from being broken. Many of those who deserted to Ṭāhir's camp returned to the town, where they enjoyed a privileged position because of the assistance they had given to Amīn's enemies. While Ma'mūn was delaying his return to the capital, the conquering armies could not be kept in it indefinitely in their full strength, for they were needed elsewhere. Ḥasan b. Sahl, Ma'mūn's representative in Baghdad, came to feel soon the power and influence of the local forces, and during the long period which passed between the conquest of the capital and Ma'mūn's entry into it, its people regained much of their former strength. There is no indication that Ma'mūn, after his entry, took any drastic measures in order to curtail that strength. From Ṭayfūr's evidence it might be deduced that there was a reconciliation between Ma'mūn and the *Abnā'*, but Ṭayfūr's wording on this subject is not fully clear (see Appendix). No wonder, therefore, that when Muᶜtaṣim tried to quarter his Mamlūk regiment in Baghdad he met with the stiff resistance of the Baghdadis, who ultimately succeeded in forcing him to leave the town and to build a new capital for himself and for his Mamlūks. The people who are mentioned by the sources as waylaying the Turkish Mamlūks in the streets of Baghdad and killing them, are the Abnāwīs, the Ḥarbīs and the mob (*ghawghā'*),

---

by the *manjanīqs* which were used amply by both sides, and which were operated by experts.

14. Often one comes to learn of the great power of the *Abnā'* by accident. This kind of unconscious evidence is always the most reliable one.

15. From the available data it is impossible to decide whether the *Abnā'* lived only in one quarter, or were scattered all over the city.

16. On some occasions it is even difficult to decide whether certain fighting elements belonged to the lower stratum of society or not.

namely, our old acquaintances from the siege of the town in Amīn's reign. The power of the people of Baghdad was still considerable during the siege of the town by caliph al-Mu^ctazz and the Turks in the year 865.

c) *The Arabs*

The Amīn–Ma'mūn struggle also sheds a very revealing light on the position of the Arabs, especially those of them who belonged to tribal confederations. Amongst other things it helps us to learn the relations existing between the *Abnā'* and the Arabs on the one hand, and between the *Abnā'* and the Khurāsānīs on the other.

The Arabs fought, as stated before, almost exclusively on Amīn's side. Their participation does not seem, however, to have been too vigorous, although Amīn was favourably disposed towards them, sometimes even in critical moments.[17] Here we shall confine ourselves to the detailed discussion of two instances in which the Arabs were intended to fight Ma'mūn's forces together with the *Abnā'*. Both instances are, in my opinion, very revealing, particulary the second one.

1) It has already been pointed out earlier in this paper that in the two first clashes between the armies of Amīn and Ma'mūn, the *Abnā'* constituted the core of Amīn's army. In the first clash the caliph's forces were headed by ᶜAlī b. ᶜĪsā, and in the second by ᶜAbd al-Raḥmān b. Jabala al-Abnāwī, both of whom were killed in battle.

Shortly after ᶜAbd al-Raḥmān's death Amīn organized an expeditionary force composed of 20,000 beduin Arabs (*Aᶜrāb*), headed by Aḥmad b. Mazyad, and 20,000 of the *Abnā'*, headed by ᶜAbdallāh b. Ḥumayd b. Qaḥṭaba and sent them to Ḥulwān, in order to fight Ṭāhir, then camped at Shalāshān. When the expedition reached Khānaqīn and camped there, Ṭāhir spread amongst its members, by means of spies, rumours alleging that Amīn was giving special pay to the units staying with him in Baghdad. These and other rumours sowed discord between the *Abnā'* and the Aᶜrāb, who started fighting each other, and then abandoned their positions and went away without giving battle to Ṭāhir, who then occupied Ḥulwān (Ṭabarī, III, p. 840, ll. 5–17).[18]

---

17. See, for example: Ṭabarī, III, p. 822, ll. 3–5; p. 847, ll. 10–11, p. 865, ll. 13–14; p. 868, l. 17. Muḥammad b. Yazīd b. Ḥātim-al Muhallabī, Amīn's governor of al-Ahwāz, seems to have been an Arab. His fight against Ṭāhir was perhaps the fiercest of all the fights in which armies from the capital were not directly involved. Unfortunately, however, the racial composition of his forces is very little known (see *ibid.*, pp. 851–855).

18. In organizing this expedition Amīn encountered great difficulties from the beginning. Asad b. Yazīd b. Mazyad, Aḥmad's nephew, was the man who was first chosen to command the Arab section of the expedition, but he was put in jail because of his

2) ᶜAbd al-Malik b. Ṣāliḥ b.ᶜAlī b. ᶜAbdallāh b. ᶜAbbās, a very prominent member of the ᶜAbbāsid family,[19] owed gratitude to Amīn, because he released him from Hārūn al-Rashīd's prison when he became caliph. ᶜAbd al-Malik decided, therefore, to stand by Amīn, and render him whatever service he could. Seeing the deterioration of Amīn's military position and the decline of his troops' morale, he suggested to the caliph that he (i.e. ᶜAbd al-Malik) should call "the people of Syria" (*Ahl al-Shām*)[20] to come and fight for Amīn. Since the people of Syria were seasoned fighters and accustomed to hardships (*ḍarrasathum al-ḥurūb wa-addabathum al-shadā'id*), there were good prospects that, with their help, the scales would be turned in Amīn's favour. Amīn accepted the offer with great enthusiasm, appointed ᶜAbd al-Malik governor of Jazīra and Syria, and sent him there with a body (*kanaf* – escort?) of his army and of the *Abnā'*. ᶜAbd al-Malik chose Raqqa, which is situated on the border of Jazīra and Syria, and which served as a temporary capital for Hārūn al-Rashīd, as the gathering place of all his supporters. He wrote to the chiefs of the Syrian armies and to the notables of Jazīra, leaving none of those who were known for their bravery and military competence, without making them attractive promises. They came to him "chief after chief and group after group, and whoever entered his audience received gifts and robes". So the people of Syria, both Zawāqīl[21] and Aᶜrāb, "came to him from all quarters and gathered there until they became numerous" (*wa-kataba ilā ru'asā' ajnād al-Shām wa-wujūh al-Jazīra fa-lam yabqa aḥad mimman yurjā wa-judhkar ba'suhu wa'ghanā'uhu illā waᶜadahu wa-basaṭa lahu fī amalihi wa-umniyyatihi fa-qadimū ᶜalayhi ra'īsan baᶜda ra'īs wa-jamāᶜa baᶜda jamāᶜa fa-kāna lā yadkhul ᶜalayhi aḥad illā ajzāhu wa-khalaᶜa ᶜalayhi ... fa-atāhu ahl al-Shām al-Zawāqīl wal-Aᶜrāb min kulli fajj wa-ijtamaᶜū ᶜindahu ḥattā kathurū*) (Ṭabarī, III, p. 843, ll. 4–8).

But at this very moment, when prospects looked so bright and hopeful, and everything seemed to be going according to plan, there came a sudden turn to the worse because of a trivial incident. A

---

demands for money (Ṭabarī, III, pp. 833–840). Amīn's request to the *Abnā'* and the Arabs, when he bid farewell to the expedition, to unite and fight side by side against the enemy, also shows that these two bodies were not inclined to cooperate with each other.

19. On this person and the various posts which he occupied under the ᶜAbbāsids see: Ziriqlī, *Aᶜlām*, IV, pp. 304–305.

20. The term *Ahl al-Shām* frequently means the Arabs who belonged to tribal confederations. Many of them might, of course, have already been partly or wholly urbanized.

21. Contrary to what has been said in Orientalistic works, the *Zawāqīl* were also Arabs, belonging mainly to Northern tribal confederations (see below).

Khurāsānī soldier (*ba*ᶜ*ḍ jund ahl Khurāsān*) from Amīn's army saw one of the *Zawāqīl* riding a mount which had been captured from him in the battle between the Umayyad rebel al-Sufyānī[22] and the governor of Syria, Sulaymān, the son of caliph al-Manṣūr. The quarrel started between the two spread quickly. The *Abnā'*, who were headed by Muḥammad b. Abī Khālid b. Hunduwān[23] (Handawān?) had the upper hand and killed off many of the *Zawāqīl*, part of whom they slaughtered in their camel saddles. The *Zawāqīl* rallied again, and the battle was resumed. ᶜAbd al-Malik asked both sides, through a messenger, to stop fighting. The messenger was stoned and the battle was continued. Again the *Abnā'* won the day, and killed many of the *Zawāqīl*. When ᶜAbd al-Malik, who was on his deathbed, was informed of the enormous dimensions of the slaughter, he clapped his hands with grief and said: "What a humiliation! Will the Arabs be wronged in their own home and in their own place and in their own country!?" (*wādhillāhu tustaḍām al-*ᶜ*Arab fi dārihā wa-maḥallihā wa-bilādihā*) (Ṭabarī, III, p. 844, ll. 2–3). This attitude had enraged those of the *Abnā'* who up till then had abstained from "doing mischief", and the situation was aggravated still more (*wa-tafāqama al-amru fīmā baynahum*). At this juncture the *Abnā'* were headed by Ḥusayn b. ᶜAlī b. ᶜĪsā b. Māhān.

Next morning the *Zawāqīl* assembled in al-Raqqa, whereas the *Abnā'* and the Khurāsānīs gathered in the neighbouring al-Rāfiqa. In al-Raqqa, however, dejection and discord prevailed. One of the people of Ḥimṣ[24] rose up and said: "To run away is easier than to perish and death is easier than humiliation. You went far away from your own country and went out of your own districts hoping for plenty after scarcity and for power and glory after weakness and humiliation. But you have fallen instead into evil and landed in the battlefield of death. There is death in the moustaches and hoods of the ᶜAbbāsid soldiers.[25] Sound the retreat! Sound the retreat! Before our ways of escape are cut off and before we are stricken by calamity … and before we are overtaken by death" (*al-harab ahwan min al-*ᶜ*aṭab wal-mawt ahwan min al-dhull innakum ba*ᶜ*udtum* ᶜ*an bilādikum*

---

22. His full name is ᶜAlī b. ᶜAbdallāh b. Yazīd b. Khālid b. Muᶜāwiya. The battle took place at the end of 195H, i.e. not long before the events described here, which happened in 196H.

23. On the important part played by this person and his numerous sons in the period immediately following the capture of Baghdad see Ṭabarī, III, pp. 998–1004.

24. What I said about *Ahl al-Shām* is true also of *Ahl Ḥimṣ*. See note no. 20.

25. For *al-Musawwida* as a term synonymous with the "ᶜAbbāsid army" see the example (in Arabic) in Dozy's *Supplement*, *s.v.*

wa-kharajtum min aqālīmikum tarjawna al-kathra ba^cda al-qilla wal-^cizza ba^cda al-dhilla alā wa-fī al-sharr waqa^ctum wa-ilā ḥawmat al-mawt anakhtum inna al-manāyā fī shawārib al-musawwida wa-qalānisihim al-nafīra al-nafīra qabla an yanqaṭi^c al-sabīl wa-yanzil al-amr al-jalīl wa-yafūr al-maṭlab wa-ya^csur al-madhhab wa-yab^cud al-amad wa-yaqtarib al-ajal), (Ṭabarī, III, p. 844, ll. 6–12. See also Fragmenta, p. 328).

After the man of Ḥimṣ finished his speech, a man of the tribe of Kalb, riding a she-camel, rose in his stirrups and said: "O people of Kalb! It is the black banner of the ^cAbbāsids! By God! This banner has never run away and never wavered. Its victories never suffered humiliation and its close friends were never weakened. *How well acquainted you are with the marks which the swords of the people of Khurāsān left in the backs of your necks and the traces which their spearheads left in your breasts.* Get away from evil before it grows too big, and shun it before your Syria goes up in flames. Go back to your homes! Go back to your homes! For death in Palestine is better than life in the Jazīra! I am going back, and whoever wants to go away may join me!" Then he went, and all the people of Syria went with him (*thumma qāla yā ma^cshar Kalb innahā al-rāya al-sawdā' wallāhi mā wallat wa-mā ^cadalat wa-lā dhalla naṣruhā wa-lā ḍa^cufa waliyyuhā wa-innakum la-ta^crifūna mawaqui^c suyūf ahl Khurāsān fī riqābikum wa-āthār asinnatihim fī ṣudūrikum i^ctazilū al-sharra qabla an ya^cẓum wa-takhaṭṭawhu qabla an yaḍṭarim Sha'mukum dārakum dārakum al-mawt al-Filasṭīnī khayr min al-^caysh al-Jazari alā wa-innī rāj^ci fa-man arāda al-inṣirāf fal-yanṣarif ma^cī thumma sāra wa-sāra ma^cahu ^cāmmat ahl al-Sha'm*) (Ṭabarī, III, pp. 844, l. 16–845, l. 2). Then the *Zawāqīl* drew near, and set on fire the fodder collected by the merchants. Ḥusayn b. Alī b. ^cĪsā b. Māhān, together with the people of Khurāsān and the *Abnā'* (*jamā^cat ahl Khurāsān wal-Abnā' ibid.*, p. 845, ll. 4–5), stayed at the gate of al-Rāfiqa for fear of Ṭawq b. Mālik[26] [the chief of the tribe of Banū Taghlib]. A man of the Banū Taghlib came to Ṭawq and said to him: "Do not you see what the Arabs experienced from these people? [i.e. the Khurāsānīs and the *Abnā'*]. Get up! [and do something!] For a person like you will not stay aloof from such a matter. The people of al-Jazīra pin their hopes to you and expect our help and succour." Ṭawq answered. "By God! I belong neither to their Qays nor to their Yaman. I had not been at the beginning of this affair, so why should I stay to see its end? I am too anxious for

26. On this tribal chief's loyalty to the ^cAbbāsids and cooperation with them see: Ṭabarī, II, p. 711, ll. 13–16; Weil, *Geschichte der Chalifen*, II, p. 203. His contention that he belongs neither to the Qays nor to the Yaman is correct, for the Taghlibis were descendants of Rabī^ca, the rivals of Muḍar, the father of Qays.

the survival of my people and too careful for the welfare of my tribe, that I should expose them to destruction because of these stupid persons of the army and because of these ignorant persons of Qays. I see safety only in staying away". (*a-lā tarā mā laqiyat al-ᶜArab min ha'ulā' inhaḍ fainna mithlaka lā yaqᶜud ᶜan hādhā al-amr qad madda ahl al-Jazīra aᶜyunahum ilayka wa-amalū ᶜawnaka wa-naṣraka fa-qāla wallāhi mā anā min Qaysihā wa-lā Yamanihā wa-lā kuntu fī awwal hādhā al-amr li-ashhada ākhirahu wa-innī laashaddu ibqā'an ᶜalā qawmī wa-anẓaru liᶜashīratī min an uᶜarriḍahum lil-halāk bi-sabab ha'ulā' al-sufahā' min al-jund wa-juhhāl Qays wa-mā arā al-salāma illā fī al-iᶜtizāl*) (Ṭabarī, III, p. 845, oo. 6–11). Now Naṣr b. Shabath[27] came forward at the head of the *Zawāqīl*. He rode a reddish-brown horse, with a blazon on its forehead, and wore a black garment (*durrāᶜa*)[28] which he tied behind his back. He held in his hand a spear and a shield, and said:

"Horsemen of Qays! Hold out against death!
Do not frighten me from meeting my end!
Stop wavering (?) with 'maybe' and 'would that'!"

Then he launched, together with his men, a very fierce attack. The opposing army held out against them. Many of the *Zawāqīl* were killed. The *Abnā'* attacked repeatedly, and in each of their attacks they killed and wounded many of their opponents. Those who distinguished themselves among the *Abnā'* (and the Khurāsānīs?) in that encounter were Kuthayyir b. Qādira, Abū al-Fīl and Dā'ūd b. Mūsā b. ᶜĪsā al-Khurāsānī. The *Zawāqīl* were routed. Their commanders (*kāna ᶜalā ḥāmiyatihim*) were then Naṣr b. Shabath [the ᶜUqaylid], ᶜAmr the Sulaymite and al-ᶜAbbās b. Zufar [the Hilālian] (Ṭabarī, III, pp. 842–845).

Before discussing the contents of the above two passages, it is essential to clarify the meaning of the term *Zawāqīl*. According to von Kremer (*Beiträge*, under *zaqala*) these are "ein syrischer Volkstamm". According to de Goeje they are "milites Syriae (et Mesopotamiae) non Arabes" (*Glossarium* to Ṭabarī, under *Zaqala*). I think that both definitions are wrong, and that the purport of the whole second passage will be misunderstood if we accept them. What I shall try to prove is that the

27. This is the first appearnce of Naṣr b. Shabath, the renowned champion of Arabdom. On his rebellion against Ma'mūn in defence of Arab rights see below.

28. The mention of the *durrāᶜa* in this context is significant, for the *durrāᶜa* was considered a typical Arab dress, whereas the *qabā'*, was considered a typical Persian dress. See Dozy, *Supplement*, *s.v.*

Zawāqīl were Arabs, and mainly Arabs who belonged to Northern (Qaysite) confederations.

The argument against von Kremer's definition is that it is highly improbable that in an area whose peoples are quite well known an entirely obscure people would suddenly spring up, play a central role in a big military gathering and fighting, and then disappear, almost completely. The contention against de Goeje is that he classified them as "non-Arabs". The sole basis for this classification is that when they are first mentioned in the passage under discussion, they appear in a context (*al-Zawāqīl wal-Aᶜrāb*) (Ṭabarī, III, p. 843, ll. 7–8) from which it might be concluded that they are different and distinct from the Arab Beduins. But one can cite numerous cases where the existence of a conjunction between two terms does not necessarily imply that they are different in meaning. In any case, the conjunction as a *sole* proof for a difference of meaning between such terms is a very flimsy argument. On the other hand, the very same passage furnishes overwhelming proof in support of the argument that the *Zawāqīl* were Arabs. Here are the proofs.

1) On the hearing of the slaughter of the *Zawāqīl* by the *Abnā'* ᶜAbd al-Malik b. Ṣāliḥ laments, in most moving words, the humiliation of the Arabs!

2) Naṣr b. Shabath, the famous chief of the Qaysite tribe Banū ᶜUqayl, who later (during Ma'mūn's reign) rebelled against the government in defence of Arabdom, is mentioned as heading the *Zawāqīl* in battle, and at the very same time reciting verses calling the *Qaysites* (!) to resist the enemy.

3) The commanders of the *Zawāqīl*, who are mentioned by name, are, without exception, chiefs of famous Qaysite tribes: Banū ᶜUqayl, Banū Sulaym and Banū Hilāl. Now, it is unimaginable under any circumstances, and especially in battle, that Arab chiefs would discard their own tribes, in order to head an anonymous element, and a non-Arab one at that. Add to this ᶜAbd al-Malik b. Ṣāliḥ's unequivocal classification of the *Zawāqīl* as Arabs, and you will arrive at the unavoidable conclusion that they were, in the passages under study, nothing but Arabs, and belonging mainly to tribal confederations.[29]

An earlier incident, in which the *Zawāqīl* are involved, offers, in my view, the explanation why certain parts of the Arab tribes were called *Zawāqīl* at that period. In the year 180/796–97, in Hārūn al-Rashīd's reign, tribal antagonism (*ᶜaṣabiyya*) among "the people of Syria" (*Ahl al-*

29. Many of the members of these confederations might have well reached various degress of urbanization.

Shām) acquired dangerous proportions. Ja^cfar b. Yaḥyā the Barmakid proceeded to Syria with the best commanders and a very well equipped army. He made peace between the rival parties, "and killed their *Zawāqīl* and robbers (*zawāqīluhum wal-mutalaṣṣiṣa minhum*). And he did not leave in it [i.e. in Syria] a lance or a horse". Then follow verses dealing with the same event, in one of which the poet says: "Its [i.e. Syria's] Qaḥṭān and Nizār have been reconciled" (Ṭabarī, III, p. 639, especially ll. 12–13 and l. 22). Here again the *Zawāqīl* are stated to have belonged to Arab tribal confederations. But there is an important addition: they are mentioned together with robbers. Now the meaning of *Zawāqīl* in Arab dictionaries *is* robbers.[30] The explanation of the term seems to be quite simple. Those Arab tribes who were more recalcitrant were named "robbers" by the authorities. Since the Qaysites were, on the whole, on worse terms with the ᶜAbbāsids than the Yamanites, this title was applied to them more frequently than to the Yamanites.[31] This application of such a designation to Arab tribal elements was facilitated by the fact that more and more of them resorted to brigandage as a result of the shrinkage of Arab influence and power. But in all probability the ᶜAbbāsids used that appellation quite liberally, without any connection with actual brigandage, as was the case with the Raqqa episode.[32]

To sum up: *Zawāqīl* is not an ethnic but a social designation. It was given to certain Arabs at that period because of the reasons and circumstances described above.

It has been necessary to give a full translation of Ṭabarī's description of the Raqqa episode and to deal with the clarification of the term *Zawāqīl* in considerable detail, because this is essential for understanding the position of the Arabs at that time, as well as their relations with the non-Arab military bodies, particularly with the *Abnā'*. What comes out so clearly from the Amīn–Ma'mūn struggle is the lack of real har-

---

30. This is a very common explanation of the term in most Arab dictionaries. Lane unfortunately omitted the whole verb *zaqala*. De Goeje alludes to this meaning. Certain Arab dictionaries do classify the *Zawāqīl* as a people living in the Jazīra and neighbouring areas (*Glossarium* to Ṭabarī, s.v.), but this cannot apply to the passages involved in the present study, where the meaning of Ṭabarī's unconscious evidence is beyond any possible doubt. In the Amīn–Ma'mūn struggle this term applied only to Arabs. Whether *Zawāqīl* developed later into meaning 'a people' is a question which I cannot answer. But even if such a development did take place, the *Zawāqīl* should not be classified as 'non Arabs', in the light of Ṭabarī's clear evidence.

31. In the case of Jaᶜfar b. Yaḥyā's operation in Syria both Northern and Southern Arabs are called *Zawāqīl*, because both of them caused trouble to the authorities.

32. The use of the term *Zawāqīl* might be similar to that of *Ṣaᶜālīq*. The last named frequently alternated brigandage with military service. The degree of similarity between the two terms has, however, still to be established.

mony and cooperation between the Arabs and the *Abnā'*. There was little cohesion between the operations of the two bodies during any stage of the struggle. On two important occasions they quarrelled in their places of gathering and scattered before even meeting the enemy. On the second of these occasions they quarrelled because of a trivial incident and parted after much bloodshed, which killed the chances of any future cooperation on a large scale between the two bodies. Amīn, who, unlike Ma'mūn, was of noble Arab descent both on his father's and mother's side, tried, from time to time, to show particular favour to the Arabs and rely on their loyalty.[33] But these were only half-hearted and ephemeral attempts. He had to comply with the *Abnā'*, because of their preponderance in general, and because of their strong position in Baghdad in particular.

The *Abnā'* are mentioned by the sources as a body which is distinctly different from the Khurāsānīs.[34] Once they are even mentioned as looking down upon the Khurāsānīs as being ᶜAjam, whereas they themselves are, by implication, non-ᶜAjam, and therefore superior to the Khurāsānīs.[35] Yet there is ample evidence for the existence of very strong ties between the *Abnā'* and Khurāsān, as I have tried to show earlier in this paper. This undoubtedly created a feeling of certain affinity and community of interests between them and the *Khurāsānīs*. In the *Zawāqīl* incident the *Abnā'* and the Khurāsānīs formed a very solid front in their fight against the Arabs.[36] Incidentally, this is the only occasion on which Khurāsānī troops are mentioned as fighting for Amīn.

The *Zawāqīl* incident also reveals the psychological transformation which the Arabs had undergone since the rise of the ᶜAbbāsids to power. Stupefaction, frustration and helplessness prevail in the Arab ranks in the face of the might of the *Abnā'* and the Khurāsānīs. The invincibility of the ᶜAbbāsid non-Arab armies is depicted in most colourful and forceful words by Arabs who took part in the conflict. The attitude of the Arabs at al-Raqqa is certainly representative and typical of their attitude in general at that time, for the strongest and best Arab elements of Syria and Upper Mesopotamia gathered there in very great numbers,

33. Cp. the references in note 17. The Abnāwī Ḥusayn b. ᶜAlī b. ᶜĪsā mentions Amīn's friendly relations with the Zawāqīl as a good reason for deposing him (Ṭabarī, III, p. 847).

34. Jāḥiẓ, *Manāqib*, p. 4, ll. 5–6. Ṭayfūr, *Kitāb Baghdād*, pp. 143–144 (see also Appendix). Ṭabarī, III, pp. 842–845.

35. Ṭabarī, III, p. 829, ll. 4–5. See the full citation above, in connection with ᶜAbd al-Raḥmān b. Jabala al-Abnāwī's activities.

36. In the last stage of the battle against the *Zawāqīl* Ṭabarī's wording gives the impression that he speaks of the *Abnā'* and the Khurāsānīs as if they constituted one body (*ibid*., p. 845, ll. 17–20).

as our source puts it so clearly. These had the explicit intention of boosting their own declining power and prestige. Yet the whole attempt ended in complete failure. The Yamanites showed total indifference. The Taghlibīs, though they were a Northern tribe, belonged to the Rabī'a branch, which had a long standing animosity with the Muḍar branch, and which supported the ᶜAbbāsids from time to time. Only some of the most important tribes of Qays–Muḍar were prepared to give battle, but they proved to be too weak to face Amīn's regular troops alone. Both the internal splits of the Arabs and the fact that they could not find any common ground with the *Abnā'* and Khurāsānīs, doomed ᶜAbd al-Malik b. Ṣāliḥ's scheme to failure from the very outset. The opportunity given to the Arabs by Amīn might look bright on paper. In reality, however, their chances of seizing at it were very meager indeed.

Such was the position of the Arabs under Amīn, who though he did not deserve the title of a champion of the Arabs, was, on the whole, quite well disposed towards them. As for Ma'mūn, the earliest chronicles dealing with his rule give only few facts which throw light on his attitude to the Arabs (with the important exception of the rebellion of Naṣr b. Shabath, who rose against him in defence of Arabdom).[37] Yet there can be little doubt left concerning his strong anti-Arab disposition. Ṭayfūr's *Kitāb Baghdād* contains a most revealing passage on this subject, which was copied verbatim by al-Ṭabarī. The passage, entitled *Akhbār al-Ma'mūn bil-Shām*, runs as follows.

> Muḥammad b. ᶜAlī b. Ṣāliḥ al-Sarakhsī told me: A man accosted Al-Ma'mūn several times in Syria and said to him. 'O Commander of the Believers! Look after the Arabs of Syria as you look after the ᶜAjam of Khurāsān'. Al-Ma'mūn answered: 'O brother of the people of Syria! *By God! I have dismounted the Qays from the backs of their horses because I discoverd that there was not left in my treasury even one dirham (wallāhi mā anzaltu Qaysan min ẓuhūr al-khayl illā wa-anā arā annahu lam yabqa fī bayt mālī dirham wāḥid*). As for the Yaman, neither did I love them nor did they love me at all! As for the Quḍāᶜa, its chiefs are waiting with expectation for [the Umayyad] al-Sufyānī and his rebellion, so that they can become his supporters. As for the Rabīᶜa, they are angry with God ever since he sent His Prophet from the Muḍar. Out of every two who revolt, one is always a Khārijite, of the Rabīᶜa. Get out! [You advocate of the Arabs of Syria!] Will God

37. See Naṣr b. Shabath's own testimony on the motives of his rebellion in Ibn al-Athīr, VI, p. 216. On the activities of this fascinating and extremely brave and proud personality, see Ṭabarī, index.

inflict punishment on you! (*i^czib fa^cala Allāh bika*)' (*Kitāb Baghdād*, pp. 266–267; Ṭabarī, III, 1142, ll. 5–13).

One important lesson of the above passage is that Ma'mūn dismissed all the Arabs, irrespective of whether they were Qaysites or Yamanites, as not deserving to enjoy his care and attention. Another lesson, of similar importance, is that there existed hard economic and financial factors which induced the ^cAbbāsids to treat the Arabs as they did. The Arabs, though very much weakened, were still very influential and enjoyed many hereditary rights, one of the most important of which was their being registered in the *Dīwān* and their receiving regular pay from the treasury. Amongst these payees there were many who were classified as soldiers. Once the ^cAbbāsids decided to reorganize their armies on new lines, and rely on non-Arab elements as the backbone of their fighting forces, they were bound, sooner or later, to oust the Arabs, both soldiers and other kinds of pensioners, from the *Dīwān*. The shrinking of revenues, and the extremely great wastage of money and treasures during the Amīn–Ma'mūn struggle, could only hasten the carrying out of such a measure by the ^cAbbāsids. From the passage under discussion it is made abundantly clear that this measure was directed, first and foremost, against the Arab military element.

Al-Mu^ctaṣim, the successor of al-Ma'mūn, and the man who introduced Mamlūk military society on a grand scale into the Muslim countries, seems to have pursued the policy of turning the Arabs out of the *Dīwān* with great tenacity. This can be deduced from the following piece of information.

> Al-Ma'mūn died ... and the Muslims elected Abū Isḥāq al-Mu^ctaṣim as caliph. His [al-Mu^ctaṣim's] letter reached Kaydar [the governor of Egypt]. He informed him of his election and ordered him to drop the names of the Arabs from the Diwan and to stop their pay. Kaydar did so (*fa-warada kitābuhu ilā Kaydar bi-bay^catihi wa-amarahu bi-isqāṭ man fī al-Dīwān min al-^cArab wa-qaṭ^c a^cṭiyatihim fa-fa^cala dhālika Kaydar*) (Kindi, *Wulāt*, etc. p. 193, ll. 13–16).

It cannot be mere chance that in the very first letter which al-Mu^ctaṣim sent to his governor, announcing his election to the caliphate, the only thing which he added to this announcement, was an order to eject the Arabs from the *Dīwān*. This proves the extreme importance which he attached to this matter.

A late historian, al-Maqrīzī (died 1442), speaks of the policy of al-Ma'mūn and al-Mu^ctaṣim towards the Arabs on the one hand and towards the Turkish-Mamlūks on the other, in the following words.

> He [al-Ma'mūn] bought numerous Turks and paid high prices for them. He sometimes paid as much as 200,000 dirhams for one

> Mamlūk. His brother Abū Isḥāq al-Muᶜtaṣim followed his example. ... He ousted the Arabs, the Prophet's people, with whom God established the Muslim religion, from the *Dīwān*, and stopped their pay. And their pay was stopped, *and ever since they have not been given pay* [from the *Dīwān*] (*wa-asqaṭa ᶜaṭā'ahum fa-saqaṭa wa-lam yufraḍ lahum baᶜdahu ᶜaṭā'*). He introduced the Turks in their stead and he took off the dress of the Arabs and their attire, and put on the dress of the ᶜAjam, against whom God sent his Prophet Muhammad, in order to kill them and fight them. Arab rule (*al-dawla al-ᶜArabiyya*) ceased to exist with him and by means of him. Since his time and his reign the Turks, against whom the Prophet called to fight became the rulers of the [Muslim] kingdoms (*Kitāb al-Nizāᶜ wal-Takhāṣum*, p. 63, ll. 5–15).

Of course, every detail of the evidence of such a late authority should be carefully checked in the light of the data furnished by earlier sources. In the context of the present paper it is particularly important to find out whether al-Maqrīzī's contention that Muᶜtaṣim excluded the Arabs from the *Dīwān*, completely and forever, is correct or not. As for the acquisition of Mamlūks in the reign of Ma'mūn, there is ample and well-known evidence that both he and his brother Muᶜtaṣim acquired them on a considerable scale before the last-named became caliph. It is worthy of note that even at that early period the Mamlūks reached the ᶜAbbāsids through the cooperation of the Ṭāhirid ᶜAbdallāh b. Ṭāhir and the Sāmānid Nūḥ b. Asad.[38] Later on, with the steady decline of ᶜAbbāsid authority in the east on the one hand, and with the corresponding rise of strong border-states in the region on the other, the dependence of the caliphs on these states for the supply of Mamlūks increased manifold.

The main conclusion to be derived from the present article up to this point is that the rise of the *Mawālī* and the eunuchs in the ᶜAbbāsid court, as well as the decline of Arab power throughout the ᶜAbbāsid Empire, which was accelerated by the determined policy of the rulers, paved the way for the introduction of the Mamlūks as a major military force in the capital and in other important centers. The military qualities of the "People of Baghdad", and particularly those of the *Abnā'*, formed a major obstacle in realizing

38. Yaᶜqūbī, *Kitāb al-Buldān*, pp. 255, l. 20–256, l. 1. Ṭabarī, III, p. 1017. Ibn Khurdādhbih, pp. 37, 39. Ibn al-Dāya, p. 4, ll. 1–4. Kindī, *Wulāt*, p. 188, ll. 6–7. See also Ḥamza al-Iṣfāhānī, *Ta'rīkh*, etc. Beirut, 1961, p. 172. M.J. Kister, of the Hebrew University of Jerusalem, called my attention to the passage in al-Maqrīzī's *Kitāb al-Nizāᶜ wal-Takhāṣum* cited above.

that object. The obstacle was circumvented by the building of a new ᶜAbbāsid capital.[39]

*

* *

The creation of the Mamlūk regiment by al-Muᶜtaṣim opened a new era in Muslim military and socio-military history. Yet the achievements of this regiment and of its successors in Baghdad were not spectacular. Some of the main reasons for this phenomenon are:

a) The reign of caliph al-Muᶜtaṣim who was, by any standard, a great man and a great military leader, was far too short (833–842) for such a grand experience to take root and be shaped according to the ideas of its creator. Al-Muᶜtaṣim was succeeded by caliphs who could not match his talents as a soldier and as a leader of men, and therefore could not command the same degree of respect and admiration which he enjoyed among his Mamlūks.

b) The appearance of the Mamlūks as a major military force under the ᶜAbbāsids roughly coincided with the beginning of the disintegration of their caliphate, a fact which prevented the caliphs from making proper use of them. They soon became embroiled in the growing intrigues of the court, and sank deeply into them. Still worse, the rise of independent and semi-independent Muslim states made the capital more and more cut off from Islam's frontiers with the unbelievers. Even under al-Muᶜtaṣim his Mamlūks never fought the Turkish and other (mainly pagan) unbelievers living beyond the Islamic frontier in the areas which stretched from the Black Sea to Afghanistan. They fought heretics in the Caspian mountainous areas who were active *within* the borders of Islam. On the Byzantine frontier circumstances were somewhat different in the days of that caliph. Al-Muᶜtaṣim penetrated at the head of an immense and extremely well equipped army deep into Anatolia and captured Amorium. But this was the last big Muslim campaign in that direction. The grip of the caliphs on Syria and even on the Jazīra gradually weakened and, as a result, their contact with the Byzantine frontier was weakened as well.

39. I have alluded to the Khurāsānīs up till now only perfunctorily, because there are still numerous points which need clarification (I mean the Khurāsānīs who served in the ᶜAbbāsid forces up to the influx of the Transoxanians. On these see below).

Being surrounded by Muslim countries, the caliphal Mamlūks did not have any important goal to strive for. In the great Muslim states which had a common boundary with Dār al-Ḥarb, and which based their might on Mamlūk or so-called "slave" armies, the "slave" soldiers had a very distinct mission and the part they took in fulfilling it was most decisive. This is true of the Sāmānid and Ghaznawid empires in the east and of the Mamlūk and Ottoman empires in the west.

The importance of the Sāmānids lay in the fact that they were, since the days of Ma'mūn, the main channel through which Mamlūks were brought to the Muslim world, and that they themselves built an extremely strong Mamlūk army, which undoubtedly served as a model for other Muslim states, especially the Ghaznawids. Furthermore, this strong Mamlūk army enabled them to penetrate deeply into "the countries of the Turks" (*Bilād al-Turk*) and thus secure the orderly supply of Mamlūks to the countries of Islam, as well as establish relations with the Turks, which must have greatly influenced the future contacts of these peoples with *Dār al-Islām* (for the special position of Transoxania and the neighbouring areas vis-à-vis the Turks see below). The importance of the Ghaznawids lay in their unique contribution to the conquest and islamization of Northern India, thus creating one of the biggest and most populous centers of Islam. Mamlūks constituted the backbone of the Ghaznawid conquering armies. The importance of the Mamlūk sultanate of Egypt and Syria lay in its elimination of the Crusaders from the Syro–Palestinian littoral, in its checking the Mongols and staving off their attacks with far greater success than any other opponent of the Mongols, and in its guarding the coast of Egypt and Syria from a possible Frankish invasion. Unlike the Ottomans, however, who for centuries first pushed the Muslim frontier deep into Europe, and later defended it against Christendom's counter attacks, the Mamlūk sultanate lost its active mission early in its history. Incidentally, out of all the four states under discussion, only the Mamlūk sultanate did not annex any new territory from *Dār al-Ḥarb* to *Dār al-Islām*. This was because on land their sultanate bordered only with Muslim countries, whereas their coast "bordered" with the Frankish naval might which was far superior to their own.

c) The rise of Muslim states between Baghdad and the Eastern and North-Eastern frontiers of Islam was detrimental to the creation by the ᶜAbbāsid caliphs of a strong Mamlūk army in yet another important way. The routes connecting the ᶜAbbāsid capital with the Mamlūks' countries of origin lay across territories of Muslim rulers, who were themselves eager, for various reasons, to emulate the caliphs and maintain strong Mamlūk armies, and who could easily cut Baghdad from it sources of supply, or control and regulate the passage of Mamlūks beyond their borders according to their own interests (the Sāmānids did regulate the passage of the Mamlūks beyond the Oxus, according to the explicit statement of al-Muqaddasī).

The fact that the caliphs suffered from grave limitations in their attempts to build and maintain their Mamlūk forces, as well as the fact that the performances of these Mamlūks were not very impressive, should not obscure the reason why the caliphs preferred them over others. The cause of the establishment of the Mamlūk institution on a wide scale in the ^c^Abbāsid capital and of its quick adoption in numerous Muslim countries was, without doubt, the Mamlūks' military superiority. There is clear evidence in the sources to this effect.

Speaking of the Turkish Mamlūks of the ^c^Abbāsid caliphs al-Iṣṭakhrī says: "and the Turks constituted their [the caliphs'] armies because of their superiority over other races in prowess, valour, courage and intrepidity" (*wa-kānat al-Atrāk juyūshahum li-faḍlihim ^c^alā sā'ir al-ajnās fī al-ba's wal-jar'a wal-shajā^c^a wal-iqdām*) (*Masālik al-Mamālik*, p. 291, ll. 16–17).[40]

Particularly instructive is the following episode told by al-Jāḥiẓ:

I [i.e. Jāḥiẓ] tell you that I witnessed from them [i.e. from the Turks] something wonderful and extraordinary. I saw in one of Ma'mūn's campaigns (*ghazawāt*) two lines of horsemen on both sides of the road near the halting place [in which the caliph and his army intended to camp]. The line on the right-hand side of the road was composed of 100 Turkish horsemen. The line on the left-hand side of the road was composed of 100 horsemen of "others" (*min sā'ir al-nās*). All were arrayed in battle-order, awaiting the arrival of Ma'mūn. [But the caliph seems to have been delayed on his way and meanwhile] it was midday and the heat became intense. When Ma'mūn reached the place he found all the Turks sitting on the backs of their horses, with the exception of three or four, whereas 'all that medley' (*jamī^c^ tilka al-Akhlāṭ*) have thrown themselves on the ground, with the exception of three or four. [Remembering that episode] I said to a friend of mine: see what happened to us! I swear that al-Mu^c^taṣim knew them better than we did when he gathered them and fostered them (*fa-qultu li-ṣāḥib lī unẓur ayy shay' ittafaqa lanā ashhadu anna al-Mu^c^taṣim kāna a^c^raf bihim ḥīna jama^c^ahum wa-iṣṭana^c^ahum*) (*Manāqib*, pp. 38, l. 21–30, l. 8).

40. Ibn Ḥawqal expresses the same idea in different words: *wa-kāna al-Atrāk rijālahum li-faḍlihim ^c^alā sā'ir al-juyūsh-Ṣurat al-Arḍ*, p. 448, ll. 9–10.

Al-Jāḥiẓ's appreciation of the contribution of the Turks serving in the ᶜAbbāsid caliph's armies, both to the strengthening of Islam and to the protection of their masters, deserves also special notice. He says,

> They became to Islam a source of reinforcement and an enormous army, and to the caliphs a protection and a shelter and an invulnerable armour and an innermost garment worn under the upper garment (*fa-ṣārū lil-Islām māddatan wa-jundan kathīfan wa-lil-khulafā' wiqāyatan wa-maw'ilan wa-junnatan ḥaṣīnatan wa-shiᶜāran dūna al-dithār*[41]) (*Manāqib*, p. 49, ll. 7–8).[42]

The inception, the growth, the structure and the character of the Mamlūk regiments of al-Muᶜtaṣim and his successors were deeply affected by the process of the final subjugation and the full islamization of Transoxania and its neighbouring areas, which took place in the days of al-Ma'mūn and al-Muᶜtaṣim. The definitive conquest of this region was accompanied by a vast recruitment of soldiers, with special stress on commanders of noble descent from amongst its population, and their inclusion in the *Dīwān*, as well as by incursions of Muslim Transoxanians into the countries of the Turks,[43] which grew with the years in scale and in intensity.

It thus happened that the Turkish Mamlūks came to Baghdad in great numbers close on the heels of the Transoxanians, for the Muslims' growing pressure on the Turks in Central Asia greatly facilitated the regular supply of Mamlūks to the Muslim countries. A central aspect of the study of the history of the caliphal Mamlūks is, therefore, the examination of their relations and antagonisms with the Transoxanian regiments, which, in their turn, were not united (there was a separate regiment of *Farāghina* and a separate regiment of *Ushrūsiyya*). The Transoxanians were ultimately overpowered and eliminated, but this was only after a long struggle, in which the Mamlūks made full use of the dissensions among the different Transoxanian racial groups.

---

41. This is a very high distinction. In a tradition relating to the Anṣār they are addressed: *antum al-shiᶜār wal-nās al-dithār*, which Lane translates "ye are the special and close friends [and the people in general are less near in friendship]." It is noteworthy that *shiᶜār* means also a coat of mail [worn under the garment]. See *Tāj al-ᶜArūs*, under *dirᶜ* and Hava's dictionary.

42. Cp. also Ibn Khaldūn's high praise of the Mamlūk institution since al-Muᶜtaṣim's reign up to his own time, and its role as a protector of Islam, especially in the Mamlūk sultanate of Egypt and Syria (*Kitāb ad-ᶜIbar*, V, pp. 370–371. On various qualities of the Turkish Mamlūks see Addenda.

43. Balādhurī, *Futūḥ*, p. 431.

Transoxania and the adjacent areas had a strong influence on the caliphal and other Mamlūks in yet another way. These areas are described by the contemporary sources as extremely rich, densely populated, with thriving commerce and agriculture, and rich in mineral deposits.[44] Besides, once their population was finally subjugated, they accepted Islam and Islamic culture with great and growing zeal. This population is described as deeply religious, immersed in Muslim culture, generous towards foreign Muslims, and especially towards those volunteers who flocked to the frontiers, very warlike and imbued with the spirit of *Jihād* against the unbelievers. The number of *ribāṭs* (fortified frontier "monasteries") in that region is said by the sources to have been immense.[45] While military preparedness and alertness in that front were at their height, on the Byzantine front they were on the wane. The geographer al-Muqaddasī, who knew both fronts and both regions, gives us a very vivid description to that effect.[46]

Such were the people with whom the Turkish nomads had contacts during long periods of peace and war, and whom the Turkish Mamlūks came to know first when they crossed the borders of Islam. Many of the choicest Mamlūks did not go further west beyond the borders of the Muslim frontier states, because they were incorporated in their armies, or bought by their well-to-do people. As for those Mamlūks who did continue their journey westward, it is only logical to think that quite a number of them did not just cross the frontier states, but stayed there for varying periods before pursuing their journey. When the Turkish Mamlūks arrived in Baghdad, they found there strong and influential Transoxanian units which must have received steady reinforcements from their own peoples, for otherwise these units could not have existed for a considerable number of decades, as they actually did. Thus, Transoxanian influence on the Mamlūks, including even those who reached Baghdad, must have been very great in the early ᶜAbbāsid period.[47]

---

44. The richness of Khwārizm was based mainly on its commerce. Its natural resources were far smaller than Transoxania's.

45. There is a certain amount of idealization in the unanimous views expressed by numerous sources on these areas, yet there is no reason to think that these views are not basically true.

46. *Aḥsan al-Taqāsīm*, p. 137, ll. 4–5; p. 160, ll. 9–13, pp. 260–261 (for the identity of *al-Mashriq*, with the Sāmānid Empire in al-Muqaddasī's terminology see *ibid.*, p. 7, ll. 20–21).

47. The sources speak of the existence of a physical resemblance between the Turks and their Khwārizmian and Transoxanian (particularly Ferghanī) neighbours. This could only stimulate the mutual influence between them. There is also the question of Turks living or roaming inside Transoxania, which will not be discussed here.

Al-Muᶜtaṣim's building of Sāmarrā and his move from Baghdad to his new capital, enabled him to effect a complete separation between his new armies, which were stationed in Sāmarrā, and many elements of the old ᶜAbbāsid armies which were left behind in Baghdad. This created a new élite, composed mainly of Turks and Transoxanians, and perhaps also of Khurāsānīs from the left bank of the Oxus (on the Maghribis see below). A new situation was created, in which the degree of nearness to the Turks served as the criterion for importance and notability. The following passage from al-Masᶜūdi is significant. He says:

> He [i.e. al-Muᶜtaṣim] built for the Turks separate quarters and made the *Farāghina*, the *Ushrūsiyya* and others from the towns of Khurāsān their neighbours, and this according to their nearness to them [to the Turks] in their countries of origin (*fa-jaᶜala lil-Atrāk qaṭā'iᶜ muta-ḥayyiza wa-jāwarahum bil-Farāghina wal-Ushrūsiyya wa-ghayrihim min mudun Khurāsān ᶜalā qadri qurbihim minhum fī bilādihim*) (*Murūj*, VII, p. 121, ll. 3–4).

Whether al-Muᶜtaṣim kept strictly to this order remains yet to be proved.[48] But the idea lying behind al-Masᶜūdī's testimony is definitely correct. The nearer a people's homeland was to the countries of the Turks, the more esteemed were this people's representatives in the capital.

Proximity to the Turks did not mean, however, merging with them into one unit. The contention of certain late Muslim chronicles that the Turks were sometimes included under the name *Farāghina* is not substantiated by the earlier sources. These sources clearly distinguish between the *Atrāk*, the *Farāghina* and the *Ushrūsiyya*, mentioning them throughout, with only few exceptions, as separate bodies alternately collaborating with, or fighting one another.

Al-Yaᶜqūbī's detailed description of Sāmarrā (*Kitāb al-Buldān*, pp. 255–268) leaves us in no doubt that al-Muᶜtaṣim's mind was set upon separating the Turks from the rest of the people, from the rest of the military racial groups and even from the *Farāghina*, who were given the privilege of being their nearest neighbours. On mentioning the Fourth Street, named after Barghāmush the Turk, al-Yaᶜqūbī says: *fīhi qaṭā' iᶜal-Atrāk wal-Farāghina fa-durūb al-Atrāk munfarida wa-durūb al-Farāghina munfarida wal-Atrāk fī al-durūb allatī fī al-qibla wal-Farāghina bi-izā'ihim bil-durūb allatī fī ẓahr al-qibla kullu darb bi-izā' darb lā yukhāliṭuhum aḥad min al-nās* (*ibid.*, p. 262, ll. 11–13). On mentioning the "Fifth

48. In any event, al-Masᶜūdī's statement is true as far as the *Farāghina* are concerned, for they, who were the Turks' nearest neighbours in their homeland, were also their nearest neighbours in Sāmarrā (see below).

Street", called Shāri^c^ al-^c^Askar, the same author says: *fīhi qaṭā'i^c^ al-Atrāk wal-Farāghina wal-Atrāk ayḍan fī durūb munfarida wal-Farāghina fī durūb munfarida* (*ibid.*, p. 262, ll. 18–20).

The main passage in al-Ya^c^qūbī's description of Sāmarrā dedicated to the special status of the Turks and the *Farāghina* runs as follows:

> He [i.e. al-Mu^c^taṣim] separated the *Qaṭā'i^c^ of* the Turks from the *Qaṭā'i^c^* of the rest of the people, and he isolated them [i.e. the Turks] from them [from the rest of the people] so that they would not mix with people of hybrid origin (*lā yakhtaliṭūna bil-muwalladīn*). Their only neighbours were the *Farāghina.* ... He built a wall stretching [over a long distance], which he called Ḥā'ir al-Ḥayr. Thus the *Qaṭā'i^c^* of all the Turks, and those of *al-Farāghina al-^c^Ajam* were placed far away from the markets and from the congestion and [were distinguished by] their wide streets and long alleys (*durūb*). In those *Qaṭā'i^c^* and *Durūb* of theirs there were no other people, like merchants or others, with whom they could mix. Then he [i.e. al-Mu^c^taṣim] bought slave-girls for them, and married them with these slave-girls and forbade them to marry or be related by marriage to any of the *Muwalladūn*, so that when their children grow up, they will intermarry [exclusively] amongst themselves. He gave the slave-girls permanent pensions (*arzāq*) and registered their names in the *Dīwāns.* None of them [of the Turks] could divorce his wife or leave her. When al-Mu^c^taṣim allotted Ashnās the Turk and his followers their *Qaṭā'i^c^* at the end of the built-up area ... and called the place al-Karkh, he ordered Ashnās not to allow any strangers, like merchants or others, to be their neighbours, and at the same time not to allow his followers to associate with the *Muwalladūn.* ... He built within the *Qaṭā'i^c^* [of the Turks] mosques and public baths and established in each place a small market (*suwayqa*) including a number of shops of grocers, butchers and the like, namely, persons of indispensable professions (*ibid.*, pp. 258, l. 15–259, l. 10).

The degree of segregation in Sāmarrā seems to me to have been exceptional in its severity. Whether that planned segregation was strictly enforced is another question. But the principles guiding al-Mu^c^taṣim come out very clearly in the above passage. I rather doubt whether any other Mamlūk society ever attempted to carry out such exclusive principles (note particularly the prohibition of a whole body of Muslim males from divorcing their wives). But although other Mamlūk societies did not go to such extremes, a wide social gulf separated them from the rest of the Muslim population. Al-Mu^c^taṣim's contribution to the creation of that gulf must have been very great indeed.

APPENDIX

The Abnā' *Excel the Khurāsānīs and the Turks in Military Qualities*

The struggle and competition between the various racial groups in the Muslim armies must have caused vivid and heated controversies between their respective protagonists. Such controversies, whether real or imaginary, offered a convenient opportunity to certain Muslim writers, to express their own opinion on the subject. The most famous instance is that of al-Jāḥiẓ in his *Manāqib al-Atrāk*. A much less known, but similarly instructive, instance is that told by Ṭayfūr.[1] Here is its translation.

> I was told that Ma'mūn and Muᶜtaṣim and another person, who was a commander, but whose name escaped me, had a discussion in which they disagreed about who was the bravest of the commanders and of the army and of the *Mawālī*. Ma'mūn said: "There is none in the world who is braver or more ferocious towards the enemy than the Khurāsānīs (*ᶜAjam Ahl Khurāsān*)". Muᶜtaṣim said: "There is none in the world who is braver or more numerous or more firm in their attacks on the enemy than the Turks. Suffice it to say that they inflict punishment on each one of the hostile enemies confronting them, and raid them in their own country, whereas they [i.e. the Turks] are raided by none." The commander said: "There is none in the world who is braver or more devastating than *Abnā' Khurāsān al-Muwalladūn*. For it was they who put [the heads of] the Turks into dogs' collars, and it was their fathers who were the leaders of the [ᶜAbbāsid] dynasty, and it was they [the *Abnā'*] who undertook the fighting against the caliph [Ma'mūn], then they obeyed him and the caliphate was kept in good order by means of them" (*wa-ābā' uhum hum alladhīna qādū al-dawla wa-hum qāmū bi-ḥarb Amīr al-Mu'minīn thumma aṭāᶜūhu fa-istaqāmat al-khilāfa bihim*). Ma'mūn said: "What will you do with our disagreement? We have [here in Baghdad] Naṣr b. Shabath.[2] We shall send for him and ask him who was the bravest of all our armies and commanders whom he met in the field of battle". He gave orders for Naṣr to be presented, and when Naṣr came he told him about their controversy and asked his opinion. Naṣr answered: "O Commander of the Faithful! There is nothing like the truth! (*al-ḥaqq awlā mā ustuᶜmila*). I met them all in battle.[3] As for the Turk, his power is in his arrows.

1. Interesting is also the controversy about who was stronger, the People of Khurāsān or the People of Syria, and Abū Muslim's verdict (Ṭabarī, III, p. 96, ll. 15–9 – A.H.137/754–55).

2. After his defeat and capture Naṣr b. Shabath was kept in Baghdad.

3. We know that he fought the *Abnā'* and the Khurāsānīs from the *Zawāqīl* incident. He must have fought the Turks as well, when he rebelled against Ma'mūn.

As soon, however, as he runs out of them 'he can be taken by the hand' (*yu'khadh bil-yad*). As for the ᶜAjamī [from Khurāsān], his power is in his sword. If, however, he gets tired, he exposes himself to death (*istabsala*). As for the *Abnā'*, I never saw the like of them. They are tireless and indefatigable and invincible. They fight in the bitterest cold wearing shabby (?) waist-wrappers, without a cuirass and without an armour and without a shield. Once [they fight] with a sword, once with a lance and once with arrows. They wade through icy rivers and they wade through fire in the midday heat. They are tireless and indefatigable.' The commander said: "we are satisfied with your verdict in our dispute" (*ḥasbunā bika ḥakaman baynanā*) (*Kitāb Baghdād*, pp. 143, l. 7–144, l. 14).

It is doubtful, of course, whether the discussion described above ever took place. Yet, had the *Abnā'* not constituted a major military force in the ᶜAbbāsid army, such a story could not have been invented. The military importance of the *Abnā'* is also confirmed by the prominent place which al-Jāḥiẓ accords them in his *Manāqib*, and far more by their share in the Amīn–Ma'mūn struggle. Ṭayfūr, if I understood him correctly, also states that it was they who fought Ma'mūn. But the same author goes much further in attributing the stability of the caliphate under Ma'mūn to the *Abnā'*, who came to terms with him and accepted his rule. The position of the *Abnā'* under Ma'mūn is very vague. Yet it is quite certain that Ṭayfūr erred on the side of exaggeration. The *Abnā'*, in all probability, though much shaken, still remained a force to be reckoned with. Their contribution to the ousting of Muᶜtaṣim's Mamlūk regiment from Baghdad was very great indeed (see, *inter alia*, Ṭabarī, III, pp. 1179–1181). At a much later date caliph al-Muhtadī (869–870) made an attempt to strengthen the *Abnā'* at the expense of the Turkish Mamlūks (Yaᶜqūbī, *Ta'rīkh*, II, pp. 618–619. See also *ibid.*, p. 604). Such an attempt had, of course, no chance of success, but the very fact that it had been made, shows that the *Abnā'* had not yet been written off as an utterly worthless ally.

Addition to the Section dealing with the Abnā'

On *Ahl Baghdād* as a military body, fighting inside and outside the capital, and receiving regular pay, during and after the Amīn–Ma'mūn contest, see: Ṭabarī, III, pp. 831, ll. 8–9; 858, ll. 1–5; 865, ll. 8–9; 866, l. 6, ll. 16–17; 898, l. 14; 1006, ll. 4, 7, 9; 1001, ll. 2–4; 1013, ll. 9–10, 17.

On *Ahl al-Arbāḍ:* Ṭabarī, III, pp. 849, l. 3; 866, l. 9; 867, ll. 13–14; 871, ll. 15–18; 872, l. 13; 934, ll. 4, 5; 935, ll. 11, 12; 936, l. 7.

On the *Ḥarbiyya* (or *Ahl al-Ḥarbiyya*): Ṭabarī, III, pp. 825, l. 18; 847, ll. 9–14; 848, l. 12; 869, l. 18; 985, ll. 16–17; 998, l. 10–1000, l. 11; 1002, ll. 2, 10; 1008–1012; Yaᶜqūbī, *Ta'rīkh*, pp. 547, 548, 564. On the founder of the Ḥarbiyya quarter (died 147/764) see Ṭabarī, III, p. 328, ll. 11–12. The population of that quarter was composed according to Yaᶜqūbī (*Kitāb al-Buldān*, p. 248, ll. 14–18. Le Strange, *Baghdād*, p. 109), mainly of Transoxanians, Khwārizmians, people from the Kabul region and people from Eastern Khurāsān. Many of those might have come at an early date, but it is reasonable to think that their numbers were greatly increased since the influx of the Transoxanians and their neighbours in the reigns of Ma'mūn and Muᶜtaṣim.

On the connection between *Abnā'*, *Ḥarbiyya*, *Ahl al-Arbāḍ* and *Ahl Baghdād*, see: Ṭabarī, III, pp. 866, ll. 16–17 (*Abnā' Ahl Baghdād*); 934, ll. 1–7; 935, ll. 11–12 (*Abnā' al-Arbāḍ*); 998, ll. 14, 16; 999, ll. 3–4; Cp. 1001, l. 20 (*Abnā'*) with 1002, l. 2 (*Ḥarbiyya*). Yaᶜqūbī, *Ta'rīkh*, II, pp. 532–33; 535;

On the rise of the *ghawghā'*, *shuṭṭār*, *fussāq*, etc. and the dependence of the rulers on them: Ṭabarī, III, pp. 867, l. 151; 872, l. 13; 873, l. 1; 881, ll. 9–11; 888, ll. 4–7; 899, l. 9; 900, ll. 11–20; 1008f; 1010, ll. 4–10, 18–19; 1012, l. 19f.

That a conjunction between two terms does not necessarily imply that the terms are different in meaning, can be learnt from phrases like: A*hl Baghdād wal-Ḥarbiyya*; *al-Jund min al-Ḥarbiyya wal-Baghdādiyyin* (Ṭabarī, III, p. 998, ll. 14, 16); *al-Abnā' wa-Ahl Baghdād* (*Ibid*., p. 846, l. 13); *al-Jund wal-Abnā'* (p. 842, l. 20).

It has been stated earlier in this paper that ᶜAlī b. ᶜĪsā went to fight Ma'mūn at the head of 50,000 horsemen and infantry men of "the People of Baghdad", and that at the critical moment of the battle he addressed his army with the phrase "*Yā maᶜshar al-Abnā'*", which proves that these constituted the most important element in that army. It should be added, in this connection, that, according to Baghdadi eye-witnesses, such a numerous and such a well equipped army had never seen before in the city (Ṭabarī, III, p. 818, ll. 12–18). Ma'mūn was proclaimed caliph only after the defeat of that army. As for the 20,000 *Abnā'* headed by ᶜAbdallāh b. Ḥumayd b. Qaḥṭaba, the same number is repeated in connection with the same expedition by Amīn himself in his above-mentioned address to the army of the *Abnā'* (Ṭabarī, III, p. 932, l. 1).

According to Jāḥiẓ there was amongst the *Abnā'* a sizable body of excellent infantrymen, whose weapons and tactics he describes (*Manāqib*, pp. 16, 33–34). I have not yet found any clear evidence corroborating Jāḥiẓ's contention. There were, indeed, infantrymen in ᶜAlī b. ᶜĪsā's army, as well as in the army sent to Raqqa, in which the *Abnā'* constituted the major element (Ṭabarī, III, p. 846, l. 9), but whether those infantrymen were *Abnā'* or not is a moot question. The passage from Ṭayfūr might hint to their being infantrymen.

For data on the *Abnā'* before the struggle between Amīn and Ma'mūn see: Ṭabarī, III, pp. 498, ll. 2, 6; 531, ll. 13–14 (Cp. the corrections in the glossary volume); 672, ll. 6–8; 703, ll. 14–16; 732, ll. 15–16. In these references they are never called just *Abnā'*, but appear in the following combinations: *Abnā' al-da^c^wa*; *Abnā' shī^c^atī wa-ahl da^c^watī*; *ibn man sabaqa ilā da^c^watika*; *a^c^qāb Abnā' hādhihi al-dawla*; *Abnā' al-shī^c^a*; *Abnā' dawlatika*. This shows how interchangeable are *dawla*, *da^c^wa* and *shī^c^a*. See also *ibid.*, p. 847 (cp. l. 1 with l. 5); p. 931, l. 18; and particularly the excellent examples to the same effect in *Manāqib*, p. 15, ll. 3–7, and pp. 8–9.

For *Abnā'* living outside Baghdad, see: Aghānī, XVIII, p. 46, ll. 20–24, and perhaps also Ṭabarī, III, p. 732, ll. 15–16.

That there must have run much Arab blood in the veins of the *Abnā'* (in addition to that resulting from intermarriage with Arabs), may be learnt from the fact, that even as late as the end of Manṣūr's rule there were very numerous Arabs in the capital's garrison (see Addenda, the paragraph on the Arabs).

The sources frequently distort *Abnā'* to *Anbār* and *Abnāwī* to *Anbārī*.

It is interesting to note that al-Rāwandī's followers were called *Abnā' al-Dawla*, after their leader's book, *Kitāb al-Dawla* (*Fihrist*, p. 204, ll. 1–3).

In concluding this part I would like to refer to the highly intelligent and extremely useful note on the *Abnā'* by de Goeje in his glossary to Ṭabarī.

ADDENDA

(Notes and References)

The Mawālī

The ordinary picture of the Khurāsānīs ousting the Arabs and the Turks ousting the Khurāsānīs, is oversimplified. In point of fact, the caliphs, who made the momentous decision of relying more and more on Turkish Mamlūks, had to act against the Arabs at least as strongly as against the Khurāsānīs. One strange thing, for which I have as yet not found any convincing answer, is that the Khurāsānīs are little noticed as a political group, fighting for its own interests and taking part in coalitions, as was the case with the Arabs (both amongst themselves and against outsiders), with the *Abnā'*, with the Turks, with the various groups of Transoxanians,[1] with the Maghribīs and with other, less significant, groups.[2] We therefore have a very vague idea of the conduct and attitude of the Khurāsānīs who served in the caliph's armies up to the appearance in great force of the Transoxanians from the days of Ma'mūn and Mu^ctaṣim onwards. We do not know the reaction of these old Khurāsānīs to the appearance of the Turks and of their more Eastern Iranian neighbours, nor do we possess much concrete information about the policy of the ^cAbbāsids towards them. The share of the *Abnā'* in the struggle for power amongst the various military racial groups in Islam and their bitter opposition both to the new oncoming wave from Khurāsān and to the Turks, has been greatly overlooked. Certain modifications and emendations must also be made in our picture of the *Mawālī.*

A significant fact about the *Mawālī* is that they are classified as distinct and different from the Khurāsānīs. We have already discussed in detail the episode in which a member of al-Mahdī's retinue expresses his fear that the caliph's preference of the *Mawālī* might antagonize the Khurāsānī commanders and army. A clear distinction between the two groups is also made in al-Manṣūr's will to his son and successor al-Mahdi (p. 444).

The *Mawālī* of the court constituted a social group, and their connections with their society greatly overshadowed their racial origins. Allusions to the racial composition of the *Mawālī* are rare. Normally they appear as a united but anonymous body, though we know the names of

---

1. Khurāsān is a flexible term. Sometimes it includes Transoxania and even Khwārizm, and sometimes not.

2. This statement is limited to specific cases of political activity in the capital and the neighbouring regions.

a certain number of their leaders, whose racial origin should be checked as far as the sources allow us to do so.[3] In all probability there were many Khurāsānīs amongst the *Mawālī* of the court, but their ties with their society seem to have been far stronger than their ties with their race.[4] The same must have been true of the *Mawālī* of other races.

The steady growth of the power of the *Mawālī* from the beginning of ᶜAbbāsid rule is very evident. Al-Manṣūr's moving speech of thanks to the Khurāsānīs, which he delivered from the pulpit (Ṭabarī, III, pp. 430–432) is really memorable. Yet it does not indicate the trend of developments under his rule. Much more indicative of that trend is a conversation between al-Manṣūr and his son and successor al-Mahdī which took place in the year of al-Manṣūr's death. On that occasion the father said to his son: "O my son! I have collected for you a fortune, the like of which has not been collected by a caliph before me. I have collected for you *Mawālī* [in quantities] the like of which has not been collected by a caliph before me. I built for you a town the like of which never had been in Islam" (Ṭabarī, III, p. 448, ll. 10–20). So these were the three main and unique assets which that caliph acquired during his reign, according to his own testimony, and which he intended to leave to his heir. To this should be added, that in his above-mentioned will al-Manṣūr gave his son the following advice concerning the *Mawālī*. "Show favour to them and increase their numbers, because they are your source of power and reinforcement in an emergency" (*wa-qarribhum wa-istakthir minhum fa-innahum māddatuka li-shiddatin in nazalat bika*) (Ṭabarī, III, p. 444, ll. 9–10.

Al-Mahdī followed the advice of his father very eagerly. From now on one can notice the existence of the *Mawālī* almost on every page of our source (at the same time one hears very little of the Khurāsānīs). They take part, as a decisive force, in almost every important event. They are mentioned, in various combinations, together with the *Ahl al-Bayt*, *Banū Hāshim*, *al-Khāṣṣa*, *al-Biṭāna*, *al-Ḥasham*, *al-Quwwād*, *al-Qarābāt*, *al-Khadam* (Ṭabarī, III, pp. 486, l. 18–491, l. 1; 493, ll. 1–2; 495, ll. 17–18; 508, l. 506–509, 514, ll. 1–4; 522, ll. 9–15; 522, l. 20–523, l. 13; 531, l. 15–532, l. 1; 545, 557, ll. 15–16; 567, l. 8; 575, ll. 3–12; 654, l. 13; 656, l. 19; 657, ll. 1–2, 10; 679, ll. 8–9, 14–15; 743, l. 19–744, l. 3; 764, l. 15–765, l. 1; 769, l. 3; 796, l. 12; 809, ll. 1–5, 876, ll. 19–20; 872,

3. It is superfluous to mention here the well-known persons, whose racial origin is not obscure.

4. There can be little doubt that among the Khurāsānīs the freeborn element was far bigger than among the *Mawālī*. This is not to say that among the Khurāsānīs there were not numerous *Mawālī*. But those did not constitute part of that strong body of *Mawālī* grouped around the person of the caliph.

ll. 13–17; 882, ll. 11–17; 1027, l. 2; 1026, l. 8. *Murūj*, VI, pp. 196–197; 211, 372).[5]

The existence of a strong group of *Mawālī*, with their special relations with the caliph, greatly facilitated the inclusion and absorption of the Mamlūks (*ghilmān, atrāk, mamālīk*) into the society which grew around the caliph's person, for reasons explained in the text of this paper. It was natural, therefore, for the *Ghilmān* and *Mawālī* to be considered as very closely-connected groups. We are told about as early an ᶜAbbāsid ruler as al-Manṣūr that he fostered *mawāliyahu wa-ghilmānahu* at the expense of the Arabs (*Murūj*, VII, pp. 291, l. 10–292, l. 2).[6] The intimate connection between the two groups finds one of its most striking expressions in the fact that both of them were included in the same pay and registration office, which was called *Dīwān al-Mawālī wal-Ghilmān*, and which was clearly distinct from the other office, bearing the name of *Dīwān al-Jund wal-Shākiriyya*[7] (Yaᶜqūbī, *Kitāb al-Buldān*, p. 267, ll. 9–10. *Ta'rikh*, II, p. 596). Equally important is the fact that the Mamlūks themselves are very often called *Mawālī* (to mention only few instances: *Murūj*, VII, pp. 324, l. 8–325, l. 7; 364, ll. 1–4; 365, l. 1; 393, l. 5. Ṭabarī, III, pp. 853, l. 20–854, l. 11). Also individual Mamlūks are often called *Mawālī*. This is the case with Bughā al-Kabīr, Bughā al-Ṣaghīr, Ashnās, Waṣīf and Ūtāmish (Balādhurī, *Futūḥ*, pp. 203, l. 14; 230, l. 16; 235, ll. 8–11; 297, ll. 10–15. Ibn al-Faqīh, p. 293). In coins bearing the name of Bajkam, he is called *Mawlā Amīr al-Mu'minīn* (*Murūj*, VIII, p. 433, notes).

The following episode is of interest. A person named Ibn Abī Maryam al-Madanī was liked by Hārūn al-Rashīd, because he used to amuse him in interesting stories. As a reward he gave him an apartment in his palace, "and mixed him with his womenfolk, his inner circle, his *Mawālī* and his *Ghilmān*" (*wa-khallaṭahu bi-ḥaramihi wa-biṭānatihi wa-mawālīhi wa-ghilmānihi*) (Ṭabarī, III, 744, ll. 1–3). These were some of the main social groups surrounding the person of the caliph. To them should be added the eunuchs.

The Eunuchs

On the high position of the eunuchs and the important and confidential tasks entrusted to them in Hārūn al-Rashīd's reign, see: Ṭabarī, III,

5. A group of the caliph's close friends, called *Ṣaḥāba*, is mentioned frequently in Manṣūr's reign, and rarely in Mahdī's reign. On one occasion their number is said to have been 700. They are also mentioned together with the *Mawālī* and the *Ahl al-Bayt* (See, for example, Ṭabarī, III, pp. 394, l. 1; 429, l. 13; 487, l. 17).

6. For the full text of this reference see the section on the Arabs in the Addenda.

7. The important military body of the *Shākiriyya* will not be discussed in this paper.

pp. 705; 712, ll. 7, 11–18; 716, ll. 7–9; 718, ll. 10–14; 720, l. 17–721, l. 41; 726, ll. 8–10; 764, l. 6; 771, ll. 3–5, 17. Special mention should be made of the central part played by the eunuchs in eliminating the Barmakids. Rashīd's topmost eunuchs were involved in this operation, namely, Masrūr al-Kabīr, Ḥusayn, Rashīd and Sallām al-Abrash (Ṭabarī, III, pp. 671–694). It was on this occasion that al-Rashīd stated that his two most trusted persons were Masrūr al-Kabīr and Harthama b. Aᶜyan (*ibid.*, p. 682, ll. 10–14). Harthama was the *Mawlā* of Rashīd (see *ibid.*, p. 716, l. 7; 913, ll. 18–19; 919, ll. 11–18; 920, ll. 10–12). On Sallām al-Abrash the eunuch see: Ṭayfūr, p. 133.[8] The eunuchs were often employed as gaolers (see, for example Ṭabarī, III, pp. 461, ll. 16–17; 766, l. 9). From al-Rashīd's reign a group of eunuchs called *khadam al-khāṣṣa* or *khuddām al-khāṣṣa*, appears in the sources (*ibid.*, pp. 731, l. 9; 749, l. 14; 969, ll. 3–4).

The *khadam*, like the *ghilmān*, are also mentioned side by side with the *Mawālī* (for *al-khadam wal-mawālī* see: *ibid.*, pp. 390, ll. 1–2; 657, ll. 1–3; 850, ll. 17–18). Many individual eunuchs are classified as *Mawlā* (*ibid.*, pp. 562, ll. 7–15; 749, ll. 13; 764, ll. 5–7; 773, ll. 1–3. *Murūj*, VII, p. 305, ll. 2–3; *Ta'rikh Baghdād*, VIII, p. 392, l. 12). The eunuch may even be called *ghulām* (*ibid.*, pp. 968, ll. 4–5). To this should be added that both eunuch and non-eunuch slave-attendants were called *wuṣafā'* (sing. *waṣīf*) (see *ibid.*, pp. 110, l. 18; 111, l. 4; 112, l. 13; 155, l. 11, 306, ll. 2–4; 393, ll. 7–16; 459, ll. 9–15; 461, ll. 16–17; 530; 536, l. 3; 545, l. 15; 547, l. 11; 562, ll. 7–15; 1016, l. 6. Yaᶜqūbī, *Kitāb al-Buldān*, pp. 252–253). Furthermore, *waṣīf* was employed as a proper name, both of eunuch and non-eunuch slaves.

Thus there was much overlapping between the terms *Mawālī*, *Ghilmān*, and *Khadam*, and there was certainly much overlapping in the functions and services of the persons included under these terms. In the text of this paper I have already pointed at the intimate connections existing between the eunuchs and the ᶜAbbāsid Mamlūks, particularly the regiment of *al-ghilmān al-ḥujariyya*. Here I shall add the following instance. An expeditionary force of 52,000 horsemen and infantrymen, sent by al-Muqtadir, included also *ḥujariyya* and *khadam al-dār* in unspecified numbers. The garrison left behind in the capital constituted of 7,000 horsemen and infantrymen. The protection of the caliph's court (*ḥirāsat al-dār*) was entrusted to the *ghilmān ḥujariyya* and to the eunuchs *in equal numbers*: One thousand persons from each group (*Nishwār al-Muḥāḍara*, VIII, p. 108, ll. 4–10).

8. On eunuchs and their functions in the early ᶜAbbāsid period, and particularly in Manṣūr's reign, see: Ṭabarī, III, pp. 27, l. 17; 34, l. 21; 389, l. 1; 390, ll. 1–4; 453, ll. 6–10; 455, ll. 4–15; 509, ll. 7, 19, 21.

According to Ibn al-Faqīh (p. 109, ll. 1–3), it was Muᶜāwiya who first introduced into Islam the eunuchs (*khiṣyān*) together with the *ḥaras* and *shuraṭ* and other innovations.

There are many indications of the influence of the Byzantines on the eunuch institution in Islam. I have not found yet similar indications of Sasanid influence on the same institution. This might be accidental. I wish to thank Professor R. Girshman for furnishing me with valuable data on the eunuchs in the Sasanid period.

The Arabs

The reason given by al-Ṭabarī for al-Manṣūr's building in 151/768 the Ruṣāfa quarter of Baghdad on the east side of the Tigris is the following one. He was afraid lest the various groups from which his army was composed would unite against him. He therefore decided to transfer part of them to the other side of the river, and thus avoid their being united against him. This he did after sowing discord between these groups which were the Muḍar, the Yaman, the Khurāsānīs and the Rabīᶜa (*fa-ṣārat Muḍar firqa wal-Yaman firqa wal-Khurāsāniyya firqa wa-Rabīᶜa firqa*) Ṭabarī, p. 366, ll. 16–17). The idea was that if one part of the city rebelled against him he could subdue it with the help of the other part, and if one group of the army rose against him he could overcome it by the help of the other groups (*wa-in fasudat ᶜalayka Muḍar ḍarabtahā bil-Yaman wa-Rabīᶜa wal-Khurāsāniyya wa-in fasudat ᶜalayka al-Yaman ḍarabtahā bi-man aṭāᶜaka min Muḍar wa-ghayrihā qāla faqabila amrahu wa-ra'yahu fa-istawā lahu mulkuhu wa-kāna dhālika sabab al-binā' fī al-jānib al-Sharqi wa-fī al-Ruṣāfa wa-iqṭāᶜ al-quwwād hunāka*) (*ibid.*, 367, ll. 4–7).

This passage shows how strong was the Arab element in the garrison which Manṣūr quartered in Baghdad. The Khurāsānīs were only one group of the four. All the rest were Arabs. This tends to support my argument that the *Abnā'* were Arabicized to a considerable extent, in spite of their strong feeling of affinity with Khurāsān and the Khurāsānīs. It should, however, be added that those Arabs who stayed in Khurāsān for a long period underwent a considerable process of change and became more and more similar to the local population (cp. Jāḥiẓ, *Manāqib*, pp. 40–41, 50 and Balādhurī, *Futūḥ*, pp. 400–401). Something comparable must have happened to the Khurāsānīs and even to the Khurāsānīzed Arabs who moved westwards.[9]

9. The term *Ahl Khurāsān* does not necessarily mean non-Arabs (cp. Ṭabarī, III, p. 291, ll. 12–13). Jāḥiẓ, in *Manāqib*, speaks several times of the Khurāsānī Arab (pp. 35, 37).

The fact that the *Zawāqīl* stayed in Raqqa and the *Abnā'* and Khurāsānīs stayed in Rāfiqa during the *Zawāqīl* incident (see the text of this paper) is by no means accidental. According to Ibn al-Faqīh, Raqqa was the heart (*wāsiṭat*) of Diyār Muḍar. When Manṣūr built *Rāfiqa* in 155/772 he stationed there a Khurāsānī army (p. 132, ll. 9–11). This was undoubtedly a measure intended to neutralize an Arab pro-Umayyad region. Rashīd's explanation of the reason for his long sojourn in Raqqa confirms this view. He said: *urīdu al-munākha ^calā nāḥiyat ahl al-shiqāq wal-nifāq wal-buhgḍ li a'immat al-hudā wal-ḥubb li-shajarat al-la^cna Banī Umayya ma^ca mā fīhā min al-māriqa wal-mutalaṣṣiṣa wa-mukhīfī al-sabīl wa-lawlā dhālika mā fāraqtu Baghdāda mā ḥayītu*) (Ṭabarī, III, p. 706, ll. 13–17). Here we have, incidentally, an additional confirmation for our explanation of the term *Zawāqīl*. Brigandage and insecurity spread in that pro-Umayyad region as a result of the ^cAbbāsids' precarious hold on it. The persistence of that phenomenon induced the ^cAbbāsids to call their opponents in that region by the name of *Zawāqīl*. The similarity of *Ṣa^cālīk* and *Zawāqīl* is confirmed by the following phrase *ru'asā' al-qabā'il wal-^cashā'ir wal-ṣa^cālīk wal-zawāqīl* (Ya^cqūbi, Ta'rīkh, II, p. 560). The chances that Amīn would be saved by such an anti-^cAbbāsid population were very poor indeed.

For the attitude of the ^cAbbāsid to the Arabs in the very beginning of their movement see: Ṭabarī, II, pp. 1974, ll. 10–11; 2004, l. 19–2005, l. 9; III, p. 25, ll. 3–6.

Policy of the ^cAbbāsids towards the Arabs from the days of al-Manṣūr onwards is described by al-Mas^cūdī: *wa-kāna [al-Manṣūr] awwal khalīfa ista^cmala mawāliyahu wa-ghilmānahu fī a^cmālihi wa-ṣarrafahum fī muhimmātihi wa-qaddamahum ^calā al-^cArab fa-imtathalat dhālika al-khulafā' min ba^cdihi min wuldihi fa-quṭi^cat qiyādāt al-^cArab wa-zālat riyāsātuhā wa-dhahabat marātibuhā* (*Murūj*, VII, pp. 291, l. 10–292, l. 2).

Ibn Sa^cd, who died in 845, cites a prediction that the Turks will oust the Arabs (*Ṭabaqāt*, VI, pp. 142, l. 21–143, l. 2).

On three Arab brothers who were commanders in Ṭāhir's army during the struggle against Amīn see: Ṭabarī, III, pp. 891, ll. 5–10; 895, ll. 18–19; 896, l. 20. On Arabs in Amīn's camp see *ibid.*, p. 826, ll. 6–8.

See also Maqrīzī (*Khiṭat*, I, p. 94; *Sulūk*, I, p. 16, ll. 14–16). and Nuwayrī (in Ya^cqūbī, p. 255, note f) on Mu^ctaṣim's policy towards the Turks and the Arabs.

II

MAMLŪK

MILITARY SLAVERY IN EGYPT AND SYRIA

This study was published in an abridged form in The Encyclopaedia of Islam (2nd edition), VI fasc. 103–104 (1987). The full version, published here for the first time, gives a more comprehensive picture of Mamlūk military slavery in Egypt and Syria under the Mamlūk sultanate.

Islamic military history and organization have not received, until very recently, even part of the attention they deserve. This in spite of the immersion of the Muslim historical sources in the subject, and in spite of its objective centrality in shaping the fate of Islam throughout its existence. This affirmation is even truer of the Mamlūk military institution, which constituted the heart and core of the military might of most of the major Muslim states during the greatest part of Islam's existence, and without which that religion's chances of becoming a world religion on its present scale and within its present boundaries would have greatly diminished.

For the purpose of laying the foundation of the study of the Mamlūk phenomenon in Islam, the Mamlūk sultanate (648–922/1250–1517) is by far the best choice, because of the richness and variety of its historical sources; because so many of them are contemporary with the events they describe, and because they contain so many definitions and descriptions of that state's institutions. The reconstruction of military slavery under the Mamlūks is bound to shed much light on practically every Mamlūk society in Islam, before, during and after the Mamlūk sultanate. However, to use what we know about the Mamlūk sultanate to draw conclusions about other reigns, of which we know less, should be done only with great caution, because of the differences in circumstances, as a systematic study will show time and time again. The abundance of definitions and descriptions, though basically most welcome, does also have its grave dangers, for so many of them are either partial or inaccurate or true only for the author's time. They have, therefore, to be constantly checked by independent, preferably unconscious, evidence.

Of all the Mamlūk societies which should be examined and reconstructed in close connection with that of the Mamlūk sultanate, it is obvious that those immediately preceding and following it (in the Ayyūbid period and in Ottoman Egypt) should have first priority.

Countries of Origin and Racial Composition

We know a good deal, relatively, about the racial composition of the Mamlūks of the Mamlūk sultanate and about their countries of origin (called quite often *al-bilād*, see e.g. Ibn al-Dawādārī, IX, p. 71, ll. 12–13). For the Ayyūbids, by contrast, though we know that the major racial component of their Mamlūks was Turkish, we do not know where they were imported from, with the certain exception of the reign al-Malik al-Ṣāliḥ Najm al-Dīn Ayyūb, the direct precursor of the Mamlūk period, and the possible exceptions of the reign of one or two of his Ayyūbid contemporaries or immediate predecessors.

The source evidence on the characteristics of the peoples inhabiting the Mamlūks' countries of origin and on the various factors which brought about those Mamlūks' sale and importation to the sultanate under discussion, clarifies the reasons for the very creation of the military slave institution, and explains its unparalleled success and durability as the major military force in the lands of Islam.

A most important description of the steppe of the Ḳipchāḳ and its people, the major source of military slaves for the Mamlūk sultanate in the first part of its existence, is that of Ibn Faḍl Allāh al-ᶜUmarī, who based it on the evidence of persons who visited the Golden Horde (K. Lech, *Das Mongolische Weltreich*, Wiesbaden, 1968, pp. 68–71 of the Arabic text, which is an excerpt of the *Masālik al-Abṣār*; al-Ḳalḳashandī, *Ṣubḥ al-Aᶜshā*, IV, pp. 456–8). There the author stresses both the very harsh circumstances in which the inhabitants of that steppe live; their primitiveness (including the primitiveness of their pagan religion), as well as their military ability, faithfulness and loyalty (see also Dimashqī, *Nukhbat al-Dahr*, pp. 264, ll. 4–11, 279, ll. 9–12). This combination of qualities made them the most suitable raw material from which a military slave fighting for Islam and for his patron could be moulded. As far as the Mamlūks of the Mamlūk sultanate are concerned, the sources testify to a unanimous conviction that they had been the decisive factor in saving Islam both from the Frankish and the Mongol threats from the time of the battle of ᶜAyn Jālūt (1260) to the later battles against the Īlkhāns of Iran and Iraq (al-Umarī, *op. cit.*, pp. 70, l. 7–71, l. 12; *Ṣubḥ*, IV, p. 458. See also D. Ayalon, "The Transfer of the ᶜAbbāsid Caliphate", pp. 58–9, and note 1; "The European–Asiatic Steppe", pp. 47–52; "The Great Yāsa", part C_1. pp. 117–130, part C_2, pp. 148–56; "From Ayyūbids to Mamlūks"). This unanimous and repeated evidence is crowned by Ibn Khaldūn's evaluation of the Mamlūk phenomenon in the lands of Islam in general and in the Mamlūk sultanate in particular (*ᶜIbar*, V, pp. 369–373; D. Ayalon, "Mamlūkiyyāt", pp. 340–343). The prestige which the Mamlūks consequently enjoyed greatly helped them in overthrowing the Ayyūbids, in firmly establishing their rule, and in thoroughly incorporating in their realm an undivided Syria, as a region with a status very inferior to that of Egypt.

The factors which led to the sale of Mamlūks by the inhabitants of the Ḳipchāḳī steppe and their rulers were the following: the general destitution of the population, which forced it, in certain years, to sell its children (ᶜUmarī, p. 70, ll. 2–4; *Ṣubḥ*, IV, p. 458, l. 2; *Sulūk*, I, p. 942, ll. 10–12); the need to sell children in lieu of taxes to the ruler (*Ṣubḥ*, IV, p. 476, ll. 11–16); the ruler's capturing and selling the children and women of his subjects (ᶜUmarī, p. 69, ll. 6–10; *Ṣubḥ*, IV, pp. 474, l. 10–475, l. 1). It was not, however, only under duress, or as a result of the intervention of the ruler of the steppe that those children were sold. The high sums paid for them constituted an immense incentive. In the third reign of al-Nāṣir Muḥammad b. Ḳalāūn (1309–1340), who was exceptionally lavish in his buying of Mamlūks, the Mongols competed with each other in selling their boys, girls and relatives to the slave-merchants. The competition was so fierce among those Mongols, that it marred their internal relations (*Sulūk*, II, p. 525, ll. 6–10).

It is true that the Mongol attacks on the lands of the Ḳipchāḳ filled the slave markets with Ḳipchāḳī Turks, thus facilitating their purchase by the later Ayyūbids, particularly by al-Ṣāliḥ Najm al-Din Ayyūb, and indirectly contributing to the establishment of the Mamlūk state (see e.g. D. Ayalon, "Le Régiment Bahriya", pp. 133–4; "The Great Yāsa, part C1, pp. 117ff.). However, prisoners of war captured by any kind of external enemy, or even by a Muslim ruler, could not guarantee the uninterrupted supply of Mamlūks, particularly children below military age, so it was necessary to have the constant cooperation of local elements, such as the ruler, the heads of the tribes, and above all the parents and relatives of those children. Furthermore, that cooperation in selling their own flesh and blood was not confined to the subjugated peoples, but also included the conquering and subjugating Mongols. But even this is not all: we are informed as well that the subjugated peoples of that region used to steal the children of their Mongol subjugators and sell them to the slave-dealers (ᶜUmarī, p. 72, ll. 16–17). Thus both the different scales of values, as well as the different relations between rulers and ruled in the steppe, should be taken into account in the study of the slave traffic from that area, as well as in the study of other subjects.

The islamization of the Mongol dynasty of the Golden Horde and many of its peoples must have contributed, in the long run, to the diminution of the Ḳipchāḳī steppe as a source of military manpower for the lands of Islam, and especially for the Mamlūk sultanate. In the short run, however, it is rather doubtful whether the adoption of Islam had any considerable effect on the slave-trade from that region. For many years those who became Muslims continued to stick to many of their old pagan habits, and numerous others remained pagan (ᶜUmarī, p. 72, ll. 12–19; *Ṣubḥ*, IV, pp. 457, l. 19–458, l. 3). Both sellers and buyers had a very strong interest the continuation of the slave-trade, which means that new converts to Islam were not necessarily excluded from becoming Mamlūks (*ibid.*). (For the effects at an earlier period of the conversion to Judaism or Christianity of nomads of the Eurasian steppe on their readiness to sell their children, see Iṣṭakhrī, p. 223, ll. 11–15.)

One of the major drawbacks of the Mamlūk system, from which almost all the Muslim states suffered – and those situated far away from the Mamlūks' countries of origin more than those nearer them – was that they had little or no control over their sources of supply (the outstanding exception was the Ottoman Empire, which recruited most of its *kullar* from the Christian peoples living within its boundaries). The states which were not contiguous to those sources of supply had an additional major problem: that they depended on the cooperation of those who commanded the routes leading to the sources in question (be they sea or land routes) see e.g. D. Ayalon, "Aspects of the Mamlūk Phenomenon", part I, pp. 207–9). The Mamlūk Sultanate was, in this respect, completely dependent on external factors both on land and on sea. No wonder, therefore, that it tried to diversify its routes (and very probably its sources) of supply as far as it could.

Its main route was by sea through the Bosphorus and the Dardanelles, which was under the complete control of Byzantium, and then the Franks and Ottomans. During the Byzantine period there is no complaint in the Mamlūk sources about Byzantine interference with the ordinary flow of slaves to the Mamlūk sultanate, in spite of Byzantium's ambivalent policy in its relations with the Mongols of the Golden Horde, the Īlkhāns of Iran and Iraq and the Mamlūks. In the correspondence between the Byzantine emperor Michael Palaeologus and sultan Ḳalāūn in 680/1281, concerning the conclusion of a pact between the two states, the slave traffic figures quite prominently. The emperor promises, *inter alia*, safe passage of Mamlūks and slave girls, on the condition that there will be no Christians among them. He also demands the release of all the Christian Mamlūks already in the sultanate, and their despatch to Byzantium. In his answer the sultan agrees to most of the emperor's suggestions, and stresses the importance of granting safe conduct to the merchants coming from Ṣūdāḳ and the Ḳipchāḳ steppe. Yet he completely ignores the emperor's demand about the Christian Mamlūks (Ibn al-Furāt, VII, pp. 229, l. 20–230, l. 16, 232, ll. 15–22, 233, ll. 3–6).

Even more important was the attitude of the Ottoman empire, which was gaining in power as Byzantium declined. With the deterioration of Mamlūk–Ottoman relations from the beginning of Ḳāytbāy's reign onwards, the Ottomans had excellent means of weakening the Mamlūks by cutting off their supply of military manpower. They seem to have used that weapon to some extent. In 895/1490, when the Ottomans wanted to conclude peace with the Mamlūks, one of Ḳāytbāy's two major stipulations was the release of the merchants of Mamlūk slaves (Ibn Iyās, III, p. 267). In 922/1516, on the verge of the Mamlūk sultanate's annihilation, sultan Selim writes to sultan Ḳanṣūh al-Ghawrī a conciliatory letter in which he states that al-Ghawrī's claim that the Ottomans prevent the slave merchants from coming to his empire is wrong. According to him, those merchants avoided bringing Mamlūks to the Mamlūk sultanate because of its debased currency (Ibn Iyās, V, p. 43, ll. 17–19). Considering the sizes of the Mamlūk regiments of Ḳāytbāy and Ḳanṣūh al-Ghawrī, it would appear that the Ottoman embargo, in as far as it had existed, had not been very thorough.

There were two additional routes by land. One led through Eastern Anatolia, about which we do not know much, but which seems to have been quite important. On this route the Mamlūks had to surmount two formidable obstacles, their enemies, the Īlkhānid Mongols, and the Mongols' staunch allies, the Christians of Little Armenia (*Bilād Sīs*). The attitude of the Mongols is unknown (for a single exception see below), but that of the rulers of Little Armenia as well as the importance of the route are revealed in the truce (*hudna*) concluded between sultan Ḳalāūn and king Leon III in Rabīᶜ II 684/June 1285. In that truce the following stipulation figures most prominently: the merchants bringing Mamlūks and slave girls to the Mamlūk sultanate will be permitted to pass through king Leon's territory without hindrance, and those of them already stopped or imprisoned should be freed and allowed to pursue their journey (Ibn ᶜAbd al-Ẓāhir, *Tashrīf al-Ayyām wal-ᶜUṣūr*, Cairo, 1960, p. 99, ll. 7–11, 15, and especially pp. 100, l. 19–101, l. 1). In all probability, sultan Baybars I, who had been bought together with others in Sīwās, arrived in the Mamlūk realm by this East Anatolian road.

The other land route seem to have been through the very heart of the Īlkhānid empire. As far as we can learn from the sources, the slave-trade along this route centered round a great merchant, named Majd al-Dīn Ismāᶜīl al-Sallāmī (or al-Majd al-Sallāmī), a native of the Īlkhānid empire, who was born in the vicinity of Mosul. He was called al-Nāṣir Muḥammad b. Ḳalāūn's "slave-dealer of the Privy Purse" (*tādjir al-khāṣṣ fī al-raḳīḳ*), and was very influential in the Īlkhānid court. He is said to have been the main instrument in the conclusion of a peace treaty between the Mamlūk and the Mongol states (723/1323). Even before that date he used to go repeatedly to Tabrīz and other places in the Īlkhānid realm and bring slaves from there. One of the Mamlūk Sulan's stipulations in that treaty was the freedom to purchase Mamlūks in the Īlkhānid dominions (*Esclavage*, p. 3; Ṣafadī, *al-Wāfī bil-Wafayāt*, IX, Wiesbaden, 1974, pp. 220, l. 9–221, l.6; Ibn al-Dawādārī, *Kanz al-Durar*, IX, pp. 312, l. 16–313, l. 10; al-Maḳrīzī, *Sulūk*, II, index, p. 1020b). It is thus very probable that the flow of Mamlūks through Īlkhānid territory increased as a result of the treaty. It is true that Dimurdāsh b. Djūbān, the Īlkhānid governor of Anatolia (*Bilād al-Rūm*), prohibited, after 1323, the dispatch of Mamlūks to Egypt from or through that area (*Sulūk*, II, p. 293, ll. 1–8). But the attitude of that highly controversial ruler, for which he paid with his life, should be considered as an exception which proves the rule. What happened to the slave trade from the Īlkhānid empire after that empire's disintegration in 736/1336 is unknown.

In the third reign of al-Nāṣir Muḥammad b. Ḳalāūn, the purchase of Mamlūks reached, perhaps, its highest peak. That sultan is said to have imported Mamlūks and slave girls from "The Golden Horde (*Bilād Uzbak*) Anatolia (*al-Rūm*), Tabriz and Baghdad *and other countries*" (*Sulūk*, II, p. 524, ll. 13–15). This reflects the maximal boundaries of the major region from which military slaves were brought to the Mamlūk sultanate, and inside which the centre of gravity of Mamlūk acquisition changed. It stands to reason that in the reign of the above mentioned sultan all the three main routes connecting his realm with the Mamlūks' countries of origin were in use.

In summing up the problem of the routes through which military manpower was supplied to the Mamlūk sultanate, it can be said that interference with the flow of slaves be it by Byzantines, Ottomans, rulers of Little Armenia, Īlkhānid Mongols, or Christian Europeans, did not seriously affect the military strength of that sultanate. An effective embargo on this item alone might have broken that strength.

One of the major events in the history of the Mamlūk sultanate, which transformed the racial composition of its military aristocracy, was the supplanting of the Ḳipchāḳī Turks by the Circassians as the main factor in that aristocracy. The Mamlūk sources attribute that transformation solely to causes internal to sultanate (D. Ayalon, "Circassians", pp. 135–6). There are, however, good reasons to suggest that the situation in the Mamlūks' countries of origin was in no small measure responsible for bringing about that result. There is a considerable amount of evidence about the comparatively flourishing situation and the dense population of the Ḳipchāḳ steppe in the thirteenth and the first half of the fourteenth centuries ("Circassians", p. 136, and note 2), although its decline seems to have started with the Mongol occupation (ᶜUmarī, p. 71, ll. 15–18). Ibn ᶜArabshāh gives a quite detailed description of how that once flourishing country had been devastated and depopulated by internal wars and the attack of Tīmūrlank (*Akhbār Tīmūr*, pp. 113, l. 5–115, l. 4, 122, l. 2, 126, l. 2–127, 1.4. See also A.N. Poliak, *REI*, ix, pp. 241–2; *BSOAS*, x, pp. 864–7). The very fact that the area under discussion had been a major source for the supply of Mamlūks must have contributed considerably to the process of its depopulation and perhaps even to the devaluation of its human material. This is because that slave traffic was confined mainly to a particular section of a special age group, namely the cream of adolescent boys and girls who still had all their reproductive years ahead of them. This must have adversely affected future generations. Although the number of Royal Mamlūks (*al-mamālīk al-sulṭāniyya*) was not very great, it should be remembered that many of the commanders, both in Egypt and in Syria, had their own Mamlūks, and that the ownership of white slaves existed well beyond the military aristocracy. Furthermore, the Ḳipchāḳī steppe supplied slaves to countries outside the Mamlūk sultanate as well. On top of all that, the rate of mortality among those Mamlūks in the countries to which they had been imported was very high, especially in times of epidemics. Thus there was a more or less constant need for the replenishment of their thinning ranks. The long-term effects of the islamization of the peoples of the Ḳipchāḳ have already been mentioned.

Before enumerating the races of the Mamlūks, the term *Turk* must be discussed. It had two meanings: one very wide, the other much narrower. We shall start with the wider meaning, leaving the other to the enumeration of the races. *Turk* or *Atrāk* in the wide sense embraced all the Mamlūk races, and was practically synonymous with Mamlūks. The Mamlūk sultanate was called *Dawlat al-Turk* or *Dawlat al-Atrāk* or *al-Dawla al-Turkiyya*. The commonest designation of the Mamlūk sultans was *Mulūk al-Turk*. But whereas the sultans of the Ḳipchāḳī period had only this designation, each of the sultans of the Circassian period had a double designation. For example, sultan Jaḳmaḳ was the thirty-fourth of "*Mulūk al-Turk* and their sons" and the tenth of the "*Jarākisa* and their sons", and so on.

To compile a list of the various races represented in Mamlūk military society is quite easy. But to evaluate the respective weight of the various racial groups, with the exception of the two major ones (*Turk* and *Jarkas*) is very difficult. This is because it is only rarely that the sources refer to the racial background of the individual Mamlūks, who usually were given Turkish names, irrespective of their racial origin; and because the mention of racial groups taking active part in any particular event or struggle (again with the exception of the two main races) is rarer still, though some lists of Mamlūk races do exist. This is in glaring contrast to the extremely rich and varied data furnished by those sources about the groups (*ṭawā*ᶜ*if*, sing. *ṭā*ᶜ*ifa*) based on slave and patron relations, such as the Ẓāhiriyya Baybars, Manṣūriyya Ḳalāūn, Nāṣiriyya Faradj, Ashrafiyya Ḳāytbāy, etc. Therefore, the picture we receive of these groups and their relations (on this see below) is far superior to that of the racial groups (*adjnās*). The racial struggle comes into prominence mainly in connection with the Circassians, from a comparatively early date in the Turkish–Ḳipchāḳī period, and reaches its peak in the closing decades of the eighth/fourteenth century. After the almost total victory of the Circassians it is brushed aside with the exception of some flickers of antagonism on the part of other races, and of repeated expressions of haughtiness towards and discrimination against those races on the part of the Circassians.

In Ottoman Egypt the racial factor is even more subdued than the Mamlūk one. Furthermore, at least as far as the chronicle of al-Djabartī is concerned, practically the only data we possess about the racial composition of the military aristocracy are references to the racial origin of a certain number of individual Mamlūks.

From the data supplied by the sources of the Mamlūk period, including the lists of races, the following general list can be reconstructed: *Turk* (or *Atrāk*), *Ḳifjāk*, *Tatar*, *Mughul* (or *Mughūl*), *Khiṭā*ᶜ*iyya*, *Rūs*, *Rūm*, *Arman*, *Āṣ*, *Abaẓa*, *Lāẓ*, *Jarkas*.

If the whole Mamlūk period is considered, the *Turk* and the *Jarkas* were by far the two most dominant races. The *Jarkas* seem already to have constituted an important element in the *Burdjiyya* regiment created by Sultan Ḳalāūn. They are the only ones who were mentioned as repeatedly challenging the supremacy of the *Turk*. The *Ḳifjāḳ* are rarely referred to in the above-mentioned data and lists, and are obviously synonym for *Turk*. The case of the *Mughul* and the *Tatar* is more complicated. The *Mugul*, who are mentioned only in the Ḳipchāḳī period, seem to have been distinct from the *Turk*, although a certain degree of overlapping between the two should not be excluded. The *Tatar*, on the other hand, especially under the Circassians, were very often synonymous with *Turk*. This can be proved in two ways: a) *Turk* and *Tatar* are never mentioned together in the same list, or in connection with the same event; b) a good number of individual Mamlūks in the Circassian period are said to have been *Turkī al-djins* on one occasion and *Tatarī al-djins* on another. The reason for this alternation is obvious. The more the Tatars advanced in the steppe, the greater was the Turkish element which they subjugated, included in their armies and mingled with. Since the Turks were much more numerous, it was they who absorbed their conquerors. Already Ibn Faḍl Allāh al-Umarī says that the Tatars were completely assimilated by the Ḳipchāḳīs and had lost their own identity (*op. cit.*, p. 73, ll. 17–20).

The *Rūm* were third in importance, but there is insufficient information for establishing the relative importance of the other racial groups. The *Rūs* are never mentioned as a racial group outside the lists, and there are hardly any individual Mamlūks who are said to have belonged to that race (the most well known individual is Baybughā Rūs, or Urus or Urūs).

The Franks (*Farandj*, *Ifrandj*) are never mentioned in the Mamlūk sources as a racial group. There are, however, a fair number of Mamlūks who are said to have been of Frankish origin. Since the Mamlūks, as already stated, did not preserve their original infidel names, especially if they had not been Turks, and since the origin of many is not mentioned, the number of the Franks amongst them might well have been considerably higher. Yet the sources' absolute silence about the Franks as a separate body does not support the claim of some European medieval writers that there was a very high proportion of Franks in the Mamlūk army. One should, however, take into consideration the possibility that there might have been a certain degree of overlapping between *Farandj* and *Rūm*.

There were some Muslim-born people, even from within the boundaries of the Mamlūk sultanate, or from the neighbouring countries (particularly the areas inhabited by the Turcomans), or from regions lying further away, who managed to join the Mamlūk military aristocracy either by fraudulent means (such as an arrangement with the slave dealer), or because they were taken prisoners, and found the status of a Mamlūk too good to give up by admitting that they had in reality been Muslim captives. Some of those whose bluff had been called, were ousted from the military aristocracy, deprived of their Mamlūk names, and forced to retake their original names. These Muslim-born Mamlūks constituted, however, only a very marginal element in Mamlūk society. A few of the Turcomans who became Mamlūks were called *Rūmīs* as well.

From Arrival in the Mamlūk Sultanate to Manumission

The crucial stage in the Mamlūk's career, from his leaving his country of origin, through his education and upbringing, and up to his manumission, can be reconstructed fairly well in the Mamlūk sultanate, despite the numerous gaps which do affect the overall picture. Still, that admittedly very deficient picture is far superior to what we know at present about the parallel career of the military slave in the whole of the rest of the Muslim world in the Middle Ages, including the Ottoman Empire up to the beginning of the sixteenth century. Yet in an attempt to outline the political and administrative organization of the Mamlūk state, that is what Gaudefroy-Demombynes has to say: "On s'étonnerait plutot que le régime de l'Etat mamelouk n'ait pas compris l'utilité des écoles d'enfants de troupe, que le sultan du Maroc, Mouley Ismail, devait plus tard organiser avec tant de soin. ... *Cependant il y en a des traces*"(!) (my italics – D.A.) (*La Syrie à l'Époque des Mamelouks*, Paris, 1923, p. XXXIII, note 5). It is very hard to imagine an assertion more at odds with reality than this one. What it reflects correctly is the wide gap which for too long existed between that reality and the state of the study of the Mamlūk institution.

In the history of each Mamlūk his slave merchant, especially the one who brought him over from his country of origin, figured most prominently. He was his first patron and protector from the hardships and dangers during the long voyage to his adoptive country. He also served as the most usual link between him and his original homeland. The Mamlūk was usually bound with strong ties of affection and veneration to that merchant. All of those merchants were Muslim civilians from outside the Mamlūk sultanate, but some of them became very influential. These merchants should not be confused with the "merchant of the Mamlūks" (*tādjir al-mamālīk*, or fully: *tādjir al-mamālīk al-sulṭāniyya*), who was generally a low ranking Mamlūk amir (amir of ten) and whose function was to supervise the commerce of the Mamlūks. He usually stayed within the boundaries of the sultanate.

While we know very little about the slave-market and its functioning, we know much more about how the sultans bought their Mamlūks, which was usually from the *Bayt al-Māl* (the treasury). Those who had not yet been manumitted before the death or dismissal of the reigning sultan, were returned to the Bayt al-Māl and bought from there by the new sultan.

The sultan's Mamlūks were brought up in a military school situated in the barracks (*ṭibāq*, *aṭbāq*, sing. *ṭabaqa*) of the Cairo citadel, of which there were twelve. It would appear that each of those barracks had a special (probably separate and secluded) section assigned to the Mamlūk novices (*kuttābiyya*, or possibly *kitābiyya*, sing. *kuttābī* or *kitābi*), and this for two arguments: a) after having finished their period of training, and as long as they had not been driven out of the citadel, the Mamlūks continued to stay in those barracks and belong to them, bearing their respective names; b) the barracks accommodated far more

Mamlūks than the number of novices staying there at any given moment.

The education of the novice was divided into two main parts: first, the study of the elements of Islam, and afterwards the military training (*anwāʿ* (or *funūn*) *al-ḥarb* (or *al-furūsiyya*)). The first part was essential; for, in spite of its unavoidably elementary character, it inculcated into the novice the conviction that he had been led in the right path from the darkness of heathendom to the light of Islam (see also Baybars al-Manṣūrī, *Zubdat al-Fikra*, B.M. MS. No. 23325, fol. 51b, ll. 5–16). This attitude on the part of the Mamlūk, even if later in his career he did not lead very strict religious life, was at least as important as his gratitude to the Muslim environment in general and to his patron in particular, for raising him from poverty to richness and from anonymity to fame and high position. As al-Maḳrīzī aptly put it in his well known passage on the upbringing of a Mamlūk, the *combination* of his identification with his new religion, and a great proficiency in the art of war (more precisely in horsemanship) were the targets of the Mamlūk's education. "[Until] the glorification of Islam and its people had been merged in his heart, and he became strong in archery, in handling the lance and in riding the horse" (*Khiṭaṭ*, II, p." 214, ll. 1–2). Curtailing the religious side of the education, or dropping it altogether, because of the need or desire to shorten the period of apprenticeship, was always a symptom of decline in the Mamlūk sultanate or elsewhere.

The most dominant element by far among the personnel of the military school were the eunuchs, who took part in the upbringing of the novices (even in the religious field, in addition to the theologians), as well as in keeping very strict discipline among them. A major reason for manning the school with eunuchs was to use them as a buffer between the young and adult Mamlūks to prevent pederasty. A novice proved to have been the object of sodomy might be sentenced to death (*Khiṭaṭ*, II, p. 214, ll. 6–8).

The eunuchs in the military school formed a kind of a pyramid, at the basis of which were the simple eunuchs called *khuddām* (or *ṭawāshiyat*) *al-ṭibāḳ*. At the head of each barrack was a eunuch called *muḳaddam al-ṭabaḳa*, and all the barracks were commanded by a eunuch who was called *muḳaddam al-mamālīk al-sulṭāniyya* and who had a deputy (*nāʾib*), also a eunuch. There does not seem to have been any distinction between the eunuchs serving in the school in some military or administrative capacity, and those serving in the harem or in religious institutions. It would appear, however, that usually they did not perform those different functions simultaneously.

The eunuchs as a body were extremely strong and influential in the Mamlūk sultanate. It is difficult to compare their power with that of the eunuchs in other medieval Muslim states, because the eunuch hierarchy of those other states cannot be reconstructed to the same degree. What is certain, however, is that *individual* eunuchs in the Mamlūk sultanate could not rise to the highest ranks, or be as powerful as those in other Muslim states, including under the Ayyūbids and in the very early decades of the sultanate. Neither could they be commanders in the field of battle, as happened so often in earlier Muslim reigns. The highest rank that a eunuch could reach under the Mamlūks was the middle one, namely, Amīr of Forty, and there was only one post at this rank to which a eunuch could be appointed: the *Muḳaddam al-Mamālīk al-Sulṭāniyya*. Only in the chaotic conditions prevailing in the years immediately following al-Nāṣir Muḥammad b. Qalāūn's third reign, and to a very great extent resulting from that reign, the eunuchs, together with the women and slave-girls of the court, accumulated unprecedented power. This kind of power could not have lasted for long, for, in addition to its running counter to the basic concepts of Muslim society, it would have destroyed the very foundations of Mamlūk aristocracy. Other evils originating from that reign (usually believed to be as good and great, with only partial justification) lasted much longer (see also below).

The eunuchs in the Mamlūk sultanate belonged mainly to four races: *Rūm*, *Ḥabash*, *Hind* and *Takrūr*, the two first-named being predominant. Thus only one race, the *Rūm*, was common to them and to the Mamlūks. Like the Mamlūks, each eunuch was considered to be Ibn ᶜAbdallāh (thus shrouding his infidel past in obscurity). Unlike them, however, they bore a special kind of Muslim name, representing the pleasant and beautiful (gems, perfumes, etc.). Only a few bore Turkish names. With all the differences, the eunuchs of the Court formed an essential part of the Mamlūk aristocracy. Without them the early stage of the Mamlūk's career, which so decisively affected his subsequent relations, would have been fundamentally different.

There is no evidence indicating the average length of the period which the novice had to stay in the military school. There is, however, much proof to show that, on the whole, that period had been considerably shortened in the later part of the Mamlūk sultanate, which adversely affected the proficiency of the Mamlūk soldier. Every single Mamlūk attending the school was manumitted on finishing his period of apprenticeship. This manumission was never performed individually; it was carried out in the presence of the sultan in a passing-out parade called *kharj*, in which 150 to 500 "graduates" took part. Each one received a manumission certificate, called *ᶜitāḳa*, which at the same time showed that he was a fully-fledged soldier.

The amirs did not have at their disposal facilities even remotely comparable to those of the sultan for the upbringing and training of their

Mamlūks, a fact which was reflected in their comparative military inferiority. There are, however, certain indications that the Mamlūks of the great amirs were brought up according to principles resembling those which were applied in the case of the sultan's Mamlūks (see e.g. *Zubdat al-Fikra*, fols. 51b, ll. 5–16, 99b, ll. 13–100a, 1.4).

All Mamlūks, on their manumission, were simple soldiers; thus all were given an equal start. However, in reality, they had a chance of rising to the highest ranks and positions only if they had been manumitted by a sultan and not by an amir. This chance was greatly improved if the Mamlūk was included in the sultan's personal guard (*al-khāṣṣakiyya*). There was no school for training officers. These rose from the rank of simple soldiers without having to undergo any special kind of training.

In a most illuminating passage, where al-Maḳrīzī contrasts the attitude of al-Nāṣir Muḥammad b. Ḳalāūn to his Mamlūks with that of the sultans who preceded him, the correct principles for creating a healthy and successful Mamlūk military body, as against the wrong ones, are highlighted. The earlier sultans, besides giving the Mamlūk the proper upbringing (already described earlier), used to dress him in comparatively simple costumes; raise his salary gradually and promote him slowly in rank and position. A Mamlūk thus treated, when reaching the top, will know how valuable is his new status, acquired with such effort, and will be able to make the right comparison between his previous wretchedness (*shaḳāᶜ*) and his present well being (*naᶜīm*). Al-Nāṣir Muḥammad b. Ḳalāūn discarded all this (*aᶜraḍa ᶜan hādhā*), and considered the policy of his predecessors to be stupid, commenting that it would lead the Mamlūk to take advantage of his patron, or vice versa. On the other hand, he argued, if the Mamlūk would be made prosperous to a degree that "would fill his eye and his heart", he would forget his country of origin and prefer his patron (*Sulūk*, II, pp. 524, ll. 3–525, l. 15).

Now there cannot be the slightest doubt which of the two was the right policy (for the policy of his father, Ḳalāūn, see e.g. *Zubdat al-Fikra*, fols. 99b, l. 13–100a, l. 4). The absurdity of al-Nāṣir Muḥammad's argumentation is self-evident. That he was capable of such a line of thinking and acting is proved by his whole attitude, based on his conviction that he could buy off both friend and foe, and immortalize his name by depleting the realm's resources on all kinds of projects, not all of them being necessarily negative. Strangely enough, he managed to combine his policy of corruption and waste with the successful enforcement of strict discipline, which he carried out mercilessly. An outward and misleading calm prevailed over the sultanate under his dominant and tyrannic personality, although ominous signs of the impending collapse under the pressure of the destructive undercurrents appeared with increasing frequency in the closing years of his reign. The chaos into which the whole realm plunged almost overnight after his death was both predictable and unavoidable. Mamlūk society was gravely shaken by the effects of his rule and its aftermath, and only partly recovered from them at a later date. Other negative aspects of the Mamlūk sultanate in the period of its decline, which affected Mamlūk society directly and indirectly, can be easily traced back to that sultan's reign. One of them was the increasing power of the bedouins, for whose temporary obedience al-Nāṣir Muḥammad paid very heavily in money and in precious gifts, thus giving them unprecedented strength (they were anyway the strongest military power after the Mamlūks in Egypt, Southern Syria and Palestine). The Mamlūks were exhausted by their constant struggle against them both in Egypt and in Syria, and by the damage these nomads and semi-nomads caused to the agricultural lands, of which the military feudal fiefs formed a central part.

The Structure of Mamlūk Society

The period of the Mamlūk's slavery, terminated by his manumission, not only affected his career (i.e. his chances of rising up the socio–military ladder) but also determined his close affiliations for life. He was bound by loyalty, on the one hand, to his manumitting patron (*muᶜtiḳ*, *ustādh*), and, on the other, to his colleagues in servitude and manumission (*khushdāshiyya*). The intensity of the Mamlūks' feelings of loyalty to their patron is revealed in those cases when things did not work according to plan, for instance when a patron-sultan died or was dismissed shortly before the date fixed for the manumission of a certain group of his Mamlūks. This group sometimes refused to be manumitted by their new patron-sultan in spite of the fact that by doing so they practically dealt a death blow to their chances of becoming part of the uppermost stratum of the military aristocracy. The patron and his freedmen developed relations very similar to those of a family. He was considered to be their father (*wālid*), and they his sons (*awlād*, sing. *walad*), and the freedmen regarded each other as brothers (*ikhwa*, sing. *akh*), with special relations between senior and junior brothers (*aghawāt*, sing. *aghā* and *iniyyāt*, sing. *inī*).

The ties binding the patron to his own freedmen and the same freedmen to each other constituted the pivot upon which Mamlūk internal relations hinged. These ties continued to be binding after the dismissal or death of a patron. That cohesive factor, most formidable in itself, was supplemented and strengthened by a rejective one: a freedman of patron A, who had been transferred to the service of patron B, would never be accepted by him and by his own freedmen on an equal footing.

He would always be considered as stranger (*gharīb*, *ajnabī*). A Mamlūk "family", or group or faction (*ṭā'ifa*, pl. *ṭawā'if*) kept outsiders serving their patron at arm's length. Such a faction, if and when separated from its patron, could either be broken by killing its members, putting them in prison, sending them into exile, transferring them to the service of other patrons, under whom they were given an inferior status; or it could remain intact and carry on until the death of the last of its members. In the Mamlūk sultanate a new sultan quite often broke up part of his immediate predecessor's group of freedmen, and let the other part stay on until it petered out after several decades. Under the Circassians, where the attempts to create a dynasty failed constantly, and sultans followed each other in quick succession, numerous factions, owing allegiance to different sultans, existed simultaneously. Many combinations of short-lived coalitions between those factions were constantly forming and dissolving.

A very instructive case in point is Ibn Taghrībirdī's account of the change in sultan Khushḳadam's position from almost complete shakiness to comparative stability as a result of the varying attitudes of the Mamlūks of the sultans who preceded him both in their relations among themselves and with the Mamlūks of the reigning sultan, al-Ẓāhiriyya Khushḳadam. The Mamlūks of the sultan who preceded Khushḳadam were, in the order of their seniority, al-Mu'ayyadiyya Shaykh, al-Ashrafiyya Barsbāy, al-Ẓāhiriyya Jaḳmaḳ and al-Ashrafiyya Aynāl (*Ḥawādith al-Duhūr*, pp. 442, l. 7–444, l. 10; 550, ll. 4–9). They formed ephemeral coalitions which changed kaleidoscopically.

The particular ties existing between the patron and his Mamlūks go back to the very beginning of Mamlūk society in Islam and have always constituted one of that society's mainstays. They were a major source of its unique power, which contributed so much to the greatness of Islam. However, they clashed quite often with interests wider than those of the specific ruler and his military slaves, thus constituting a source of weakness as well. Yet their balance sheet, from a Muslim point of view, was unequalled in its positiveness. The great drawback of the whole system in the end was that it had outlived its purpose. It could not cope properly with the progress of technology and with the unavoidable military changes which that brought about, as was so decisively demonstrated by the annihilation of the Mamlūk army and empire at the hands of the Ottomans. In Ottoman Egypt the antiquated character of the Mamlūks' "Art of War" was only accentuated. At the same time the internal dissensions within Mamlūk society were greatly intensified, and reached an unprecedented peak. The reason for that intensification was that a strange merging of hereditary and one-generation nobilities took place. Mamlūk "houses" (*buyūt*, sing. *bayt*) did not peter out as they had done in the Mamlūk sultanate but went on living indefinitely, so long as they were not crushed by a factor external to the specific "house". The longer they lived, the more deep-rooted and vehement became their mutual hatreds. The incidents necessitating the taking of blood revenge (*al-akhdh bil-tha'r*) grew in number, ultimately leading to the unflinching determination to physically annihilate (*qaṭʿ*, *izāla*) the rival "house". When the Fiḳāriyya wiped out the Ḳāsimiyya in 1142/1729 the causes which brought about the inevitably uncompromising struggles within the Mamlūk society were not removed. The "houses" which grew out of the Fiḳāriyya continued their fights according to the old pattern.

Mamlūk society in the Mamlūk sultanate was a very exclusive one. In order to become a member of it a person had to fulfil very definite requirements. He had to be: fair-skinned; (in most cases) an inhabitant of the area stretching to the north and to the north east of the lands of Islam; born an infidel; brought over to the Mamlūk sultanate as a child or young boy (preferably at the age of puberty); bought, brought up and manumitted by a patron who was a member of the military aristocracy (preferably a Mamlūk as well, and ideally the sultan himself). The chances of a Mamlūk bought and manumitted by a civilian joining the aristocracy, and particularly rising high within it, were very meager indeed.

What greatly helped in making the Mamlūks so easily distinguishable, distinct and exclusive was a practice which started long before the creation of the Mamlūk sultanate, namely, that all of them, with but a few exceptions, bore Turkish names, irrespective of their origin. This was also true in the case of the Circassians, when they constituted the major factor in the military aristocracy. The fact that most of the Mamlūks' sons (*awlād al-nās*) bore Muslim names greatly helped in their smooth ousting from that aristocracy, thus facilitating its preservation as a one generation aristocracy. In Ottoman Egypt the adoption of Muslim names by the overwhelming majority of the Mamlūks was an important factor in the creation of a society where hereditary and one-generation nobilities merged into one.

Another important aspect of the exclusiveness of that society was that its members mainly married slave-girls from their own countries of origin, or daughters of Mamlūks. Most of their concubines were also from the same regions, although black girls were by no means excluded from that category. Marriages between Mamlūk amirs and local girls (mainly the daughters of high ranking officials, great merchants or distinguished *ʿulamā'*) were quite rare. This would mean that the number of slave-girls imported from the areas which served as the source for military slaves was at least as great as the number of Mamlūks. Marriages between the sons of the Mamlūks and local girls were much more numerous, and this represents one facet of the assimilation of the Mamlūks' offspring into the local population.

The Mamlūks were also distinguished by their dress, which was considered to be much more respectable than that of any other class. This dress distinction goes back to the Mamlūk regiment of the ᶜAbbāsid caliph al-Muᶜtaṣim (al-Masᶜūdi, *Murūdj al-Dhahab*, VIII, p. 119).

The owning of Mamlūks was the prerogative of the Mamlūks, although cases of Mamlūks owned by civilians were quite frequent. Another prerogative was the riding of horses, and orders prohibiting civilians from buying Mamlūks were rarer than those forbidding them to ride horses (some of the highest civilian officials were explicitly exempted from the riding prohibition).

The language which the Mamlūks predominantly used among themselves was Turkish. Their knowledge of Arabic in most cases seems to have been very superficial, although a more systematic study of this question may change that impression to a certain extent. Their Islamic awareness, however, was very strong. It was expressed, *inter alia*, in the numerous religious institutions which they built. This activity had also its material aspect, as stated by Ibn Khaldūn: to assure the future of the Mamlūks' descendants, who could not join the upper class, they appointed them as administrators or superintendents of the *waḳfs* assigned to those institutions for their maintenance (*al-Taᶜrīf bi-Ibn Khaldūn*, p. 279).

The main body of the Mamlūk sultanate's army, namely, all the Royal Mamlūks (*al-mamālīk al-sulṭāniyya*) – who formed the backbone of the Sultanate's might – and most of the armies of the first-ranking amirs, were stationed in Cairo. It was very difficult to make any part of the Royal Mamlūks serve as a garrison anywhere outside the capital. Units of the corps which were forced to stay in Syria, for example, soon declined in power and importance. Some minor exceptions to this rule did not affect the general picture. Considering the comparatively limited number of Mamlūks, keeping their élite element together must have been the only way of preserving its military might. This, in its turn, considerably increased the already great weight of the capital vis-à-vis the rest of the realm. Nothing could move the Royal Mamlūks, of their own choice, from Cairo, not even epidemics, which wrought havoc among them.

This concentration in the capital had its grave drawbacks. Any serious revolt by the Bedouins or Turcomans anywhere in the realm could not be quelled without the participation of the Royal Mamlūks, who were stationed so often far away from the scene of the revolt. Worse still, all the major wars of the Mamlūks took place in its northern part or beyond it, a great distance from the main centre of military might.

This was always a very great handicap, and it became critical in the closing decades of Mamlūk rule, when the Mamlūks had to cope with the Turcomans beyond their borders, who lived contiguously to the Turcomans of their own realm, and who were supported by the ominously growing power of the Ottoman empire.

The Mamlūk sultanate served as an example to other Muslim states, including the reliance on Mamlūk soldiers, many of whom were acquired in Egypt. For the ruler of Yanbu^c, see Ibn al-Furāt, IX, p. 43, ll. 6–9; for the ruler of Mecca, *Ḍaw' al-Ṣubḥ*, p. 332; Ibn Iyās, IV, p. 456, ll. 10–12; *Nudjum* (ed. Popper), V, p. 117, ll. 18–23; Ibn al-Furāt, IX, pp. 208, ll. 12–15, 308, ll. 7–20; for the ruler of Yemen, *Ṣubḥ*, V. p. 35, ll. 15–17; *Nudjum*, V, p. 81, ll. 1–2; for the ruler of *Bidjāya*, *Ṣubḥ*, V, p. 137, l. 9; for the Sultan of Takrūr, *Ṣubḥ*, V, p. 300, ll. 7–9. In 669.1464–5 the army of the ruler of Shirwān and the adjacent areas, whose capital was Shamākhī, was estimated at 20,000 combat soldiers (*mukātila*) of whom 1,000 were Circassian Mamlūks (*Ḥawādith al-Duhūr*, pp. 579, l. 16–580, l. 13). This does not necessarily imply influence from the Mamlūk sultanate, but what it certainly reflects is the great competition from other Muslim states which that sultanate had to face in drawing manpower from the same source, especially from states situated much nearer to that source.

The character, structure and development of military slavery in the Mamlūk sultanate can be more properly understood if it is studied in connection with its Ayyūbid predecessor. The Kurdishness of the Ayyūbid regime and its army has been greatly exaggerated. The Turkish, and even more so the Turkish–Mamlūk element in its armed forces was the dominant one throughout its history, as was only natural for a dynasty whose founders came from the ranks of the Zankid army. Shīrkūh's private army, the Asadiyya, who counted 500, and who were, most probably, the main factor which enabled Saladin to succeed his uncle, had been – contrary to what students of the Ayyūbids have written about them – a pure Mamlūk unit (see e.g. Abū Shāma, I, p. 173, l. 1–2; al-Maḳrīzī, *Itti^cāẓ al-Ḥanafā'*, III, p. 308, ll. 9–10). So were the other private armies of the Ayyūbid sultans, like the Kāmiliyya Muḥammad, the Ashrafiyya Mūsā, the Nāṣiriyya Yūsuf, etc.

The reign of al-Malik al-Ṣāliḥ Najm al-Dīn Ayyūb, the founder of the Baḥriyya regiment, which toppled the Ayyūbids and established the Mamlūk sultanate, strengthened the Ayyūbid impact on that sultanate. That sultan was venerated by his Baḥriyya, and they looked upon him as the example which should be followed. It is very rare that a ruler belonging to a deposed dynasty would leave such an impress on its deposers. It took the Baḥriyya quite long to disconnect themselves from the direct heritage of their patron; from their general Ayyūbid heritage they disconnected themselves only partly. Mamlūk military slavery certainly evolved in comparison with its Ayyūbid prototype, but the changes were quite slow, and each of them has to be traced and identified separately.

BIBLIOGRAPHY

This bibliography is restricted to studies dealing in some detail with Mamlūk military slavery and a few related subjects discussed in the present article. Works based on European sources are only perfunctorily mentioned.

G. Wiet, "L'Egypte Arab ... 642–1517", in *Histoire de la nation égyptienne*, vol. IV (1937), pp. 387–636 (esp. pp. 387–392); MM. Ziada, "The Mamlūk Sultans", *History of the Crusades*, Philadelphia, vol. II (1962), pp. 735–758; vol. III (1975), pp. 486–512, passim; ᶜA. ᶜĀshur, *Miṣr fi ᶜAṣr Dawlat al-Mamālīk al-Baḥriyya* (Cairo 1959); I. ᶜA. Tarkhān, *Miṣr fī ᶜAṣr Dawlat Mamālīk al-Djarākisa* (Cairo 1960); E. Quatremère, *Histoire des Sultans Mamlouks de l'Egypte* (Paris 1837–1842) (the notes on Mamlūk terms are still very useful; see indexes); M. Van Berchem, *CIA, Egypte* (Paris 1894–1929) (many relevant terms; indexes); W. Björkman, *Beiträge zur Geschichte der Staatskanzlei im islamischen Ägypten* (Hamburg 1928) (much relevant terminology; index); Gaudefroy-Demombynes, *La Syrie à l'époque des Mamelouks* (Paris 1923) (esp. pp. XIX–CXIX); M. Mostafa, "Beiträge zur Geschichte Ägyptens zur Zeit der türkischen Eroberung", *Zeitschrift der Deutschen Morgenländischen Gesellschaft* 89 (1935), pp. 194–224 (esp. 208–224); J. Sauvaget, *La poste aux chevaux dans l'Empire des Mamelouks* (Paris 1941); —*La Chronique de Damas d'al-Jazari* (Paris 1949) (terms in the index); —"Noms et surnoms de Mamelouks", *Journal Asiatique* 238 (1950), pp. 31–58; A.N. Poliak, "Le caractère colonial de l'état mamelouk dans ses rapports avec la Horde d'Or", *Revue des Etudes islamiques* 9 (1935), pp. 231–248; —"The influence of Chingiz-Khān's Yāsa upon the general organization of the Mamlouk State", *Bulletin of the School of Oriental and African Studies* 10 (1940–1942), pp. 862–876; —"Some notes on the feudal system of the Mamlūks", *Journal of the Royal Asiatic Society* (1937), pp. 97–107; —*Feudalism in Egypt, Syria, Palestine and Lebanon (1250–1900)* (London 1939); S.B. Pevzner, article in Russian on the *Iḳṭāᶜ* analysed by M. Canard in *Arabica* VI–VII (1960–1961); L.A. Semenöva, *Salakh ad-Din i Mamlūki Egypte* (Moscow 1966); M.C.S. Tekindag, *Berkuk devrinde Mamlūk Sultanligi* (Istanbul 1961), pp. 151–157 and passim; A. Darrāg, *L'Egypte sous le régime de Barsbāy 825–841/1422–1438* (Damascus 1961), pp. 33–55; P.M. Holt, "The Sultanate of al-Manṣūr Lāchin (696–698/1296–1299)", *Bulletin of the School of Oriental and African Studies* 36 (1973), pp. 521–532; —"The position and power of the Mamlūk sultan", *Bulletin of the School of Oriental and African Studies* 38 (1975), pp. 237–249; H.M. Rabie, *The Financial System of Egypt 564–741/ 1169–1341* (Oxford 1972) (numerous relevant terms; index); —"The training of the Mamlūk Fāris", *War, Technology and Society in the Middle East* (London 1975), pp. 153–163; R.S. Humphreys, "The Emergence of the Mamlūk Army", *Studia Islamica* 45 (1977), pp. 67–99; 46 (1977), pp. 147–182; —*From Saladin to the Mongols* (Albany 1957), passim; B. Flemming, "Literary Activities in Mamlūk Halls and Barracks", *Studies in Memory of Gaston Wiet* (Jerusalem 1977), pp. 249–260, and the studies quoted there; N. Haarmann, "Alṭun Hān and Cingiz Hān bei den ägyptischen Mamluken", *Der Islam* 51 (1974), pp. 1–36; D.P. Little, "Notes on Aitamis, a Mongol Mamlūk", *Die Islamische Welt zwischen Mittelalter und Neuzeit* (Beirut 1979), pp. 387–401; G. Guémard, "De l'armement et de l'équipement des Mamelouks", *Bulletin de l'Institut d'Egypte* 8 (1926), pp. 1–19; L.A. Mayer, *Saracenic Heraldry* (Oxford 1933) (esp. pp. 1–43); —*Mamlūk Costume* (Geneva 1952); G.T. Scanlon, *A Muslim Manual of War* (Cairo 1961); J.D. Latham and W.F. Paterson, *Saracen Archery* (London 1970); S.H. Labib, *Handelsgeschichte Ägyptens im Spätmittelalter* (Wiesbaden 1965) (index: Sklaven, Sklavenhandel, etc.); W. Heyd, *Histoire du commerce du Levant* (Leipzig 1885–1886) (index: Esclaves, Mamelouks); A. Schaube, *Handelsgeschichte der romanischen Völker des Mittelmeergebiets bis zum Ende der Kreuzzüge* (Munich 1906) (index: Sklaven and Sklavenhandel); G.I. Bratianu, *Recherches sur le commerce Génois dans la Mer Noire au XIIIe siècle* (Paris 1929), passim; R.S. Lopez and W. Raymond, Medieval Trade in the *Mediterranean World* (New York 1955) (index: slaves, slave trade); P.H. Dopp, *Traité d'Emmanuel Piloti sur le Passage en Terre Sainte (1420)* (Louvain–Paris 1958) (esp. pp. 51–56); D. Ayalon, three collections of studies: *Studies on the Mamlūks of Egypt (1250–1517)* (London 1977) (includes: Circassians; Le régiment Baḥriyya; The Transfer of the ᶜAbbāsid Caliphate); —*The Mamlūk Military Society* (London 1979) (includes: Aspects of the Mamlūk Phenomenon; Esclavage; European-Asiatic Steppe); —*Outsiders in the Lands of Islam* (London 1988) (includes: Egypt as a Dominant Factor in Syria and Palestine; The Great Yāsa; Mamlūkiyyat); —*Gunpowder and Firearms in the Mamlūk Kingdom – A Challenge to the Medieval Society* (London 1978); —"The Mamlūk Army in the First Years of the Ottoman Conquest (in Hebrew)" (*Tarbiz*, Jerusalem 1952), pp. 221–226; —"From Ayyūbids to Mamlūks", *Revue des Etudes islamiques* 49 (1981), pp. 43–57 (included in the present volume; see also studies IV, V, VI); —articles in *Encyclopaedia of Islam* (2nd ed.), which are summaries of as yet unpublished studies: Baḥriyya, the navy of the Mamlūks; Burdjiyya; Ḥarb; Ḥiṣār; M. Sobernheim, art. Mamlūks, *Encyclopaedia of Islam* (1st ed.).

III

FROM AYYUBIDS TO MAMLUKS

The transition from the Ayyūbid to the Mamlūk reign constitutes an inseparable part of the history and development of the Mamlūk institution in Islam, and should be studied against that background. The immenseness of the subject, however, as well as its being a comparatively new target of systematic research, make a constant revision of the emerging picture of that institution quite unavoidable. Yet it seems to me that the more one studies the subject, the more one must become convinced that without the Mamlūks the chances of Islam to become a world religion on *such* a scale and within *such* wide boundaries, would have greatly diminished.

For the purpose of the present paper, the lot of the Mamlūks under the Saljūqs is of cardinal importance, because the Zangids, the Ayyūbids, and even the Mamlūks, were, to this or that extent, successor states of the Saljūqs.

The problem of the Mamlūks under the Saljūqs is this. When the Saljūqs crossed the boundaries of the lands of Islam, the Mamlūks had already been firmly established as a most formidable force, at least over the lands of the Eastern Caliphate. The Saljūqs were, for quite a long time, too weak to destroy or even to seriously weaken them. In fact, they are never said to have done so, or even to have intended to. Yet as far as the data in the *sources* are concerned, the Mamlūks are in the shadow in the early decades of Saljūq history inside the Muslim borders. Some of the reasons for that situation were, in my view: the preoccupation of the sources with the big events and wars of the time; the fact, that for the first time in Muslim history one can

---

* This is a brief summary of one part of an extensive study on the transition process from the Ayyūbid to the Mamlūk reign, now in preparation. Only a tiny fraction of the scholary apparatus of that study is given here.

not be certain whether *Turk* or *Atrāk* well inside Muslim territory were Mamlūks or those freeborn newcomers; and, perhaps, also because these newcomers, just fresh from the steppe, counterbalanced the Mamlūks militarily to some extent for some time. One has, therefore, to make an exertion in order to trace the Mamlūks in that early Saljūq stage, and when one does, he discovers their centrality and decisiveness. I have already shown elsewhere that the great Niẓām al-Mulk could not have even dreamt of accumulating such power and influence, certainly not maintaining them, without his immense private Mamlūk army (the Niẓāmiyya)[1]. This was in full keeping with his view of the Mamlūks as expressed in the Siyāsat Nāmeh, and which certainly reflects a much earlier Saljūq attitude to this military class.

Indeed, Mamlūks of the Saljūqs come to the forefront as a decisive factor well before the first mention of Niẓām al-Mulk's Mamlūks in the reign of Malikshāh. There are Mamlūk soldiers serving the Saljūqs already in the reign of Sultan Tughril, and playing a no mean role in defeating al-Basāsīrī. In this juncture I shall refer specifically only to one major event in the reign of Tughril's successor, Alp Arslān, the father of Malikshāh. The historian Ghars al-Ni'ma Abū al-Ḥasan Muḥammad, the son and continuator of Hilāl al-Ṣābī, who, I believe, gives the best account of the battle of Manzikert, which paved the way to the conquest of Anatolia and to the rise of the Ottoman empire, says that Sultan Alp Arslan relied in that battle only on the 4,000 Mamlūks *(ghilmān, mamālīk)* who did not leave him on the way to the battlefield, whereas the rest of his army melted away[2].

What I wanted to demonstrate in this most central instance (to which a good number of other instances, including earlier ones, can be added) is that there was no serious break in the predominance of the Mamlūk element since the time of Caliph al-Mu'tasim, which had not been shaken even by the influx of the Turkish tribes under the Saljūqs. It is against this background of the overwhelmingness and continuity of the Mamlūk phenomenon and its crucial role in the internal and external relations of Islam that the Ayyūbid and Mamlūk empires should be studied.

But before going into that, another class of people has to be discussed: the eunuchs. These are not only closely connected with the Mamlūks, but their important element constitutes an inseparable part of them. The subject of the eunuchs and their place in Islam was neglected even more than that of the Mamlūks (the study of that subject in the Ottoman empire might be excepted). A major reason for that neglect, apart from an inherent reluctance to deal with such a topic, belongs to the realm of terminology: *khā-*

---

1. D. Ayalon, Aspects of the Mamlūk Phenomenon. A. The Importance of the Mamlūk Institution, *Der Islam,* 1976, p. 212-217.

2. See Ghars al-Ni'ma's account in Sibṭ Ibn al-Jawsī, *Mir'āt al-Zamān,* Ankara, 1968, p. 147-152. Compare especially p. 147, 11. 14-18, with p. 148, 11. 15-18 and 152, 11. 6-9.

dim, the main and most constant term designating « eunuch » in Medieval Islam, and well into later centuries, was, in too many cases, not understood as such. I collected elsewhere a host of proofs in support of that meaning, which, I believe, are many times more than needed. That is why I considered that hoarding of proofs as an unavoidable « overkill »[3]. In view of the unique importance of that term I shall do here a « superoverkill » by presenting yet another proof which seems to me to be conclusive. I collected data on *many* hundreds of prominent persons called *khādim.* Not a single one of them is said to have had an offspring, or that he had been, or died, childless. Take any dozen or score of prominent *non-khādims*, chosen at random, and follow their history, and you will see how quickly the existence of the offspring of a substantial part of them will emerge. To this should be added, that any political group in the court or in the military society which bears the name *khadam* or *khuddām* consists of nothing but eunuchs. What should also be pointed out is that *khadam* in the sense of eunuchs goes far beyond prominent people and prominent groups bearing that designation.

The power accumulated by the formidable combination of Mamlūks and eunuchs and the decisive role played by them, are astounding. The key positions held by eunuchs under the Caliphs, the Saljūqs, the Fāṭimids and a number of other states of the East from Tranoxania to Egypt, up to the Ayyūbid reign, are extremely numerous. Under the Ayyūbids the power of the eunuchs continued to be as strong as ever. We shall quote here only few instances. The Ayyūbids started their career in Takrīt under the auspices of the famous and very powerful eunuch Bihrūz. When Saladin succeeded his uncle Asad al-Dīn Shīrkāh in Egypt, it was the eunuch Mu'taman al-Dawla, the Grand Master of the Fāṭimid palace, who instigated and conducted the great rebellion of the blacks and the Armenians against the new regime. When the rebellion was crushed, Saladin put at the head of the same palace the eunuch Bahā' al-Dīn Qarāqūsh al-Asadī, the Mamlūk of Shīrkūh, entrusting to him all the Fāṭimid treasures and the Fāṭimid family. It was the same Qarāqūsh who had been given the task of building the wall and citadel of Cairo. In a time of great despair it was he who had been appointed to command the garrison of Acre, besieged by the Franks. And these are not all his feats. When al-Ṣāliḥ Najm al-Dīn Ayyūb showed in Egypt signs of disobedience in the reign of his father, al-Kāmil, he had been dispatched beyond the Euphrates, and stayed there under the vigilant eye of the most faithful eunuch, Ṣawāb al-'Ādilī, who had also been a well known military commander. Both Mamlūks and eunuchs were the main factor in ousting al-'Ādil Abū Bakr II and putting al-Ṣāliḥ Ayyūb on the throne (637/1240). It was

3. D. Ayalon, On the Eunuchs in Islam, *Jerusalem Studies in Arabic and Islam,* Jerusalem, 1979, p. 74-92.

eunuchs who were entrusted with murdering Abū Bakr in prison. When Najm decided to live in seclusion, it was through eunuchs that he kept his contacts with the outside world. It was a eunuch who imitated his handwriting in order to conceal his death in a time of critical Frankish danger to Egypt and Islam. When the huge and superbly equipped army of Louis IX was defeated and captured by the Baḥriyya Mamlūks, it was a eunuch, Muḥsin, who gave them safe conduct, and another eunuch was appointed as the chief guardian in prison of the French king and his retinue. Other eunuchs had their important share in the struggle of Sultan Tūrānshāh and the Bahriyya, and in the reign of Shajar al-Durr and Aybak.

As for the eunuchs under the Mamlūks, in no other Muslim Medieval state their hierachy and functioning can be reconstructed to the same or similar degree as in the Mamlūk Sultanate (this is true of so many other subjects and institutions). Therefore, a full comparison is impossible. In general one can say that their power as a class remained very great. Yet their chances as individuals considerably diminished in comparison with the past. They could not rise to the highest ranks, neither do we meet them as commanders in the field of battle.[4] But it should be stated that this had been the result of a quite slow process, which continued well into the Mamlūk reign, and well beyond the time of Sultan Baybars I.

In dealing with the transition from the Ayyūbid to the Mamlūk reigns, the identification of the character of the Ayyūbid regime is of primary importance. In a word: it was overwhelmingly Turkish and Turkish-Mamlūk, the weight of the Kurdish element in it being greatly exaggerated by the students of the subject. I have already brought elsewhere numerous proofs to this effect, of which I shall mention only few. In speaking about the extinction of the Fāṭimids, Ibn al-Athīr says *twice* that the rule passed from them to the *Atrāk*. A contemporary praising Saladin calls his reign *Dawlat al-Turk,* precisely the name of the later Mamlūk Sultanate. In a letter sent by the Fāṭimid Caliph to Nūr al-Dīn, he begs to rid him of the Atrāk, of whom he is afraid, and to leave with him only Saladin and his retinue. There could not be a better proof to the might of the *Atrāk* vis-à-vis that of the *Akrād*, who are not even mentioned in that correspondence. The belief about the Kurdish character of the Ayyūbid reign led to the identification of the *Ghuzz* under the Ayyūbids with *Kurd.* I have already shown that this identification, repeated since Quatremère onwards, is unfounded. *Ghuzz* is, as always, synonymous with *Turk*[5]. Since than I found numerous additional proofs to this

---

4. D. Ayalon, The Eunuchs in the Mamluk Sultanate, *Studies in Memory of Gaston Wiet,* Jerusalem, 1977, p. 267-295.

5. D. Ayalon, Aspects of the Mamluk Phenomenon: B. Ayyūbid's Kurds and Turks, *Der Islam,* 1977, p. 2-8, 10-13.

effect, of which I shall mention only one. A Mamlūk contingent sent to Upper Egypt in 651/1253, shortly after the extinction of the Ayyūbid Sultanate, is alternately called *Ghuzz* and *Turk*[6]. An additional piece of evidence, unmentioned yet by me in print, is this. Ibn al-Furāt includes in his chronicle a verbatim description of the occupation of Egypt by Nūr al-Dīn's army, written by a contemporary anonymous source (already published by C. Cahen). In this description the *Turk* or *Atrāk* are mentioned *eleven* times; the Kurds, not even once. Furthermore, the commander of the Nūrid forces is called Shīrkūh al-Turkī[7].

The overwhelming superiority of the Turks and Turkish Mamlūks over the Kurds under the Ayyūbids becomes more than evident by just an ordinary comparison between the two racial groups. But such a kind of comparison does not do justice to the *real* preponderance, which was certainly far bigger. The crux of the matter lies in the answer to the question: who were the private armies of the Kurdish amirs under the Zangids and Ayyūbids, a point which I raised in a note in a previous study[8]. I shall concentrate here on the composition of the private army of the Kurd Asad al-Dīn Shīrkūh, for this is *pivotal* to the proper understanding of the very establishment of the Ayyūbid rule in Egypt, as well as of the character of all those whom I call the *iyya* groups (Asadiyya, Ṣalāḥiyya, Ashrafiyya, Ẓāhiriyya, 'Azīziyya, Nāṣiriyya, Ṣāliḥiyya, Mu'izziyya, Muṣaffariyya, Manṣūriyya, Mu'ayyadiyya, etc.), from the very begining of the Ayyūbid rule, up to the very end of Mamlūk rule, groups which constituted the very core of the two reigns.

The early chronicler Ibn Abī Ṭayy says in connection with the death of Shīrkūh: « He left much money and property and he left many horses and riding animals and camels, *and he left a group of ghilmān, five hundred Mamlūks, and these are the Asadiyya (wa-khallafa jamā'a min al-Ghilmān khamsmi'at mamlūk wa-hum al-Asadiyya)*[8a].

The whole credit, and a great one, for bringing this uniquely important evidence to the knowledge of the students of the Ayyūbids goes to H.A.R. Gibb. However, this is how he translates it. « Shirkuh's own regiment... *consisting of 500 mamlūks and Kurds* »[9] (my italics — D.A.). There can hardly be a more conclusive proof for the Kurdish complex dominating the students of the Ayyūbid period, than that a scholar of Gibb's stature and command of Arabic would see Kurds in a passage of such clearness and simplicity, where they just do not exist.

---

6. IBN AL-FURÂT, ms. Vatican. Or. 726, vol. VII, fol. 163a; cf. also *Sulūk*, I, p. 386, ll. 16, 17; 387, ll. 7, 9.

7. IBN AL-FURÂT, ms. Vienne, A.F. 119, vol. III, fol. 184b-189b.

8. Aspects., etc., B, p. 29, note 105.

8a. ABŪ SHĀMA. *Kitāb al-Rawḍatayn,* Cairo, 1287/1871, p. 172, l. 37-173, l. 1.

9. The Armies of Saladin, *Studies on the Civilization of Islam,* Boston, 1962, p. 74, and note 3 on p. 85.

What is of no smaller significance is that every scholar I know, who used the selfsame evidence, directly or indirectly, explicitly or implicitly, made the same mistake like Gibb, or at least considered the Asadiyya as a non purely Mamlūk unit. The contentions of some of them (including Gibb) that a commander or commanders of the Asadiyya or Ṣalāḥiyya (the private regiment of Saladin) were Kurds, are erroneous, either because those specific amirs were not the commanders of those two bodies, or because they were not Kurds.

What Ibn Abī Ṭayy says in so few words is that the Asadiyya were a purely Mamlūk body, and this is the simple truth. In the future history of the Asadiyya there is nothing to refute or modify that evidence, and there is much to strengthen it. The same is true of the Ṣalāḥiyya (or Nāṣiriyya) of Saladin, and of all the *iyya* military groups or factions that followed, up to the end of Mamlūk rule. There might; of course, be on the margin *iyya* persons who were not the Mamlūks of that particular patron, but this was only by extension or by mistake.

There is yet another proof, and, in my view, a very convincing one, for the Mamlūk character of the *iyya* groups. It is only the Mamlūk adhesive (the mutual solidarity existing between the patron and his Mamlūks and between the Mamlūks towards each other) which can explain the long survival of so many of these groups after the death or deposition of their patrons, with the members of each such group sticking together until it peters out. This adhesive was complemented and strengthened by an anti-adhesive or rejective, namely: any member of such a group, who had, after having been manumitted, to leave it and serve another patron, would never be accepted as an equal by the *iyya* group of that new patron. Furthermore, what a systematic collection of the very rich data on these groups easily demonstrates is that they are very often called not just *iyya* but *al-mamālīk al-iyya,* like *al-mamālīk al-Ṣāliḥiyya, al Kāmiliyya, al-Ashrafīyya,* etc.

The Asadiyya had undoubtedly been the most compact and, in all probalility, the strongest single military body in the Nūrid expeditionary force to Egypt (in this I fully share Gibb's views)[10]. In order to understand what a body of 500 Mamlūks means one should remember that the whole regiment of the Baḥriyya, which had been the major factor in the resounding victories of al-Manṣūra against the Franks and of ʻAyn Jālūt against the Mongols, and in between toppled the Ayyūbids and the Mamlūk Sultanate, numbered 750 to 1 000 horsemen, according to the various sources. To return to the Asadiyya: *all* of them supported Saladin in his bid for nomination as their patron's successor. No other actual or potential contender to this succession,

---

10. *The life of Saladin,* Oxford, 1973, p. 6, note 2. Yet Gibb's assertion that the Asadiyya numbered 2,000 (*ibid.,* p. 5) is erroneous.

be he a Kurd, a Turk or a Turkoman, had a comparable support. Thus, in the very establishment of the Ayyūbid rule and in the very creation of the Ayyūbid dynasty, the share of a purely Mamluk unit was most decisive.

Thus, looking at the founding of a Kurdish dynasty in Egypt as the outcome of a struggle between just Kurds and Turks, in which the Kurds had the upper hand, as might be inferred from the expression: « the rule should not move from the Kurds to the Turks » *(lā yakhruj al-amr ʻan al Akrād ilā al-Atrāk)*[11] is a very misleading oversimplification. For the power of the Kurdish side was based to a very great extent on Turkish Mamlūks. In the case of Shīrkūh, any non-Mamlūk groups which might have been under his aegis, did not seem to have been worth mentioning. Now Shīrkūh was one of the two or three topmost commanders in the army of Nūr al-Dīn. The type of private army which he built certainly represents the *ideal*, to which equal or lower commanders, be they Mamlūks or non-Mamlūks, would crave, if they had the means or if they had been allowed to (or both). Unfortunately, the sources speak up to (and not including) the Mamlūk period, very little about the amirs' armies. Yet, on rare occasions they do mention them. Thus we know, usually by accident, of the Mamlūk private bodies of non-Mamlūk amirs (Kurdish and other). It is very noteworthy that only because of the particular circumstances of Shīrkūh's end, the very existence of his private Mamlūk army, as well as its size, were made known. Otherwise the chances that that information would come down to us would be almost zero. In spite of the fact that Shīrkūh is mentioned so frequently in the sources and in connection with such mighty military events, there is no allusion whatsoever to his Asadiyya or to any single Mamlūk of his until after his death[12].

Throughout the Ayyūbid reign the *iyya* groups, almost all of them relating to Ayyūbid Sultans and princes in Egypt, Syria and beyond the Euphrates, were Mamlūk bodies, with (as I said) insignificant exceptions on the margin (such exceptions existed also in the reign of the Mamlūks). It was they who had been the decisive factors and the Kurds, who had been, on the whole, discriminated against, trailed far behind them. I believe I have already proved this on the basis of a quite partial data.[13] Additional reading substantiates and greatly strengthens that conclusion.

Thus there was a much wider and stronger continuity between the

11. Abū Shāma, *op. cit.*, p. 161, 11. 10-11.

12. There are very strong grounds in support of the conclusion that Saladin's Ṣalāḥiyya existed already before Shīrkūh's death. They also were an important factor in maintaining Saladin in his office soon after his appointment to it. However, they must have been at that early stage much weaker than the Asadiyya. This, as well as the Mamlūk private armies of the amirs under the Ayyūbids, are discussed in detail in the more comprehensive study mentioned above.

13. « Ayyūbids Kurds and Turks », *op. cit.*, the whole article, as well as p. 8-10.

Mamlūk institution of the Ayyūbids and that of the Mamlūks, than I assumed or implied in my earlier studies, where I concentrated on the Mamlūk period (a thing which, under the circumstances, was unavoidable) and read only perfunctorily some of the then available sources dealing with the Ayyūbids. I accepted some general statements of these sources, or interpreted them inexactly, as I came to learn in the light of further reading. It was a grave oversight on my part that in a recent article of mine in *Der Islam*[14], I forgot to mention the revision of some of my earlier conclusions.

The impact of the Ayyūbids on the Mamlūks was, I believe, far wider than as it is reflected in the existence of a very solid Mamlūk backbone going through both reigns. This brings me to two important works of R.S. Humphreys published recently. In a book on the Ayyūbids of Damascus[15] he brings a very intelligent order in the intricate and most confusing internal relations of the Ayyūbids. This is a very welcome departure from any previous study, and its implications are considerably beyond that particular subject. I have, however, to disagree with some basic aspects of his view of the transition from Ayyūbids to Mamlūks expressed in this book and in an earlier article of his[16]. He tends to minimize the Ayyūbid impact, arguing that Sultan Baybars I introduced far reaching changes in the structure of the army[17]. I cannot accept that view, because there is no direct or indirect evidence to uphold it. Fortunately for that Sultan's reign we do possess most of the major contemporary sources dealing with it. These sources speak about quite a good number of Baybars' enterprises and exploits, including his building of the navy, and creation (or, more precisely, reorganization) of the *barīd* with its obvious military implications. As for the army, they do mention the increase in its numerical strength, but say nothing about its reorganization. From the indirect evidence one can perceive a certain change, but which does not seriously affect the continuity existing between the Ayyūbid and Mamlūk armies.

In the context of the present subject H. analyzes in considerable length three terms, or institutions: *'askar, ḥalqa* and *ṭulb.* Here I shall dwell in some detail only on *ḥalqa.* The other two, together with few additional subjects, will be dealt with only briefly.

H. says: « *It is hard to see any but a verbal relationship* (my italics -D.A.) between the elite Ayyūbid *ḥalqa* sultaniyya and the low paid reserve troopers who made up the Mamlūk ḥalqa »[18]; and then: « the Ayyubid *ḥalqa* has so

---

14. See notes 1 and 5.

15. *From Saladin to the Mongols — The Ayyubids of Damascus 1193-1260,* Albany, 1977.

16. The Emergence of the Mamluk Army, *Studia Islamica,* fascicle XLV (1977), p. 67-99; fascicle XLVI (1977), p. 147-182. In the present paper I shall refer mainly to this article.

17. Emergence, etc., II, p. 153-180.

18. Emergence, etc., *op. cit.,* part I, p. 68.

little in common with its immediate descendent in the Mamlūk army[19] ». The sole reference which he brings in support of these two assertions is my study (« on the contrast between the Ayyūbid and Mamluk periods see Ayalon »[20]) but what I say is not quite exactly so. After pointing at the *ḥalqa*'s immense importance in the reign of Saladin, I state that I did not examine systematically its development under the Ayyūbids. Then I say: « As for the Mamluk era, its early years saw the *ḥalqa* preserve its power and lofty position[21]. From the source references and instances which follow, it is clear that I mean a period which continues considerably beyond the reign of Baybars I, and then I state that until the [third] reign of al-Nāsir Muḥammad b. Qalāūn we find no clear indication of the decline of the *ḥalqa*[22]. Then I add that under Qalāūn we still hear of 4,000 soldiers of the Sultan's *own ḥalqa*, participating as *elite* troops (italics in the original - D.A.) in the uniquely important battle against the Mongols in 1281[23]. They fight, like in Saladin's time[24], in the center *(qalb),* whereas the number of Qalāūn's own Mamlūks fighting in the center was only 800 *(wa-waqafa al-sulṭān tahta al-ṣanājiq wa-ma'ahu khāṣṣatuhu wa-alzāmuhu wa-arbāb al-waẓā'if fa-kānat 'iddat ḥalqatihi arba'at ālāf fāris wa-hiya aqwā wa-ashadd wa-'iddat mamālīk al-sultān thamān mi'at mamlūk)*[25]. Note the *ḥalqa's* being described as « stronger and more powerful », and that it is mentioned before the Sultan's Mamlūks, which is not the only instance.

In his conviction that Baybars I « *created* »[25a] (my italics - D.A.), among other military institutions, a quite thoroughly new kind of *ḥalqa,* H. writes: « The *ḥalqa* in its classical Mamlūk form as a distinct structure, appears from the earliest years of Baybars' reign... already we see the characteristic, *but hitherto unexampled* (my italics - D.A.) terminology of this institution — *ajnād al-ḥalqa, mufradī/mafārida, muqaddamū ḥalqa, a'yān al-ḥalqa*[26].

As for *mufradi/mafārida,* I found them in the Ayyūbid reign already in Saladin's time and several times after him[27], and even more frequently in Ayyūbid and Rasūlid Yemen. *Muqaddam ḥalqa* I found for the first time in

---

19. *Ibid.*, p. 82.

20. *Ibid.*, p. 82. The reference here is to my: Studies on the Structure of the Mamluk Army, *BSOAS,* XV, part II, p. 448-456. In support of his first assertion H. refers to the same article of mine, p. 448-50 (Emergence, etc., p. 68, note 1).

21. Studies on the Structure, etc., *op. cit.,* p. 449.

22. *Ibid.,* p. 451.

23. See my: Ḥims (the battle of) in EI², vol. III, p. 402-403.

24. See my: Aspects, etc. *op. cit.,* part B, p. 15.

25. AL-MAQRIZI, *Sulūk*, Cairo, 1939, p. 693, ll. 3-5.

25a. Emergence, etc., II, p. 164.

26. Emergence, etc., Part II, p. 162 and note 2.

27. 'Imād al-Dīn AL-ISFFAHĀNĪ, *al-Fatḥ al-Qussī*, Leiden, p. 103, l. 16; IBN WĀSIL, *Mufarrij al-Kurūb* (ed. Shayyāl), vol. III, p. 93, 98, 239. See also IBN AL-FURAT, vol. IV, part II, Cairo, 1969, p. 155, 160; vol. V, part I, Cairo, 1970, p. 200.

the siege of Damietta in 615/1218[28]. Then just before al-Ṣāliḥ Ayyūb's accession to the throne, and several times during his reign[28a]. There is an indication to the existence *ajnad al-ḥalqa* in Ayyūbid Yemen. *A'yān al-ḥalqa* I would discard, because, in my view, it is not a term at all.

Within his attempt to prove that the *ḥalqa* of the first Ayyūbid, Saladin, and the *ḥalqa* of the last of them, Najm al-Dīn Ayyūb, were much the same, and constituted a *corp d'élite* in contrast to the transformed *ḥalqa* of Baybars, H. suggess that the Ṣalāḥiyya regiment of Saladin might be identical with his *ḥalqa,* and does not exclude the possibility that the Baḥriyya of Najm al-Dīn were included in *his ḥalqa*[29]. As for Saladin, the maximum that can be said at the present state of our knowledge, as I have already pointed out elsewhere[30], is that there might be some overlapping between the two. The Baḥariyya and the ḥalqa of Najm's time were two distinct and antagonistic bodies. In the struggle between Sultan Tūrānshāh and the Baḥriyya the *ḥalqa* were, according to our best contemporary source, Ibn Wāṣil, on Tūranshāh side. The same author says afterwards explicitly that he heard that a dispute took place between the ḥalqa and the Baḥriyya *(balaghana annahu waqa'a khalf bayna al-ḥalqa wal-Baḥriyya)*[31]. This excludes any difference in this respect between the *ḥalqa* of the Ayyūbids and that of the Mamlūks, where the Baḥriyya regiment constituted always an entity most distinct from the *ḥalqa.* Neither can I see why the *ḥalqa* of Qalāūn is less of an élite than the *ḥalqa* of al-Najm Ayyūb. Never did the *ḥalqa* of Najm appear in circumstances of prominence which are even remotely similar to those of Qalāūn's *ḥalqa.* Incidentally, the epithet *al-ḥalqa al-manṣūra,* which H. considers as a sign of the elitist character of Saladin's[32] *ḥalqa,* continues well into the Mamlūk reign[33]. I cannot see the connection between H.'s impression that the *ḥalqa* under Sultan al-Mu'izz Aybak still kept its traditional character as a *corps d'élite,* and the passage he quotes in support of this impression from Ibn Wāṣil[34]. What this passage certainly proves is that the *ḥalqa* and the Baḥriyya were both different and antagonistic groups. According to H.'s conjecture, Saladin's *ḥalqa* « numbered no more than 1,000 at the outside »[35]. In fact, no figure of the *ḥalqa* as a whole under the Ayyūbids is

---

28. IBN AL-DAWĀDĀRĪ, Cairo, 1972, vol. VII, p. 200, l. 17.

28a. See e.g. C. CAHEN, *La Chronique des Ayyoubides d'al-Makīn b. al-'Amīd*, Damas, 1955-7, p. 39, ll. 21-26; 45, ll. 9-10; al-Maqrīzī, *Sulūk,* p. 281, l. 11.

29. Emergence, etc., cp. I, p. 62-3 and p. 98.

30. Aspects, etc., B, p. 15-16.

31. *Mufarrij al-Kurūb,* BN, ms. Arabe 1703, fol. 89 b, especially 11. 15-16; 90 b, 11. 8-9.

32. Emergence, etc., I, p. 82.

33. In addition to the reference in « Studies on the Structure, etc. », see also, Ibn al-Dawādārī, vol. VIII (Cairo, 1971), p. 283, l. 15; l. 303, ll. 9-10, 345, l. 10.

34. Emergence, etc., II, p. 103, in the note.

35. *Ibid.,* I, p. 73. See also, *From Saladin to the Mongols,* p. 18.

mentioned in the sources, and we have no way of reasonably estimating it. Therefore, a comparison of the numerical strength of the *ḥalqa* between the two reigns should be ruled out at the present state of our knowledge.

The way Baybars I reformed the *ḥalqa* within H.'s suggestion of that Sultan's reorganization of the army, was this. « Second, there were Syrian troops who had fled to Egypt as refugees; these represented the numerous but disorganized remnant of the Ayyubid military establishment »... This « second group, partly reassigned to Syria and partly permitted to remain in Egypt, must have become the basis of the new *ḥalqa* [36] and then: « The unification of Syrian and Egyptian forces and the reform of the *ḥalqa* altered the social and political character of the army » [37].

Ar far as the unit under discussion is concerned, there was no « reform »; there was no « new *ḥalqa* », and the suggestion that Baybars « created » a *ḥalqa* of his own from the Syrian troops who found refuge in Egypt, not only lacks any foundation whatsoever, but runs counter to whatever we know about this unit.

The *ṭulb* (pl. *aṭlāb)* was a formation of the highest importance, which existed from the very beginning of Ayyūbid and up to the very end of Mamlūk rule (unlike the *ḥalqa* which petered out round about the middle of the Mamlūk period). Incidentally, since the days of Quatremère no trace of that formation was found before the Ayyūbids. Quite recently I came across it in the reign of 'Imād al-Dīn Zaukī, in the year 528/1134 (his siege of Āmid) [38]. H. calls it « the basic combat formation »; « the basic structural unit of the Ayyubid military system, and « its most important parade and field unit » [39]. I agree, on the whole, to these definitions, but they fit quite well the Mamluk *ṭulb*. True, the term is flexible as far as the size of the formation is concerned, but this is typical of both reigns. We do not know whether al-Qāḍī al-Fāḍil's statement about the size of the *ṭulb* at the beginning of Saladin's rule (70 to 200 horsemen) holds good even up to the end of that rule. The *ṭulb* could also designate a formation of a non-Muslim enemy, but even this applies to both Ayyūbids and Mamlūks (from Saladin's time onwards). There is no doubt that during the long period of its existence, the *ṭulb* had undergone changes, but these can in no way be tied to the change of regimes in Egypt and Syria, certainly not to the reign of Baybars. H. says that he found the mention of the *ṭulb* under the Ayyūbids only once after Saladin's death (in 616/1219) [40]. I can furnish a good number of additional instances

---

36. *Ibid.*, II, p. 163.
37. *Ibid.*, p. 105.
38. Ibn al-Furāt, ms. Vienne, A.F. 118, vol. II, fol. 54b-55a. It can only be hoped that sources earlier than Ibn al-Furāt will corroborate this evidence of his.
39. Emergence, etc., I, 79, *From Saladin to the Mongols*, p. 23.
40. Emergence, etc., I, p. 80, and note 2.

for that period, which proves the unbroken continuity of that formation from Ayyūbids to Mamlūks. In searching for characteristics of the Mamlūk *ṭulb,* which distinguish it from its Ayyūbid predecessor, H. brings the evidence of Ibn Faḍl Allāh al-'Umarī, from which, he believes, it can be deduced that the Mamlūk *ṭulb* might also refer to the major field unit of the Mamlūk army, the division of one thousand under the command of a senior amir[41]. At this stage I shall confine myself to this particular evidence, without expressing any view about whether the *ṭulb* had been an *ad hoc* formation or a unit of a more permanent character. Quite unfortunately, and in contrast to his usual approach, H. looks at this evidence through the eyes of another scholar (Al-'Umarī speaks there about *Mongol,* not *Mamlūk ṭulbs (tarattaba al-Mughul aḥad 'ashar ṭulban kull ṭulb yazīd 'alā alf fāris)*[42].

In addition to the *iyya* Mamlūk bodies we have thus two most formidable mainstays of Ayyūbid army and military society, which continue without break and without any discernible drastic change very deeply into the Mamlūk reign. True, there is much ambiguity left about those two institutions, a considerable part of which might never be removed, but this is another matter.

Whereas the *ḥalqa* and the ṭulb constitute a very good choice for the study of Ayyūbid-Mamlūk connections, *'askar*[43], in my view, is not so. It is too general and loose and I personally do not see what can be done with it.

A sentence epitomizing H.'s idea of the respective composition of the Ayyūbid and Mamlūk armies is this. « Whereas the Ayyubid princes used Mamlūk recruits chiefly as a supplement to the free-born troops who were the bulk of their armies, the Mamlūks made slave recruitment the very foundation of the army and state »[44]. This runs counter to my main thesis in this paper, as well as in recent articles, about the Mamlūk preponderance. Again he cites me as his sole source, but this time with full justification, for this is in keeping with what I wrote many years ago. Such an erroneous appreciation of the Mamlūk institution is bound to lead to other mistakes. For the sake or clarification it will, perhaps, be worthwhile to point out that the Mamlūks were a minority in any army, including the army, or armies, of the Mamlūk Sultanate. This did not undermine their position as the focal power in those armies.

H. found few court offices assigned to amirs under the Ayyūbids, which continued into the Mamlūk period[45]. The number of such offices is considerably bigger. But what is at least as necessary to do is to collect the data on

---

41. *Ibid.,* p. 82, and note 2.
42. QUATREMÈRE, *Histoire des Sultans Mamluks,* Paris, 1837, vol. I, part I, p. 34, note 41.
43. Emergence, etc, I, p. 77-79.
44. *Ibid.,* p. 68.
45. *Ibid.,* p. 83.

offices assigned to military men lower than amirs which survived under the Mamlūks from the Ayyūbid period. Their number is quite high. Moreover, any office connected with the army and military society, even if occupied by a civilian, should be included in such a collection.

H. says that the division of the amirs into three rigid ranks (*amīr 'ashara; amīr arba'īn or tablkhana; amīr mi'a)* is a phenomenon of the Mamluk period[46]. To this I quite agree. Yet even here we should be cautious. He says, for example, that « the very word *ṭablkhāna* never appears in Ayyūbid texts »[47]. It does. For example: the well known incident in 640/1242 connected with the *ṭablkhāna* of Mu'īn ad-Dīn Ibn Shaykh al-Shuyūkh[48]. It is also mentioned quite often in Ayyūbid Yemen. And there is this astounding piece of evidence, which seems to come completely out of the blue. Year 615/1218 — Sultan al-Kāmil rewarded Shamā'īl for his feats in the siege of Damietta by making him *amīr ṭablkhāna* with forty horsemen *(ammara Shama'ila ṭablkhāna bi-arba'īn ṭawāshiyan)*[49]. The possibility of anachronisms will always bedevil us, but I have no doubt that quite a few surprises in the contrary direction lie still in store to the students of the subject.

It is true that under Baybars one can already discern the rudiments of the three basic ranks of amirs. Yet side by side with them, and on a far larger scale, continues the old loose system of appointments to the ranks of amirs, including the term *ṭawāshī*, which, in this context, is equivalent to *fāris,* and has nothing to do with « eunuch ». This loose system lasts until well after Baybars' reign, and crysralyzes gradually. It is difficult to point even at the approximate date of its crystalization. I dealt in considerable detail with the development of the ranks in the early Mamlūk reign, including the period of transition to that reign, and showed, inter alia, how the term *ṭablkhāna* was still not exclusively confined to the rank of amir of forty. I also discussed the very important term *ṭawāshī* = *fāris*[50]. H. does not refer to the term *ṭawāshī* at all, and seems to have overlooked my discussion of the early military ranks.

In dealing with the Mamlūk vis-à-vis the Ayyūbid regime, what we call the non-hereditary character of the Mamlūk Sultanate should be viewed in its right perspective.

A considerable number of states had already been established in Islam by Mamlūks *before* the creation of the Mamlūk Sultanate. It was dynasties

---

46. *Ibid.*, II, 167-173.

47. *Ibid.*, p. 168.

48. *Mufarrij al-Kurūb*, vol. V (Cairo, 1977), p. 303, ll. 13-15; *Sulūk*, I, p. 312, ll. 6-13.

49. Ibn al-Dawādārī, VII, p. 201, l. 1.

50. *BSOAS*, XV (1953), p. 464-7, 471-3 (for *tablkhāna* and the amir's rank see especially p. 472, note 2).

springing from those Mamlūks who ruled those states. It might well be that the dynastic character of the Caliphate encouraged that phenomenon. Whatever the reason, we witness dynasties of Mamlūks basing their power on a nucleus of a mainly non-hereditary military aristocracy. Among those dynasties there were very strong and respectable ones, not less respectable than those descending from free-born rulers. One of them was the very respectable dynasty of the Zangids, the patrons of the founders of the Ayyūbid dynasty.

Now there is no indication whatsoever that the Mamlūks, when they came to power, ever dreamt, individually or collectively, of creating a non-hereditary Sultan's office. This, as far as it materialized, came about, at least in the Baḥrī-Qipohaqī period, without any planning. During most of that period the Mamlūk Sultanate was ruled by the Qalāūnid dynasty, which lasted longer than the Ayyūbid, any if only its uninterrupted rule is considered, almost as long. Only Ibn Taghrībirdī, in the third quarter of the fifteenth century, questions the wisdom of the reigning Sultan in appointing his son as his successor, knowing full well that he would be quickly overthrown.

Few rulers in Islam made such a concentrated effort like Baybars I in order to make his son, Abū Sa'id Berke Khān, his successor. Two of the reasons of his failure were his untimely death, which affected the whole course of the Mamlūk Sultanate, and the worthlessness of that son. Baybars had nothing to do, at least intentionally, with weakening the hereditary character of the Mamlūk Sultan's Office.

The hindsight *we* possess about that office was not available to the contemporary Mamlūks until very late. The character of the office in question in the transition period should be studied in that light.

I shall now allude to a subject in a brevity which is in inverse proportion to its importance. The Mamlūk soldiery continued to wear practically the same dress as their Ayyūbid predecessors, and this went beyond the strict dress. The Mamlūks also adopted the Ayyūbid banner, which, from the time of Saladin, had been yellow. There was, however, one important difference. Sultan-Qalāūn, when he formed the Burjiyya regiment, discarded that dress, substituting it for a new one, presumably in order to rid himself of the impact of Sultan Najm al-Dīn Ayyūb, his Baḥriyya and Baybars. He preserved, however, the yellow flag.

There is little need to stress the importance of the Mamlūk army preserving the outward appearance of the Ayyūbid army for so long, and having the Ayyūbid flag flutter over it for much longer. This is also a very strong indication (apart from other ones) that the Mamlūks were in no great hurry in making meaningful changes in the Ayyūbid military structure. After all, changing the dress and the flag is both very easy and most conspicuous if a departure from the older pattern is intended.

Another kind of continuity, and a meaningful one, between the two regimes, was the absence of any weighty body of black soldiery. Under the Fāṭimids and before them the blacks constituted a very important element in the army, inspite of their inferior social status. After Saladin had crushed their great rebellion, that element stopped to be of any consequence thenceforward.

An inheritance of unique importance which the Ayyūbids left to the Mamlūks was the Cairo citadel *(qalʿat al-jabal),* which served as the seat of power and government for many centuries to come. The impact of the citadel on the political and military life of the ruling class was immeasurable.

IV

BAḤRĪ MAMLŪKS, BURJĪ MAMLŪKS—INADEQUATE NAMES FOR THE TWO REIGNS OF THE MAMLŪK SULTANATE

I

THE TERMINOLOGY

The Mamlūk sultanate was one of the most important Muslim empires and by far the most important and the most stable one in the later Middle Ages. Its history, structure, and institutions are, however, insufficiently known, and its systematic scholarly study is still at its early stage. Yet it is "a matter of common knowledge" (or more precisely, of common acceptance) that the names of the two well-known consecutive reigns of that sultanate were "Baḥrī" (648–784/1250–1382) and "Burjī" (784–922/1382–1517), respectively, after the names of the two famous Mamlūk "regiments," the first created by the Ayyūbid Sultan al-Malik al-Ṣāliḥ Najm al-Dīn Ayyūb (637–647/1240–1249) and the second by the Mamlūk Sultan al-Malik al-Manṣūr Qalāūn (678–689/1279–1290). The foremost scholars who studied the sultanate in question used that terminology constantly and without hesitation, and students who had just started learning Islamic history became acquainted with it already in the introductory literature to that history. The combination of these two names might vary: [Baḥrī, Burjī] "period," "reign," "dynasty," "line," "Mamlūks," etc.; but the two elements of "Baḥrī" and "Burjī" would remain constant.

These names are very inadequate and misleading (although admittedly not to the same degree—see below). I have stressed that fact on various occasions. I did it for the first time in 1949, when I stated that "its [the Mamlūk Sultanate's] earlier period is erroneously styled 'the period of the Baḥrī Mamlūks,'" and that "the Circassian period is erroneously styled by Orientalists 'the period of the Burjī Mamlūks.'"[1] I repeated this statement in the

[1] "The Circassians in the Mamlūk Kingdom," *JAOS* (1949): 137, nn. 19, 20.

articles "Baḥriyya" and "Burdjiyya" in the *Encyclopaedia of Islam*,[2] and, I believe, in other studies as well.[3] However, all this was to no avail. Nobody seems to have referred to these statements, either in acceptance or in contradiction. It is quite indicative of the prevalence and predominance of Baḥriyya and Burjiyya in the sense under discussion, that I myself used them (especially the first of the two) more than once. In the article in which I pointed out for the first time the error of that terminology I used the term "Baḥriyya period" (or a similar one) *nine* times, once on the very page where I took exception to it![4]

In the present section of this study I would like to prove the erroneous usage of these two terms in the above senses and suggest the terms which should replace them. This necessitates, first of all, a brief review of the relevant Islamicist literature, and then a more detailed review of the Mamlūk sources.

The Islamicist Literature

I shall confine myself here, first and foremost, to the introductory literature, namely, the one which initiates the beginner into Islamic history, emphasizing once more that on the particular matter under discussion there is full agreement between it and the more specialized studies:

P. K. Hitti: "Baḥrī and Burjī Mamlūks";[5] C. Brockelmann: "Baḥrī Mamlūks," "Burjī Mamlūks";[6] Gaston Wiet: "De toute évidence aussi la première dynastie est très dissemblable de la seconde, non pas parce que les uns sont Turcs ou Baḥrides, les

---

[2] *EI*², 1:944b–945a, 1325a.

[3] I stress it once more in "The Auxiliary Forces of the Mamlūk Sultanate," *Der Islam* 65 (1988): 13–14. See also my reservation concerning that terminology in "The Great Yāsa of Chingiz Khān—A Reexamination," *Studia Islamica* 36 (1972): 130, 145.

[4] "The Circassians," pp. 137b, 140b, 142b (four times on the same page), 144a, 145b, 146a.

[5] *History of the Arabs* (London, 1943), pp. 672–674. On p. 672, n. 6, Hitti states that what he calls "the Baḥrī dynasty" is designated as the "Turkish dynasty" by Ibn Khaldūn and al-Suyūṭī. This is his translation of *dawlat al-turk*. There is no reason whatsoever to single out those two authors in connection with that term. For the double meaning of *dawlat al-turk* in the Mamlūk sources see below.

[6] *History of the Islamic People* (London, 1949), pp. 234, 236.

autres Circassiens ou Bordjites";[7] and then: "pendant la dynastie Bahride";[8] "sous la dynastie Bahride";[9] "les mamlouks Bahrides."[10] His list of the sultans of the first Mamlūk reign has the title "Les Mamlouks Bahrides."[11] But, quite significantly, that of the second Mamlūk reign is entitled "Les Mamlouks circassiens."[12]

Noteworthy is Stanley Lane-Poole's name of the Mamlūk reigns. In his *History of Egypt* he divides the early Mamlūk reign into two reigns and calls them "The First Mamlūks, 1250–1279" and "The House of Ḳalaʾun, 1279–1382." The later reign he calls "The Circassian Mamlūks, 1382–1517."[13] But when he gives the lists of the sultans of the two reigns he calls them "The Baḥrī Dynasty" (twice on the same page), and "The Burgī Dynasty" or "Burgī Mamlūks" (on the same page).[14]

The same author, in his book *The Mohammedan Dynasties*, calls the two reigns "Baḥrī Mamlūks" and "Burjī Mamlūks."[15] E. de Zambaur calls them "Mamluks Bahrites" and "Mamluks Burjites," respectively.[16] C. E. Bosworth calls them "Baḥrī line" and "Burjī line."[17]

M. Sobernheim's terminology in the first edition of the *Encyclopaedia of Islam* deserves special note. In the article "Mamlūks," published in 1936, he speaks about "the two dynasties" . . . "the Baḥrī and the Burdjī Mamlūks."[18] Twenty five years earlier (1911), in his brief note on the Baḥriyya, he speaks about "the Burdjī Mamlūk Barḳūḳ"![19] In another brief note on the Burjiyya ["Burdjī Mamlūk corps"] the same author says in the same year: "From the time of Sultan Barḳūḳ the sultan was chosen from their ranks

---

[7] *Précis de l'histoire d'Egypte* (Cairo, 1932), 2:237.

[8] Ibid., p. 245.

[9] Ibid., p. 257.

[10] Ibid., p. 258.

[11] Ibid., pp. 329–330.

[12] Ibid., pp. 330–331.

[13] *A History of Egypt in the Middle Ages*, 5th ed. (London, 1936), pp. 242, 276, 323.

[14] Ibid., pp. 254, 324.

[15] (1893; reprint Paris 1925), pp. 81, 83.

[16] *Manuel de généalogie et de chronologie pour l'histoire de l'Islam* (Bad Pyrmont, 1927), pp. 103–105.

[17] *The Islamic Dynasties* (rev. ed., Edinburgh, 1980), pp. 63, 64.

[18] *EI*², 3:216b.

[19] Ibid., 1:586b.

[i.e., the ranks of the Burjiyya]. Baibars II was the first Burdjī Mamlūk to occupy the throne of Egypt. Their last ruler Ṭūmān Bey was executed in 1517."[20] These statements leave no doubt that according to Sobernheim the sultans of the later Mamlūk period (at least those of them who were Mamlūks) were actual members of the Burjiyya "regiment."[21] This is so absolutely wrong that I cannot refrain from giving here a summary of one of the arguments which I bring later on in this study. The truth is that Barqūq arrived in Egypt well after the last member of that "regiment" had already died, in all probability at a very advanced age. And if this is the case with Barqūq, it is much more so with his successors. Baybars II (al-Jashnakīr) (708–709/1308–1309) belongs, of course, to a very different category.

The prevalence in the Islamicist literature of Baḥrī and Burjī as designations of the two consecutive Mamlūk reigns is, of course, most important. Also very important, although not to the same degree, is the question of who was the first Islamicist who introduced that terminology. A much more systematic examination of this question should be made. Here I shall only say that I did not find that terminology in Quatremère's translation of al-Maqrīzī's chronicle of *al-Sulūk*,[22] although I cannot say that my checking was very thorough.

The earliest scholar whom I found using the terminology under discussion, or part of it, is Gustav Weil. The title page of the first volume of his classical history of the Mamlūk sultanate reads *Das Chalifat unter den Bahritischen Mamlukensultanen von Egypten.*[23] However, he does not connect the later Mamlūk reign with the Burjiyya. The second volume of that history reads *Das Chalifat unter den Cirkassischen Mamlukensultanen von Egypten.*[24] This is meaningful, in my view; the same goes for Lane-Poole's and Wiet's histories, mentioned earlier in this study (see also below).

Now the obvious question which poses itself is whether there is any support in the Mamlūk sources for the terminology in question. The answer is in the affirmative but only for the first of the

---

[20] Ibid., 1:796b.

[21] For the reason why I put "regiment" in quotation marks when referring to the Baḥriyya and Burjiyya, see below.

[22] *Histoire des sultans Mamlouks* (Paris, 1837–44).

[23] *Geschichte des Abbasidenchalifats in Egypten* (Stuttgart, 1860), vol. 1.

[24] Ibid. (Stuttgart, 1862), vol. 2.

two reigns. However, that support is very flimsy, and on the basis of the overwhelming evidence in those sources a different terminology should replace it.

In the following section Mamlūk source evidence will be presented and analyzed, and we shall start with the seemingly supporting evidence.

Mamlūk Source Evidence

As far as I could check, the source which seems to have been the cause of that erroneous designation for the two Mamlūk reigns is al-Maqrīzī's opus *al-Khiṭaṭ*; and, to the best of my knowledge, this is the only source.

In the section dealing with the rulers of Egypt since the building of the Cairo citadel (*Dhikr mulūk Miṣr mundhu buniyat Qalᶜat al-Jabal*),[25] the description of the first Mamlūk reign opens with the title "The Account of the Reign of the Baḥriyya Mamlūks (*Dhikr dawlat al-mamālīk al-Baḥriyya*),"[26] and the account itself opens with the words "And these are the Turkish kings [= sultans] (*wa-hum al-mulūk al-atrāk*)."[27] Later on, in the note about the last sultan of this reign, al-Malik al-Ṣāliḥ Ḥājjī, it is stated that "with him ended the reign of the Baḥriyya Turkish Mamlūks and their descendants (*wa-bihi inqaḍat dawlat al-mamālīk al-baḥriyya al-atrāk wa-awlādihim*)."[28]

My comments on the above quoted evidence from al-Maqrīzī are as follows:

a) In the section which contains that evidence, al-Maqrīzī's identification of the reign with the "regiment" is confined to the first of the two. The second has the title "The Account of the Reign of the Circassian Mamlūks (*Dhikr dawlat al-mamālīk al-jarākisa*)."[29] I never met in any Mamlūk source *al-burjiyya*, *al-mamālīk al-burjiyya*, etc., as meaning the second Mamlūk reign. *Al-dawla al-burjiyya*, or *dawlat al-mamālīk al-burjiyya*, does not exist in those sources in that sense.[30]

---

25 *al-Mawāᶜiẓ wal-iᶜtibār fī dhikr al-khiṭaṭ wal-āthār* (Cairo, 1853–54): 2:232ff.

26 Ibid., 2:236, l. 23.

27 Ibid., l. 24.

28 Ibid., p. 240, l. 38.

29 Ibid., p. 241, l. 6.

30 For its existence in a very different and much narrower sense see below.

b) The term Baḥriyya Mamlūks as designating the first Mamlūk reign is unique to those two instances from the same passage of *al-Khiṭaṭ*. Even in the selfsame source of *al-Khiṭaṭ* the usual terminology is the one which is current in the rest of the Mamlūk sources, including al-Maqrīzī's own chronicle (*Kitāb al-sulūk*).

We shall now start with examples from al-Maqrīzī's two works and continue with instances from other Mamlūk sources.

Very instructive are al-Maqrīzī's references to the transition from the Ayyūbid to the "Baḥrī" and from the "Baḥrī" to the "Burjī" reigns, both in his *al-Khiṭaṭ* and in his *al-Sulūk*, in passages other than the one just quoted.

In the chapter of his *al-Khiṭaṭ* dealing with the Egyptian army chancellery since the pre-Islamic period up to his own time (*Dhikr dīwān al-ᶜasākir wal-juyūsh*),[31] he says describing that transition:

> Then they [the Ayyūbids] were split and at variance with one another until their reign was ended by the coup of their Turkish Mamlūks (*bi-qiyām ᶜabīdihim al-mamālīk al-atrāk*). These latter followed the example of their Ayyūbid masters and confined themselves to [the recruitment] of Turks and some Kurds. They recruited great numbers from amongst the Mamlūks imported from the lands of the Turks . . . until the reign of Banū Qalāūn was ended . . . by al-Malik al-Ẓāhir Barqūq, who started wiping out the Ashrafiyya [Shaᶜbān] Mamlūks[32] and created for himself a reign [composed] of Circassian Mamlūks (*ilā an zālat dawlat Banī Qalāūn bil-Malik al-Ẓāhir Barqūq fa-akhadha fī maḥwi al-mamālīk al-ashrafiyya wa-anshaᵓa li-nafsihi dawlatan min al-mamālīk al-jarākisa*).[33]

In the chapter describing the construction of the Cairo Citadel (*Qalᶜat al-Jabal*) he says:

> Until the Ayyūbid reign became extinct, and the Turkish Mamlūks established their reign in Egypt (*fa-qāma bi-mamlakat Miṣr al-mamālīk al-atrāk*). The first of them was al-Malik al-Muᶜizz Aybak. When he died, his son ᶜAlī did not succeed [in

[31] *al-Khiṭaṭ*, 1:91–95.

[32] The Mamlūks of sultan al-Malik al-Ashraf Shaᶜbān (764–778/1363–1376).

[33] *al-Khiṭaṭ*, 1:95, ll. 2–8.

holding onto the throne], and therefore Quṭuz became sultan. The person who established Circassian reign was al-Ẓāhir Barqūq (*wa-awwal man qāma bil-dawla al-jarkasiyya al-Ẓāhir Barqūq*).[34]

Speaking of the rules of inheritance of the Fāṭimids as compared with those of their successors, the Ayyūbids and the Mamlūks, he says: "When their [the Fāṭimids'] days ended and the Ayyūbids became rulers and then [followed] the Turkish reign . . . (*fa-lammā inqaḍat ayyāmuhum wa-istawlat al-ayyūbiyya thumma al-dawla at turkiyya*)."[35]

As is well known, and as al-Maqrīzī clearly states, he wrote that chronicle as a continuation of his works dealing with the earlier periods of Muslim Egypt, and particularly that of the Fāṭimids. In his foreword of *al-Sulūk* he states:

> I wanted to follow this up by relating [the history] of those who ruled Egypt after them [i.e., after the Fāṭimids], that is to say, the Kurdish Ayyūbid kings and the Mamlūk Turkish and Circassian sultans (*aḥbabtu an aṣil dhālika bi-dhikr man malaka Miṣr baᶜdahum min al-mulūk al-akrād al-ayyūbiyya wal-salāṭīn al-mamālīk al-turkiyya wal-jarkasiyya*).[36]

Al-Maqrīzī's account of the Ayyūbid reign ends with the words, "And with the killing of al-Muᶜaẓẓam [Tūrānshāh] the reign of the Ayyūbids came to an end in the land of Egypt (*inqaraḍat dawlat Banī Ayyūb min arḍ Miṣr*)."[37] And a few lines later on the same page, "Shajar al-Durr is the first of the Turkish Mamlūk kings who ruled Egypt (*Shajar al-durr hiya awwal man malaka Miṣr min mulūk al-turk al-mamālīk*)."[38]

In describing the ouster of the Qalāūnid dynasty and the coming of Barqūq to power, our author says, after speaking about the dismissal and internment of Sultan al-Malik al-Ṣāliḥ Ḥājjī: "The reign of the Turks was finished in Egypt and the reign of the Qalāunids came to an end (*fa-inqaḍat dawlat al-atrāk min Miṣr*

---

34 Ibid., 2:204, ll. 16–18.

35 Ibid., 1:111, l. 19.

36 *Kitāb al-sulūk fī maᶜrifat al-duwal wal-mulūk* (Cairo, 1934), 1:9, ll. 4–5.

37 Ibid., 1:361, ll. 8–9.

38 Ibid., l. 14.

wa-zālat dawlat Banī Qalāūn)."[39] And on the next page the inception of the new reign is presented thus: "Sultan . . . Barqūq . . . the Circassian . . . the founder of the reign of the Circassians (*al-sulṭān al-Malik al-Ẓāhir Sayf al-Dīn Abū Saᶜīd Barqūq ibn Anaṣ al-Jarkasī al-ᶜUthmānī al-Yalbughāwī al-qāᵓim bi-dawlat al-jarākisa*)."[40]

In the obituary of Barqūq he is said to have been "the first of the Circassian Kings (*awwal mulūk al-jarkas*),"[41] and his son Sultan Faraj is called "the second of the Circassian kings in Egypt (*thānī mulūk al-jarākisa fī Miṣr*)."[42]

In both *al-Khiṭaṭ* and *al-Sulūk* (and much more frequently in the first of these two) the term *dawlat al-turk* (more rarely *al-atrāk*) or *al-dawla al-turkiyya* is employed either in the sense of the Mamlūk reign (or sultanate) as a whole, or as meaning only the first Mamlūk reign.

The following are instances of the employment of the term in its narrower sense.

Sultan ᶜImād al-Dīn Ismāᶜīl (743–746/1342–1345), the son of Sultan al-Nāsir Muḥammad, decided to revive the office of the viceroy (*nāᵓib al-salṭana*), which had been abolished by his father, "as was the custom [in relation to that office] during the time of al-dawla al-turkiyya (*ka-mā kānat al-ᶜāda fī dhālika fī muddat al-dawla al-turkiyya*)."[43]

That only the narrower sense of the term is meant here is proved both by the language of the text and by the fact that that office died out long before the end of the "Baḥrī" period, in spite of the rather furtive attempts to revive it.

Speaking of the office of the chief of police (*niqābat al-jaysh* or *al-juyush*)[44] our author says: "that office was in *al-dawla al-turkiyya* one of the high offices[45] . . . today that office has de-

[39] Ibid., 3:475, ll. 3–5.

[40] Ibid., p. 476, ll. 1–3.

[41] Ibid., p. 915.

[42] Ibid., p. 959, l. 3.

[43] *al-Khiṭaṭ*, 1:425, l. 18.

[44] The holder of that office was called *naqīb al-jaysh* (see my "Studies on the Structure of the Mamluk Army, Part III," *BSOAS* 16 [1954]: 64–65).

[45] See also A. N. Poliak, *Feudalism in Egypt, Syria, etc.* (London, 1939), index.

clined (*hādhihi al-rutba kānat fī al-dawla al-turkiyya min al-rutab al-jalīla . . . thumma inḥaṭṭat al-yawm hādhihi al-rutba*)."[46]

In both these instances only the narrower meaning of *dawlat al-turk* makes sense, because the wider meaning would imply that in the time of al-Maqrīzī that sultanate did not exist any longer.

The following is another interesting example. After the Mamlūk victory in Cyprus in 828/1425, al-Maqrīzī describes the great procession in Cairo and the immense amount of booty which was displayed in it, and comments: "This was a memorable day, the like of which was unknown in the Turkish and the Circassian reign (*fa-kāna yawman mashhūdan lam yuᶜhad mithlahu fī al-dawla al-turkiyya wal-jarkasiyya*)."[47]

In this particular case it is clear that *al-dawla al-turkiyya* applies only to the first Mamlūk reign. For a very clear case of al-Maqrīzī's calling the first Mamlūk reign *dawlat al-atrāk* and the second *dawlat al-jarākisa*, see the passage above.

There is a considerable number of other cases in *al-Khiṭaṭ* where *al-dawla al-turkiyya* is mentioned, and where one part might mean the early reign and the other part the whole reign, with varying degrees of probability.[48] There are, however, other cases in the same source where there is no doubt that the whole Mamlūk reign is meant, up to the time of al-Maqrīzī: *Wa-fī hādhihi al-dawla al-turkiyya . . .*[49] *Mā ᶜalayhi al-ḥāl al-yawm fī ajnād al-dawla al-turkiyya . . .*[50] [*Al-khuddām*] *alladhīna yuᶜrafūna al-yawm fī al-dawla al-turkiyya bil-ṭawāshiya.*[51]

What is made so evident from the passages quoted from al-Maqrīzī's two works is that it was the Turkish Mamlūks who took over the rule from the Kurdish Ayyūbids and that later it was the Circassian Mamlūks who replaced the Turkish Mamlūks.

---

[46] *al-Khiṭaṭ*, 2:223, ll. 1 and 5.

[47] *al-Sulūk*, 4:696.

[48] See, e.g., *al-Khiṭaṭ*, pp. 95, l. 9; 440, l. 35; 2:22, ll. 9–11; 61, l. 6; 98, ll. 32–39; 102, ll. 35–36; 103, ll. 23–38; 109, l. 5; 134, l. 32; 136, ll. 32–33; 211, l. 31; 216, l. 39; 217, l. 1; 220, l. 8; 221, l. 35; 223, ll. 17, 18; 226, ll. 6–7; 227, l. 11; 245, l. 5; 295, ll. 26–27; 296, l. 20; 314, ll. 18–19, 20; 443, l. 10. See also *al-Sulūk*, 3:772, ll. 1–3.

[49] Ibid., 1:469, l. 29.

[50] Ibid., 1:85, l. 36.

[51] Ibid., 2:380, l. 11. See also al-Maqrīzī's description of the army of *al-dawla al-turkiyya* (ibid., p. 215, ll. 31, 34, and the whole passage pp. 215–219).

Al-dawla al-turkiyya, even in its narrower sense, is never considered by him as synonymous with the Baḥriyya (with the sole exception quoted above), in spite of his very frequent use of that term. Within the first Mamlūk reign the Qalāunid dynasty (*dawlat Banī Qalāūn*) is mentioned sometimes separately by him, with full justification.

Data from other Mamlūk sources fully corroborate the conclusions drawn above from al-Maqrīzī's works. Here are some examples arranged in chronological order:

Ibn al-ᶜAmīd (602–672/1205–1274)

The chapter entitled: "The beginning of *dawlat al-turk* and their seizure of power in the country of Egypt (*ibtidāᵓ* [spelled ابتدى] *dawlat al-turk wa-istīlāᵓihim* [*sic!*] *ᶜalā al-diyār al-miṣriyya*)."[52] And then "al-Manṣūr Nūr al-Dīn ᶜAlī, the second of *mulūk al-turk* in the land of Egypt";[53] and "Quṭuz, the third of *mulūk al-turk*."[54]

Al-Yūnīnī (640–726/1242–1326)

In his obituary of Sayf al-Dīn Balabān al-Zaynī al-Ṣāliḥī al-Najmī (died 677/1278), the author states that at the beginning of *dawlat al-turk* in the land of Egypt, he was the commander of the *Baḥriyya* (*kāna fī awwal dawlat al-turk bil-diyār al-miṣriyya muqaddam al-Baḥriyya*). Then he was imprisoned for a [considerable] number of years, and after being released, he was given an amir's rank in Damascus, where he lived until his death.[55]

This piece of evidence deserves immediate comment. It shows that the name of the reign and the name of the "regiment" are completely distinct.[56]

Al-Nuwayrī (677–733/1278–1333)

This author says about Ibn Salᶜūs, the vizier of sultan al-Ashraf Khalīl, in the account of the year 690/1291, that the

---

[52] *La "Chronique des Ayyoubides" d'Al-Makīn b. al-ᶜAmīd* (Damas, 1955–57), p. 53.

[53] Ibid., p. 58.

[54] Ibid., p. 62.

[55] Al-Yūnīnī, *Dhayl mirᵓāt al-zamān* (Hyderabad, 1955), 3:301.

[56] My student and colleague Reuven Amitai called my attention to this important passage. It is noteworthy that al-Yūnīnī, in his obituary of sultan Aybak (died 655/1257), says nothing about his being the founder of a new reign, or that

sultan made him more powerful than any other vizier who preceded him in *dawlat al-Turk.*[57]

Ibn al-Dawādārī (died after 736/1335)

This author entitles the eighth volume of his chronicle (*Kanz al-durar*), with which he starts the history of the Mamlūk sultanate, *al-Durra al-zakiyya fī akhbār al-dawla al-turkiyya,*[58] and repeats the same title in the preface to that volume.[59] In the first line of that preface he calls it *Dawlat al-atrāk,*[60] and somewhat later in the same preface *Dawlat al-turk.*[61] He opens the actual narrative of the history of that sultanate with the heading "The Account of the Beginning of *al-dawla al-turkiyya* (*Dhikr ibtidāʾ al-dawla al-turkiyya*)."[62] On the same page he states: "The Account of the Sultanate of al-Muᶜizz Aybak, the First of the Turk Kings (*awwal mulūk al-turk*)."[63] In his preface to the ninth volume of the same chronicle,[64] dedicated to the reign of al-Nāṣir Muḥammad b. Qalāūn, Ibn al-Dawādārī dwells on the great merits of that sultan, whom he calls *sayyid mulūk al-atrāk.*[65]

Al-Mufaḍḍal b. Abī al-Faḍāʾil (died after 749/1348)

This continuator of Ibn al-ᶜAmīd opens his chronicle with the reign of al-Ẓāhir Baybars, whom he calls the fourth of the *mulūk al-turk* in the land of Egypt.[66] His son al-Malik al-Saᶜīd Nāṣir al-Dīn Berke Khān is called the fifth of *mulūk al-turk;*[67] his other son, al-Malik al-ᶜĀdil Salāmish, the sixth of *mulūk al-turk.*[68] Sultan Qalāūn is called the seventh of *mulūk al-turk;*[69] and

---

he had been the first of *mulūk al-turk*. This kind of evidence is discussed later in this study.

[57] Al-Nuwayrī, *Nihāyat al-arab fī funūn al-adab*, MS Leiden, Ar 2n, fol. 486.

[58] *Kanz al-durar* (Cairo, 1971).

[59] Ibid., p. 11, ll. 5–6.

[60] Ibid., p. 2, l. 3.

[61] Ibid., p. 7, l. 7.

[62] Ibid., p. 12, l. 1.

[63] Ibid., l. 15.

[64] *Kanz al-durar* (Cairo, 1960).

[65] Ibid., p. 6, l. 1.

[66] *al-Nahj al-sadīd*, in *Patrologia Orientalis*, 2:408, ll. 4–5.

[67] Ibid., 14:452.

[68] Ibid., p. 471, l. 1.

[69] Ibid., p. 475, l. 7.

Qalāūn's son Khalīl—the eighth of *mulūk al-turk.*[70] Sultan Qalāūn died a certain number of years and days after the beginning of *al-dawla al-turkiyya.*[71]

Ibn Ḥābīb (710–779/1310–1377)

This author entitles his chronicle *Durrat al-aslāk fī dawlat al-atrāk.*[72] He begins it thus: "This is a book which comprises [the history of] *dawlat al-atrāk* and their descendants."[73] In his account of the year 648/1250, the first year of his chronicle and of the Mamlūk reign, he says: "And in this year Sulṭan al-Malik al-Muᶜizz Aybak al-Ṣāliḥī became the ruler of the country of Egypt, and he is the first of the *atrāk* who ruled it (*wa-huwa awwal man malakahā min al-atrāk*)."[74]

Ibn al-Furāt (735–807/1335–1405)

The chronicle of this historian contains much information on the terms under discussion in his account of the first years of the Mamlūk sultanate. He entitles the events of 648/1250 "The Account of the Beginning of *dawlat al-turk* in the Land of Egypt . . . The Account of the Accession to the throne (*salṭana*) of ᶜIzz al-Dīn Aybak al-Turkumānī in Egypt and his Riding with the Royal Banners (*al-ṣanājiq al-sulṭāniyya*)."[75] The events of 650/1252 he entitles "The Account of ᶜIzz al-Dīn Aybak Becoming the Sole Ruler in Egypt . . . , and the Complete Expiry of *al-dawla al-ayyūbiyya.*"[76] Then: "[Aybak] was the first ruler (*awwal mutamallik*) of the Turkish people [or faction] (*min al-ṭāʾifa*[77] *al-turkiyya*)."[78] And: "*al-dawla al-ayyūbiyya* was completely eradicated from Egypt, and *al-dawla al-turkiyya* started as its sole master."[79] Under the events of 655/1257, summing up the life of Aybak after his assassination, he is stated to have been the first of

---

[70] Ibid., p. 533, l. 8.

[71] Ibid., p. 533, l. 6.

[72] B.N., MS Arabe, Nº 4680.

[73] Ibid., fol. 11b.

[74] Ibid., fol. 12a.

[75] *Taʾrīkh al-khulafāʾ wal-mulūk*, MS Vat., Ar. 726, 7:130b.

[76] Ibid., fol. 153a.

[77] The term *ṭāʾifa* is discussed later on in this article.

[78] Ibid., fol. 153c.

[79] Ibid., fol. 155a.

the *mulūk al-turk* in the land of Egypt.[80] His son and successor al-Malik al-Manṣūr Nūr al-Dīn ᶜAlī is said to have been the second of the *mulūk al-turk* in the land of Egypt, twice on the same page.[81]

The evidence of Ibn al-Furāt is important because he copied, on the whole very accurately, from numerous earlier sources.

Ibn Khaldūn (732–808/1332–1406)

Ibn Khaldūn's title for that part of his chronicle which deals with the history of the Mamlūk sultanate is "The Account of *al-dawla al-turkiyya* which Sustains *al-dawlah al-ᶜAbbāsiyya*[82] in Egypt and Syria from after Banū Ayyūb and up to this Time (*min baᶜd Banī Ayyūb ilā hādhā al-waqt*)."[83] A few pages later he says: "The *turk* became the sole rulers in Egypt (*wa-istaqallat al-dawla bi-Miṣr lil-turk*) and the *dawla* of *Banū Ayyūb* became extinct."[84] Then about the incorporation of Syria in the Mamlūk sultanate, "the possession of Syria by the *turk* (*ḥuṣūl al-Shām fī mulk al-turk*)."[85] He ends his account of the history of the Mamlūk sultanate with the description of Sultan Barqūq's arrival in Damascus in 796/1394 in preparation against an impending attack by Tīmūr (which did not materialize), and states: "That is the last event which took place in the history of *dawlat al-turk* (*wa-hādhā ākhir mā intahat ilayhi dawlat al-turk*), and no one knows what will happen tomorrow."[86]

It is important to see in this context what Ibn Khaldūn has to say about the accession to the throne of Sultan Barqūq, in whose reign Ibn Khaldūn arrived in the Mamlūk sultanate and remained until the end of his life, that is to say, seven years after that sultan's death. He does stress his Circassian origin (*aṣl hādhā al-amīr Barqūq min qabīlat Jarkas*),[87] and quotes in some detail the

---

80 Ibid., fol. 184a.

81 Ibid., fol. 186a.

82 Ibn Khaldūn refers here, of course, to the transfer of the ᶜAbbāsid caliphate to Egypt after its extinction by the Mongols in Baghdad.

83 *Kitāb al-ᶜibar* (Cairo, 1867): 5:369, ll. 1–2.

84 Ibid., p. 374, l. 1.

85 Ibid., p. 379. See also, in the same source, "the chamberlain (*ḥājib*) in *dawlat al-turk*" (ibid., p. 484).

86 Ibid., p. 508.

87 Ibid., p. 472, l. 4.

tradition about the Circassians' descent from the Arab tribe of Ghassān,[88] but he says nothing about the racial transformation of Mamlūk society, and the establishment of a new Mamlūk reign as a result of that transformation. One reason might be that he did not live long enough after that transformation, and therefore could not grasp its full meaning. This is true of some others of his contemporaries.

Another matter which is very instructive in our context is how Ibn Khaldūn connects Barqūq with the Ayyūbid Sultan al-Malik al-Ṣāliḥ Najm al-Dīn Ayyūb, by demonstrating his Mamlūk "descent" from him. He draws the following direct perpendicular "lineage" between the two: al-Ẓāhir Barqūq, the Mamlūk (*mawlā*) of al-Ashraf the son of Shaᶜbān, the son of [al-Nāṣir] Ḥasan, the son of al-Nāṣir Muḥammad, the son of [al-Manṣūr] Qalāūn, the Mamlūk (*mawlā*) of Najm al-Dīn Ayyūb. All the other sultans, be they Mamlūks or not, are mentioned on the two sides of that direct perpendicular line.[89] There are two mistakes in this lineage: Barqūq's patron was not al-Ashraf, the son of Shaᶜbān, but al-Ashraf Shaᶜbān; al-Ashraf Shaᶜbān was not the son but the grandson of al-Nāṣir Ḥasan. His father was Ḥusayn, who was not a sultan.

This lineage is very important in the context of Najm al-Dīn Ayyūb's place in Mamlūk society, which will be discussed in a different study (see also below).

Ibn Duqmāq (750–809/1349–1407)

In his *Nuzhat al-ānām*, under the events of 650/1252, Ibn Duqmāq says that in that year the reign of the *turk* began (*wa-fīhā kāna mubtadaᵓ mulk al-turk wa-mabdaᵓ aḥwālihim*).[90]

Ibn Qāḍī Shuhba (779–851/1377–1447)

In speaking of Barqūq's accession to the throne Ibn Qāḍī Shuhba says that he was the twenty-fifth of the *mulūk al-turk*

[88] Ibid., ll. 5–17. See also my "The Circassians," p. 137.

[89] Ibid., p. 509. Ibn Khaldūn uses very frequently the term *mawlā* in the sense of Mamlūk, also in his account of the history of the Mamlūk sultanate. See *Kitāb al-ᶜibar*, 5:373, 377 (five times), 381 (twice), 382, 393, 394 (twice), 395, 396, 398, 406, 408, 409, 411 (twice), 422, 442 (twice), 446 (three times), 447 (twice), 451 (four times), 452, 455, 459, 460, 461, 476, 482, 506. I have already pointed out that usage of the term *mawlā* by Ibn Khaldūn in *L'esclavage du Mamelouk* (Jerusalem, 1951), p. 57, note 188, where a much smaller number of instances is cited.

[90] *Nuzhat al-ānām*, B.N., MS Arabe N° 1597, fol. 91c, l. 9.

who ruled Egypt; the twenty-third of them who ruled Syria as well; and the eighth of those of them who were themselves slaves (*mimman massahu al-riqq*).[91] But he says nothing about his being the founder of the Circassian reign.

Ibn Taghrībirdī (813–874/1410–1470)

Aybak is "the first of the *turk* kings in the land of Egypt (*awwal mulūk al-turk bil-diyār al-miṣriyya*)."[92] The second was Nūr al-Dīn ᶜAlī,[93] the third was Quṭuz,[94] and so on.

Sultan Barqūq was "the twenty-fifth of the *turk* kings in Egypt . . . and the first of the *jarākisa* kings (*wa-huwa al-sulṭān al-khāmis wal-ᶜishrūn min mulūk al-turk . . . wal-awwal min mulūk al-jarākisa*)."[95] Sultan Faraj, Barqūq's son, was "the twenty-sixth of the kings of the *turk* and the second of the *jarākisa* (*al-sādis wal-ᶜishrūn min mulūk al-turk wal-thānī min al-jarākisa*),"[96] and so on.

Ibn Bahādur al-Muᵓminī (836–877/1432–1472)

Sultan Aybak is the first of the *turk* kings (*huwa awwal mulūk al-turk*).[97]

Al-Sakhāwī (831–902/1427–1497)

Sultan Barqūq was "the first of the *jarākisa* kings (*awwal mulūk al-jarākisa*)."[98]

Al-Suyūṭī (849–911/1445–1505)

Sultan al-ᶜĀdil Badr al-Dīn Salāmish "is the sixth of *dawlat al-atrāk*, since the first of them is Sultan Aybak (*huwa al-sādis min dawlat al-atrāk fa-inna awwalahum al-Muᶜizz Aybak*)."[99]

---

[91] Ibn Qāḍī Shuhba, B.N., MS Arabe N° 1598, fol. 276a.

[92] *al-Nujūm al-zāhira* (Cairo, 1934–42), 7:37, ll. 5–8.

[93] Ibid., p. 41, ll. 5–6.

[94] Ibid., p. 72, ll. 2–3.

[95] Ibid., ed. Popper (Leiden, 1909–), 5:362, ll. 2–7. Here Ibn Taghrībirdī has a problem in deciding whether Barqūq was the first or the second of the Circassian kings, in view of the fact that Sultan Baybars II (al-Jashnakīr) was a Circassian.

[96] Ibid., 6:1, ll. 6–7.

[97] *Futūḥ al-naṣr fī taᵓrīkh Miṣr*, Aya Sofia, MS N° 3344.

[98] *al-Ḍawᵓ al-lāmiᶜ* (Cairo, 1353–55 A.H.), 3:12, ll. 23–24.

[99] *Ḥusn al-Muḥāḍara* (Cairo, 1968), 2:106. See also *Tāᵓrīkh al-khulafāᵓ* (Beirut, n.d.), p. 537.

Barqūq "is the first of the *jarākisa* sultans (*huwa awwal al-salāṭīn min al-jarākisa*)."[100]

Ibn Iyās (852–930/1448–1524)

Ibn Iyas entitles two chapters of his chronicle, "The Beginning of the Mamlūk Reign (*ibtidāᵓ dawlat al-atrāk*),"[101] and "The Beginning of the Circassian Reign (*Dhikr ibtidāᵓ dawlat al-jarākisa*)."[102]

"Barqūq, the Circassian . . . the first of the Circassian kings in Egypt and the twenty-fifth of the *turk* kings and their descendants in Egypt (*Barqūq . . . al-jarkasī wa-huwa awwal mulūk al-jarākisa bil-diyār al-miṣriyya wal-khāmis wal-ᶜishrūn min mulūk al-turk wa-awlādihim bil-diyār al-miṣriyya*)."[103] Sultan al-Muᵓayyad Shaykh is the twenty-eighth in the line of *mulūk al-turk* and the fourth in the line of *mulūk al-jarākisa*,"[104] and so on.

It should be pointed out at this time that some authors, especially those who lived in the first reign, either forgot completely to mention the fact that there had been a change of rule from the Ayyūbids to the Mamlūks, or alluded to that fact in a rather vague way.

Al-Dhahabī (673–748/1274–1348)

In his short survey of the Islamic states al-Dhahabī does speak about the wiping out of the [Fāṭimid] ᶜUbaydite *daᶜwa*,[105] but does not say that the Fāṭimid dynasty had been replaced by the Ayyūbid dynasty.[106] Neither does he mention the replacement of the Ayyūbids by the Mamlūks,[107] in spite of the fact that he tells the history of these two reigns!

Abū al-Fidāᵓ (672–732/1273–1331)

This author, himself an Ayyūbid ruler, glosses quite elegantly over the replacement of the Ayyūbids by the Mamlūks in his

---

[100] Ibid., 2:120.

[101] *Badaᵓiᶜ al-zuhūr* (Cairo, 1311–12 A.H.), 1:90.

[102] Ibid., 1:252.

[103] Ibid., 1:258–259, and again on p. 258.

[104] Ibid., ed. M. Mostafa (Wiesbaden, 1972), p. 3, ll. 4–5.

[105] *Duwal al-Islām* (Hyderabad, 1365 A.H.), 2:58.

[106] Ibid., 2:56, 60.

[107] Ibid., 2:115–121.

account of the years 648–650/1250–1252.[108] When he speaks about the accession of Shajar al-Durr and later of Aybak,[109] he does not state that the reign of the Ayyūbids came to and end and that a new reign began in Egypt.[110]

Al-Ṣafadī (696–764/1276–1363)

In the whole long biography of Sultan Aybak there is no reference to the fact that he was the first Mamlūk ruler, neither is the Mamlūk reign mentioned in it under any name.[111] In the biography of the Ayyūbid Sultan al-Ṣāliḥ Ayyūb, on the other hand, it is stated that his slave-wife Shajar al-Durr became ruler for two months or more, that her name was mentioned in the Friday sermon, and that after him his Turkish Mamlūks became the rulers "up to this day" (*wa-baqiya al-mulk baᶜdahu fī mawālīhi*[112] *al-atrāk*).[113]

Al-Ṣuqāᶜī (died 726/1326)

In his biographical dictionary the Baḥriyya are mentioned only in the sense of "regiment." There is no mention of the Burjiyya. The term *turk* is a designation of the Mamlūks but, as far as I could check, there is no name in this source for the Mamlūk reign.[114]

Ibn al-Wardī (691–749/1292–1349)

This author does not mention the change of rule from Ayyūbid to Mamlūk in connection with the accession to the throne of either Aybak,[115] Quṭuz,[116] Baybars,[117] or Qalāūn.[118]

---

[108] *Kitāb al-Mukhtaṣar fī taʾrīkh al-bashar* (Cairo, 1325 A.H.), 3:181–190.

[109] Ibid., pp. 182, 183.

[110] The term *mulūk al-turk* as designating the Mamlūk sultans does appear in his chronicle (ibid., 4:19), but not in connection with the Mamlūks' ousting of the Ayyūbids.

[111] *al-Wāfī bil-wafayāt* (Wiesbaden, 1974), 9:469–474.

[112] Note the use of *mawālī* here in the sense of Mamlūks, already mentioned before in connection with Ibn Khaldūn.

[113] Ibid., 10:56–57.

[114] *Tālī kitāb wafayāt al-aᶜyān* (Damascus, 1974).

[115] *Tatimmat al-mukhtaṣar fī taʾrīkh al-bashar* (Beirut, 1970), 2:268.

[116] Ibid., p. 290.

[117] Ibid., p. 301.

[118] Ibid., pp. 335–336.

Ibn ᶜAbd al-Ẓāhir (620–692/1223–1292)

Of great interest is the account of this historian, who is a major authority on the history of the early decades of Mamlūk rule. In his preface to Sultan Baybars's biography he speaks about the events which took place since the death of al-Malik al-Ṣāliḥ Najm al-Dīn Ayyūb, through the succession and murder of his son Tūrānshāh, the sultanates of Shajar al-Durr, Aybak, Quṭuz, and up to and including Baybars's coming to power. Yet in all this account he never mentions the change of rule. Neither does he give a name to the new reign.[119] I think that the reason for this way of presenting Baybars's beginnings was Ibn ᶜAbd al-Ẓāhir's desire to glorify his hero at the expense of the Mamlūk sultans who preceded him, and his wish to stress Baybars's direct ties with al-Ṣāliḥ Ayyūb, the venerated founder of the Baḥriyya, in whose footsteps he wanted to follow.

Also significant is the same author's way of presenting the decline of the standards of the official correspondence at the beginning of the Mamlūk period, until their return to the old level in the reign of al-Ashraf Khalīl (in his biography of that sultan). This is what he says about the start of that decline: "And when the reign of Al-Ṣāliḥ Ayyūb ended, and Aybak . . . took up [the reins of government] he let matters grow lax (*fa-lammā inqaḍat al-dawla al-Ṣāliḥiyya wa-bāshara al-malik al-Muᶜizz Aybak al-Turkumānī sahhala al-umūr*)."[120] Here there is again no reference to the change of regime.

Sibṭ Ibn al-Jawzī (581–654/1185–1256) and Abū Shāma (599–665/1202–1267)

These two historians constitute a special category. Both died at the very beginning of the Mamlūk reign, and lived in Syria, which was finally incorporated in the new sultanate shortly after the death of the first and a few years before the death of the

[119] *Baybars I of Egypt*, ed. S. F. Sadeque, (Dacca, 1956), pp. 1–20 of the Arabic text.

[120] *al-Alṭāf al-khafiyya min al-sīra al-sharīfa al-sulṭāniyya al-malikiyya al-ashrafiyya*, ed. Moberg, (Lund, 1902), p. 36. The extant part of Ibn Shaddād's (613–684/1217–1285) biography of Sultan Baybars I (*Taᵓrīkh al-malik al-Ẓāhir* (Wiesbaden, 1983) covers only the last years of his reign. We therefore cannot know if and what that author says about the transition from the Ayyūbid to the Mamlūk reign.

second. They were clearly pro-Ayyūbid, and it is quite uncertain whether they realized that the Mamlūks came to stay. Therefore they could not be expected to give a name to the new reign. Sibṭ[121] has nothing good to say about the Mamlūks and their feats during the period which he covers. Aybak is called only al-Malik, but not al-Malik al-Muᶜizz, and certainly not *al-sulṭān.*[122] Abū Shāma is somewhat more generous but still very grudging. In connection with the liquidation of sultan Tūrānshāh he says that the Baḥriyya Mamlūks of his father became the rulers, "and they made ᶜIzz al-Dīn Aybak al-Turkmānī their chief, and he is called now (*al-mulaqqab al-āna*) al-Malik al-Muᶜizz."[123]

This reserved attitude of Abū Shāma to the new rulers did not prevent him, however, from lauding in his famous verses the selfsame Turkish Mamlūks of Egypt, who, as he says, by their self-sacrifice and bravery defeated the invincible Mongols.[124]

Ibn Faḍl Allāh al-ᶜUmarī (700–749/1301–1349)

Quite extraordinary is this author's way of designating the Mamlūk sultanate in his most important and unique contemporary description of it (he wrote that description, according to his own testimony, in 738/1338). He calls it "the realm of Egypt, Syria, and the Ḥejaz. These realms are one realm (*mamlakat Miṣr wal-Shām wal-Ḥijāz hādhā* [sic!] *al-mamālik hiya mamlaka wāḥida*)."[125] Throughout that description it is never called *al-dawla al-turkiyya* or the like, or given any other name. It is repeatedly called "this realm (*hādhihi al-mamlaka*)."[126] Since (as he makes it clear in the title of his description) he uses *mamlaka* also for each of the main countries of the sultanate, he calls Syria

---

[121] *Mirᵓāt al-zamān* (Chicago, 1907), pp. 518–529.

[122] Ibid., p. 527, ll. 5, 10.

[123] *Tarājim rijāl al-qarnayn al-sādis wal-sābiᶜ* (Cairo, 1947), p. 185. See also pp. 188, 196, and the way Abū Shāma mentions Sultan Quṭuz on the eve of the battle of ᶜAyn Jālūt (ibid., p. 207).

[124] See my "The European-Asiatic Steppe: A Major Reservoir of Power for the Islamic World," *Proceedings of the 25th Congress of Orientalists* (Moscow, 1963), 2:49.

[125] *Masālik al-abṣār*, B.N., MS Arabe N° 2325, fol. 139a.

[126] See, e.g., ibid., fols. 166b, 181b, 185a, 188a, 202a.

separately by the same name: *Dhikr al-mamlaka al-thāniya wa-hiya mamlakat Dimashq.*[127]

CONCLUSIONS

Although the foregoing list of citations is far from complete and could be greatly augmented without difficulty, I think it constitutes quite a representative sample of the terminology relating to the two successive Mamlūk reigns, as used by the sources. Whatever revisions a wider reading of the sources may bring in the foregoing picture, one thing seems to me to be certain: Baḥrī and Burjī are not at all the terms which those sources employ to designate these two reigns. Baḥrī as meaning the first of the two is, to the best of my knowledge, never used by any Mamlūk writer who lived all or most of his life in that reign. Al-Maqrīzī, the only one to use it, spent all his adult life in the second reign. Burjī, as designating the second reign, is not found in any Mamlūk source that I know of.[128] And in this context it would be worthwhile to point out that the users of these two terms for the two reigns did not seem to be aware of the fact that these names are practically nonexistent in the Mamlūk sources. Therefore, the users did not deem it necessary to explain why they prefer them to the ones which are current in those sources.

As far as the sources themselves are concerned, the terms current in them, which the reader encounters with great frequency (examples, in addition to those cited above, can be multiplied with great ease) are: *dawlat al-turk*, *dawlat al-atrāk*,[129] *al-dawla al-turkiyya*, *mulūk al-turk*, *mulūk al-atrāk*, and the like, as well as *dawlat al-jarkas* (or *al-jarākisa*), *mulūk al-jarkas*, etc. *Dawlat al-turk*, etc., might mean either the entire Mamlūk reign or only the first reign; and *mulūk al-turk*, etc., may refer either to the Mamlūk sultans in general, or only to the sultans of the first reign. *Turk* and *atrāk* (sing. *turkī*) might mean Mamlūks of any

---

[127] Ibid., fol. 203c. For the date of the compilation of this description of the sultanate see ibid., fol. 184a.

[128] If—for argument's sake—one instance or two in the sources is unearthed with Baḥrī or Burjī mentioned in the sense adopted by the Islamicists, a matter which I very much doubt, it can hardly affect the general conclusion.

[129] For *Dawlat al-atrāk* as the name given to the Mamlūk sultanate see B. Lewis, *The Cambridge History of Islam* (Cambridge, Eng., 1976), p. 214.

ethnic group, or only Turkish Mamlūks. As far as the term *jarkas* is concerned, there is obviously no ambiguity involved in it.

As a matter of principle, I think that the terminology of the contemporary sources should be adopted, unless there are weighty considerations against it. Under no circumstances should it be replaced by a terminology which has little foundation and may be misleading.

In our particular case the sources lay special stress on the ethnic element: first on the transformation from Kurdish Ayyūbids to the Turkish Mamlūks, and then from the Turkish Mamlūks to the Circassian Mamlūks. And this seems to me to be the logical stress.[130] The decisive contribution of the Baḥriyya Mamlūks to the creation of the new sultanate did not induce these sources to call it after them. The justification for calling the second reign Burjī is infinitely smaller (see above, and also part II). This fact is reflected even in the terminology adopted by some of the Islamicists, which had already been presented and discussed.

The confusing element in the sources' terminology (and this applies not only to the Mamlūk period) is that the terms *turk*, *atrāk*, *turkī* have a double meaning: Turk and Mamlūk. So the designations which, in my view, Islamicists should prefer, and which will be the nearest to that of the sources would be: the reign of the Turkish Mamlūks and that of the Circassian Mamlūks (or in an abbreviated form, the reign of the Turks and that of the Circassians). For the first reign Turkish-Qipchaqi may also be considered.

On the other hand, a literal translation of *dawlat al-turk*, or one of its variants, should not be adopted, if only because of the double meaning of the term *turk*. "The Mamlūk sultanate" seems to me to be the most appropriate name. "The Mamlūk kingdom," which I used on several occasions, should be discarded.[131]

Another important reason for avoiding the adoption of the literal translation of that name is that in European languages the word "Turk" would cause in that context additional confusion to

---

[130] Those sources which do not employ the current Mamlūk terminology in the obvious places belong to a different category. In any case, they do not offer alternative terms, and at least some of them do use that terminology in less obvious places.

[131] It was Professor Paul Wittek who suggested to me "the Mamlūk sultanate" many years ago.

that caused by the double meaning of the word. The confusion will be particularly great when dealing with the Ottomans and their relations with the Mamlūks.[132]

In light of what has been said up to now, the Baḥriyya and Burjiyya should be studied only within the narrow limits of their existence as Mamlūk bodies, and treated as such. This raises the very difficult question of how to classify them, and what is the most suitable name which should be given to them in their capacity as socio-military Mamlūk bodies. The same question applies to all the other Mamlūk groups which are based on identical, or almost identical, principles, for all of them have no real parallel in any civilization outside Islam. It is misleading therefore to call any of them "regiment" or "corps," as I and others did on so many past occasions (that is why I put "regiment" in quotation marks in this study). Somewhat better is the term "household" used by P. M. Holt, but even this term is unsatisfactory because it does not reflect the Mamlūk relation between patron and slave, and between comrades in slavery and manumission. There is also great difficulty and ambiguity with the usual term which the Mamlūk sources use, *ṭāʾifa* (pl. *ṭawāʾif*), because it has so many meanings, a good part of which is outside the military society. The nearest translation I could find is "faction," but this word represents only one facet of that kind of Mamlūk body. In short, I cannot offer a satisfactory translation for that term, and for lack of a better choice I shall use in the following pages *ṭāʾifa* and "faction" alternately.

II

Now that we can look at the Baḥriyya and the Burjiyya within their more realistic dimensions, a comparison between the two seems to me to be quite necessary. Since such a comparison should be made within the framework of the structure of Mamlūk

---

[132] To give here just one example, in the account of the conquest of Egypt by Sultan Selim I the Ottomans are called *ʿuthmāniyya*, *rūm*, *turkmān*, or *tarākima*, whereas the Mamlūks are called *jarākisa* or *atrāk* (see my short article "The Mamlūk Army at the Beginning of the Ottoman Conquest" [in Hebrew], *Tarbiẓ* 23 (1962): 221, n. 2, and the completely revised version of it in the *Festschrift* in honor of Prof. Bernard Lewis, *The Islamic World* (Princeton, 1989), pp. 413–431. For a wider treatment of the use of the term *turk* by the Mamlūk sources in connection with the Ottomans and Anatolia, see Appendix B.

society, some of the basic principles on which that society was built should be mentioned briefly in advance.

This was a one-generation nobility of fair-skinned people, who had been brought to the *dār al-Islām* from beyond its borders as youthful slaves. They were taken especially from pagan populations of high warlike qualities and on a quite primitive cultural level. Besides being brought up in devotion to Islam, each one of them was bound by extremely strong ties of loyalty to both his patron and his comrades in servitude and (usually, though not always) in manumission.

That society, in its various and varying forms, constituted the backbone of Islam's strength during the greater part of its existence, and throughout that very long period it bore the brunt of Islam's expansion and defense, especially against the steady technological and military rise of Christian Western Europe.

It is against this background, which in my view, is axiomatic, that the comparison has to be made.

Before starting with the comparison, however, a brief remark should be made about Mamlūk ties of loyalty. These were a source of both great power and great weakness, and the internal relations of Mamlūk society developed to a very great extent around them. As a matter of fact, they affected almost every important aspect of Mamlūk rule.

As far as Mamlūk ties are concerned, the Baḥriyya, the Mamlūks of al-Malik al-Ṣāliḥ Najm al-Dīn Ayyūb (637–647/1240–1249), and the Burjiyya, the Mamlūks of al-Malik al-Manṣūr Sayf al-Dīn Qalāūn (678–689/1279–1290), were bound by exactly the same ties as the other Mamlūk factions (*ṭawāʾif*, sing. *ṭāʾifa*) which existed throughout the history of that sultanate.[133] One major element of these ties was that each member of the *ṭaʾifa* had to be the freedman of its patron. This meant that no other person, be he a freeman or a freedman of another patron, could join that particular *ṭāʾifa*. He certainly could not be equal to the patron's own freedmen in case he was transferred to his service, because he was an outsider, a foreigner (*gharīb*, *ajnabī*). Since loyalty to both patron and colleagues in servitude and manumission did not stop with the death of the patron (*ustādh*) and lasted till the very end of the life of each single colleague (*khushdāsh*),

[133] See above, and my "Studies on the Structure of the Mamlūk Army," *BSOAS* 15 (1953): 217–220.

the *ṭāʾifa*, with the absence of new recruits, had to peter out and finally disappear with the passing away of its last member. That is exactly what happened with the Baḥriyya and the Burjiyya (see also below).

Another feature common to all the *ṭawāʾif* was that those of them which constituted the dominant element in Mamlūk aristocracy would perforce decline and be pushed aside. The death or the final removal of the patron constituted a watershed in the history of each *ṭāʾifa*. It might have an immediate (usually bad, much less frequently beneficial) effect on it, depending on the circumstances. Within a somewhat longer period, however, the *ṭāʾifa* was bound to lose its power, and not only because of the inevitable diminution of its numerical strength and the aging of its members. Amongst other things it had to struggle against other *ṭawāʾif*, whose patrons were still living and influential. These competing *ṭawāʾif* and patrons were not necessarily unrelated to that *ṭāʾifa*. They might well have grown from within in several forms. And that is what mainly happened in the case of both the Baḥriyya and the Burjiyya.

In some matters, however, the Baḥriyya and Burjiyya were similar, fully or partly, to each other and different from the ordinary *ṭāʾifa*. Both of them were called after the places in which they were originally housed, the Baḥriyya after the barracks of the citadel on the island of al-Rawḍa in the Nile (Baḥr al-Nīl), and the Burjiyya after the barracks in the towers (*abrāj*, sing. *burj*) of the Cairo citadel. The usual naming of a *ṭāʾifa* was made after the epithet of the patron, Ẓāhiriyya [Baybars], Nāṣiriyya [Faraj], etc., and much more rarely after the personal name of the patron, Khushqadamiyya, for example. This does not imply at all that our two "regiments" were not called in the sources Ṣāliḥiyya [Ayyūb] or Manṣūriyya [Qalāūn] as well. Both the Baḥriyya and the Burjiyya formed only part of the Mamlūks of their respective patrons. The ordinary *ṭāʾifa* included all the patron's Mamlūks.

Neither the Baḥriyya nor the Burjiyya are mentioned during the lifetime of their patrons. The Baḥriyya appear for the first time in the battle of al-Manṣūra, after the death of al-Ṣāliḥ Ayyūb, and then in his obituary. The Burjiyya appear only in the obituary of Qalāūn.

There are, at the same time, both similarities and great differences between the two. The sources do mention the number of both the Baḥriyya (between 800 and 1000) and the Burjiyya (3,700), but while they say nothing about the total of all of al-Ṣāliḥ Ayyub's Mamlūks, they give the number of Qalāūn's Mamlūks (between 7,000 and 12,000). Thus we can form an approximate idea only about the relative numerical strength of the Burjiyya within the al-Manṣūriyya Qalāūn, but not of that of the Baḥriyya within al-Ṣāliḥiyya Ayyūb.

(The evidence about the creation of the Burjiyya causes difficulties and raises questions which do not exist in connection with the Baḥriyya. This subject will be discussed later in the present study.)

In spite of the fact that the number of the Burjiyya was about four times larger than that of the Baḥriyya, the importance, centrality, and military feats of the latter was incomparably larger.[134]

At present I shall confine myself to a single instance, which might look marginal but which, in my view, puts in bold relief the uniqueness of the Baḥriyya within Mamlūk society on the one hand, and the attitude of that society towards non-Mamlūks on the other.

[134] There is such an overwhelming mass of evidence about the feats of the Turkish Mamlūks in general and of the Baḥriyya in particular during the transition period from Ayyūbid to Mamlūk rule and in the early decades of the Mamlūk Sultanate that I decided to deal with that subject separately (in *From Ayyūbids to Mamlūks*, in preparation). Here I shall confine myself to saying that the greatness of the Baḥriyya's patron (*ustādh*), Sultan al-Ṣāliḥ Najm al-Dīn Ayyūb, was an essential element in their success. A by-product of the study of that personality is the following one. The mother of that sultan was a black slave-girl (*jāriya sawdāʾ*) (Abū al-Fidāʾ *al-Mukhtaṣar fī taʾrīkh al-bashar* [Cairo, 1325 A.H.], 3:180, ll. 4–5; Ibn Faḍl Allāh al-ʿUmarī, B.N. MS Arabe N° 2328, fol. 91b, chronicle of the years 541–744 A.H.). There is no indication that this fact acted as an obstacle in his personal career, nor did it diminish his unique prestige among his fair-skinned Mamlūks. While male blacks were hermetically excluded from Mamlūk society, blackness of the Mamlūks' patron on his mother's side was something very different. In this connection I would like to note that the dark complexion of the scion of the ʿAbbāsids who survived the Mongol carnage and fled to Egypt to establish there the Egyptian ʿAbbasid dynasty, is not proof of his being an impostor—it rather proves the contrary. If the Mamlūks did not shrink from having a pseudo-caliph under their suzerainty, they could have easily found a less swarthy person. That caliph was said to have been *shakhṣ aswad al-lawn*, and was called *al-khalīfa al-aswad* (Abū al-Fidāʾ, 3:212–213).

One of the most indicative expressions of the outstanding position and status of the Baḥriyya, not only in comparison with the Burjiyya but also in comparison with any other Mamlūk *ṭāʾifa*, is the following. Sultan Qalāūn, a prominent member of the Baḥriyya Mamlūks, collected the sons of these Mamlūks and formed them into a unit which bore exactly the same name as that of their fathers. The sources furnish quite rich data about that unit, which lasted for a relatively long period of time, as I have shown long ago.[135]

Out of the data which I have quite haphazardly gathered since then about those later Baḥriyya,[136] the most revealing evidence is that included in the chronicle of Ibn al-Dawādārī (died after 736/1335). Here is a translation of it:

The year 689/1290 (obituary of Sultan Qalāūn):

> He gathered the children of the Baḥriyya from various places,[137] even from Bāb al-Lūq, from the storehouse (*ḥānūt*) of al-Sharāyijī, and from the dunghill [used] for heating the public bath (*mustawqad al-ḥammām*),[138] and bestowed upon them [military] service-coats (*qumāsh*),[139] military belts (*ḥawāʾis*, sing. *ḥiyāṣa*),[140] and swords (*suyūf*), and gave them

---

[135] In my article "Le Régiment Baḥriya," the section entitled "Les Baḥrīya postérieurs," pp. 138–141.

[136] See, e.g., *al-Sulūk*, 3:676, ll. 6–9; 679, ll. 1–6; 807, ll. 5–7; al-Qalqashandī, *Ṣubḥ al-aʿshā*, (Cairo, 1913), 3:182; Jawharī, *Nuzhat al-nufūs* (Cairo, 1970), p. 271. To the list of Syro-Palestinian fortresses which were manned by late-Baḥriyya garrisons, according to the specific evidence of the sources ("Le Régiment Baḥriya," p. 140) that of Sidon should be added (*Ṣubḥ*, 4:202). In the summary of al-Jazarī's chronicle, under the year 698/1298, Sauvaget says, "et même les mamlouks royaux (*baḥriya*) de la citadelle [de Damas]" (*La Chronique de Damas d'al-Jazarī* [Paris, 1949], p. 75, paragraph 482). This is a mistake, because the later Baḥriyya who belonged to the *ḥalqa* are meant here, not the original Baḥriyya, who were royal Mamluks. See also the following discussion in the text.

[137] In the source, *min sāʾir al-amākin*, literally: "from the rest of the places," which might mean "from all the places."

[138] Dozy explains *mustawqad* thus: "amas de fumier (mazbala) qui, en Egypte, sert de combustible dans les étuves," and cites references for *mustawqad ḥammām* from *Thousand and One Nights*. *Supplement aux dictionnaires arabes* (Leiden, 1927), 2:828b.

[139] L. A. Mayer, *Mamluk Costume* (Genève, 1952), pp. 75–80, especially p. 77.

[140] Ibid., pp. 25–27.

> monthly salaries (*jawāmik*, sing. *jāmakiyya*).[141] He also bestowed upon them fiefs (*akhbāz*) in the victorious *ḥalqa* (*al-ḥalqa al-manṣūra*),[142] stationed them (*ajlasahum*) by the citadel's gate [of Cairo], and called them al-Baḥriyya, after the name of their fathers (*bi-asmāʾ abāʾihim*). All this was done in spite of the opposition (*bi-ghayr riḍā*) of the amir Ḥusām al-Dīn Ṭurunṭāy, who hated the sons of the Mamlūks (*fa-innahu kāna yakrah awlād al-nās*).[143]

Now throughout the history of the Mamlūk sultanate there is no parallel case of creating a special unit to which the sons of members of any Mamlūk *ṭāʾifa* were recruited, let alone giving it the name of the *ṭāʾifa* of their fathers. This is an incontestable proof of the uniqueness of the Baḥriyya, its greatness, and its particular esprit de corps. Without all this there would have been little need to perpetuate its name. At the same time the case of the later Baḥriyya clearly demonstrates the extremely poor chance of the descendants of the Mamlūks, even if they were the sons of the strongest and most prestigious *ṭāʾifa* of the Royal Mamlūks, of reaching (especially as a group) anything resembling, however remotely, the status and power of their parents. The pure Mamlūks could not tolerate the establishment of strong, or even weak, socio-military bodies from among their own offspring, for this would eliminate the principle of single generation nobility on which the whole system was based, and thus would bring an inevitable end to that system. In the very isolated case of the later Baḥriyya, a compromise was reached between the indebtedness of Qalāūn to the greatness of the *ṭāʾifa*, of which he was a member (mingled with a feeling of guilt because of his own share in accelerating its decline and removal from power) and the stubborn Mamlūk antagonism to its creation (Ṭurunṭāy was the strongest person in the realm in the closing years of that sultan's reign). The result was, at best, a second rate military unit. Its inclusion

---

[141] D. Ayalon, "The System of Payment in the Mamlūk Military Society," *JESHO* 1 (1958): 48–56.

[142] See my "Studies on the Structure," *BSOAS* 15 (1953): 448–459. It continued to be called *al-ḥalqa al-manṣūra* long after it had begun to decline.

[143] *al-Durra al-zakiyya fī akhbār al-dawla al-turkiyya* (Cairo, 1971), p. 303, ll. 7–11.

in the Ḥalqa determined its insignificance from the very outset. Even so, the attempt to create a similar unit with a name of its own was never repeated.

As I have already pointed out, sultans Ḥasan (748–752/1347–1351 and 755/762/1354–1361) and al-Muʾayyad Shaykh (815–824/1412–1421) tried to give preference to the *awlād al-nās* but quickly failed.[144]

In addition to the antagonism of the Mamlūks there was another important cause for the failure of *awlād al-nās* to become a military body of any real consequence. They lacked something similar to the "glue" which united the pure Mamlūks (*khushdāshiyya-ustādh* relations) and which helped them to struggle together, and on the whole quite consistently, in a common cause. In all the three cases just quoted (the late Baḥriyya, sultans Ḥasan and al-Muʾayyad Shaykh) it is always the ruler who is the active factor in their advancement, whereas their own initiative is little noticed. For another very important cause which put the *awlād al-nās* in an inferior position, see the following section.

Although the *awlād al-nās* component of the *ḥalqa* outlived in Egypt the general *ḥalqa*, and remained up to the very end of the Mamlūk sultanate,[145] it underwent a process of more or less steady decline. The lot of individual members of that body need not have been the same. All kinds of conditions might have been created, from which those individuals could benefit. A stalemate between two powerful Mamlūks or Mamlūk groups might help an *ibn nās* or a number of *awlād nās* to rise to a high position or office, *because* they did not have a military-political body to support them. This would not usually turn those individuals into a group of much consequence. In addition, we learn from the above-quoted passage that many of the sons of the original Baḥriyya were destitute, humble, and scattered, in spite of the great achievements of their fathers and the opulence of many of them; and that but for the personal and firm intervention of Qalāūn they would have disappeared and many of them would have sunk into complete oblivion.

The importance of this aspect of the cited passage is that it speaks about the lot of the offspring of a whole Mamlūk *ṭāʾifa*, a

---

[144] "Studies on the Structure," p. 457.

[145] Ibid., p. 457. See also my "The Mamlūk Army at the Beginning of the Ottoman Conquest," cited above, n. 132.

piece of evidence to which I know of no parallel. Even if I am mistaken, such evidence is extremely rare. The whole body of the sons of the Baḥriyya fared quite badly, and there is little reason to believe that the bodies of the sons of any of the other *ṭawāʾif* in Mamlūk history fared much better. Now when we try to reconstruct the history of the *awlād al-nās* in the Mamlūk sultanate, we cannot escape the question of how big was the proportion of the successful individuals of that class in comparison with those who remained anonymous. This is, in my view, a crucial question. Whatever the case may be, a separate study of the *awlād al-nās* is long overdue, and it should embrace a domain much wider than their socio-military role.[146]

Ibn Khaldūn and Awlād al-Nās

The antagonism of the Mamlūk body as a whole to the creation of socio-military units of real power and significance from amongst their own descendants and the lack of "glue" binding those descendants to one another—each one of these factors was sufficient in itself to prevent such a creation. There was, however, yet another and even more important factor. The sons of the Mamlūks, "who were born and grew up in very advanced civilized areas, in countries abounding with luxury and comfort . . . were usually inferior to those who were born in the steppe, endured its hardships, and were toughened by them."[147] After having written these sentences (in Hebrew) almost forty years ago I found a similar view expressed by Ibn Khaldūn in a passage of his *Muqaddima*, which I very regrettably mislaid, and which Professor Franz Rosenthal kindly helped me to rediscover quite recently. Although the number of admirers and panegyrists of the Mamlūk socio-military system among medieval Muslim writers was very great, none of them showed such a deep and comprehensive understanding of it and of its unequalled contribution to the preservation and increase of the might of Islam during many centuries as did Ibn Khaldūn. He did this in a quite long introduction to his account of the history of the Mamlūk sultanate, an

[146] I understand that Professor U. Haarmann is now finishing a detailed study of that important subject.

[147] See D. Ayalon, "Mamlūkiyyat: (A) A First Attempt to Evaluate the Mamlūk Military System," *JSAI* 2 (1980): 327–330, especially p. 329, passages *a* and *c*.

introduction which remained completely unnoticed.[148] The introduction and the passage should be read and studied together. Here is a translation of the passage in question followed by the transliterated Arabic original.

After stating that the ruler of a realm affected by senility sometimes chooses outsiders as helpers and partisans, who are used to toughness and whom he employs as an army which can better withstand the hardships of war, hunger, and privation, and thus succeeds in curing his realm of its senility, Ibn Khaldūn adds:

> And that is what happened to the Mamlūk sultanate in the East, for most of its army is [composed] of Turkish Mamlūks. Their rulers choose from amongst these Mamlūks, who are imported to them, horsemen and soldiers. These [Mamlūks] are more courageous in war and endure privations better than the sons of the Mamlūks who had preceded them and who were reared in easy circumstances and in the shadow of rulership (*wa-hādhā ka-mā waqaᶜa fī dawlat al-turk*[149] *bil-mashriq fa-inna ghālib jundihā al-mawālī*[150] *min al-turk fa-tatakhayyar mulūkuhum min ūlāʾika al-mamālīk al-majlūbīn ilayhim fursānan wa-jundan fa-yakunūna ajraʾ ᶜalā al-ḥarb wa-aṣbar ᶜalā al-shaẓaf min abnāʾ al-mamālīk alladhīnu kānū qablahum wa-rubbū fī māʾ al-naᶜīm wal-sulṭān wa-ẓillihi*).[151]

---

[148] D. Ayalon, "Mamlūkiyyāt:" (B) Ibn Khaldūn's View of the Mamlūk Phenomenon," *JSAI* 2 (1980): 340–349.

[149] For *dawlat al-turk* as the name of the Mamlūk sultanate (also according to Ibn Khaldūn's own terminology) see above, p. 15.

[150] For Ibn Khaldūn's constant employment of *mawālī* in the sense of *mamālīk*, at least in his account of the history of the Mamlūk sultanate, see the numerous references collected in note 89, above. Here he uses the two terms alternately as synonyms in the same sentence.

[151] *Kitāb al-ᶜibar* (Beirut, 1971), 1:142. On the same page Ibn Khaldūn gives another example of the prevention of senility in the realm by the recruitment of outsiders: the employment of Berber and Beduin tribesmen by the Muwaḥḥidūn. But this example belongs to a completely different category. See also F. Rosenthal's translation in *The Muqaddimah* (New York, 1958), 1:342. The introductory words to the translated passage from Ibn Khaldūn's *Muqaddima* in this article are a paraphrase of Rosenthal's translation. My translation of the passage itself differs in several points from that of Rosenthal, in order to adapt it to the circumstances in the Mamlūk sultanate as I see them. I translated the last words of the passage rather freely, because of their difficulty.

Ibn Khaldūn asserts here in most unequivocal words that the sons of the veteran Mamlūks could not have the basic warlike qualities possessed by Mamlūks newly arrived from their countries of origin. This is a very important addition to his general view of the Mamlūk phenomenon as expressed in his introductory note already cited.

After having discussed the passages from Ibn al-Dawādārī and Ibn Khaldūn, we shall now return to our comparison between the two *ṭāʾifa*s.

As I have already stated, both the Baḥriyya and the Burjiyya are mentioned only after the death of their patrons. The Burjiyya, however, unlike their predecessors, is mentioned only in very few biographies of Qalāūn and as far as I could check only by quite late Mamlūk writers. When I wrote the first version of the chapter on the Burjiyya (1945) in my work on the Mamlūk army, I was only partly aware of this state of affairs.[152]

The only Mamlūk historians that I know who speak about the formation of the Burjiyya by Qalāūn are al-Maqrīzī (766–845/1365–1441) and Ibn Taghrībirdī (813–874/1410–1470). They give also its numerical strength at that stage. Each of these two historians does it twice, the first in his chronicle[153] and in his topographical work,[154] and the second in his chronicle[155] and in his biographical dictionary.[156] The lateness of the evidence of these two authors is, however, not their only drawback. Al-Maqrīzī asserts in his *al-Khiṭaṭ* that it was al-Ashraf Khalīl, Qalāūn's son, who formed that body(!), whereas Ibn Taghrībirdī quotes Ibn Kathīr as his source about the creation of the Burjiyya by Qalāūn and about their numerical strength; but Ibn Kathīr says nothing of the kind! (see also below).

Here is a list of Mamlūk sources, most of them early ones, who pass in complete silence over Qalāūn's role as the creator of the

[152] The original chapter on the Burjiyya, written in Hebrew, is much shorter than the chapter on the Baḥriyya (published in full in 1951) for obvious reasons. It was never published, but a detailed summary of it appeared in EI^2, as already stated.

[153] *al-Sulūk*, 1:762, ll. 1–2.

[154] *al-Khiṭaṭ*, 2:214, ll. 22–26.

[155] *al-Nujūm* (C), 7:330, ll. 1–2.

[156] *Manhal*, B.N. MS 5:33a, ll. 1–2.

Burjiyya, either in the account of his reign or in his obituary notice:

Ibn ᶜAbd al-Ẓāhir (see below); al-Nuwayrī;[157] al-Dhahabī;[158] al-Yūnīnī;[159] al-Mufaḍḍal b. Abī al-Faḍāʾil;[160] Abū al-Fidāʾ;[161] al-Ṣafadī;[162] Ibn al-Dawādārī (see below); al-Kutubī[163] (see also below); al-Ṣuqāᶜī (see below); Ibn al-Wardī;[164] Ibn Ḥabīb;[165] Ibn al-Furāt[166] (see also below); Ibn Khaldūn;[167] al-Suyūṭī.[168]

Most significant is the case of Ibn ᶜAbd al-Ẓāhir, the contemporary of Sultan Qalāūn. He wrote the longest and most detailed biography of that sultan (covering the years 680–689/1281–1290 of his reign), yet there is not a single word about the Burjiyya in the whole book![169] Neither is there any reference to it in that part of the same author's biography of Qalāūn's son, al-Ashraf Khalīl, published by A. Moberg.[170]

Also noteworthy is the complete silence of Ibn al-Dawādārī about the Burjiyya throughout his long account of the reign of Qalāūn.[171] What is also most remarkable is that while that same author does speak in the same book with great sympathy and appreciation about Qalāūn's formation of the quite insignificant later Baḥriyya (see the passage analyzed above), he fails to mention his forming of the infinitely more important Burjiyya. Fur-

---

[157] B.N., Suppl. Ar. 739, fol. 136.

[158] *Taʾrīkh al-Islām*, B.M. MS Or. 1540, 32:92a–b.

[159] Topkapı, A III 2967, fols. 296a–b.

[160] *al-Nahj al-sadīd* (in *Patrologia Orientalis*), 14:475–533 and 533, ll. 1–7.

[161] *Mukhtaṣar*, 4:12–24.

[162] *Wāfī*, Tunis, Bibliothèque Historique, MS Nº 4850b, pp. 349–353 (an added pagination!). Al-Ṣafadī's *Aᶜyān al-ᶜaṣr* does not have a biography of that sultan (Aya Sofia, Nº 2967).

[163] *Fawāt al-wafayāt*, 1:408; 3:203–204.

[164] *Tatimmat al-mukhtaṣar fī akhbār al-bashar*, 2:335–336.

[165] In both of his books: *Tadhkirat al-nabīh* (Cairo, 1976), 1:135; *Durrat al-aslāk*, B.N., MS Ar., Nº 4680, fol. 157b.

[166] *Taʾrīkh al-duwal wal-mulūk*, 8:94–98.

[167] *Kitāb al-ᶜibar*, 5:394–403.

[168] *Ḥusn al-muḥāḍara*, 2:106–111. See also *Taʾrīkh al-khulafāʾ* (Beirut, n.d.), pp. 514–515.

[169] *Tashrīf al-ayyām wal-ᶜuṣūr fī sīrat al-Malik al-Manṣūr* (Cairo, 1961).

[170] *al-Alṭāf al-khafiyya al-sharīfa al-sulṭāniyya al-malakiyya al-ashrafiyya* (Lund, 1902).

[171] *al-Durra al-zakiyya fī akhbār al-dawla al-turkiyya* (Cairo, 1971), pp. 231–303.

thermore, the Burjiyya do not figure even once in the account of the reign of Qalāūn's son and successor al-Ashraf Khalīl, included in the same book.[172] Only immediately after that sultan's death does Ibn al-Dawādārī refer to them for the first time, and he does it in a very negative way.[173] And his attitude towards them is the same throughout his chronicle. The antagonism between them and his hero Sultan al-Nāṣir Muḥammad ibn Qalāūn is undoubtedly a major cause of this attitude.

In al-Ṣuqāᶜī's work the Burjiyya are not mentioned at all, not even in the biography of Baybars al-Jashnakīr, let alone the biography of Qalāūn. Neither do I remember coming across their name in al-Kutubī's biographical dictionary, certainly not in connection with their formation.

The silence of Ibn al-Furāt about the Burjiyya, both in the account of Qalāūn's reign and in the obituary of that sultan is of particular weight; for as already stated, that author had used many sources, the evidence of which he very often incorporated in his chronicle in great detail and with a considerable degree of accuracy.

The evidence of Ibn Kathīr, on which Ibn Taghrībirdī claims to rely, deserves special treatment. Here is what Ibn Taghrībirdī says:

> Ibn Kathīr also says: "al-Malik al-Manṣūr [Qalāūn] set aside 3700 from among his Mamlūks, both amirs and Circassians, placed them in the [Cairo] Citadel, and called them al-Burjiyya. He appointed his Mamlūks as governors in the various provinces, and it was they who changed the dress of the ruling class (*qāla Ibn Kathīr ayḍan wa-kāna al-Malik al-Manṣūr afrada min mamālīkihi thalāthat ālāf wa-sabᶜmiᵓat mamlūk min al-umarāᵓ wal-jarākisa wa-jaᶜalahum bil-qalᶜa wa-sammāhum al-Burjiyya wa-aqāma nuwwābahu fī al-buldān min mamālīkihi wa-hum alladhīna ghayyarū malābis al-dawla*)."[174]

No such statement about Qalāūn and the Burjiyya is found in Ibn Kathīr's account of Qalāūn's reign and in his short obituary note.[175]

---

[172] Ibid., pp. 303–350.

[173] Ibid., p. 350, l. 17.

[174] *al-Nujūm* (C), 7:330, ll. 1–3.

[175] *al-Bidāya wal-nihāya*, 23:288–318 (and pp. 317–318). On the change of the Mamlūk dress by Qalāūn and his successors and on his reliance on his own

On the other hand, Ibn Taghrībirdī quotes Ibn Kathīr in the same passage as saying that Sultan al-Ṣāliḥ Najm al-Dīn Ayyūb was the one who bought Qalāūn, and criticizes him for mentioning a wrong sum as his price.[176] In both cases he was right. This makes our problem even more enigmatic.

Al-Maqrīzī did not bother to mention any of his sources about the formation of the Burjiyya by Qalāūn.

In concluding this long presentation of the source evidence concerning the creation of the Burjiyya, I did not intend in any way to shed the slightest doubt on the close connection between it and Sultan Qalāūn. There may well be other such early sources which I did not consult and which do mention that connection. Some of the sources I consulted might mention it outside the obvious places where they would be expected to do so (where the ruler's outstanding achievements are enumerated).[177] Furthermore, there is a very long array of Burjī Mamlūks (particularly amīrs) each of whom is said to have been a Mamlūk of Qalāūn, and more than once the Burjiyya are called Manṣūriyya. The main point I wanted to demonstrate is that the attitude of those early sources toward the formation of the Baḥriyya and its consequent history was completely different. The reason for this was the great disparity in importance between these two bodies. A contributory yet quite weighty factor was the animosity of the Burjiyya to one of the most venerated sultans of the Qalāūnid dynasty, al-Nāṣir Muḥammad b. Qalāūn. The fact that the Burjiyya had nothing to do with the establishment of the "Burjī" reign, as I am trying to prove (for this see above and below), also helps to look at them in the right perspective, and to bring down to its real size their inflated image, created to no small extent by students of the Mamlūk sultanate.

The examination of a few major aspects of the Burjiyya's career is also of great help in establishing their place in Mamlūk history, and sheds additional light on the correctness of the claim that the second Mamlūk reign was named after them.

The Burjiyya began to be noticed after the death of Sultan al-Ashraf Khalīl (689–693/1290–1293), the son of their patron, and

---

Mamlūks in key positions there is other evidence as well in earlier sources, but all of those sources keep quiet about his founding the Burjiyya.

[176] Compare *al-Nujūm* (C), 7:329 with *al-Bidāya*, 23:317, ll. 20–21.

[177] This might be true also of Ibn Kathīr.

their power grew gradually, albeit with interruptions, until it reached its peak during the reign of one of their own members, Baybars al-Jashnakīr (708–709/1308–1309).[178] In that short period of predominance covering only a few years we do indeed find the term "the Burjiyya reign" (*al-dawla al-Burjiyya*) in a sense confined to that period alone.[179] When al-Nāṣir Muḥammad, the son of Qalāūn, returned from exile and ascended the throne of the sultanate for the third time, he conducted a most determined and most cruel policy, the major aim of which was to stay in power to the end of his life, an aim in which he succeeded.[180] The obvious main danger to the fulfillment of that policy was the Burjiyya. Therefore, "the first thing which he [al-Nāṣir Muḥammad] did when he came back (*awwal mā*[181] *badaʾa bihi baʿda qudūmihi min al-Karak*)" was to arrest "in one day (*fī yawm wāḥid*)" some thirty of the leading (*kibāsh*) amirs of the Burjiyya and send them to the prison in Alexandria.[182] Another great step which he took in order to break the power of the Burjiyya was an economic one: the well-known land measurement (*rawk*) of Egypt (715/1315), which enabled him, inter alia, to redistribute the feudal fiefs according to his will. The Burjiyya were the immediate target of that step, as al-Maqrīzī clearly puts it:

---

[178] The prestige of the Burjiyya and of their leaders must have been considerably enhanced in the second of the two great battles against the Mongol army of Īlkhān Ghāzān. In the first battle (December 23, 1299) they seem to have constituted the main element of the Mamlūk center (*al-umarāʾ al-burjiyya ahl al-qalb*), but were defeated (*al-Sulūk*, 1:887, ll. 13–16). In the second (April 21, 1303) they were the major cause of the Muslim victory (*wa-ṣāḥa Sallār halaka wallāhi ahl al-Islām wa-ṣarakha fī Baybars wal-Burjiyya wa-ṣadama bihim Qaṭlūshāh* [the Mongol chief commander] *wa-ablā dhālika al-yawma huwa wa-Baybars balāʾan ʿaẓīman ilā an kashafa al-tatār ʿan al-Muslimīn*) (ibid., p. 933, ll. 7–13).

[179] *Thumma innahu kāna tawallā al-Qāhira fī dawlat al-burjiyya marratayn* (Ibn al-Dawādārī, *Kanz al-durar* [Cairo, 1960], 9:354, l. 17); *lammā kāna mutawallī al-Qāhira ayyām al-Burjiyya* (ibid., p. 364, ll. 4–5).

[180] In a study entitled "The Expansion and Decline of Cairo under the Mamlūks and its Background," I deal with the policy of al-Nāṣir Muḥammad and its immediate and long range consequences. The picture emerging from that study of that sultan is much less favorable than the accepted one. Certain facets of his policy are discussed in the Appendix to my article "The Auxiliary Forces of the Mamlūk Sultanate," *Der Islam* 65 (1988): 32–37.

[181] Mistakenly spelled *man* in the text.

[182] *al-Sulūk*, 2:524, ll. 8–10; Ibn al-Dawādārī, 9:196; *al-Nahj al-sadīd*, 14:170, ll. 1–2; Ibn Kathīr, 14:55, 58, 65, 73.

In the last ten days of Sha^c^bān the measurement of the land of Egypt began. The reason for it was that the sultan found the incomes from the feudal fiefs of those Mamlūks who were the followers of Baybars al-Jashnakīr, the viceroy Sallār, and the rest of the Burjiyya, to be too large (*wa-fī al-ᶜushr al-akhīr min Shaᶜbān waqaᶜa al-shurūᶜ fī rawk arḍ Miṣr wa-sabab dhālika anna al-sulṭān istakthara akhbāz al-Mamālīk aṣhāb Baybars al-Jashnakīr wa-Sallār al-nāᵓib wa-baqiyyat al-Burjiyya*).[183]

Thus al-Nāṣir Muḥammad managed to put an abrupt end to the Burjiyya's might, for since the *rawk* and onward they ceased to constitute a socio-political body of real consequence. Individual Burjī amirs could occupy this or that important position, but that was all. Those and other individual Burjiyya lingered on for some time, until all of them passed away towards the middle of the eighth/fourteenth century. Here are the names of the latest surviving Burjiyya which I found in the sources, and the dates of their death:

Qujmās al-Jūkandār (died 734/1334);[184] ᶜIzz al-Dīn Aydamūr al-Khaṭīrī, amir of a hundred (died 737/1337);[185] Baybars al-Aḥmadī, amir of a hundred (died 746/1346, in the eighth decade of his life);[186] Baktāt al-Kirmānī, amir of forty (died 749/1348).[187]

This list does not in any way claim to be full, but for our purpose it is sufficient and quite instructive.

While the sources cared to mention who was the last of the Baḥriyya, and agreed unanimously, or almost so, that it was

[183] *al-Sulūk*, 2:146, ll. 4–7. See also ibid., p. 156, ll. 1–5. In my "Studies on the Structure of the Mamlūk Army" I laid stress on the strengthening of the royal Mamlūks at the expense of the *ḥalqa* by means of the *rawk*. This is correct. But I overlooked the fact that within the royal Mamlūks the Burjiyya served as a major and immediate target for destruction. An excellent description and analysis of the various *rawks* in medieval Egypt is included in Hassanein Rabie's *The Financial System of Egypt—A.H. 564–741/A.D. 1169–1341* (London, 1972), pp. 51–56, and index. A detailed examination of al-Nāṣir Muḥammad's policy towards the Mamlūks, including the Burjiyya, is found in "The Expansion and Decline of Cairo," mentioned above in n. 47.

[184] *al-Sulūk*, 2:377, ll. 3–4.

[185] Ibid., p. 426, ll. 1–5.

[186] Ibid., p. 698, ll. 16–19.

[187] Ibid., p. 793, ll. 14–16.

Baybars al-Jāliq,[188] none of them seems to have singled out the last of the Burjiyya. It was so much less important!

Another matter which comes to the fore in connection with the total disappearance of the Burjiyya is their supposed connection with Sultan Barqūq. Barqūq, as is well known, was brought over to Egypt by the slave-dealer ᶜUthmān ibn Musāfir, and was bought from him by amir Yalbughā al-ᶜUmarī al-Khāṣṣikī. Al-Sakhāwī says that this occurred in 764/1363, and that Barqūq became part of Yalbughā's novices (*kāna min jumlat mamālīkihi al-kuttābiyya*).[189] This means that when Barqūq started his career as a Mamlūk novice—75 *hijra* years after Qalāūn's death—there was no trace in the Mamlūk sultanate of any Burjī for quite some time—this on top of the fact that the Burjiyya lost their importance several decades before their total disappearance.[190] Barqūq himself never claimed any connection with the Burjiyya, neither did the other Circassian sultans or amirs, or even Mamlūks. During the whole Circassian reign there is no glorification of them; neither is there the slightest nostalgia for them (this applies also to the only Burjī Circassian sultan, Baybars al-Jashnakīr). They simply did not exist as far as that reign is concerned.

From the point of view of the thesis presented in this study, the absence of any link between the Burjiyya and the reign established by Sultan Barqūq has thus been proved. However, since the

---

[188] See "Le Régiment Baḥriyya," p. 138, and note 33.

[189] *al-Ḍawʾ al-lāmiᶜ* (Cairo, 1354 A.H.), 3:11, ll. 1–2.

[190] According to al-Maqrīzī, Barqūq was born, "by conjecture (*takhmīnan*)," in 741/1340 "because it was said (*fa-innahu dhukira*)" [by whom?] in the year 798/1396 that he was on that date fifty seven years old (*al-Sulūk*, 3:476, ll. 7–8. See also ibid., 2:698, ll. 16–19). Of course the date of Barqūq's arrival in Egypt is much more certain than the date of his birth in his country of origin. The language of our author also makes the accuracy of that date quite doubtful. In addition, if that date is the correct one he came to Egypt at the age of 23, which practically excludes him from starting his career as a novice at that time. Whatever the case may be, this argumentation, necessary in itself, has no bearing on the issue raised here. On Barqūq's purchase by Yalbughā al-ᶜUmarī see also *al-Sulūk*, 3:476, ll. 4–7; *al-Khiṭaṭ*, 2:240, ll. 29–30; 241. After the murder of his patron Yalbughā, Barqūq served with the viceroy of Damascus, and then in Egypt with ᶜAlī ibn al-Ashraf Shaᶜbān until the murder of that sultan. Thus he was for some time the Mamlūk of a *sayyid* (*aḥad mamālīk al-asyād*) (ibid., 3:485; 943, ll. 6–7), a rather poor position to rise from to the throne of the sultanate. On the *asyād* see "Studies on the Structure," p. 458.

Burjiyya were overwhelmingly Circassians, it would be appropriate to follow the rise of the Circassians in the Mamlūk sultanate within a wider context, and to do this in connection with the effects of the ethnical and other factors on Mamlūk relations.

Outline of the Rise of the Circassians until Their Final Victory

As I have already shown in the article on the Circassians,[191] we have a fairly good picture—albeit with some serious gaps—of their history in the Mamlūk sultanate in the period preceding their final ouster of the Qipchaqi Turks.[192] Ibn Khaldūn's claim, however, that al-Ṣāliḥ Najm al-Dīn Ayyūb already had Circassian Mamlūks serving in his army[193] is doubtful, because it is not supported by any corroborative evidence.[194] The undoubted beginning of the grand history of the Circassians took place with the creation of the Burjiyya. An outline of its vicissitudes and quite abrupt end has just been given above.

The fear felt by the other ethnic elements about the aggressiveness of the Circassians, which led to their replacement or even extermination, is dominant throughout their history in the Mamlūk sultanate. It finds its earliest and very illuminating expression on the eve of Baybars al-Jashnakīr's reign in the words of the Turkish amir al-Ḥājj Bahādur about the Burjī Circassian amir Aqūsh al-Afram.[195]

After the Burjiyya had been crushed by al-Nāṣir Muḥammad ibn Qalāūn, a relative silence about the Circassians prevails in the sources. Suddenly, however, towards the end of 748 (in the months

---

[191] "The Circassians," pp. 135–147.

[192] Ibid., pp. 137–138.

[193] *Kitāb al-ᶜibar* 5:373, l. 8.

[194] "The Circassians," p. 137a.

[195] For the details see "The Circassians," p. 138a. In that article I could cite only later sources for that unusually important piece of evidence. Now we have the early original source for it: Khalīl b. Aybak al-Ṣafadī (died 764/1362), who learned it from a close friend of Ḥājj Bahādur, the historian Ibn Faḍl Allāh al-ᶜUmarī (died 749/1348). See *al-Wāfī bil-wafayāt*, 10:296, ll. 1–5. The significance of al-Ṣafadī's evidence lies in the fact that it makes certain that Bahādur's statement is not a concocted story created during the Circassian reign in order to prove that the ugly character of the Circassians was revealed long before they came to power (784/1382), but is a true story. Al-Ṣafadī died twenty years and al-ᶜUmarī forty four years before that reign.

of Ramaḍān and Shawwāl/December 1347 and January 1348), an attempt at a coup d'état by the Circassians against Sultan Ḥasan was nipped in the bud. The Circassians had been brought over "from all quarters (*jalabahum min kulli makān*)" by the sultan who preceded him, his brother al-Muẓaffar Ḥājjī (747–748/1346–1347), with the purpose of giving them precedence over the *atrāk* (*wa-arāda an yunshiʾahum ʿalā al-atrāk wa-adnāhum ilayhi*). Their haughtiness and their troublesomeness are particularly stressed.[196] The purge was not confined to Egypt. Amir Fakhr al-Dīn Iyāz, the governor of Aleppo, was also arrested and imprisoned in Shawwāl 748/January 1348 by order of the sultan:

> That was because he is a Circassian, and these [Circassians] are the opponents of the Tatar race. Al-Muẓaffar [Ḥājjī] turned away from the Tatar race towards the Circassians and their like (*fa-innahu min al-jarkas wa-hum aḍdād al-jins* [sic!] *al-tatār wa-kāna al-Muḍaffar* [sic!] *qad māla ʿan jins al-tatār ilā al-jarkas wa-naḥwihim*).[197]

When I wrote my article on the Circassians I did not notice this piece of evidence from Ibn al-Wardī, the importance of which goes beyond the subject of our discussion,[198] and I therefore was not aware of the wide dimensions of the conspiracy against the *atrāk*. How Sultan Ḥājjī managed during his short reign to make the Circassians so powerful, is really amazing. In any case, there is no mention of any link, direct or indirect, between Ḥājjī's Circassians and the Burjiyya. Neither is there any traceable link between them and the Circassians of Barqūq.

We thus have three peaks of different heights in the history of the Circassians in the Mamlūk sultanate, separated from each

---

196 "The Circassians," p. 138a–b.

197 Ibn al-Wardī on the margin of Abū al-Fidāʾ *al-Muhtaṣar*, 4:149.

198 It is significant that those whom Ibn Taghrībirdī calls *atrāk* are called by the much earlier Ibn al-Wardī *tatār*. In the later Mamlūk period the synonymity and interchangeability of *turk* and *tatār*, as well as of *turkī* and *tatārī* in Mamlūk military society, are frequent. I have discussed this at some length in the as yet unpublished chapter of my work on the racial composition of that society. I also mentioned that phenomenon briefly in *Mamlūk*, *EI*², 6:316b. However, I did not yet find such an early example as the one reproduced here from Ibn al-Wardī. This interchangeability makes it very difficult to distinguish between Turks and real Tatars (or Mongols) among the Mamlūks.

other by a number of decades. The wide gaps between these three peaks might or might not be filled. But whatever the result may be, they indicate two things: a) justification for designating the reign of Barqūq and his successors as Burjī remains as invalid as ever; b) ethnic loyalty was a competitor of Mamlūk loyalty, and under certain circumstances it combined with other factors to endanger the Mamlūk institution. This will be discussed on the following pages.

The Mamlūk institution, unique in Islamic civilization, took many shapes and always had to struggle against a number of factors of varying degrees of strength working against it. As I put it long ago (in 1950), "The method developed during a long period through contact with the circumstances existing in each region and through adaptation to them. As a result, different Mamlūk systems developed in different regions. The military slave system of the Ottoman sultanate was not identical with that of the Mamlūk sultanate. In spite of the common elements there were big differences. Moreover, there was in Mamlūkdom much which had been contrary to human nature. What actually resulted was a compromise between the system and human nature."[199]

The major factor working against the Mamlūk system was of course the obvious antagonism to the principle according to which the Mamlūks constitute a one generation aristocracy, a principle clearly contradictory to human nature, and one which has no real parallel outside of Islam. I tried elsewhere to find a partial and tentative explanation of how this factor was subdued or at least tamed:[200] in a nutshell, in my view the Mamlūk "family," in its wider sense: the "father" (*ustādh*); his "sons," who were each other's "brothers" (*khushdāshiyya*); the "sons" of these *khushdāshiyya*, who were the "grandsons" of the *ustādh*; the "father" of the *ustādh* (i.e., *ustādh al-ustādh*) and his "brothers" (*khushdāshiyyat ustādh al-ustādh*), and so on—all were strong enough to stop or minimize an attempt by any member of the

---

[199] "*Mamlūkiyyāt* (A): A First Attempt to Evaluate the Mamlūk Military System," *JSAI*, 2 (1980): 325–326 (the article is a translation of a lecture in Hebrew delivered in Jerusalem on May 15, 1950); ibid., p. 322.

[200] "Mamlūk Military Aristocracy—A Non-Hereditary Nobility," *JSAI* 10 (1987) [Festschrift in Honor of Prof. M. J. Kister]: 205–210. There (p. 205) I repeat in different words the ideas set forth in the lecture mentioned in the immediately preceding note.

"family" to include one's natural son in that "family." The fact that the Mamlūk "family" had only a "father" who, unlike the father in a natural family, did not have to cope with the ambition of competing mothers to advance their own sons, greatly facilitated the carrying out of a policy of one generation nobility. On the other hand, the great size of the Mamlūk "family" made it quite unwieldy, and created different kinds of difficulties.

Another factor important in itself but which gains additional weight when linked with the factor which I shall mention immediately thereafter, is this: The main cause for the ultimate success of the Mamlūk system was the fact that the Mamlūk youth or novice was separated from his original milieu in his country of origin and, above all, from his family and close relatives at the very beginning of his apprenticeship. However, this separation was not absolute. The slave-dealer, who went back and forth between the Mamlūk's adoptive country and his country of origin, was the obvious connecting link between him and his natural family, and there might well have been other links as well. The proof for this argument, which is not the only one, is that a considerable number of Mamlūks, especially those who rose to high ranks and positions, could bring over members of their family to their new homeland.[201]

Yet another significant factor was that the Mamlūks belonged to a very specific ethnic group. Now most of those Mamlūks arrived at their countries of destination at the age of puberty or thereabout, and they served a patron who quite often had in his service a substantial number of Mamlūks of the same stock.[202] At the age of puberty a Mamlūk had already acquired not only the essential warrior qualities of the people of his mother country but

---

[201] After all, the Mamlūks, or most of them, were given an equal start at the bottom of the socio-military pyramid. None of them had been given any guarantee that he would rise to a position which would enable him to bring over his relatives from abroad.

[202] Al-Maqrīzī, in his well known account of the Mamlūk military school, says that the sultan used to lodge a Mamlūk recently bought from a slave dealer together with [recruits] of his own race (*nazzalahu fī ṭabaqat jinsihi*) (*al-Khiṭaṭ*, 2:213, ll. 32–33). See also *Esclavage du Mamelouk*, p. 19. If this statement is correct, it would mean that the newly arrived novice was given the opportunity to form close ties with his fellow countrymen from the very beginning of his career in the Mamlūk sultanate. Unfortunately, however, this is an isolated piece of evidence which I could not corroborate by any other proof.

also important elements of their outlook and way of life. It would be most natural for him to cling to his compatriots, whose habits were identical with or similar to his and, what is more important, whose mother-tongue was like his own. Thus the facts that a Mamlūk's ties with his people in his homeland were not completely severed, and that in his adoptive country he was naturally inclined to cling to Mamlūks of his own stock, supplemented each other and strengthened his feeling of ethnic affinity.

The dominant element in most of the important Mamlūk societies since the first half of the third/ninth century and long afterward were the Turks. It would be only natural for them to try and keep their dominance as long as they could, and they were successful in this to a very great extent. The lingua franca of the Mamlūks was Turkish, and in the Mamluk sultanate it continued to be Turkish even after the *atrāk* lost their first place in the ruling class of that sultanate.[203]

The same is true of the names of the Mamlūks. Irrespective of whether they were Turks or belonged to other ethnic groups, most of them bore Turkish names.[204] Thus ethnic affinity played a central role in Mamlūk society from its very inception. What certainly helped the ethnic Turks to keep their mastery, in addition to other factors, was that non-Turkish Mamluks, in spite of bearing Turkish names, could be recognized by their on the whole deficient Turkish speech, their accent, and perhaps also by their different physiognomy and habits. These differences from the true Turks must have caused the non-Turks to keep together, as far as they were allowed to, each in his own ethnic group, where they must have felt much more at home.[205]

---

[203] I do not discuss here the problems raised in connection with the replacement of Qipchaqi Turkish by Ottoman Turkish in the Mamlūk sultanate. From the point of view of the non-Turkish speakers it makes little difference.

[204] The non-Turks certainly had to change their names, but whether the Turks kept their original names which they bore in their homelands or were now given Turkish names which were in vogue in the sultanate at the time of their arrival, is unknown. What can be said with a high degree of certainty is that in different periods in the history of the sultanate some Mamlūk names were more popular than others. The subject of Mamlūk names, titles, etc., is of the highest importance and deserves a much more comprehensive study than "Names, titles, and *nisbas* of the Mamlūk," *IOS* 5 (1975): 189–232, which should also include a special statistical section.

[205] The clash between Mamlūk and ethnic loyalties was particularly dangerous when there was more than one strong ethnic group in the field. In a Mamlūk

There was yet another dividing line within a Mamlūk group which owed allegiance to the same patron, and that was the original religion of its members. But here the dividing line was not between the Turks and the others, but between those who had been pagans and those who were originally monotheist, namely Christians.[206] The conversion from paganism to Islam could not have been the same as that from another monotheistic faith to Islam. To turn a pagan into a devout and convinced Muslim was much easier than to do the same to a Christian who before his conversion had been brought up in a creed whose believers were convinced of its absolute superiority over the other brands of monotheism.[207] The existence side by side of Mamlūks with such different religious backgrounds in the pre-Islamic part of their lives must have detracted from their homogeneity and thus must have contributed to some extent to the weakening of the Islamic and Mamlūk loyalties.

The great power of the ethnic factor finds its strongest expression in the victory of the Circassians over the Turks in the Mamlūk sultanate. It was caused by a combination of elements, one of them was the intense feeling of mutual affinity among the Circassians, which came into prominence repeatedly before and after their final success. A very helpful factor was the ability and determination of their leaders. Even more important was the change of circumstances in the Mamluks' countries of origin, the growing islamization of the Turks in their original homelands and the disintegration of the Golden Horde, which were accompanied by devastating internal and external wars.[208]

Thus a whole set of formidable factors, like the Mamlūk's ties with his biological family, his feeling of ethnic affinity, his pre-Muslim monotheistic background (if he had one), as well as other

---

society where one ethnic group was overwhelmingly strong, joining that society by members of other ethnic groups became much more difficult. But internal Mamlūk relations were considerably less affected.

[206] There is hardly a trace of a Mamlūk of Jewish origin in the Mamlūk sultanate. I deal with this subject briefly in the as yet unpublished chapter on the racial composition of the Mamlūk society.

[207] This does not fully apply to peoples who were on the fringes of the domain of Christendom, who were primitive, and whose Christianity was relatively young, like that of the Circassians. These, as is well known, later on converted to Islam in their own country.

[208] See also "The Circassians," pp. 135–136.

factors, combined sometimes to undermine the foundations of the Mamlūk system. Not the least of those foundations were the *ustādh-khushdāsh* relations. In view of this state of affairs one should wonder not at the convulsions which overtook that system and the weaknesses from which it suffered, but at its immense vitality and resilience, and above all, at its longevity and great achievements.

There is a tendency among some scholars who study the history and other aspects of the Mamlūk sultanate to detract from the centrality and minimize the importance of these *ustādh-khushdāsh* relations. This is, to say the least, a very erroneous and most unwelcome tendency. Because of the great importance of the subject, I intend to deal with it separately. Here I shall only emphasize in the strongest terms two things: a) such an approach would be an attempt to push the center away into the margin, and force the margin into the center; b) without that double Mamlūk link there would have been no Mamlūk institution, no Mamlūk sultanate, no Baḥriyya and no Burjiyya; and consequently there would have been left no *ustādh-khushdāsh* ties to belittle.

APPENDIX A

A Correct Criticism Based on a Wrong Argumentation

Professor Muḥammad M. Ziyāda, to whom we owe so much for his contribution to the study of the Mamlūk period and for undertaking the great project of the publication of an excellent edition of al-Maqrīzī's chronicle *Kitāb al-Sulūk*, is the only scholar that I know who has expressed doubt about the adequacy of the name Burjiyya as designating the second Mamlūk reign, but his argumentation is unacceptable.

In the *Kitab al-Sulūk*, in the obituaries of the year 707/1307, it is stated that amīr Baybars al-Jāliq, one of the *Burjiyya Ṣāliḥiyya*, died in that year.[1] From this statement Prof. Ziyāda has concluded that the founder of the Burjiyya might have been the

[1] *al-Sulūk*, 2:40, l. 15.

earlier al-Ṣāliḥ Najm al-Dīn Ayyūb and not the later al-Manṣūr Qalāūn, "which is the basis for the agreement among the historians to call the second Mamlūk reign al-Burjiyya, after Qalaūn's Mamlūks who are known by that name (*wa-yanbanī ᶜalayhi mā tawāḍaᶜa ᶜalayhi al-muᵓarrikhūn min tasmiyat dawlat al-mamālīk al-thāniya bi-ism al-Burjiyya nisbatan ilā mamālīk Qalāūn al-maᶜrūfīn bi-dhālika al-ism*)."[2] Ziyāda does mention in this connection that, according to Ibn Taghrībirdī,[3] Baybars al-Jāliq was one of the Baḥriyya,[4] but he adds that this does not disprove al-Maqrīzī's evidence, and only the evidence of earlier sources will decide the matter.[5]

All this reasoning and argumentation are unnecessary, for the simple reason that there cannot be any doubt about the fact that Baybars al-Jāliq was the Baḥrī Ṣāliḥī and not the Burjī, as I have already shown in my article on the Baḥriyya.[6] There I also bring the evidence of the early historians Abū al-Fidāᵓ and al-Mufaḍḍal ibn Abū al-Faḍāᵓil to this effect, thus eliminating the possibility that evidence of an earlier source might support Ziyāda's theory. As a matter of fact, I know of no early or late Mamlūk source which attributes the formation of the Burjiyya to the sultan who created the Baḥriyya. In that article I state emphatically that al-Maqrīzī's version is wrong, and I see no reason to change my statement today.[7]

What Ziyāda, like almost all other students of the Mamlūk period, failed to notice was that the historians who identified the name of Qalāūn's "regiment" with the name of the reign of Sultan Barqūq and his successors were all, without exception, not Mamlūk historians but European historians of Islam who lived

---

[2] Ibid., n. 5.

[3] *al-Nujūm* (C), 8:227.

[4] *al-Sulūk*, 2:40, n. 5.

[5] Ibid., n. 5.

[6] "Le Régiment Baḥriyya," p. 138, and n. 33.

[7] This mistake of al-Maqrīzī might well have been a slip of his own pen or of that of his copyist. Quatremère, in his translation of this passage calls Baybars al-Jāliq "Burjī Ṣāliḥī" without comment (*Histoire des Sultans Mamlouks*, 2b:281). On this personality see also al-Ṣafadī, *al-Wāfī bil-wafayāt*, 10:348; Ibn al-Dawādārī, 9:151, ll. 17–152, l. 5; M. van Berchem, *CIA*, *Jerusalem, ville*, II, N° 72; G. Wiet, *Les Biographies du Manhal Safi* (Cairo, 1932), N° 710.

centuries after the demise of the Mamlūk sultanate. He also disregarded the fact that whether Qalāūn did or did not create that "regiment" has nothing whatever to do with that identification.

The main thing, which in my view the argumentation of Ziyāda brings into bold relief, is the practically unanimous lack of awareness among students of the Mamlūk sultanate of the absolute wrongness and baselessness of the terminology which they use to designate the two consecutive reigns of that sultanate.

APPENDIX B

ATRĀK *and* TURKIYYA *as relating to the Ottomans and their Like in the Mamlūk Sources*

The names *turk* and *atrāk* as designating the Mamlūks have lasted up to the very end of the Mamlūk sultanate. The Ottomans, their state, and their lands have other names in the Mamlūk sources. Even during their conquest of Syria and Egypt the Ottomans are called *ᶜUthmāniyya*, *rūm* (or *arwām*), and quite frequently *tarākima* or *turkmān*.[1]

However, *atrāk* and *turkiyya* in connection with the Turkish speaking peoples and their lands in and about Anatolia do appear in those sources, albeit very rarely. Already Ibn Faḍl Allāh al-ᶜUmarī, in the first half of the fourteenth century, speaks about *mamlakat al-atrāk bil-rūm* and *bilād al-atrāk bil-rūm*.[2] A later historian of the mid-fifteenth century, Ibn Taghrībirdī, calls those lands *al-turkiyya*, *bilād al-turkiyya*, and *barr al-turkiyya*, in connection with the import of wood and flour from Iljūn and the supplying by sea of the Mamlūk forces fighting the Turkmen Shāh Siwār.[3]

---

[1] See my "Mamlūk Military Aristocracy during the First Years of the Ottoman Occupation of Egypt," n. 3 (see above, Pt. I, n. 132).

[2] *Masālik al-abṣār*, B.N., MS Arabe N° 2328, fols. 109b, 139a.

[3] *al-Nujūm* (P), 7:486, ll. 15–487, l. 1; 522, l. 10; Ibn Taghribirdī, *Ḥawādith* (Berkeley, 1942), pp. 96, ll. 12–14; 115, ll. 10–11, 13–14; 129, l. 9; 301, ll. 4–5; 700, ll. 18–20). Anatolia as a source of wood for the Mamlūks (mainly for their navy) is discussed in the as yet unpublished chapter on the Mamlūk navy.

APPENDIX C

Some Supplementary Notes on the Circassians of the Mamlūk Sultanate

I believe that the main conclusions of my study on the Circassians of that sultanate, published forty years ago, still hold good. However, the availability today of published and unpublished sources, to which I had no access then, necessitates certain additions and modifications. Some modifications should have been made even on the basis of the sources I could consult at that time.

In this context I shall confine myself to very few subjects, the main one being the attitude of Sultan Faraj, the son of Barqūq, to the Circassians.

I shall begin with the quotation of three short passages, which will help us in dealing with two of these subjects.

1. 784/1382: "He [Barqūq] had a great number of *Jarākisa* Mamlūks, who were brought over to him (*julibū*) from their countries of origin (*al-bilād*),[1] and he raised them to [a status] the like of which they never dreamt of (*raqqāhum ilā mā lam yakhṭur lahum bi-bāl*). He bestowed the rank of officers (*imriyyāt*) on a group (*jamāᶜa*) from amongst them."[2]

2. 784/1382: "He [Barqūq] annihilated (*afnā*) the Ashrafiyya Mamlūks [in Shaᶜbān (764–778/1363–1376)] by means of banishment and killing, and he favored (*qarraba*) the *Jarākisa* and disfavored (*abᶜada*) the *Turk*."[3]

3. 801/1398: "He [Barqūq] loved to have numerous Mamlūks and he gave preference (*qaddam ᶜalā*) to the *Jarākisa* over the *Atrāk* and the *Rūm*."[4]

What might be implied from passage 1 is that in spite of the fact that the Circassians were so aggressive and determined in their attempts to seize power before the reign of Barqūq, they

[1] This is the meaning of the term *al-bilād* in its Mamlūk context. See also my "Mamlūk," *EI*², 6:314a.

[2] *al-Sulūk*, 3:474, ll. 7–9.

[3] al-ᶜAsqalānī, *Inbāʾ al-ghumr* (Cairo, 1969), 1:257.

[4] *al-Sulūk*, 3:943.

seem to have been quite weak and to have carried little weight in the period preceding their successful coup. After all, as already stated, there is hardly any indication of Circassian political power after 748/1347. This would mean that the personality and leadership of Barqūq were particularly decisive in the final victory of the Circassians, as far as factors within the sultanate are concerned.

From the combination of passages 2 and 3 it can be concluded, and rightly so, that the major opponents of the *Jarākisa* were the *Turk*, as might be expected, but that these were not the only ones. The *Rūm* were also an important factor,[5] although that name might be omitted sometimes (as is the case with the passage from al-ᶜAsqālanī). As far as my own research on the Circassians is concerned, there was an additional reason for my lack of awareness of the intensity of the antagonism between the *Jarkas* and the *Rūm*, and this is the state of the source materials which were then at my disposal.

The main sources which were available to me for the study of the Circassians' rise to power and for their early reign were Ibn al-Furāt and Ibn Taghrībirdī. The first of these two is by far the best and most detailed of all the sources that I know for the reconstruction of the ethnic struggle during the transition period between the two reigns. Unfortunately, however, it ends with the year 799/1397, that is to say, about two years before Barqūq's death. By contrast, Ibn Taghrībirdī had good reasons to dilute to some extent the Jarkasī-Rūmī struggle, because he himself was a Rūmī. Now with the availability of additional sources, especially the chronicle of al-Maqrīzī, a better picture of the antagonism between these two ethnic groups can be drawn. This is particularly relevant to the reign of Sultan Faraj, Barqūq's son, who was a Rūmī on his mother's side and who, through his mother, was a relative of Ibn Taghrībirdī.[6]

During his reign Faraj made repeated attempts to weaken the Circassians. The first attempt of this kind was made only a few

---

[5] They occupied a third place after the *Turk* and the *Jarkas* (Mamlūks), *EI*², 6:316b. The full account of the place of the Rūmīs within the corps of the Royal Mamlūks is found in the yet unpublished chapter on the Mamlūk races of my work on the Mamlūks.

[6] Faraj's mother, Shīrīn, was the cousin on the father's side of Taghrībirdī, the historian's father (*al-Nujūm* [P], 6:149, ll. 1–6). Faraj also married that historian's daughter (ibid., p. 129, l. 14).

months after his enthronement by his *atābak al-ᶜasākir* Aytmish (Rabīᶜ I 802/November 1399).[7] In this case it is not clear whether the sultan himself was involved.

The antagonism between Faraj and the *Jarākisa*, because of his Rūmī affiliations, comes to the forefront most forcefully on the eve of his short abdication (for about seventy days):

> On Tuesday the sixth (of Rabīᶜ I 808/September 1, 1405) relations between the sultan and the Mamlūks became strained. A group of *Jarākisa* Mamlūks demanded the arrest of the amirs Taghrībirdī, Dimurdāsh, and Arghūn because of their Rūmī ethnicity (*min ajli annahum min jins al-Rūm*). The sultan favored them [i.e., the Rūm] (*ikhtaṣṣa bihim*) and married the daughter of Taghrībirdī,[8] and he turned away from (*aᶜraḍa ᶜan*) the *Jarākisa* and imprisoned Aynāl Bīh. The *Jarākisa* feared lest the *Rūm*[īs] should surpass them (*khāfa al-Jarākisa min taqaddum al-Rūm ᶜalayhim*). They wanted the sultan to remove them (*ibᶜādahum*), but he refused, so they united against him (*taḥazzabū ᶜalayhi*), and made common cause with *atābak al-ᶜasākir* Baybars.[9]

Less than three weeks later, on the eve of the 24th of the same month (September 19), during the Nawrūz festivities, the sultan got drunk in the company of his *khāṣṣakiyya* and jumped into a water pond. Some of his boon companions followed him into the pond, with the intention of drowning him, and almost succeeded. However, one of them, who was a Rūmī, saved him when he was on the verge of death. At first Faraj tried to keep silent, but since he could not keep a secret, he disclosed it, and started vilifying the *Jarākisa*—who were the people of his own father, and who constituted the might of his reign and formed the bulk of his army (*wa-hum qawm abīhi wa-shawkat dawlatihi wa-jull ᶜaskarihi*). He began to praise the *Rūm*[īs], siding with them, and stressing his affiliation with them (*wa-yamdaḥ al-Rūm wa-yataᶜaṣṣab lahum wa-yantamī ilayhim*), for his mother Shīrīn was a Rūmiyya. This

---

[7] *al-Sulūk*, 3:987.

[8] According to Ibn Taghrībirdī, Faraj married his (the historian's) daughter (see above, note 6), and on this particular subject his evidence is reliable.

[9] *al-Sulūk*, 3:1174.

was too much for the [Circassian] people (*fa-shaqqa dhālika ᶜalā al-qawm*)[10] . . . so they went to the *atābak al-ᶜasākir*, amīr Baybars, the son of al-Ẓāhir [Barqūq's] sister, and brought him to their side. The sultan took fright and planned to run away.[11]

As for Ibn Taghrībirdī's evidence about these two incidents, he does speak, and with considerable detail, about both of them,[12] but he either ignores or thoroughly dilutes the antagonism between the *Rūmī*s and the *Jarkas*. In view of the fact that Ibn Taghrībirdī knew al-Maqrīzī's chronicle very well, used it extensively, and referred to it frequently, either in praise or in criticism, it can be said with absolute certainty that he was well acquainted with that author's version of events in both cases. Yet he preferred to disregard it for obvious reasons.[13]

Thus the ethnic conflict in the reign of Faraj was much more fierce than I thought many years ago, and the stress during part of that reign was on the antagonism between the *Jarākisa* and the *Rūmī*s, rather than between them and the *Atrāk*.

There are some important obstacles which hinder an attempt to give a full picture of the ethnic struggle and transformation in the period in which that struggle took place. One of them is the fact that the sources do not mention the ethnic origin of numerous Mamlūks. This difficulty is greatly aggravated by yet another fact, namely, that the overwhelming majority of the Mamlūks were given Turkish names.[14] Thus it is quite often difficult to

---

[10] For the special meaning of the term *al-qawm* in our context see my "The Circassians," pp. 142–143.

[11] *al-Sulūk*, 3:1177. For the actual flight see ibid., pp. 1177–1178.

[12] *al-Nujūm* (P), 6:129, 1-8–130, l. 3; 131, l. 3–135, l. 4.

[13] It should be pointed out, however, that if one follows the biographies of the persons involved in the two incidents, one can easily discover the reality even in Ibn Taghrībirdī's own works which that author tried to disguise, or at least to tone down, in his narrative account.

[14] Note, for example, the Turkish names of the three leading *Rūmī* amirs in the incident of 6 Rabīᶜ I 808 (Taghrībirdī, Dimurdāsh, and Arghūn). They certainly had different names in their country of origin. Whether Turkish Mamlūks kept their original Turkish names or were given new ones at a certain stage after leaving their homelands, is a moot point. The case of the Circassian sultan Barqūq is of special interest. We are told that when Yalbughā al-ᶜUmarī bought him from his slave-dealer, ᶜUthmān b. Musāfir, his name was Alṭunbughā, but because of an outgrowth (*nutūʾ*) in his eye he changed it into Barqūq (see, e.g., al-Sākhāwī, *al-Ḍawʾ al-lāmiᶜ* 3:11, l. 2). Now Barqūq certainly did not bear a

decide to what degree the activity of this or that Mamlūk was decided by his being part of this or that ethnic group. Still, in this particular and important domain much more can be done by a systematic scrutiny of the history and careers of the individual Mamlūks.[15] Another obstacle is that in that period there is much overlapping and interchangeability in the terminology current in the sources between the Mamlūk groups and the ethnic groups (for example, in passage 2: Ashrafiyya [Shaᶜbān] and *Turk*).[16] Yet another obstacle is the accelerated economic decline with which Egypt, Syria, and other neighboring regions were afflicted in those years, and which diverted to a certain extent the attention of some of the writers from developments inside Mamlūk society.

These are only preliminary remarks to a subject which needs much more thorough and systematic discussion.[17]

Turkish name in his homeland. This might indicate that sometimes the original name of a Mamlūk might have been changed into a Turkish one while he was on his way to the Mamlūk sultanate, possibly already by the slave-dealer. I do not know the usual procedure of naming the Mamlūks. Speaking of Barqūq, it should be pointed out that in paving the way to his and his Circassian Mamlūks' seizure of power, Barqūq had to deal not only with the Mamlūks of the preceding Qalāūnid sultans but also with the Mamlūks of those sultans' descendants (*al-asyād*), as well as with those descendants themselves (see, e.g., *al-Sulūk*, 3:473, 474, 594; Jawharī, *Nuzhat al-nufūs* [Cairo, 1970], p. 188). Interestingly enough, Barqūq himself was employed in the service of one of those *asyād*, amir ᶜAlī, the son of al-Ashraf Shaᶜbān, up to the time when al-Ashraf was killed (*al-Sulūk*, 3:943, ll. 6–7). As already stated, it was mainly against the Mamlūks of that Sultan, al-Ashrafiyya, that Barqūq had to fight in order to establish Circassian rule (for the *asyād* see my "Studies on the Structure," p. 458).

[15] This remark applies not only to the period under discussion but also to the whole Mamlūk reign.

[16] To mention a few instances out of many selected at random: *al-Sulūk*, 3:501, 551, 649, 650, 651, 658. And these are not the best examples.

[17] The Mamlūk and the ethnic affinities might either work against each other or complement each other, as was the case in the struggle of Barqūq and his Circassians against the Turkish Mamlūks of the sultans who preceded him.

V

THE MAMLŪK NOVICE
(ON HIS YOUTHFULNESS AND ON HIS ORIGINAL RELIGION)

When one studies a certain phenomenon for many years, one tends to believe that he had reached a point in which considerations of elementary simplicity and obviousness, pertaining to matters of first ranking importance in his field of research, had not been overlooked by him. Yet time and time again one discovers that this kind of belief is not always well founded.

Here is an instance to this effect based on my own experience.

The fact that the mamlūks, or at least their overwhelming majority, were brought over to the lands of Islam at a relatively tender age, is well known. Some obvious reasons for that practice were already enumerated and discussed by me on various occasions [1]. The most important of them was that at that age the mamlūk could be best moulded as a devoted Muslim, as a faithful bondsman of his patron and as an able soldier.

In the following lines I shall reproduce and translate two passages, the first of which highlights and adds yet another angle to the elements mentioned above, and the second stands by itself ; and, to the best of my conviction, reveals a factor of the first magnitude. A third passage, which complements these two, within the framework of the subjects dealt with in the present paper, will be reproduced and translated later on.

---

1. See e.g. *L'Esclavage du Mamelouk*, Jerusalem, 1951, pp. 1-8 ; A First Attempt to Evaluate the Mamlūk Military System, *Jerusalem Studies in Arabic and Islam*, Jerusalem, II (1980), pp. 324-330 ; The Muslim City and the Mamluk Military Aristocracy, *Proceedings of the Israel Academy of Sciences and Humanities*, Jerusalem, II (1968), pp. 319f.

Passage I

Text

[*al-Kīmāk*] ... *fa-idhā wulida lil-rajul walad rabbāhu wa-'ālahu wa-qāma bi-amrihi ḥattā yaḥtalim thumma yadfa' ilayhi qawsan wa-sihāman wā-yukhrijuhu min manzilihi wa-yaqūlu lahu iḥtall li-nafsika wa-yuṣayyiruhu bi-manzilat al-gharīb al-ajnabī wa-minhum man yabī'u dhukūra wuldihi wa-ināthahum bi-mā yunfiqūnahu*[2].

Translation

[The Kīmāk] ... If a man [of the Kīmāk] begets a son, he would bring him up and provide for him and take care of him until he attains puberty. Then [i.e. on attaining puberty] he would hand him a bow and arrows and would drive him out of his abode telling him : 'fend for yourself !', and he would treat him [thenceforward] as a stranger and foreigner. There are amongst them [amongst the Kīmāk] those who sell their sons and daughters in order to cover their expenses.

Passage II

Text

Ḥākā ba'ḍ al-tujjār qāla kharaja min Khwārizm qafal 'aẓīm fa-lammā dhahabū ayyāman wa-ba'udū 'an Khwārizm sārū dhāta yawmin fa-lammā nazala al-qawm ra'aw mamālīkahum al-Turk kharajū 'an wasṭ al-qawm wa-kāna 'adaduhum akthar min 'adad al-tujjār yarmūna al-qawm bil-nushshāb qālū mā sha'nukum qālū nurīdu qatlakum wa-na'khudh hādhihi al-amwāl nashtarī minhā al-khayl wal-silāḥ wa-namshī ilā khidmat al-sulṭān fa-qāla al-qawm lahum antum lā tuḥsinūna bay' hādhā al-qumāsh fa-utrukūhu ma'anā ḥattā nuḥsin nashtarī lakum minhā al-khayl wal-silāḥ wa-naj'al aḥadakum amīran wa-tamshūna ilā khidmat al-sulṭān fa-khada'ūhum wa-ba'athū ilā Khwārizm man yukhbir shiḥnat Khwārizm bil-ḥāl fa-mā kāna illā ayyām qalā'il ḥattā waṣala al-shiḥna qabaḍa 'alā al-mamālīk wa-radda al-qafal ilā Khwārizm wa-ṣalaba al-mamālīk wa-nādā fī Khwārizm an lā yashtariya min al-tujjār aḥad mamlūkan rajulan[3].

Translation

A merchant recounted [the following event] : A huge caravan went out of Khwārizm. After travelling for several days, when a considerable distance

2. Yāqūt, *Mu'jam al-Buldān*, Leipzig, I (1866), p. 839, ll. 18-22.
3. Al-Qazwīnī, *Āthār al-Bilād wa-Akhbār al-'Ibād*, Beirut, 1960, p. 514, ll. 14-23.

had already separated them from Khwārizm, they halted and pitched their camp. When they did so, they saw that their Turkish Mamlūks, *whose number had been bigger than that of the merchants,* went out of the middle of the camp, pelting the merchants with arrows. The merchants asked them : 'what is the matter ?'. They answered : 'we want to kill you and take all these goods ; buy with them horses and arms and go to the sultan's service'. The merchants said to them : 'you are not qualified for selling these fabrics [for a good price]. Leave them with us, and we shall do it for you. We shall buy you, as well, horses and arms and appoint one of you as your commander. Then you will go to serve the sultan'. They thus succeeded in duping them, and in the meantime they sent to Khwārizm a person who informed its governor about what had been going on [in the caravan]. Within a few days the governor arrived, arrested the mamlūks and returned the caravan to Khwārizm. He crucified the mamlūks and announced in Khwārizm that *nobody should buy an adult mamlūk from the merchants*[4].

These two passages are most illuminating, each in its own way.

The first of them, though dealing only with the Turkish Kīmāk tribal group, describes a situation which certainly applies, with this or that modification, to the majority of the tribes of the Eurasian steppe, from whom mamlūks had been imported to the countries of Islam. What it so clearly demonstrates is that the decisive stage in the parents-children relations in the steppe is the age of puberty. This is the stage when ties between father and son loosen, and the son has to fend for himself, or at least start doing so. The rift between father and son need not always be as sharp as in the case under discussion, but the basic situation is correctly reflected in that account.

What could be derived from the evidence of other sources and from logical considerations was that the peoples, particularly the pagan peoples, from amongst whom mamlūks had been recruited to the armies of Islam, did not have many qualms in parting with their children for a good remuneration. This is, of course, true. But what the evidence in passage I reveals, is that at that particular age of puberty the estrangement between the child and his parents made that parting much easier. *It is no mere accident that our source speaks in the same breath about the boy's being ousted from his father's abode and about the tribesmen's selling their offspring !*

Thus there was a most welcome coincidence between the phase of the maximum readiness of the people of the steppe to part with their children and the military needs of Islam. For the age of puberty was the ideal one for the formation of a mamlūk. On the one hand he was sufficiently young to be shaped and moulded, militarily and otherwise, according to the lights of his new faith and of his patron. On the other hand, he was sufficiently old to absorb in the steppe or the mountainous rugged area the basic warlike qualities which could be acquired in the special conditions of his country of

4. Most of the translation of the passage from al-Qazwīnī is literal. Some of the sentences are paraphrased. I found this combination unavoidable.

origin. As we learn from our passage, at that age not only could he already stand on his own feet, but also use the bow, i.e. the weapon which was the essential one both in his homeland and in the elite army of his future adoptive country.

The evidence quoted in passage I furnishes, perhaps, an additional reason for the preference of pagans over monotheists for recruitment as Mamlūks. But this point needs a preliminary explanation, which we shall open with a third passage, from the tenth century geographical work of al-Iṣṭakhrī.

Passage III

Text

Wa-alladhī yaqaʿ min raqīq al-Khazar hum ahl al-awthān alladhīna yastajīzūna bayʿ awlādihim wa-istirqāq baʿḍihim baʿḍan fa-ammā al-yahūd minhum wal-naṣārā fa-innahā tadīn bi-taḥrīm istirqāq baʿḍihim baʿḍan mithla al-muslimīn[5].

Translation

The Khazar slaves who arrive [in the lands of Islam] are from those of them who are pagans, and who deem it permissible to sell their children and enslave each other [within their own people]. As for the Jews amongst them and the Christians, these consider unlawful the enslavement of each other, like the Muslims[6].

This evidence of the relatively early source al-Isṭakhrī is a very revealing one, but it reflects only one side of the coin. Its other side is that a Mamlūk who was born into and grew up in a monotheistic environment (to all intents and purposes : a Christian one) is not at all the ideal muslim choice, because his religious past, in which antagonism to Islam played a no mean part, could not be wiped out so easily and so thoroughly as that of a Mamluk of pagan origin. His unwavering faithfulness to his new religion would, therefore, be quite uncertain. The problem of faithfulness would become particularly acute when the Mamlūk would have to fight his own ex-coreligionists[7]. That

---

5. Al-Iṣṭakhrī, *al-Masālik wal-Mamālik*, Leiden, 1927, p. 223, ll. 11-15.

6. This highly significant passage from al-Iṣṭakhrī had already been reproduced and translated by me in : Aspects of the Mamluk Phenomenon, part A, *Der Islam*, Berlin, 1976, at the end of that article (pp. 224-225). But it was brought there in a different context, and was neither discussed nor analyzed.

7. According to the accepted standards of those times the Turks and their likes were considered to be better soldiers than those Christians from amongst whom most of the Mamlūks of monotheistic origin were recruited. Whether those standards were the correct ones, wholly or partly, is another matter.

is how things had to be considered from the *Muslim* standpoint. From the *Christian* standpoint the fact that at the age of puberty the relations between parents and children, especially in more advanced centres of civilization, was, on the whole, so fundamentally different from those prevailing in the pagan steppe, could only intensify their already existent strong reluctance to part with their children.

The above statements necessitate some additional explanation. There *were* Mamlūks of Christian origin in the armies of Islam, and their number grew steadily. The main reason was that the pagan reservoir of Turkish peoples and their like, gradually diminished, chiefly, though not solely, because of the Islamization of those peoples[8], and, as Muslims, they could not be enslaved[9]. Another reason, almost as important, was the geographical proximity or remoteness of the various Muslim rulers from the sources of Mamlūk supply, and the obvious clash of interests between those rulers in their competition to acquire the best Mamlūks. The Turks, for example, were considered as superior to the Ṣaqāliba as far as military qualities are concerned. It is, therefore, no mere accident that the Ṣaqāliba constituted such important military element in remote Spain, and (to a lesser extent) the Maghrib, whereas in the Eastern part of the lands of Islam they serve almost exclusively as eunuchs[10]. Muslim rulers in the East recruited Christian Mamlūks because they had easier access to their countries of origin, or because stronger rulers, or rulers better situated geographically, did not permit them to recruit Turks. A Mamlūk private army, even if it consisted of military elements which were not classified as first rate according to the criteria of those times, was considered far superior to any other kind of army. This state of things is highlighted by the following instance. The Saljūq sultan

---

8. Other causes were internal wars in the steppe, or attacks on it by outsiders ; the depletion and deterioration of the human material, as a result of the constant departure to "the Abode of Islam" of numerous young males and females constituting the flower of their age group ; the emigration of whole tribes from their original homeland to other places, including the Muslim countries. The regions lying beyond those depleted areas were less accessible and did not always contain the needed proper stuff for the formation of a Mamlūk.

9. There was, in addition, the gradually decreasing inclination of the family or tribe to be separated from their youngsters. On this see also below.

10. The study of the ethnic composition of the Ṣaqāliba went absolutely astray because of R. Dozy. Not only did he totally misinterpret a passage in the geographical work of Ibn Ḥawqal, but he also presented it in a shockingly mutilated form. A host of Islamists, amongst them most eminent ones, accepted, for well over a century, both his misleading translation and the theory which he formed around it. I have alluded to Dozy's erroneous interpretation in Aspects, etc., B, p. 224 (1976), and proved its absolute wrongness in "Remarks on the Ṣaqāliba within *Dār al-Islām*" (*Jerusalem Studies in Arabic and Islam*, vol. I, 1979, pp. 92-124) which forms part of my article "On the Eunuchs in Islam". There I also discuss various other aspects of the Ṣaqāliba. Although this term still remains ambiguous, one thing is certain. In the Islamic East the Ṣaqāliba as non castrated soldiers constituted a minor factor. There are contradicting views about their prowess, some of which I bring in that article. The evidence about the prowess of the Turks is incomparably richer. The process of the adoption of Christianity by the Ṣaqāliba necessitates further investigation.

did not permit Caliph al-Muqtafī (530-555/1136-1160) to buy Turkish Mamlūks, so he recruited Greek and Armenian Mamlūks during the lifetime of that Sultan. Other kinds of army which that Caliph had or wanted to have are not even mentioned, and this is one instance out of many[11]. The Ottomans recruited their slave army mainly from amongst the Christians of their realm, and in glaring violation of the *sharī'a*, because of the Islamization of the south Russian steppe in their neighbourhood and because they wanted to eliminate one of the main drawbacks of the Mamlūk system : dependence on a source of supply on which they had no control.

In addition to the above clarification concerning monotheism versus paganism in the Mamlūk countries of origin, the following modification has to be made. In those countries of origin where monotheism existed, or even became prevalent, it did not have a uniform strength. Its strength depended on various factors : the degree of civilization in those countries ; the recentness or otherwise of the penetration of monotheism into each of them, and the extent of its spread. There must have transpired quite a long period between the beginning of the penetration of a monotheistic religion until its firm establishment down to the bottom of the social ladder. Even then many pagan practices will remain, especially in primitive and marginal areas, as so many of those countries had actually been. For this we have numerous examples, up to the present day. The practice of selling children by their parents and relatives or by the chieftains of their tribes and by the ruler of the region would certainly not stop overnight. This is true even of countries which adopted Islam[12]. A case in point is that of the lands of the Golden Horde. As is well known, these lands had been for a long time the major source of Mamlūks for the Mamlūk Sultanate. At the same time their population, including its various nomad elements, underwent a process of Islamization. There cannot be any doubt that all those involved in the slave trade, be they the sellers or the buyers, were not too strict, for quite a long time, in distinguishing between the pagan boys and the boys already converted to Islam and in avoiding the enslavement of the new converts. Slavery was too profitable to all parties concerned, including the young slaves themselves[13].

Yet, in spite of all that, the spread of monotheism in the Mamlūks' countries of origin, made their recruitment there far more difficult and

---

11. I am discussing this subject in considerable detail in a study on the transition from the Ayyūbid to the Mamlūk reign, of some parts of which a very brief summary is given in a forthcoming issue of *REI*.

12. The enslavement of Muslims in countries where Islam had been the dominant religion for many generations is not discussed here. This important subject deserves a special study.

13. There are quite a few instances of persons belonging to veteran Muslim families, within the old boundaries of *Dār al-Islām*, who penetrated, or tried to penetrate, the Mamlūk aristocracy under false pretences, because it conferred on its members so many advantages. The temptation to do the same among new converts to Islam must have been much greater.

problematic. Ultimately it proved to be a quite formidable, though not absolute, barrier against enslavement.

Passage no. II reveals a factor of the highest importance, which, I have to admit, never came to my mind before reading it[14]. The Mamlūks had to be imported at the tender age of puberty not only because that had been the ideal age both from the point of view of the sellers and the buyers, but also for the most simple and the most obvious reason : importing adult Mamlūks in great numbers, constantly and over a long period, in ordinary caravans and under peaceful conditions, was absolutely impossible. This means that building a permanent, large-scale Mamlūk institution, based on the importation of adult slaves was doomed to failure from the very outset, because of that reason alone. Let me explain that assertion.

The Muslim campaigns into "the Abode of War" brought numerous slave-captives from that "Abode" into the lands of Islam. The influx of those captives had a major share in building up the slave institution, including its Mamlūk part. However, the constant and uninterrupted supply of numerous Mamlūks for maintaining and enlarging the Mamlūk armies could be guaranteed not by means of irregular wars, but by means of a very regular commerce, namely, by means of the ordinary caravans, plying their way back and forth between the two "Abodes". And that is what actually took place. The Mamlūks were brought over in this kind of caravans, which carried a whole variety of other imported commodities. The slave dealers in those caravans — not to mention the other merchants — usually did not confine themselves to the importation of Mamlūks alone.

Now the transportation of many captives by an expeditionary force posed no problem. The soldiers, who were numerous, and who, in addition, did not have to protect any kind of merchandise, could take care of the unarmed captives, whatever their numbers. With a commercial caravan the story was completely different. Though there certainly were caravans protected, for particular reasons, by strong military forces, this could not have been usually the case. A considerable number of adult Mamlūks distinguished by their superb military qualities would have had many opportunities to overcome the caravan and rob it, or at the very least, to cause much trouble to the guards. This would have been unwelcome to all participants in the caravan, particularly to the merchants who had no Mamlūks in their possession. These merchants would be very reluctant to join again a caravan carrying Mamlūks of this kind[15].

---

14. The degree of the accuracy of al-Qazwīnī's account is not important. What can be deduced from it, however, is both obvious and of the highest significance.

15. Transportation of adult Mamlūks by sea might have caused less difficulty than by land. However, there hardly existed a pure sea route in the case of this particular commodity. Before embarkation and after disembarkation the Mamlūks had to be carried on land, quite often over long distances. Besides, the ship's crews and the merchants, be they Franks or Muslims, would be much more at ease with adolescent children than with grown up men.

By contrast, Mamlūks of tender age constituted no danger to the caravan. They were very much dependent on the slave-dealer and clung to him [16]. They were grateful to him up to the end of their lives. The instance of the Khwārizm caravan is an excellent illustration for the impracticality of building a great and permanent slave army based on adult Mamlūks, even if only the problem of their transportation to "the Abode of Islam" is taken into account [17].

---

16. The adolescent Mamlūks were, indeed, more independent in various ways than their counterparts in the more civilized countries. But when they were uprooted from their natural environment they became completely dependent on those who carried them away from home, especially the slave dealers.

17. Adult Mamlūks were often imported in certain quantities into the Muslim countries, and part of them joined the military aristocracy. But this was, on the whole, a marginal and transitory phenomenon. I have alluded to the damage caused to the Mamlūk institution by that practice on several occasions.

VI

MAMLŪK MILITARY ARISTOCRACY – A NON-HEREDITARY NOBILITY

To M.J. Kister
On the occasion of his seventieth birthday

As I have repeatedly emphasized in earlier studies on the Mamlūk institution, that institution has no parallel worthy of its name outside Muslim civilization.[1] Of its very specific characteristics, one of the most important is that Mamlūk aristocracy was confined to a single generation only, which means that the sons of the Mamlūks could not belong to that aristocracy. Without that particular feature all its other characteristics would have been of little value, and the formidable Mamlūk military might would have disappeared quite quickly. This would have certainly changed the whole course of Islamic history, by affecting most negatively both its power of expansion and its ability to resist the onslaught of external enemies.

The obvious question which poses itself in connection with such a unique aristocracy, based on the principle of non-heredity, is how that aristocracy came into being, survived and flourished for so long, when the said principle is so decidedly contradictory to human nature?

Before answering that question an important qualification should be made: human nature did have its very weighty share in shaping the various Mamlūk societies in the diverse parts of the Muslim world. The outcome was different kinds of compromises between it and the principle of non-heredity. Furthermore, it did happen that as a result of the clash between the hereditary interests of the individual Mamlūk and the said principle, the Mamlūk system was greatly transformed or might have even crumbled.

[1] See especially: *L'Esclavage du Mamelouk*, Jerusalem, 1951, pp. I-V; "The Muslim City and the Mamluk Military Aristocracy", *Proceedings of the Israel Academy of Sciences and Humanities*, II, Jerusalem, 1968, pp. 311ff.; "Preliminary Remarks on the Mamluk Military Institution in Islam", *War, Technology and Society in the Middle East*, London, 1975, pp. 48ff.; "Aspects of the Mamlūk Phenomenon: The Importance of the Mamlūk Phenomenon in Islam", *Der Islam*, 1976, pp. 196ff.; "A First Attempt to Evaluate the Mamlūk Military System", *JSAI*, II (1980), pp. 321-349.

However, after having made that essential qualification, and having emphasized the impact of hereditary trends on the structure and functioning of Mamlūk society, it still remains true that the principle of non-heredity loomed large and was decisive throughout its history. Therefore, the question posed here loses nothing of its pertinence.

The answer which I can give at present is both partial and tentative.[2] Our knowledge of the creation and development of Mamlūk societies before the formation of the Mamlūk Sultanate is, with but few exceptions, very fragmentary. We cannot follow yet in any systematic way the inescapable changes which those societies underwent as well as the process of their crystalization. In all probability non-heredity suffered many setbacks before it could establish itself with comparative firmness, thus prolonging Mamlūk aristocracy's existence for many centuries. We have no choice but to skip the formative period of Mamlūk society and confine ourselves to the stage of its relative maturity. We shall therefore have mainly to explain how it managed to preserve itself during that advanced stage of its development.

Before starting, however, with our explanation several background remarks are needed. First of all, the Mamlūk institution, although unique in its character, constitutes an inseparable part of the Muslim slave institution. The person to whom the Muslim slave owed allegiance and loyalty was the patron by whom he had been manumitted. That kind of allegiance was expressed in the famous phrase "allegiance goes to the manumitter" (*al-walā', li-man a'taq*).[3] The freedman was bound by that allegiance for life, even when the manumitting patron died before him. It is very significant that the term *mawlā* has two opposite meanings which complement each other so nicely: the freedman and his manumitter. As I have already stated on numerous occasions, the relations between the Mamlūk and his manumitting patron were analogous to those existing between father and son, and the relations between the Mamlūk and his colleagues in servitude and manumission under the same patron were similar to the ones which are common among brothers. And, indeed, a considerable part of the

2 Although I have mentioned very often the non-hereditary character of Mamlūk society, I never tried to explain that phenomenon. I am offering the following tentative and preliminary explanation for the first time. An explanation of this particular and central aspect of Mamlūk society by somebody else is unknown to me, but I may be mistaken.

3 See R. Brunschvig's excellent article *ʿAbd* in *EI*². At this stage I shall not speak about military slaves who rose to high positions without being enfranchised.

ogy: "son" (*walad* or *ibn*), "father" (*wālid* or *ab*), "brother" and "brothers" terminology marking those relations is identical with the family terminol- (*akh*, *ikhwa*), "family" or "clan" (*bayt*, *ᶜā'ila*). A Mamlūk who did not belong to the specific Mamlūk "family" was considered by that "family" as "foreigner" or "stranger" (*gharīb*, *ajnabī*). This implies that once a certain Mamlūk had been freed by patron X, he could never become a real member of the "family" of the freedmen of patron Y; and if, for whatever reason, he became affiliated to that "family", he always remained, up to his very death, an "outsider".[4]

We shall turn now to our partial and tentative answer or explanation. Every Mamlūk, be he a high commander or a simple soldier, belonged to two circles, which controlled his actions in the most decisive way: the big circle, namely, the whole Mamlūk aristocracy; and the small circle, namely, his Mamlūk "family". And when I say his Mamlūk "family", I do not mean only his "father" and "brothers", but also the "sons" (i.e. the Mamlūks) of the selfsame Mamlūk, as well as his "uncles" (i.e. the colleagues in servitude and manumission of his patron, in case that patron had been a Mamlūk), and sometimes even his "grandfather" (his patron's patron) and the "brothers" of his "grandfather". For the purpose of carrying out any plan beneficial to himself[4a] the Mamlūk would have to mobilize first of all the support of the small circle, or of important elements of it. He might succeed or fail in accordance with the degree of help he received or of the opposition he raised in both circles. If he tried, however, to implement heredity in his own biological family he would meet with the prompt and most resolute opposition from both circles. What would have been sufficient to nip his attempt in the bud is the certain opposition of the small circle alone.

This statement needs clarification, but before offering it I have to mention two terms. Although terminology analogous to the one pertaining to a biological family is very common in connection with Mamlūk ties, the most common terms are: *ustādh* for the purchasing and manumitting

[4] *Esclavage etc*., pp. 27-37; "Studies on the Structure of the Mamluk Army", part I, *BSOAS*, XV (1953), pp. 203-228; "Studies in al-Jabartī, I: Notes on the Transformation of Mamlūk Society in Egypt under the Ottomans", *JESHO*, vol. III (1960), pp. 158-174, 275-299.

[4a] I mean, of course, any kind of plan which does not involve the transfer of the Mamlūk's basic socio-military privileges and attainments to his offspring. It is true that, as far as the Mamlūk Sultanate is concerned, instances of sons of Mamlūks who rose to high ranks and acquired great power are mentioned in the sources. But these were not very numerous and did not change the general picture. I deal with them in other studies of mine.

patron, and *khushdāshiyya* (sing. *khushdāsh*) for the colleagues in slavery and manumission of the same patron.[5]

Now we come to the clarification: The small circle as a whole, on all its components, would stand up against any intention of a Mamlūk to hand down to his offspring anything which might have seriously jeopardized the non-hereditary principle on which Mamlūk society was based, because discarding that principle, or even thoroughly shaking it, would have spelt the end of that society.[6] Such an intention would have been opposed by the Mamlūk's Mamlūks; by his *khushdāshiyya*; by his *ustādh*; by the *khushdāshiyya* of the *ustādh* (irrespective of whether that *ustādh was* still alive or dead); by the *ustadh* of the *ustādh* and by the *khushdāshiyya* of the *ustādh* of the *ustādh*, as far as that "grandparent" and his "brothers" were still alive. Even the possibility that our Mamlūk would have been opposed by the Mamlūks of his own Mamlūks, i.e. by his "grandsons", should not be completely excluded. That opposition would have resulted not only from the danger of the ultimate extinction of that particular Mamlūk society, but also — and to a no lesser degree — from the fact that the immediate self interest of each Mamlūk who did not benefit from the inheritance would have been gravely affected to this or that degree. This means that those very elements who were usually expected to support a member of their "family" when he wanted to have something which was acceptable by Mamlūk standards, would, in this case, unite against him. The intervention of the big circle, whose interests concerning heredity were identical with those of the smaller circle, might well have been unnecessary.

The character and circumstances of the Muslim biological family constituted also, in my view, a very important factor in strengthening and perpetuating the Mamluk society. The fact that a Muslim man could have four wives at a time and divorce them easily; and on top of that could own an unlimited number of concubines, must have affected that society in the following way. A Mamlūk who reached a certain socio-military status, which was usually accompanied by a fair income and property, had quite often a considerable number of children from different mothers who, because of their contradictory interests, neutralized each other. Many a

5 See the reference in note 4.

6 For the circumvention of the non-hereditary principle in the domain of the inheritance of considerable properties by means of the *waqf* institution, see "The Muslim City, etc.", p. 327. There existed other kinds of circumventions as well, which deserve a special study. All these, however, did not seriously endanger Mamlūk society.

time those competing mothers had to ask the Mamlūks of their husband for help in furthering their own and their children's interests against each other. This in itself gave the Mamlūks immense influence. But this was by no means their only source of power. The Mamlūks of a certain patron had the great advantage of having all of them the same sole "parent" and of being absolutely "motherless". Their usually anonymous biological parents were far (sometimes thousands of miles) away, and did not exist as a factor of influence. The allegiance and loyalty of those Mamlūks was directed towards one person only: their "father", who did not have to share it with anybody else. In this important respect the Mamlūk "family" was much more united and compact than the biological family of their patron and, therefore, could usually push and foster its own interests, at the expense of their master's real family, which was often beset by contradictory tendencies concerning the inheritance of that family's head.

In the formation and crystalization of the non-hereditary Mamlūk aristocracy there was one outstanding exception, which was of first ranking importance. The ruler of a Muslim empire, or state or province, if he himself had been a Mamlūk, or of Mamlūk origin, would establish a dynasty.[7] This phenomenon was repeated time and time again in the history of Medieval Islam. Most probably it was the example of the hereditary Caliphate which was followed by the various Muslim rulers, be they non-Mamlūks or Mamlūks. Thus the phenomenon with which we have to deal, at least in the lands of Medieval Islam, is a hereditary ruler, belonging to a dynasty, served by a non-hereditary Mamlūk aristocracy as the nucleus of his military power. Even the sultans of the Mamlūk Sultanate should not be totally excluded from that formula or pattern. The so-called non-hereditary office of the Sultan under the Mamlūks was not a thing which had been planned in any way. It just came about; and it does not apply to the whole Mamlūk reign. A Mamlūk succeeding (or almost succeeding) another Mamlūk on the Sultan's throne is a thing which occurred only in the few early decades of the Mamlūk reign, and during most of the Circassian period. In between there was the Qalā'ūnid dynasty,

7 In most cases it was the provincial governor, usually (though not always) appointed by the Caliph, or one of his descendants, who became an independent ruler, and created a dynasty. The process of independence was ordinarily gradual. In this respect there was no difference between a Mamlūk or non-Mamlūk ruler. I am dealing with the dynastic principle in the Mamlūk Sultanate from a rather different angle in "From Ayūbids to Mamlūks" (*REI*, in the press).

which lasted considerably longer than the preceding non-Mamlūk Ayyūbid dynasty, if the brief interruptions in its rule are ignored, and more or less during a similar period if those interruptions are taken into account. That dynasty was replaced under very special circumstances of ethnic upheaval and transformation, and was succeeded by a Circassian dynasty, which lasted for about 30 years, with a short gap, which was filled by a Sultan belonging to the older Qalā'ūnid dynasty.

Even about the two periods of Mamlūk rule, in which the Sultan's office might be considered (only to a certain extent!) as non-hereditary, the following most instructive qualification should be made. Almost all those pure Mamlūks who became Sultans appointed their sons as their heirs, and in most cases those heirs did ascend the throne, which they usually occupied for short periods. It was quite rare that a pure Mamlūk would follow another pure Mamlūk in immediate succession on the Sultan's throne. Furthermore, throughout the history of the Mamlūk Sultanate there is not the slightest mention of the non-hereditary character of the Sultan's office, or of the intention of turning it into such. Only very late in the Circassian period one single historian (Ibn Taghrībirdī) laments the fact that the reigning Sultan appoints his son as his successor, knowing full well that he would be deposed after a short period.[8]

The same applies to the "slave kings" of the Sultanate of Dihlī in India (602-686/1206-1287), which was ruled for more than eighty years by Mamlūk dynasties. That of Iltermish lasted for about fifty five years, and was preceded and succeeded by two other Mamlūk dynasties.

[8] "The Circassians in the Mamluk Kingdom", *JAOS*, 69 (1949), p. 139, note 32. For the gradual erosion of dynasticism in connection with the Sultan's office, see *ibid.*, pp. 145b-146a. Some of my statements there should be somewhat mitigated.

VII

The Auxiliary Forces of the Mamluk Sultanate*

The regular Mamluk army was frequently assisted in its wars and campaigns by irregular forces, both cavalry and infantry. In times of peace this kind of forces was charged with guard duties in certain regions, including some of the coastal areas; with the protection of the Royal postal system (*barīd*), and, quite often, with the supply of relay horses to it, etc.[1]) The most important of all these auxiliary armies were the Turcoman tribesmen. Approaching them in military status were the Kurds; but the Kurds, who were so important in the Ayyūbid period, declined steadily under the Mamluks. In the early Turkish-Qipchaqi period (wrongly called "Baḥrī") they are still noticeable, but in the later Circassian period (wrongly called

---

*) This chapter of my work on the Mamluk army and military society had been written many years ago (1945). Since I shall not be able, in the foreseeable future, to develop it as thoroughly as it deserves and as I would like to, I decided to translate it from the Hebrew original more or less as it is. The only updating is the reference to a good number of relevant conclusions, to which I arrived in some other, published and yet unpublished, studies of mine. The main theme of the present study is the auxiliary forces as part of the whole Mamluk army; the relations between the regular and the auxiliary elements of that army; and the auxiliaries as an asset or a liability in the Mamluk military machine. I do not think that I have to change anything substantial relating to these subjects. Furthermore, this paper is an essential complement to "Studies on the Structure of the Mamluk Army", published in *BSOAS*, XV (1953), pp. 203–228, 448–476, and XVI (1954), pp. 57–90; and it is preferable that both will be written by the same person. Data included here on the nomads of the Mamluk Sultanate, which are not confined to the theme under discussion, are certainly meager and inadequate. They might, however, be of some use to those who do or will study those nomads in a wider context, a task which is badly needed.

[1]) Various aspects of the auxiliary forces are dealt with in other chapters of my work, some of them yet unpublished. A brief summary of those aspects is given in the Appendix to this study. The Appendix contains also a brief allusion to two corrected conclusions of mine.

"Burjī")[2]) they cease almost completely to constitute a military power of any weight. As for the beduins (and semi-beduins), it is mainly those of Syria and Palestine who are intended, as far as taking part in the major wars of the Mamluks is concerned. These tribesmen lived in or near the areas where those wars took place. It was, therefore, much easier to mobilize them for battle, than do the same with the tribes of Lower Egypt, let alone those of Upper Egypt.[3]) The fact that the beduins of the country of the Nile lived near the main body of the Mamluk military power was for them a source of strength, but also a source of great suffering (see below).

Needless to say that in the category under discussion only tribes obeying the central power and cooperating with it are included.[4]) The Turcomans answering that definition were called *Turkmān al-Ṭāʿa.*[5]) This was their ususal name. Sometimes they were designated *al-Turkmān al-Ṭāʾiʿa*[6]) or *al-Ṭāʾiʿīn.*[7]) The loyal beduins were called *ʿArab* (or *ʿUrbān*) *al-Ṭāʿa.*[8])

[2]) It is high time that the misnomers "Baḥrī" and "Burjī" as denoting respectively the earlier and later Mamluk reigns, should be discarded. They are totally inadequate names given to these two reigns by Orientalists, and have hardly any foundation in the sources. I have already stressed that fact in each of my two articles on the Baḥriyya and Burjiyya regiments in *EI*². I am dealing in greater detail with the inadequacy of these two terms in the fuller version of my short study of the Burjiyya regiment which is now in preparation.

[3]) I have already discussed the military advantages of the inhabitants of Syria, where I did not confine myself to the nomads alone. See: The Muslim City and the Mamluk Military Aristocracy, *Proceedings of the Israel Academy of Sciences and Humanities*, II, Jerusalem, 1968, pp. 328–329; Egypt as a Dominant Factor in Syria and Palestine during the Islamic Period, *Egypt and Palestine — A Millenium of Association (868–1948)*, Jerusalem, 1984, pp. 34–35. The military power of the Syrian towndwellers and their contribution to the Mamluk war machine, especially in siege warfare, deserves a special and very detailed study.

[4]) Obedience and cooperation could be, and actually were not so rarely, quite temporary.

[5]) Ibn Taghrībirdī, *al-Nujūm al-Zāhira* (ed. Popper), Leiden 1909 and onwards, vol. V, p. 548, l. 12; VI, pp. 210, l. 7, 732, l. 10; VII, pp. 96, l. 1, 7, 706, l. 6; *Ḥawādith al-Duhūr*, pp. 292, l. 13, 293, l. 9, 427, l. 4, 500, ll. 16–17, 607; l. 20, 635, ll. 6–7; Ibn Taghrībirdī, *al-Manhal al-Ṣāfī* (B.N. MS Arab, Nos. 2068–2072), vol. II, fol. 14b, l. 11 al-Sakhāwī, *al-Tibr al-Masbūk*, Cairo, 1896, p. 323, l. 12.

[6]) Ibn al-Furāt, *Taʾrīkh al-Duwal wal-Mulūk*, Beirut, 1936–1942, Vol. IX, p. 50, l. 8.

[7]) Idem, p. 405, l. 14.

[8]) Al-Maqrīzī, *Kitāb al-Sulūk*, Cairo, 1934 and onwards, vol. I, p. 92, l. 9; II, 408, ll. 1–2; Ibn Kathīr, *al-Bidāya wal-Nihāya*, Cairo, 1351–8 H, vol. XIV, p. 272, l. 26; *Ḥawādith*, pp. 190, l. 2, 431, l. 23; *Nujūm* (Popper), VII, pp. 84, ll. 10–11, 711, ll. 3–7; *Tibr*, p. 389, l. 15.

Disobedient tribes were named *al-ʿĀṣiya* or *al-ʿUṣāt*. Other kinds of auxiliary forces will be discussed at the end of the present paper.

The Turcomans

The Turcomans were usually called in the Mamluk sources *Turkmān*. But quite often they were named *Tarākmīn*[9]) or *Tarākima*.[10]) I came across *Tarākimiyya*[11]) only once.

The Turcomans were entrusted with a very important military task already during the early part of the reign of Sultan Baybars I (658–676/1260–1272), when considerable parts of the Syro-Palestinian coast were still dominated by the Crusaders. That sultan settled Turcomans in the coastal area to protect it from Crusader incursions.[12]) In 661/1263 the Sultan took care of the affairs of the Turcomans, bestowed robes of honour on their amirs and on the amirs of ʿUrbān al-ʿĀbid, Jarm and Thaʿlaba, charged them with guarding the country; taking care of their own equipment (*al-qiyām bil-ʿidād*); serving the *barīd* network and supplying horses to the Royal stables.[13]) Turcoman and Kurdish tribesmen served as military settlers in all parts of Syria, Palestine and the Lebanon.[14]) At the beginning of the 7th/14th century Turcomans are settled in Kisrawān, in Northern Lebanon, instead of the local inhabitants, who had been exiled from their homeland because they attacked the retreating army of Sultan al-Nāṣir Muḥammad b. Qalāūn after its defeat by Īlkhān Ghāzān (699/

---

[9]) Abū al-Fidāʾ, *Kitāb al-Mukhtaṣar*, Cairo, 1325H, vol. IV, pp. 27, l. 21, 82, l. 8; *Sulūk*, I, p. 931, l. 8; II, p. 428 and note 6; *Nujūm* (Popper), VI, pp. 127, l. 7, 185, l. 19, 186, l. 2, 187, l. 10, 331, l. 21; VII, p. 262, l. 3; *Ḥawādith*, p. 549, l. 18; *Manhal*, II, fol. 10a, l. 10; III, fol. 136b, l. 11; VIII, fol. 467a, l. 7; al-Qalqashandī, *Ṣubḥ al-Aʿshā*, Cairo, 1913–1919, vol. XIII, p. 37, l. 101; Abū al-Fidāʾ, *Taqwīm al-Buldān*, Paris, 1840, p. 29.

[10]) Ibn Iyās, *Badāʾiʿ al-Zuhūr*, Cairo, 1311–1312H, vol. II, p. 19, l. 14; Ibn ʿArabshāh, *Akhbār Tīmūr*, p. 53, l. 8.

[11]) Ibn Iyās, *Badāʾiʿ al-Zuhūr*, ed. Kahle-Mustafa, Istanbul, 1931–6, vol. III, p. 170, l. 1.

[12]) *Sulūk* (Quatremère's translation), Paris, 1837–1844, vol. I, part II, p. 51; *Ṣubḥ*, XII, p. 218, l. 16; A. N. Poliak, *Feudalism in Egypt, Syria, Palestine and the Lebanon*, London, 1939, p. 9. Certain aspects of the Turcomans and beduins in the Mamluk Sultanate are discussed in that book.

[13]) *Sulūk*, I, p. 481, ll. 9–11.

[14]) Ibn Iyās, I, p. 105; *Ṣubḥ*, III, p. 182; VII, pp. 190, 282; XII, p. 218; *Nujūm* (Popper), VI, p. 364; Ibn al-Shiḥna, *al-Durr al-Muntakhab*, Beirut, 1909, pp. 228, 264; Ṣāliḥ b. Yaḥyā, *Taʾrīkh Bayrūt*, Beirut, 1927, pp. 107, 182.

1299).[15]) The task of these Turcomans was to guard the coastal strip up to the boundaries of the province of Tripoli.[16]) Thenceforward these Turcomans were called *Turkmān Kisrawān*. The Turcomans inhabiting the coastal area, who were called *al-Tarākmīn alladhīna min ʿaskar al-sāḥil*, were sent to fight as far as the northern end of the coast of the Mamluk sultanate.[17]) According to one isolated evidence, however, it was in the reign of Sultan Baybars I, that a substantial part of the Turcomans had to leave the Mamluk sultanate as a result of the following developments: When the Tatars entered Northern Syria under the command of Īlkhān Hūlākū *all* the Turcomans had to run away to the coastal area. Their tribes got together in the neighbourhood of Safed (*kāna al-Turkmān . . . kulluhum qad ajfalū ilā al-sāḥil wa-ijtamaʿat aḥyāʾuhum bil-Jūkān qarīban min Ṣafad*). In a fight between them and the Franks of Safed, which, according to our source, the Franks initiated, the Turcomans had the upper hand, captured some of their leaders and released them for ransom. The Turcomans feared, however, that Sultan Baybars would take retaliatory measures against them, because of the treaty of peace he had with the people of Jaffa, Beirut and Safed, which had also been ratified by the king of France. They decided, therefore, to find refuge in Byzantine territory (*Bilād al-Rūm*), "and Syria became emptied of them" (*wa-aqfara al-Shām minhum*).[18]) I found this piece of information only in the chronicle of Ibn Khaldūn, and it is impossible to decide whether this emigration affected in any appreciable way the numerical strenght of the Turcomans in the sultanate, even in the short run. In the long run its impact seems to have been quite negligible.

The Turcomans always occupied the most important place among the auxiliary forces, and the Mamluk sultans made their best, as far as circumstances allowed, to treat them with the greatest consideration. During the Turkish-Qipchāqī period there existed, in addition, the factor of (a real or supposed) close ethnical kinship between them and the dominant element in the Mamluk ruling class. In an official decree from the reign of al-Nāṣir Muḥammad b. Qalāūn, which exempts the Turcomans from paying taxes, it is stated that they are "pure Qipchāqī" (*al-Qafjāq al-Khullaṣ*).[19]) The Mamluk sources preserved orders exempting the Turcomans from tax payment,

---

[15]) Al-Dhahabī, *Duwal al-Islām*, Hyderabad, 1337H, vol. II, p. 164, ll. 2–3; *Taʾrīkh Bayrūt*, pp. 29–30, 169, ll. 3–6, 197, l. 3, 198, l. 1.

[16]) *Taʾrīkh Bayrūt*, pp. 33, 37, 42, 169.

[17]) Abū al-Fidāʾ, IV, p. 88, ll. 14–15.

[18]) Ibn Khaldūn, *Kitāb al-ʿIbar*, Cairo, 1284H, vol. V, pp. 383, l. 24–384, l. 2.

[19]) Ibn Faḍl Allāh al-ʿUmarī, *al-Taʿrīf fī al-Muṣṭalaḥ al-Sharīf*, Cairo, 1312H, p. 113, ll. 4–5. The same decree is found also in al-Qalqashandī's *Ṣubḥ al-Aʿshā*.

or reducing them considerably, in recognition of their military prowess.[20]) They derived their strength and their relatively great independence from other factors as well: Their overwhelming majority inhabited the northern part of the realm, and it was extremely difficult, nay, almost impossible, to control them from remote Cairo, where the *élite* of the Mamluk units was permanently stationed. Moreover, the region in which the Turcomans were either predominant, or formed a very important element, stretched contiguously far beyond the northern boundaries of the Mamluk sultanate: to its north-west, north and north-east. The Turcomans within the sultanate could easily threaten to cooperate with their brethren beyond the border against the Mamluks and carry out that threat. There is no better proof to the particularly strong power enjoyed by the Turcomans than the extremely bloody wars which the Mamluks had been forced to wage against Shāh Siwār who had been supported by the Ottomans. These wars cost the Mamluks very dearly and greatly contributed to the decline of the sultanate's prestige among its neighbours. They also constituted a direct preliminary to the wars against the Ottomans, which ended with the annihilation of the Mamluk empire.[21])

The power of the Turcomans in northern Syria reached formidable dimensions already in the last decades of the 8th/14th century. It has been considerably increaased in the early 9th/15th century, as a result of the internal conflicts in the Mamluk society (which led, *inter alia*, to the replacement of the Qipchāqīs by the Circassians), and of the attack of Timurlank. Acording to al-Qalqashandī, the Turcomans and the Kurds[22]) became the dominant factor in the greatest part of the Aleppo region following the Timurid wars, until Sultan al-Mu'ayyad Shaykh (815–824/1412–1421) attacked and defeated them.[23]) The Turcomans, however, recovered very quickly from their defeat, and thenceforward the northern areas of Mamluk Syria became more and more unruly. Sultan Barsbāy's (825–842/1422–1438) failure in 836/1433 to capture Āmid from the Turcoman Qarā Yuluk

---

[20]) *Ṣubḥ*, XIII, p. 37, ll. 2–5, 10–16; Sulūk, II, p. 483, ll. 12–17.

[21]) In spite of the decline of the Mamluk Sultanate both economically and militarily, it is extremely doubtful whether the Ottomans could have beaten them at all in the field of battle, without their absolute preponderance in firearms, and especially in the use of the handgun. They certainly would not have been able to route them with such swiftness. See my *Gunpowder and Firearms in the Mamluk Kingdom*, London, 1956 (reprinted 1978), especially pp. 108–111.

[22]) I did not find any evidence of a noticeable and continuous strengthening of the Kurdish element in that region in the period mentioned by al-Qalqashandī. They certainly did not play then a very significant role.

[23]) Al-Qalqashandī, *Ḍaw' al-Ṣubḥ*, Cairo, 1966, p. 300, l. 18–22.

considerably increased the power and independence of the Turcomans in that region.[24]) Long before that date Turcomans were appointed as governors in northern fortresses.[25]) The country inhabited by the Turcomans also served as a place of refuge for Mamluks of Turcoman origin, who were out of favour with the central government.[26]) In the struggle for power between Sultan Barqūq and the Mamluk amir of Turcoman origin, Minṭāsh, the Turcomans constituted a mainstay of that amir's power. They formed a substantial part of his army when he marched to Cairo.[27]) Sultan Jaqmaq (842–857/1438–1453) maintained excellent relations with the Turcomans, very probably as a result of the failure of his predecessor, Barsbāy, in his campaign against them. Consequently, "his reign was quiet, without wars and without military expeditions". He bestowed on their amirs many gifts, and even intermarried with them. "That is why they obeyed him throughout his reign". He used to claim that all the money he had spent on the Turcomans and their leaders would not have been sufficient to cover even the expenditure on horse-shoes for his cavalry, had he been constrained to fight them.[28]) Now, this might work as a short-term policy. In the long run, however, such a handling of the Turcoman problem could only weaken the Mamluks' hold on their northern province, as it really did. A noteworthy manifestation of the "Turkmanization" of northern Syria is to be found in the evidence of a contemporary eyewitness from the reign of Qā'itbāy in the second half of the 9th/15th century, according to which the dominant language from Latakiya to al-Bīra (today's Biredjik on the Euphrates) was not Arabic but Turkish.[29])

The following episode is quite instructive. At a certain stage during the abortive siege of al-Āmid (836/1433), when the morale in the Mamluk camp was very low, the Mamluk amir Uzbak Khujā, speaking to Sultan

---

[24]) *Nujūm* (Popper), VI, pp. 231–232.

[25]) See e.g. *Sulūk*, II, p. 415, ll. 4–6.

[26]) See e.g. *Nujūm* (Popper), VII, p. 98, ll. 4–6. The Turcomans could not become Mamluks, because they were born Muslims. However, some of them managed to smuggle themselves into the Mamluk aristocracy, often with the aid of a slave dealer.

[27]) *Nujūm* (Popper), V, pp. 373, ll. 11–12, 374, l. 1, 500; *Ḥawādith*, p. 176, l. 3. On the struggle between Barqūq and Minṭāsh see also my "The Circassians in the Mamluk Kingdom", *JAOS* (1949), pp. 140f.

[28]) Al-Sakhāwī, *al-Ḍaw' al-Lāmi'*, Cairo, 1353–5H, vol. III, p. 73, ll. 15–17; Ibn Iyās, II, p. 34, ll. 25–27.

[29]) Abū al-Baqā' Ibn al-Jī'ān, *Al-Qawl al-Mustaẓraf fī Safar Mawlānā al-Malik al-Ashraf*, Torino, 1878, p. 17 (already cited in "Egypt as a Dominant Factor, etc., p. 37).

Barsbāy, praised the Turcomans and the beduins (*'Urbān*) highly, stating that "this is the kind of army by means of which kings win victories. They and no others". These words infuriated his Mamluk colleagues, "because he spoke the truth".[30]) The statement just quoted certainly portrays correctly the bad performance of the Mamluks in that siege. The suggestion, however, of replacing the Mamluks by the Turcomans was impractical from any point of view, and the rulers of the Mamluk sultanate never contemplated doing so. The policy of the Seljuks and their successors developed in the contrary direction: strengthening the Mamluk element at the expense of the Turcomans and of other military bodies.[31]) The mention of the *'Urbān* in the Āmid context is out of place.

The strength of the Turcomans lay in their great military ability and in the geographical position which they occupied, as explained above. Since the individual Turcoman, however, did not, and, in fact, could not, pass through the stages which were an inseparable part of the career of the individual Mamluk (especially that stage which covered his being bought in his infidel country of origin up to his manumission by his Muslim patron), with all the implications which such a career entailed, they could never equal, let alone replace, the Mamluks *even in the best circumstances*. In the circumstances of the Mamluk sultanate they had yet another disadvantage. As far as vying with the Mamluk aristocracy or influencing it are concerned, their geographical position was a source of weakness. Whereas the *'Urbān* were omnipresent in the sultanate (in Syria, in Egypt and in the Ḥijāz) the Turcomans were concentrated almost exclusively in the North. The *élite* Mamluk units, the Royal Mamluks (*al-Mamālīk al-Sulṭāniyya*) and a very substantial part of the Mamluks of the important amirs was stationed in Cairo. There, and in Egypt as a whole, these Mamluks had to handle the less mighty *'Urbān* and the less warlike townspeople (in comparison with those of Syria), elements which never managed to act in unison.[32]) In addition, there existed the language barrier between the Mamluks and the local inhabitants, together will all the prejudices which the Mamluks had against people who did not come from their own (or from neighbouring) countries of origin. Had there been in Egypt, and especially in the vicinity of the capital, Turcomans in great numbers, the situation would have become substantially different. The Mamluk rival factions would have been more inclined to form, in their internal struggles, alliances against each other with

30) *Nujūm* (Popper), VI, p. 704, ll. 18–21.

31) See e.g. my "Aspects of the Mamluk Phenomenon", part A: *Der Islam*, Berlin, 1976, pp. 196–225.

32) See my "The Muslim City and the Mamluk Military Aristocracy", pp. 325–6.

this or that Turcoman tribe, and that is because of common origin and similar language (the inhibition of the Mamluks to involve the neighbouring *'Urbān* in those struggles is discussed below). Even the possibility that such a close and constant neighbourhood between the main body of the Mamluks and the Turcomans might have affected the internal structure of Mamluk aristocracy should not be completely discarded. As a rule, Mamluk society in the environment of warlike Turkish speaking peoples could not develop on exactly the same lines as in a different kind of environment.

All in all, the status of the Turcomans in the Mamluk sultanate was very much lower than that of the Mamluks, and especially that of the Royal Mamluks. They were not allowed to put on the Mamluk dress, and they had a special dress of their own. Only in very exceptional cases a Mamluk dress would be bestowed on a Turcoman amir.[33]) The Turcoman chieftain could never rise to the highest rank in the Mamluk ladder of promotion: that of an Amir of a Hundred, Commander of a Thousand Soldiers in the field of battle (*Amīr Mi'a Muqaddam Alf*). They did receive all the other lower ranks: Amīr of Ten (*Amīr 'Ashara*), Amīr of Twenty (*Amīr 'Ishrīn*) and Amīr of Forty (*Amīr Arba'īn* or *Amīr Ṭablkhāna*), but these ranks were not equal to the correspondng ranks of the Mamluk amirs. The difference was expressed already in their feudal charters (*manāshīr*, sing. *manshūr*).[34]) It is noteworthy that one of the duties of the chief commander of the Turcomans was to take care that the Turcoman amirs under his supervision should observe all the ceremonies connected with their ranks, and that the orchestras would play in front of the entrances to their abodes every evening.[35]) This commander was called *Muqaddam al-Turkmān*[36] (I do not know whether this title is identical with that of *Amīr al-Turkmān*).[37]) Among the duties mentioned in his letter of appointment were the following ones: to bring the Turcomans together when called to participate in the Holy War; to make them obey the sultan, for he [i.e. the *Muqaddam*] had been appointed to that post, specifically for that purpose; and to inform the sultan or the governor nearest to the Turcoman habitations of the death of Turcoman

---

[33]) Al-Qalqashandī, *Ṣubḥ*, IV, p. 182, ll. 10–12; Ibn al-Furāt, IX, p. 382, ll. 24–25; A. N. Poliak, The Influence of Chingiz-Khān's Yāsa upon the General Organization of the Mamluk State, *BSOAS*, X (1940–2), p. 867.

[34]) *Ṣubḥ*, VII, p. 190, ll. 6–7; XIII, pp. 158, l. 19, 198, ll. 10–11. See also Poliak, *Feudalism, op. cit.*

[35]) *Ta'rīf*, p. 113, ll. 5–6.

[36]) *Nujūm* (Popper), VI, p. 379, l. 9; *Manhal*, VIII, fol. 395a, ll. 16–19; *Ḍaw' al-Ṣubḥ*, p. 348; *Ṣubḥ*, V, p. 468, ll. 11–12; XI, p. 121, ll. 13–16.

[37]) *Nujūm* (Popper), VI, p. 382, ll. 14–5; Ibn Iyās (Kahle), IV, pp. 191, l. 16, 378, ll. 13–16.

soldiers or amirs who received salaries or feudal fiefs from the state, so that their legal heirs could be ascertained. In case of the absence of heirs, the deceased's property should be transferred to the State Treasury (*Bayt al-Māl*).[38]

According to al-Qalqashandī the important Turcoman tribes were eleven (my vocalization of their names is somewhat arbitrary): al-Būzaqiyya; Awlād Ramaḍān; al-'Ūshāriyya (the Turcomans of Aleppo); al-Dalkariyya; al-Kharbandaliyya; al-Aghājiriyya; al-Warsaq (the Turcomans of Ṭarsūs); al-Qunuqiyya (al-Qiniqiyya?); al-Bābandariyya; al-Bakrliyya; al-Bayāḍiyya.[39]) A more detailed list of the Turcoman tribes inhabiting the area streching from Gaza to Diyār Bakr is given by Khalīl b. Shāhīn al-Ẓāhirī (according to him they could mobilize 180,000 horsemen).[40]) In the chronicles I came across the following Turcoman tribes, mentioned in connection with specific events: al-Īnāliyya; al-Bayāḍiyya; al-Ūshāriyya; al-Ūjāqiyya; al-Bazāwqiyya; al-Aghājiriyya; al-Kabakiyya; al-Yārūqiyya.[41])

The Kurds

Al-Maqrīzī says that the Mamluks, when they rose to power and built their army, "confined themselves to Mamluks and to a few Kurds".[42]) The exclusion of the Kurds, however, from the Ayyūbid army and the preference of the Mamluks over them, because they [i. e. the Mamluks] proved to be more loyal to their patron, was made already by the Ayyūbid sultan al-Ṣāliḥ Najm al-Dīn Ayyūb (637–647/1240–1429).[43]) The Kurds constituted, in all the military echelons, a minor factor from the very beginning of the

---

38) *Ta'rīf*, pp. 112–113.

39) *Ṣubḥ*, VII, pp. 281–282; *Ḍaw' al-Ṣubḥ*, pp. 326–327.

40) *Zubdat Kashf al-Mamālik*, Paris, 1894, p. 105, ll. 10–15. I have already discussed the list of al-Ẓāhirī, which deals with the numerical strength of the whole army of the Mamluk Sultanate, including the Turcomans (Studies on the Structure of the Mamluk Army, *BSOAS*, 1954, pp. 71–73), and stressed its exaggerated and quite unreliable character.

41) *Nujūm* (Popper), VI, pp. 127, l. 6, 225, l. 14, 389–557, ll. 15–16; *Manhal*, II, fols 53, 138a, ll. 10–11; III, fols. 38b, l. 6, 136a, ll. 19–20; VIII, fol. 395a, ll. 16–19; Ibn Iyās, V, 327. One of the effective measures used by the Turcomans and *'Urbān* in a war was to let off their herds into the fields of the besieged city (see e. g. *Ta'rīkh Bayrūt*, p. 107, ll. 2–5). It is noteworthy that in the Mamluk naval campaigns against Cyprus the Turcomans helped the Frankish inhabitants of the island against the Mamluks (*Nujūm*, VI, pp. 606, l. 222–607, l. 3; *Manhal*, II, fol. 56a, ll. 4–5).

42) Al-Maqrīzī, *Khiṭaṭ*, Cairo, 1270H, vol. II, p. 95, l. 4.

43) Le Régiment Bahriya dans L'Armée Mamelouke, *REI*, 1951, pp. 133–134.

Mamluk reign; and, indeed, they are usually little noticed in the Mamluk sources throughout that reign. The coming over of the Shahrazūriyya Kurds in 656/1258 somewhat strengthened the position of the Kurds.[44]) Together with the Ḥalqa soldiers and the Wāfidiyya Tatars, the Shahrazūriyya comprise the army of Sultan Kitbughā (694–696/1294–1296) in his fight against amir Sanjar al-Shujāʿī.[45]) Sultan Baybars I, in his famous letter to his Mongol ally, Berke Khān, the ruler of the Golden Horde, mentions the Kurds among the elements from which his army is composed.[46]) But the purpose of that letter was to impress that ally with the great might of the Mamluk Sultanate, and such circumstances are not good for evaluating the real share of any component of that army. The low status and marginal share of the Kurds in the Mamluk military machine is revealed in the following instance. In expectation of an impending attack by Īlkhān Ghāzān, when the realm had to mobilize all its resources, Kurds are mentioned as being called up together with soldiers out of employment (*al-ajnād al-baṭṭālūn*). What is even more instructive is *that they receive the same pay*![47]) Sultan al-Nāṣir Muḥammad b. Qalāūn used to go to the hippodrome (*al-maydān*) in an impressive procession. A group of Kurdish axe-bearers (*ṭabardāriyya*) went on foot in front of him with their drawn axes (*aṭbār*).[48]) In the march of amir Minṭāsh against Sultan Barqūq 800 Kurds and Turcomans take part.[49]) Although al-Qalqashandī states that after Tīmūrlank's attack on Syria the Turcomans as well as the Kurds dominated the region of Aleppo,[50]) the presence, and even more so, the impact, of the Kurds there is not much noticed, whereas the Turcomans are encountered practically everywhere in that region.[51]) The head of the Kurds was called *Muqaddam al-Akrād*. His duties were similar to those of *Muqaddam al-Turkmān*, as far as can be learnt from the letters of appointment (*waṣāyā*, sing. *waṣiyya*) of

---

[44]) Th Wāfidiyya in the Mamluk Kingdom, *Islamic Culture*, Hyderabad, 191, p. 97.

[45]) Ibn al-Furāt, VIII, p. 180, ll. 21–22; *Ṣubḥ*, IV, p. 373, ll. 17–20. On the Shahrazūriyya see also Ibn Ḥajar al-ʿAsqalānī, *al-Durar al-Kāmina*, Hyderabad 1348–1350H, vol. I, p. 425, l. 10. All the three elements supporting Sultan Kitbughā were inferior to the Mamluks in the military hierarchy of the Sultanate.

[46]) *Sulūk*, I, p. 479, l. 16.

[47]) Zetterstéen (ed.), *Beiträge zur Geschichte der Mamlukensultane*, Leiden, 1919, p. 83, ll. 6–7.

[48]) *Khiṭaṭ*, II, p. 202, ll. 16–17.

[49]) *Nujūm*, V, pp. 373, ll. 11–12, 374, l. 1.

[50]) *Ḍaw' al-Ṣubḥ*, p. 306, ll. 18–22.

[51]) For a limited Kurdish activity in the Northern part of the Sultanate see *Ḥawādith*, p. 467, ll. 8–10.

both of them. In the *waṣiyya* of *Muqadam al-Akrād* it is stated, inter alia, that he has to convince his fellow-Kurds that in the Mamluk Sultanate they would be better off than in their countries of origin.[52])

The 'Urbān

In 659/1261 Sultan Baybars I invited the amirs of the *'Urbān*, gave them feudal fiefs (*iqṭā'āt*) and charged them with guarding the roads of the Mamluk Sultanate up to the borders of Iraq. As the head (*Amīr*) of all the *'Urbān* he appointed the Syrian Sharaf al-Dīn 'Īsā b. Muhannā.[53]) It would appear that *'Urbān* were also responsible for the safety of the roads leading from Egypt southwards, to the lands of the blacks, but these did not receive feudal fiefs.[54]) The *'Urbān* road-guardians were called *Arbāb al-Adrāk*.[55]) Every amir of those *'Urbān* was responsible for a fixed territory (*darak*), and the guards lived in tents by the roads. One of their duties was the punishment of robbers.[56]) The amirs appointed for that duty were called *mudarrikūn*[57] or *mutadarrikūn*.[58]) In times of emergency they furnished an auxiliary force of cavalrymen.[59]) The heads of the *'Urbān* of al-Sharqiyya and of the Sinai peninsula were charged with an additional task: the supply of horses for the Royal horse-post (*barīd*) in the lines Bilbays-Damietta and Bilbays-al-Kharrūba.[60]) The amirs of the *'Urbān* received, like their Turcoman counterparts, ranks which were not higher than that of amir of forty (or *Ṭablkhāna*).[61]) In the Turkish-Qipchāqi period the most important of

---

52) *Ta'rīf*, pp. 111–112. For additional data on the Kurds see: *Sulūk*, I, pp. 4–6; *al-Nujūm al-Zāhira*, Cairo, from 1934 onward, vol. VI, p. 4, l. 1; VII? p. 40, l. 1; *Ṣubḥ*, IV, pp. 373–379; VII, pp. 190, 283–289; *Ta'rīf*, pp. 37–39. The Kurds are mentioned together with Bayāḍiyya Turcomans after the annihilation of the Mamluk Sultanate (Ibn Iyās, V, p. 327, l. 4).

53) *Sulūk*, I, p. 465, ll. 1–3.

54) *Ṣubḥ*, VIII, pp. 5–6.

55) *Nujūm* (Cairo), VIII, p. 205, ll. 4–6; *Nujūm* (Popper), pp. 292, ll. 2–5, 481, ll. 8–9. See also 'Alī Bāshā Mubārak, *al-Khiṭaṭ al-Tawfīqiyya*, Cairo, 1305–1306 A.H., vol. IX, p. 19, l. 29, 25, l. 33; Popper's Glossarium to vol. VI, p. XXVIII; and Dozy, Supplement, *s. v.*

56) *Ṣubḥ*, VIII, p. 95, ll. 14–19; *Nujūm*, VI, pp. 292, l. 3, 481, l. 8.

57) Ibn Iyās, II, p. 110, l. 9; III, p. 31, l. 20; IV, p. 327, ll. 4–17.

58) Ibn al-Furāt, IX, p. 250, ll. 3–4; *Ta'rīkh Bayrūt*, pp. 182, l. 10, 168, l. 3, and note 1. For additional data on *Arbāb al-Adrāk* see Poliak, *Feudalism*, p. 9.

59) *Nujūm*, VI, pp. 71, l. 15–72, l. 14; Ibn Khaldūn, V, p. 6, l. 19; Ibn Iyās, I, p. 331, ll. 7–10.

60) *Ṣubh*, III, p. 458, l. 4; XIV, p. 377, ll. 1–3.

61) Poliak, *Feudalism*, pp. 9–11.

those amirs was Ibn al-Muhannā.[62] The general name of the Beduin tribal heads was *Mashāyikh al-'Urbān.*[63]) Most of them were not amirs.

Before describing the relations between the Mamluk sultanate and the *'Urbān,* a very brief review of their tribes and the areas of their habitation will be given.

The Mamluk Encycopaedias give a quite detailed description of the *'Urbān* tribes in the various parts of the Mamluk Sultanate.[64]) I have no intention to repeat here that description (the summary of which had already been given by A. N. Poliak),[65]) for within the framework of the present study only those tribes which I encountered in the chronicles in connection with specific events are the relevant ones. Even so the following enumeration of the 'Urbān tribes is certainly very deficient.

The 'Urbān in Egypt

A. Lower Egypt

Al-Buḥayra

In the early Mamluk period Jābir and Mirdās are mentioned as fighting each other.[66]) In this area were also 'Arab al-Akhmās.[67]) An immense damage was caused to the region of al-Buḥayra by 'Urbān Labīd, who roamed between Alexandria and al-'Aqaba. Because of the drought in their own country they asked permission to settle in the province of al-Buḥayra, but their request was rejected. Consequently, a series of bloody wars was conducted between them and the Mamluks.[68]) Before 'Arab Labīd the incursion of 'Arab Muḥārib took place.[69]) 'Urbān al-Zuhūr also revolted in this area.[70]) On the Hawwāra see: Upper Egypt.

---

[62]) Idem.

[63]) Ibn Iyās, III, pp. 4, ll. 14–20, 31, l. 20; IV, p. 327, ll. 4–17.

[64]) See e.g. *Ta'rīf,* pp. 76–77, 79–80; *Ṣubḥ,* IV, pp. 67–72, 203–215, 231–232, 242–243; VII, pp. 160–162, 184–189. The treatises of al-Qalqashandī and al-Maqrīzī on the beduins were not available to me when this chapter was originally written.

[65]) *Feudalism,* pp. 10–12.

[66]) *Sulūk,* I, p. 914, ll. 3–7.

[67]) Ibn al-Furāt, IX, p. 157, l. 10. See also Ibn Iyās, III, p. 11, ll. 10–14; IV, pp. 256–257; *Ḥawādith,* p. 220, ll. 12–14.

[68]) *Nujūm,* VI, p. 728, and the note; VII, p. 9, ll. 3–8; *Ḥawādith,* pp. 190, 210, ll. 1–4, 213, ll. 1–3, 218, ll. 11–14; Ibn Iyās, III, p. 48, ll. 10–13.

[69]) *Ḥawādith,* pp. 47, ll. 14–15, 70, ll. 10–11, 70–71.

[70]) Ibn al-Furāt, IX, p. 248, ll. 17–28. It is not clear whether 'Arab al-Yasār, who were transferred to the area situated just below the Cairo citadel, inhabited originally al-Buḥayra (Ibn Iyās, IV, p. 190, l. 14).

Al-Sharqiyya (and al-Gharbiyya)

It is not always easy to decide, according to the evidence of the sources, whether the tribes belonging to the province of al-Sharqiyya wandered in al-Gharbiyya as well. Wide areas in al-Sharqiyya were desert-like.[71]) Already in 577/1181, in the reign of Saladin, the Sultan ordered to confiscate the estates of the 'Urbān in al-Sharqiyya, and especially those belonging to Judhām and Tha'laba, because they sold grains to the Franks. As a punishment, they were exiled to the Buḥayra region.[72]) 'Urbān Judhām, however, are mentioned in al-Sharqiyya at a much later period.[73]) 'Arab al-'Ā'id lived in the neighbourhood of both al-Ṣāliḥiyya and Qaṭyā.[74]) It would appear that the most important of all the Sharqiyya tribes were Banū Ḥārim and Banū Wā'il, between whom the bloodiest and bitterest wars broke out. The intervention of the Mamluk army between the two adversaris was usually of no avail.[75]) Towards the end of the Mamluk reign the predatory incursions of the 'Urbān of Banū 'Aṭiyya and al-Na'ā'im are mentioned in al-Sharqiyya.[76])

Al-Manūfiyya

Banū Ṣūra fought each other in al-Manūfiyya.[77]) It would appear that Banū Sālim, who are sometimes called 'Arab al-Sawālim, also lived in al-Manūfiyya or its vicinity.[78])

B. Upper Egypt

Al-'Arab al-Aḥāmida rob Aswān together with 'Arab al-Kanz.[79]) In the area of Asyūṭ lived 'Urbān 'Arak and Tawrīk.[80]) Other tribes of Upper

---

[71]) *Ṣubḥ*, III, p. 404, ll. 15–19; *Zubda*, p. 34, ll. 9–11.

[72]) *Sulūk*, I, p. 71, ll. 9–11.

[73]) Ibn Khaldūn, V, p. 377; Ibn Iyās, III, p. 164, ll. 3–4.

[74]) *Nujūm*, V, p. 410, ll. 13–16; VI, pp. 112–113; Ibn al-Furāt, IX, pp. 78, l. 20, 381, ll. 5–7.

[75]) *Nujūm*, VI, p. 235, l. 2; Ibn Iyās, III, pp. 67, ll. 21–23, 101, ll. 7–8, 353, ll. 3–5, 365, ll. 10–14.

[76]) Ibn Iyās, V, p. 77, ll. 18–19. On 'Urbān Banī 'Aṭā' and Banī 'Aṭiyya see *ibid.*, p. 370, ll. 8, 10.

[77]) Ibn al-Furāt, VII, p. 226, ll. 20–25.

[78]) *Ḥawādith*, p. 654, l. 10; Ibn Iyās, V, pp. 253, l. 21, 254, l. 13.

[79]) Ibn al-Furāt, IX, pp. 440, l. 20–444, l. 7; Ibn Qāḍī Shuhba, fol. 115a, ll. 1–13. On them see also Ibn Iyās, III, pp. 234, l. 22–235, l. 5. On 'Arab al-Kanz in the Aswān area see Ibn Khaldūn, V, p. 474, l. 26; *Tibr*, p. 93, ll. 12–19.

[80]) Ibn al-Furāt, IX, pp. 468, l. 23–469, l. 7, 471 – l. 19–472, l. 5.

Egypt were: Awlād Abū Bakr, Awlād 'Umar, Awlād Sharīf, Awlād Shībā and Awlād al-Kanz (already mentioned),[81]) as well as 'Arab Qatīl, Fazāra and Muḥārib.[82]) The tribes of Juhayna and Rifā'a fought each other in the desert of 'Aydhāb.[83]) 'Arab Juhayna settled in Nubia (*Bilād al-Nūba*), and became its masters. They put an end to its majestic glory, and brought upon it disturbances and disorganization.[84]) 'Arab Ḥazanbal were brought from Upper Egypt to al-Jīza by amir Yashbak al-Dawādār, as a reward for the help they extended to him in the period he had been the governor of Southern Egypt (*Kāshif al-Wajh al-Qiblī*). In spite of their being considered as *'Arab al-Ṭā'a*, they caused immense damage to their new area of settlement. They raided al-Manūfiyya as well.[85]) In the vicinity of the oases of Egypt, in the Western Desert, wandered, as it seems, 'Arab Sulaym.[86])

But the most important and most prestigious of all the tribes in Upper Egypt was, without question, the tribe of al-Hawwāra, which moved there from al-Buḥayra in the 8th/14th century. Al-Qalqashandī says about this tribe: "But in our time, since al-Hawwāra moved from al-Buḥayra to Upper Egypt and settled there, they spread in it like locusts, and stretched their hand from the district of Behnesa up to the end of Upper Egypt, where Aswān and the area adjacent to it are situated. All the other 'Urbān in the south, without exception, obeyed them and were at their beck and call".[87]) 'Umar b. 'Abd al-'Azīz, the amir of 'Arab Hawwāra, who died in 799/1397 was the father of the dynasty of the amirs of Upper Egypt called Banū 'Umar, and, according to Ibn Taghrībirdī, he seems to have been the first of them who received the title of amir.[88]) Dā'ūd b. Sulaymān, of the Awlād Banī 'Umar, was made amir in Upper Egypt in 898/1493.[89])

[81]) *Sulūk*, I, p. 737, ll. 1–2.

[82]) *Ḥawādith*, pp. 193, ll. 20–22, 501, l. 18–502, l. 8.

[83]) Ibn al-Furāt, VII, p. 226, l. 14.

[84]) Ibn Khaldūn, V, pp. 420–440.

[85]) *Ḥawādith*, pp. 632, ll. 3–15. They are also mentioned later both in al-Jīza and al-Ṣa'īd as helping Āqbirdī al-Dawādār together with Banū Wā'il (Ibn Iyās, III, pp. 355, ll. 17–18, 407–410; IV, pp. 371, ll. 22–23, 372, ll. 5–6).

[86]) Ibn Duqmāq, *Kitāb al-Intiṣār*, Cairo, 1893, pp. 13, l. 26 – 14, l. 1. On 'Arab Banī Sulaym's habitations in Tunisia see Ibn Khaldūn, V, p. 480.

[87]) *Ṣubḥ*, IV, p. 49, ll. 7–10.

[88]) *Nujūm*, V, p. 635, ll. 12–14.

[89]) Ibn Iyās, III, p. 290, ll. 4–6. See also *Nujūm*, VII, p. 622, ll. 1–5; *Ḥawādith*, pp. 322–323; Ibn Iyās, III, pp. 116, ll. 18–19, 141–142, 143, 353, ll. 1–3; IV, p. 193, ll. 5–8. Al-Sakhāwī, *al-Ḍaw' al-Lāmi'*, Cairo, 1353–5H, vol. X, p. 341.

Syria and Palestine (al-Bilād al-Shāmiyya)

Of the tribes of *al-Bilād al-Shāmiyya* particularly important were Āl Faḍl, who wandered in the northern part of the Syrian desert, and whose head, al-Muhannā, was called *Malik al-ʿArab*, or *Amīr al-ʿArab bil-Shām.*[90]) In the reign of al-Nāṣir Muḥammad b. Qalāūn he joined the Mongols of Iran and persuaded them to attack the Mamluk Sultanate. He was also involved in the flight of amirs Qarāsunqur and Āqūsh al-Afram to Īlkhān Kherbenda. Finally he made peace with the Mamluk Sultan.[91]) Āl ʿAlī, who formed a branch of Āl Faḍl roamed in the vicinity of Damascus.[92]) Banū Kilāb wandered in the Aleppo area.[93]) Banū ʿĀmir, also called Aʿrāb al-Shām, wandered in the Jerusalem mountains, in the district (*wilāya*) of Jenin and in Marj Ibn ʿĀmir (the Valley of Esdraelon).[94]) In the Ḥawrān were Āl Marā (or Mirā).[95]) In al-Karak and its vicinity – Banū ʿUqba.[96]) Banū Lām wandered at first in Northern Ḥijāz,[97]) and afterwards in the areas of al-Karak and al-Shawbak.[98] They are mentioned in the Mamluk sources very frequently, because of their constant attacks on the pilgrims' caravans to Mecca.[99]) Two great wars between the Qays and the Yaman tribes in the Turkish-Qipchāqī period are described by the sources: one in al-

---

[90]) *Sulūk*, II, p. 87, 160, ll. 17–18; Ibn al-Furāt, VIII, p. 155, l. 6.

[91]) See e.g. Ibn Khaldūn, V, pp. 438, l. 28–439, l. 3. Much of the data on this subject is included in the yet unpublished chapter of my work on the Mamluks who escaped from the Mamluk Sultanate and found refuge in the Īlkhāmid state. For additional data on al-Muhannā see: Zetterstéen, *Beiträge*, p. 188, ll. 23–25; *Sulūk*, II, pp. 407, l. 4–408, l. 2; *Manhal*, IV, fol. 202; VIII, fols. 270–271; Ibn Khaldūn, V, p. 459; Ibn al-Furāt, IX, p. 133; Ibn Iyās, III, pp. 109, ll. 12–15, 188, ll. 19–22, 216, ll. 507, 344, ll. 8–9; *Durar*, IV, pp. 368–370, 382; Poliak, *Feudalism*, pp. 10–11.

[92]) Poliak, *Feudalism*, p. 11; Ibn Khaldūn, V, pp. 496, l. 29–497, l. 1.

[93]) *Sulūk*, II, p. 3; Ibn Abī al-Faḍā'il, *al-Nahj al-Sadīd* (in *Patrologia Orientalis*), vol. XX, p. 103; Ibn Khaldūn, V, p. 386, ll. 17–18; *Manhal*, V, fol. 22b. Ibn al-Furāt specifies the boundaries of the wandering area of Banū Kilāb al-Kalbiyyūn (Ibn al-Furāt, VIII, pp. 67–68).

[94]) *Ḍaw'*, III, p. 258, l. 20; VII, p. 244; Ibn al-Furāt, VII, p. 191, l. 7.

[95]) Poliak, *Feudalism*, p. 11.

[96]) Ibn al-Furāt, IX, p. 139, ll. 2–3; *Sulūk*, II, p. 472, note 3; *Ṣubḥ*, VIII, p. 221, l. 1.

[97]) Abū al-Fidā', IV, p. 74.

[98]) Ibn Iyās, III, pp. 274, ll. 22–23, 291, ll. 6–7, 299, ll. 11–15, 422, ll. 20–25, 438, ll. 18–19; IV, pp. 35, l. 22–36, l. 7, 38, ll. 5–7, 99, ll. 8–11, 117, ll. 3–8. The ʿArab of Wādī Banī Sālim were also among the robbers of the Ḥajj caravans (*Sulūk*, II, p. 5).

[99]) See the references in the two previous notes.

Ḥawrān,[100]) and the other in the ʿAjlūn area.[101]) Very frequent is the mention of ʿUrbān Jabal Nāblus.[102]) It is not clear, however, whether this name denoted various tribes or only one tribe (or a tribal group). In *al-Bilād al-Shāmiyya* there were also the tribes of Banū Mahdī, ʿArab Jarm and ʿArab Zabīd.[103])

The Struggle between the ʿUrbān and the Mamluks

During most of the Turkish-Qipchāqī period the problem of the ʿUrbān did not preoccupy the Mamluk army very much. It is true that soon after the rise of the Mamluks to power the ʿUrbān refused in 651/1253 to pay taxes, claiming that they were the masters of the land, because they served the Ayyūbids more than enough, and that they deserve to be the rulers more than the Mamluks. According to them, the Ayyubids are *Khawārij*, and the Mamluks are nothing but the slaves of the *Khawārij*.[104]) But in the great campaign which the Mamluks waged against the ʿUrbān of Upper Egyps in reply to their insurgence, the ʿUrbān were completely routed. After that defeat the Mamluks inflicted similar defeats on the ʿUrbān of al-Manūfiyya and al-Gharbiyya, and since then they had been subdued for a long time.[105]) Sultan Aybak (648–655/1250–1257), however, did not content himself with those victories. He decided to break the power of the ʿUrbān completely, and in order to carry out that decision he used the following stratagem. He invited the heads of the ʿUrbān of Upper Egypt to visit him in Bilbays under the pretext that he wanted to come to terms with them. They swallowed the bait, and arrived at the head of 2000 horsemen and 600 infantrymen. All of them were caught and hanged on wooden structures (*akhshāb*) which were erected along the whole road connecting Cairo with Bilbays.[106]) Only when the Mamluk army was defeated by Īlkhān Ghāzān, and later, during the reign of Sultan Baybars II and his chief lieutenant amir Salār, the ʿUrbān tried to revolt against the central government, but

---

[100]) Ibn Kathīr, XIV, p. 55, ll. 10–14.

[101]) Idem, p. 289, ll. 24–26.

[102]) See e. g. *Tibr*, p. 102, l. 27; Ibn Iyās, III, pp. 172, ll. 3–12, 220, ll. 11–17; 226, ll. 8–9; IV, p. 468, l. 14. This is only a tiny selection of source references.

[103]) *Ṣubḥ*, XI, p. 110, l. 10; Nujūm, VI, p. 520, l. 20; Poliak, *Feudalism*, p. 11.

[104]) *Sulūk*, I, p. 386, ll. 12–18.

[105]) Idem, p. 387, ll. 6–9.

[106]) Idem, p. 388, ll. 1–9. On the retaliatory measures of Baybars I in 661/1263 against the fellahs of Nāblus and the coastal area mainly because of their furnishing information to the Franks, see *Sulūk*, I, p. 488, ll. 2–7.

their uprisings were quelled with relative ease.[107]) There were other isolated attempts by the 'Urbān to throw off the government's yoke during the Turkish-Qipchāqī period.[108]) But in most of that period they supplied the Mamluks with auxiliary forces both from Syria and from Egypt (from Egypt mainly, though not exclusively, for duties inside the boundaries of Egypt).

Signs of unrest among the 'Urbān became more and more evident in the last decades of Qipchāqī rule, and in the Circassian period things went from bad to worse. With the steadily weakening hold of the central government on the countryside and the general decline of the Sultanate, the 'Urbān became one of its greatest afflictions. Not only did the 'Urbān cease, or substantially curtail, the supply of auxiliary forces and the performance of other duties of theirs, but the Mamluk army, which had been quite small in size, had to send repeatedly punitive expeditions against the 'Urbān, who rose up in arms each time in a different part of the realm. This is true mainly for Upper and Lower Egypt. In al-Bilād al-Shāmiyya the situation was, on the whole, somewhat better, with the very noticeable exception of Jabal Nāblus. The Mamluks did not refrain from employing the harshest and cruellest measures in order to suppress the revolting 'Urbān. Those whom they caught they would roast alive; impale (*khawzaqa*) on stakes; flay while still alive;[109]) bury alive in the ground and sell their wives into slavery;[110] cut them in two (*tawsīṭ*); sever their heads and hang those heads over the gates of Cairo and other Egyptian towns;[111]) nail their (dead ?) bodies and then send their flayed skins to the abodes of their respective tribes to serve as a most convincing reminder.[112])

But all these measures were of no avail. The mastery of the 'Urbān in Upper Egypt started already in the beginning of the 9th/15th century.[113]) In 873/1468 it is stated that the 'Urbān dominate Lower Egypt.[114]) Any unrest in Cairo or a general crisis in the Sultanate was exploited by the 'Ur-

---

107) See e.g. *Al-Nahj al-Sadīd* (in Patrologia Orientalis), XX, pp. 38, ll. 4–8; *Sulūk*, I, p. 914, ll. 8–16; Ibn Khaldūn, V, pp. 415, l. 25–416, l. 1; *Khiṭaṭ*, II, p. 84, ll. 36–37.

108) *Sulūk*, I, pp. 920, l. 4–922, l. 15; II, p. 157, ll. 5–9.

109) Ibn Iyās, III, p. 40.

110) Ibn Iyās, III, pp. 23, ll. 17–21, 234, l. 22–235, l. 5.

111) Ibn al-Furāt, IX p. 20, ll. 15–19; *Ḥawādith*, pp. 684, ll. 3–5, 695, l. 16–696, l. 7; Ibn Iyās, III, pp. 59, ll. 20–24, 102, ll. 14–16, 220, ll. 3–4, 229, ll. 6–11, 346, l. 7–347, l. 2, 350, l. 23–351, l. 2, 401, ll. 5–8, 406–407; IV, pp. 55, ll. 7–11, 63, ll. 3–6, 116, ll. 7–11, 121, ll. 9–11, 123–124, 187, ll. 7–9.

112) *Ḥawādith*, p. 210, ll. 8–12.

113) *Khiṭaṭ*, I, pp. 198, l. 35–199, l. 13.

114) *Ḥawādith*, p. 678, ll. 19–20.

bān in order to increase their power and foment disorder. That is what they did when the Mamluk army was defeated by Shāh Siwār,[115]) and when Ismāʿīl al-Ṣafawī was believed to have made preparations to attack the Mamluk realm. The Sultan was then faced with the very bad alternative: either send his army against the external enemy, or against the internal one: the ʿUrbān.[116]) One of the revolts of the ʿUrbān in al-Buḥayra (872/1468) reached such immense dimensions, that the Sultan decided to send against them a military expedition of 2,000 Royal Mamluks, which was considered to be a very impressive force even in a war against a major enemy. On the occasion of the dispatch of this expedition, the historian Ibn Ṭaghrībirdī states that he does not know of any time or of any period when the ʿUrbān accumulated in Egypt so much power. They spread over al-Sharqiyya, al-Gharbiyya and al-Manūfiyya and took possession of the property of the inhabitants. As for al-Buḥayra, they treated it like their own feudal fief (*ṣārat lahum kal-iqṭāʿ*).[117]) Security was precarious even in the approaches of Cairo. The ʿUrbān used to seize the horses of the Mamluks pasturing near Cairo, and nobody could stop them.[118])

In the Circassian period the ʿUrbān were on the way of becoming a military factor even in the struggles inside the Mamluk aristrocracy. Sultan Khushqadam wanted in 872/1467 to use ʿArab Ḥazanbal, whom amir Yashbak al-Dawādār brought over from Upper Egypt to al-Jīza, as a counterbalance to the Ashrafiyya Mamluks (the Mamluks of the late al-Ashraf Aynāl). Our historians comment on the sultan's intention is that *there could hardly be a greater disgrace than that of the Mamluks calling for beduin succour against each other*! (*wa-hādhā min aʿarr mā yakūn min kawn al-Turk tastanjid bil-ʿArab ʿalā baʿḍihim*).[119])

The growing power of the ʿUrbān and its effects is discussed in other chapters of our work on the Mamluk army and military aristocracy, especially in the yet unpublished chapters: "The Mamluk Army in the Field of Battle" and "The Decline of the Mamluk Sultanate".

The great power which the ʿUrbān of Egypt accumulated under the Circassian Mamluks had its far reaching effect under the Ottomans. Neither

---

[115]) Idem, p. 653, ll. 19–22.

[116]) Ibn Iyās, IV, p. 257, ll. 11–15.

[117]) *Ḥawādith*, p. 631, ll. 6–23.

[118]) *Ḥawādith*, p. 537, ll. 11–15; Ibn Iyās, II, pp. 54, ll. 13–15, 156; III, p. 101, ll. 9–12. The disruption of communications between al-Ḥijāz and the other parts of the Sultanate by the beduins, especially during the pilgrimage season, has already been mentioned before. See also *Njūm*, VII, pp. 10–11; *Ḥawādith*, p. 222, ll. 5–18; Ibn Iyās, III, pp. 287, ll. 2–4, 376, ll. 5–13.

[119]) *Ḥawādith*, p. 632, ll. 14–15.

they, nor the Mamluks of that country succeeded in reducing or even curbing and containing that power. Up to the reign of Muḥammad ʿAlī, who eliminated the Egyptian beduin factor for good, it played an even much more dominant role than in the second half of the Mamluk reign. Alliances between rival Mamluk factions and beduin tribal factions were no more an isolated or rare phenomenon. Nor were they considered to be shameful in any way. These alliances became constant and every day facts of life. In Lower Egypt the relations between the two main Mamluk factions of the capital and the two main tribal bodies in the Delta area became so close, that the Mamluk factions sometimes received the names of their respective beduin allies. Furthermore, in Upper Egypt a center of opposition to the central government grew up, where ʿUrbān and (mainly exiled) Mamluks fought together against the rulers in Cairo.[120]) Without the preliminary developments in the Mamluk Circassian period, such a situation could not have been created.

Al-ʿAshīr

In *al-Bilād al-Shāmiyya* there was a special kind of tribes who, according to A. N. Poliak's suggestion, lived on agriculture.[121]) They were called *al-ʿAshīr* or *al-ʿUshrān*, and rarely *al-ʿAshāʾir*. They also took quite often part, as auxiliary forces, in the wars of the Mamluks. Their commanders were called *Muqaddamū al-ʿAshīr.*[122])

Al-Jabaliyya

Among the auxiliary forces in the service of the Mamluk army there was a body called al-Jabaliyya. These were also mainly in *al-Bilād al-Shāmiyya.* Their commanders were called *Muqaddamū al-Jabaliyya.* They took part in various military operations. I do not know the exact character of that body, and whether its members were mountain dwellers or not. They

---

[120]) I have already discussed in some detail the Mamluk-nomad relations in Ottoman Egypt in Studies on al-Jabartī: Notes on the Transformation of Mamluk Society in Egypt under the Ottomans, *JESHO*, III (1960), pp. 148–174, 275–325.

[121]) *Feudalism*, p. 11.

[122]) *Sulūk*, I, pp. 689, l. 21 and note 3, 699, l. 21–700, l. 2; II, p. 80, l. 14; *Nujūm* (Cairo), VIII, pp. 5. ll. 12–13, 274, l. 10; *Nujūm* (Popper), V, pp. 482, l. 21, 493, l. 4; VI, pp. 114, ll. 3-4, 613, ll. 1–2, 778, l. 1; VII, p. 91, ll. 12–13, l. 17; *Ḥawādith*, pp. 53, ll. 16–18, 109, ll. 9–10; Ibn al-Furāt, VII, pp. 225–226; IX, pp. 147, ll. 25–26, 349, ll. 9–16; *Tibr*, pp. 268, l. 11, 351, l. 1; Ibn Iyās, II, p. 123, ll. 26–28; III, pp. 226, ll. 7–8, l. 9, 449, l. 2; V. pp. 80, 86; *Ṣubḥ*, VII, p. 410, ll. 6–7; *Taʾrīkh Bayrūt*, pp. 64, l. 4, 74, 105, ll. 2–4; *Zubda*, p. 105, l. 16.

are mentioned also as policemen and as hangmen.[123]) It is noteworthy that in the *waṣiyya* of *Muqaddam al-Jabaliyya* special stress is laid on his function as arbiter in disputes between Qays and Yaman.[124]) It would appear that that office was considered to be a very low one, for Ibn Taghrībirdī, speaking of the corruption which spread in the Sultanate, states that everybody was contaminated by it, from the Great Amir [i. e. Atābak al-'Asākir] [down] to the *Muaqddam al-Jabaliyya.*[125])

Al-Muṭṭawi'a

In addition to the compulsory participation in war of the auxiliary forces, there was also a voluntary participation. These volunteers were called *Muṭṭawi'a* or *Mutaṭawwi'a*. Some of them had some kind of a previous military background. Others were ordinary citizens. The number of volunteers was particularly great in the naval campaigns against Cyprus and Rhodes (they are discussed in the yet unpublished chapter "The Mamluks and Naval Power").[126])

The auxiliary forces had both cavalrymen and infantrymen (*mushāt, rajjāla*). As infantrymen they marched in front of the army (*quddām* or *amām a-'askar*).[127])

Appendix

A. In almost any subject pertaining to the Mamluk Sultanate as a whole, our information on Egypt usually far exceeds in richness, variety and quality its equivalent on Syria. This is also true, and particularly regrettable, of the subject of the present article. The auxiliary forces of Syria were, within the framework of the whole army of the realm, much more important than those of Egypt for the reasons

---

[123]) Ibn Kathīr, XIV, p. 243, ll. 7–10; Sulūk, I, p. 554, l. 13; II, p. 83, l. 22; *Nujūm*, VI, pp. 22 and the note, 229, l. 1; Ibn al-Furāt, IX, pp. 204, ll. 9–11, 258, ll. 17–18, 335, l. 22, 387, l. 13; *Ta'rīkh Bayrūt*, p. 90, l. 11; Ṣubḥ, IX, p. 254, ll. 19–20.

[124]) *Ta'rīf*, pp. 113–115.

[125]) *Nujūm*, VII, p. 150, ll. 11–12.

[126]) See e. g. *Nujūm* (Cairo), VIII, p. 5, ll. 12–13; Ibn Kathīr, XIV, pp. 6, ll. 22–23, 13–17, 108, l. 16; Ibn Khaldūn, VIII, p. 550, l. 15; *Zubda*, p. 140, l. 5. The article Baḥriyya (navy) in *EI*[2], and the lecture bearing the same name as that of the whole chapter (*Proceedings of the Israel Academy*, vol. I (1965), pp. 1–12) are only very brief summaries of that chapter.

[127]) *Nujūm*, VI, pp. 50, 364, ll. 11–12, 613; *Ḥawādith*, p. 348; Ibn Iyās, IV, pp. 408, 448, 451; V, p. 63. See also *Nujūm* (Cairo), VI, p. 36, l. 7. See also Poliak, *Feudalism*, pp. 11–12 (on the auxiliary forces). Sometimes the auxiliary cavalry units went also at the head of the main army (Ibn Iyās, III, p. 263, ll. 12–16).

already mentioned. Yet we know about them relatively little. Sources which are more available today might well improve that situation.

The role played by the al-Muhannā (or Abū al-Muhannā)[1]) dynasty of amirs of the Āl-Faḍl between the Mamluks and the Īlkhāns of Iran, which started on a large scale with the antecedents to the battle of Ḥimṣ[2]) in October 1281 (the Sunqur al-Ashqar affair), bears some resemblance to the role played by the Turcomans between the Mamluks and the Ottomans. There were, however, fundamental differences, of which three will be mentioned. a) there was not a territorial contiguity of Arab tribes beyond the Mamluk border on a scale similar to the one existing in the Turcoman region; b) there was not a feeling of affinity between the Mongols and the Arabs; c) last but not least, the Īlkhānid empire was relatively short lived, and its decline was quite swift, whereas the Ottoman Empire was on the ascendant when it cooperated with the Turcomans against the Mamluks. At exactly the time when al-Nāṣir Muḥammad b. Qalāūn, with his short-sighted policy (on this see also below), tried to buy off the Āl-Faḍl, thus strengthening them immensely, the Īlkhānids could not benefit from the growing power of such a potential ally, because their empire had already been well on the way of disintegration.

B. The third reign of al-Nāṣir Muḥammad b. Qalāūn was, without doubt, one of the most important in the history of the Sultanate. About this there is full agreement among students of that history. What is almost completely ignored, however, is the very negative aspects of the reign in question, which had far-reaching, and unwholesome, effects on subsequent developments in the realm, including developments connected with the ʿUrbān. For this there is overwhelming evidence.[3])

In a nutshell: al-Nāṣir Muḥammad, a man with an exceptionally strong personality and devouring ambition, and full of revengeful hatred against those who dethroned him twice, when he was too young and too weak to fight them back, ascended the throne for the third (709–741/1309–1340) time with the unwavering determination that this would never happen to him again, and that he would prove to the whole world that he is the greatest of them all, especially greater than the almost legendary Baybars I.

Since the period of great wars against formidable external enemies was over, the obvious alternative for becoming great and famous was building on an immense scale. What characterized that activity was that it had not been confined to state or religious construction, but embraced the whole population, or at least that part of it which could afford joining the building spree, instigated and unremittingly encouraged by the Sultan. In the third reign of that ruler the Egyptian capital expanded at an unexampled pace, and reached unprecedented dimensions, which were surpassed only by modern Cairo (from the reign of khedive Ismāʿīl onwards). The building craze was by no means confined to the capital.

---

[1]) See Gaston Wiet, *Les Biographies du Manhal Safi*, Cairo, 1932, the genealogical tree of the Muhannā family, p. 263.

[2]) See my Ḥimṣ (the battle of) in *EI*², III, pp. 402–403.

[3]) I deal with this subject in great length in a detailed study now in progress called "The Expansion and Decline of Cairo under the Mamluks and their Background".

That branch of activity was not the only one where money had been spent so lavishly and so indiscriminately. One of al-Nāṣir Muḥammad's main targets was the destruction of the power of the Mamluks of his father, Qalāūn, who treated him so badly, and build a big corps of his own Mamluks. This was an extremely expensive project in itself. What aggravated the situation manifold – a matter not confined to sheer expenditure and to economy alone – was that that Sultan was a great believer in buying off friend and foe, and at the same time an even greater disbeliever in the loyalty to himself of anybody, not even in the loyalty of his own Mamluks. For some time he would trust a certain person or persons blindly, and then discard him or them most cruelly, often without previous warning. This was done within the framework of a much more general attitude, which shook the very foundations of Mamluk society and Mamluk military might by his constant purges, and even more so by his disregard of the basic principles guiding a healthy Mamluk society, and observed so strictly by his predecessors, namely: bringing the Mamluk novice up on frugality, slow promotion and modest reward for real achievement.[4])

Amongst others whom al-Nāṣir Muḥammad bought off were the ʿUrbān, who kept quiet and accumulated great strength which they used to their great advantage after his death.

Perhaps the brightest spot in our Sultan's record was his great care for agriculture, and for widening and preserving the irrigation system of Egypt. But even this most welcome policy did not have only its positive aspects (for this see below).

In order to carry out his great projects and cover his lavish expenditures (he imself lived quite modestly) he bled his realm and his subjects white by his cruel extortions, which increased every year, and which reached frightful dimensions in the last decade or so of his more than thirty years' rule. Signs of unrest in the realm, in the court and in Mamluk society were very visible, and steadily growing, but he managed to crush them with an iron hand up to his very last moment. His third reign was one of the quietest and outwardly most prosperous periods in the whole history of Muslim Egypt. As soon as he died, however, the whole realm was plunged into anarchy, caused mainly by the immediate outburst of the pent-up hatred, bitterness, antagonism and frustration of an impoverished society and a pulverized military aristocracy which accumulated during many years and which was suppressed by the Sultan. There were, however, additional factors which had their no mean share in accelerating and augmenting the anarchy and the decline. One of them was the constant sturggle of succession between the immature sons of the deceased monarch, most of whom were totally unfit for rule. Each of these sons was supported by his ambitious mother and a group of Mamluk amirs belonging to an aristocracy

---

[4]) In a passage of unique importance (*Sulūk*, II, pp. 524, l. 13–525, l. 15) al-Maqrīzī describes al-Nāṣir Muḥammad's attitude towards his own Mamluks and his view of how they should be brought up and advanced. I discuss it in "The Expansion, etc." In my opinion it is far more important than the well known passage in Niẓām al-Mulk's *Siyāsat Nameh*, describing the training and advancement of the Mamluk under the Samanids. This passage of al-Maqrīzī and the one in his *al-Khiṭaṭ*, II, pp. 213–214 (see also *L'Esclavage du Mamelouk*, pp. 13–14) overlap and complement each other.

which had been torn to pieces by their father. An outstanding result of that unceasing tug of war inside the Royal family was that within barely twenty two years *eight* of al-Nāṣir Muḥammad's incapable sons (with the conspicuous exception of al-Nāṣir Ḥasan) followed each other in quick succession. There could hardly be a worse thing for the Sultanate than such a line of misfits ruling it under such critical conditions. As if all that was not enough, a series of misfortunes which were beyond human control, and were topped by the Black Death, afflicted the realm (particularly Egypt) thus greatly aggravating the chaos and quickening the pace of decline.

From the very moment that al-Nāṣir Muḥammad closed his eyes, the sad plight of the realm occupies a major place in the sources' narrative of events. What was not, and, in fact, could not, be noticed immediately was the effects of the decline on the expanded capital, for the simple reason that buildings do not start falling down as soon as a great economic crisis sets on. But this is bound to come if the crisis lasts for a long period. And, indeed, several decades later the capital starts shrinking, and shrinks more and more as a result of the progressive ruin of great parts of the suburbs and other sections of the town, and their abandonment by their inhabitants.[5]) Such a shrinkage on such an immense scale without war or conflagrations, etc., is, as far as I know, a unique phenomenon. One of its main causes was al-Nāṣir Muḥammad's squander mania, one of its most conspicuous manifestations being unbridled building craze.

The study of the Mamluk economy and its decline made an appreciable progress in recent years. What has been ignored completely, or almost so, is the negative contribution of al-Nāṣir Muḥammad's third reign to that economy. In my view, *any* aspect of the economy under discussion should be examined with reference to that reign. This does not imply that a connection will be established in every single case, but only that such an examination is essential. This is also true of the impact of the ʿUrbān on the resources and the economy of the realm.

C. Speaking of the ʿUrbān, the problem with them in Egypt was that their overwhelming majoirty inhabited the cultivated or cultivable areas in that country, all of which could be fed only by the Nile. Considering the delicacy of the Nile irrigation system, the damage which can be caused to it by the ʿUrbān when they succeed in freeing themselves from government control, is obvious; and this happened time and time again in Egypt. The damage was greatly enhanced by the fact that the Nile constituted the main means of communication in the country. In times of urest, and even in more quiet periods, the ʿUrbāns' domination of key points on the river, its branches and canals, was a common phenomenon.

As far as the irrigation system which al-Nāṣir Muḥammad left behind is concerned, it is extremely doubtful whether its overhead expenses had been covered, before it started declining. Already in the first reign of Sultan Ḥasan (748–752/1347–1351) the decay of the irrigation system (*talaf al-jusūr*)[6]) in Egypt is mention-

[5]) Al-Maqrīzī repeatedly speaks about the year 806/1403–4 as the year of calamity after which everything went from bad to worse. This is a rather exaggerated evaluation. I discuss it in "The Expansion, etc."

[6]) The office of *kashf al-jusūr* was not confined to the supervision of the dams, but denoted the irrigation system as a whole.

ed, as part of a very sombre description of the chaotic conditions (*ikhtilāl fāḥish*) prevailing in both Egypt and Syria. This is in accordance with the repeated evidence of the sources along a period of about 15 years since al-Nāṣir's death, studied systematically by me: emptiness of the treasury on the one hand, and extortions equalling or even exceeding those of the deceased Sultan; misgovernment, which was accentuated in the provinces; internal struggles within the military aristocracy; 'Urbān unrest and revolts; utter chaos and corruption in the distribution and management of fiefs (*iqṭā'āt*); the rapid decline of the postal (*barīd*) system, which was a major means of the government's control over the provinces (the *barīd* never really recovered afterwards).[7]) The 'Urbān were closely connected with the postal services, as already stated before. From time to time they had also a say in the bestowment and control of feudal fiefs, because many of them were situated in their territories. The irrigation system suffered heavily from a combination of the 'Urbāns' unruliness and the corruption and neglect of the government officials responsible for its upkeep. In the first reign of Sultan Ḥasan the district governors of Egypt are said to have ruined the operation of the irrigation system (*aḍā'a al-wulāt 'amal al-jusūr*). Amongst other things they sold out the rakes (*jarārīf*) vital for the maintenance of that kind of irrigation.

Thus the unruliness of the 'Urbān and the damage caused by them in the period under discussion were considerably bigger than it is reflected in the text of this article. Though they did not reach the dimensions of later periods, they constituted an ominous preliminary to future developments.

In view of the fact that of the two main countries of the Mamluk Sultanate Egypt was by far the richest, its decline was of particular significance, and the contribution of its 'Urbān to that process made them a far more decisive factor than their pure military ability justified.

D. The sizes of the expeditions against the rebellious 'Urbān varied between 100 (or 150) and 500. Very rarely they reached 600. Most of them were Royal Mamluks.[8]) Thus the expedition discussed above of 2,000 Royal Mamluks against the 'Urbān of al-Buḥayra in 872/1468 was an exceptionally big one.

In the internal struggles between the Mamluk factions it *did* happen very rarely that each side mobilized its loyal 'Urbān for battle, but then the fighting was conducted between the Mamluks separately and between the 'Urbān of each faction separately (*fa-ṣāra al-Atrāk yattaqi'ū ma'a ba'ḍihim wal-'Urbān yattaqi'ū ma'a ba'ḍihim*).[9]) Shortly after that encounter, and in reliance on it as a precedent, the participation of other 'Urbān in another Mamluk internal conflict was contemplated, but this time the idea was rejected, on the ground that *this would cause utter*

---

[7]) The temporary upsurge of the eunuchs and the women in the court, which took place at exactly the same time, both reflected and enhanced the deteriorating situation. Amongst other negative effects, it contributed considerably to the indiscriminate and irresponsible distribution of the fiefs. For this see "The Eunuchs in the Mamluk Sultanate", Jerusalem, 1977, especially pp. 282–295.

[8]) These numbers are taken from the yet unpublished chapter on the Mamluk Army in the Field of Battle. There a detailed list is given.

[9]) This statement is repeated twice (Ibn Iyās, III, pp. 356, ll. 8–0, 358, l. 2).

depravity! (*hādhā yaḥṣul minhu ghāyat al-fasād*).[10]) Sultan Barqūq asked, at an earlier date, the 'Urbān of Upper Egypt to help him against amirs Minṭāsh and Yalbughā during his Cairo struggle, but they excused themselves stating that they are incapable of fighting the Mamluks. Had his adversaries been 'Urbān they would have come and fought them! (*i'tadharū annahum lā yuḥṣinū al-qitāl ma'a al-Turk wa-annahum law kānū 'Arab ḥaḍarū wa-qātalūhum*).[11])

These instances clearly demonstrate the inferior socio-military status of the Egyptian 'Urbān under the Mamluks, and accentuate the great transformation which Mamluk-'Urbān relations underwent in Ottoman Egypt. In Mamluk Syria the relations between the ruling class and the 'Urbān and other local military elements were very different from the outset.

E. When I originally wrote the chapter on the auxiliary forces in the Mamluk Sultanate I more or less accepted the prevalent view about the predominance of the Kurds in the Ayyūbid reign and this is reflected in the text of the present article. My change of view, namely, that the core of the Ayyūbid army was always its Mamluk component, is to be found in later studies.[12]) However, what remained true is that at the very end of the Ayyūbid rule the position of te Kurds was greatly weakened, and that under the Mamluks that weakening continued, although not necessarily without interruption.

---

[10]) Idem, p. 450, ll. 8–10.

[11]) Ibn al-Furāt, IX, p. 72, ll. 12–14.

[12]) See: Aspects of the Mamluk Phenomenon: Ayyubids, Kurds and Turks, *Der Islam*, vol. 54 (1977), pp. 1–32, and From Ayybids to Mamluks, *REI* (in the press).

VIII

SOME REMARKS ON THE ECONOMIC DECLINE OF THE MAMLŪK SULTANATE

Introductory Note

In a study of the Mamlūk army and military society, reference to the economic conditions of the Sultanate is, quite obviously, unavoidable. It is also obvious that within the framework of such a study the main stress would be on those economic aspects which had a bearing on that army and that society, and, to a lesser extent, on bodies and problems closely connected with them. This fact alone indicates the limitations of an approach to the economy of the Mamlūk Sultanate from such a relatively narrow angle. Another drawback, in my view, is that what follows the present introductory note was written a very long time ago, when the available sources, and particularly those available in Jerusalem, were considerably fewer than they are today.

There are, however, certain mitigating circumstances. First, the contemporary source-material available for the later Mamlūk period, in which most of the economic decline took place, was at that time better than that for the earlier period. Second, in some important respects a period of decline can be studied more thoroughly than a period of prosperity. The sources pay much more attention to many central subjects during times of weakness and tension. As far as the army and military society are concerned, I was able to reconstruct many major aspects concerning them more reliably and more fully on the basis of the accounts of later sources, for just that reason. A more or less full picture of the system of payment of the Mamlūk army and of some other inferior units, could be drawn mainly for the time when pay was below standard and irregular, a fact which caused constant tensions and much discussion in the sources. For example, those sources repeatedly mention the sums to which the soldier, commander, etc., was entitled, as against the sums which he actually received. By contrast, when the army receives its full pay regularly, there is no need to refer to this subject at all; and, therefore, the information about it is next to negligible.[1] For the same reason the structure of the whole Mamlūk military aristocracy is revealed when antagonisms between its various components are frequent, a phenomenon which repeats itself more often under conditions of stress and decline.[2] There are, of course, numerous other examples to this effect.

So much for the relation between the economic decline of the Sultanate and its Mamlūk military society. The subject should, however, be studied in a much wider context, wider even than the boundaries of the Mamlūk Sultanate. The reason is that, in fact, the decline was not confined to that Sultanate alone, but affected numerous other countries, especially those lying to its east.[3] Therefore, the study should embrace that whole vast area.

In this connection, I would like to repeat what I have already emphasized on other occasions, namely, that the Mamlūk sources contain immensely rich and valuable information about countries lying beyond their Sultanate. In more than one instance this information is considerably more significant than that furnished by the local sources. This is also true of the subject just discussed.

I have been occupied for some time now, gathering material for certain aspects of the above-mentioned subject in its widest context. Yet I find it justified to publish my initial version, which was written within the limits and limitations of the study of Mamlūk society, because I believe that it may be of some help for future research.

Before reproducing that initial version, however, I would like to enumerate some guidelines, which, in my view, the student of the subject, both in its narrower and wider sense, should take into consideration.

---

1 See my "The System of Payment in Mamlūk Military Society", *JESHO*, vol. I (1958), pp. 37–65, 257–296.

2 See "Studies on the Structure of the Mamlūk Army", *BSOAS*, vols. XIV (1953), pp. 203–228, 448–476; XVI (1954), pp. 57–90. The same is true, on the whole, of units of more inferior status ("The Auxiliary Forces of the Mamlūk Sultanate", *Der Islam* vol. 65 (1988), pp. 13–37).

3 The decline of North Africa started much earlier, as is well known.

a) The visible roots of the decline in the Mamlūk Sultanate are considerably earlier than the end of the eighth/fourteenth – beginning of the ninth/fifteenth centuries. They are clearly found in the third reign of Sultan al-Nāṣir Muḥammad b. Qalāūn (709–741/1309–1340).[4]

b) One should not accept at its face value the claim of al-Maqrīzī and some others, who assert that the year 806/1403–1404 was the one in which the turning point to the worse took place (see below). It should, however, be considered as one of the important milestones in the process of decline.

c) In the study of the Mamlūk Sultanate's decline three matters should be taken into account: 1) The nostalgic idealization, by some of the late Mamlūk historians, of the early Mamlūk period, as compared with their own time. This idealization led them to paint a somewhat exaggerated picture of the size of the gap between the glorious past and the wretched present; 2) Although the general outline of the decline is undeniable, there may well have been periods of slowdown and stoppage in that process, or perhaps even ameliorations;[5] 3) The terms *khariba, kharraba, kharāb* and the like used frequently by our sources (see below) do not necessarily always mean total destruction. Hence the economic situation might have been somewhat less sombre than that suggested by contemporary historians.[6]

d) Towards the end of the fifteenth century, and less than twenty

---

4 I am dealing with this subject comprehensively in a detailed study called "The Expansion and Decline of Cairo under the Mamlūks and its Background", which is now in progress. A brief summary of the paper on that subject which I read in the 1973 Congress of Orientalists in Paris was published in *Résumés des Communications Sections 1–5. XXIX Congrès International des Orientalistes*, Paris, 1973, pp. 64–65. The lecture itself was not published. Some of the conclusions of this study were published as an Appendix to my study "The Auxiliary Forces, etc.", *op. cit.*, pp. 32–37.

5 Sumptuous buildings and other imposing constructions do not necessarily serve as a proof of economic change for the better.

6 I have already called attention to that point in *Gunpowder and Firearms in the Mamlūk Kingdom — A Challenge to a Medieval Society*, London, 1956, p. 131, note 280.

years before the Mamlūk Sultanate's demise, the appearance of the Portuguese, headed by Vasco da Gama, took place in the Indian Ocean and beyond, as a result of the circumnavigation of the African continent. This was part of the expansion of Christian Western Europe in both the Western and Eastern hemispheres, an expansion which changed the face of the globe. Few events in human recorded history can be compared in their importance and their far-reaching results to that expansion. The long-range decisive impact of that circumnavigation, be it political, strategic or economic, cannot be contested. But what was its impact on the economy of the Sultanate which was, at that time, nearing its end? For an answer to this difficult question two facts should be taken into consideration: 1) Very little is said in the Mamlūk sources about that impact; 2) The appearance of the Christian Europeans in the Indian Ocean occurred a long time after the economic deterioration had already set in, and quite shortly before the disappearance of the Mamlūk Sultanate (its effects could be felt in Egypt for fifteen years or thereabouts). Even if it could be established that, according to non-Mamlūk, and particularly to Christian European, sources, the impact was considerable, these two formidable facts should not be forgotten and should be given much weight.

e) There cannot be any doubt whatsoever that the Turkish peoples and their like, and particularly the Mamlūks in all their variations, were the main factor in Islam's defence and expansion during the greatest part of its existence. On the other hand, their contribution, generally speaking, to the flourishing of the Islamic economy does not seem to have been so welcome. Now, economic conditions have always affected military ability and the war machine to a very great extent. However, in those states which had a relatively small elite army, the economic factor did not play such a decisive role as in the states of our own time, whose armies are based on general conscription and on the mobilization of a very great part of the available resources. Thus, states or empires whose economy was quite weak or declining, could still have very strong armies. In the case of the Mamlūk Sultanate, its economic deterioration was, indeed, no small factor in its defeat by the Ottomans. It was not, however, the major cause. The Sultanate was defeated, first and foremost, because the Ottomans employed a revolutionary weapon — firearms — on a very large scale, and used it properly.[7]

f) The results of the study of our subject in its widest sense (which should require the work of numerous scholars), will put us, among other things, in a better position to assess the relations between Islam and Christian Europe as well as the relations between the Ottoman Empire and its Muslim neighbours. The Mamlūk sources should occupy a central place in such a study, for the reasons already stated.

The following is a translation from Hebrew of the initial version mentioned above. It does not include any reference to additional source material.[8]

The Decline

The late Mamlūk sources are literally replete with very rich and very detailed information about the economic decline of Egypt and Syria, and especially of the former. The reader of the sources of the Circassian period becomes easily aware of the deep conviction of the Mamlūk writers that they live in a period of decline and disintegration. Clear statements to this effect are scattered in the

---

7 They equipped a very great number of warriors (mainly infantry men) with the hand-gun which was used in a *field* battle and not in a siege (see *Gunpowder and Firearms*, pp. 108–112, as well as pp. 97–108).

8 Not even to those volumes of al-Maqrīzī's chronicle *Kitāb al-Sulūk*, which were not yet published at the time of my writing. As far as reference to evidence included in them is made, it is through other sources which quote it. There is, indeed, a certain degree of overlapping between the general guidelines of the introductory note written today and some of the ideas expressed in the first pages of the text which follows it, written long ago. I decided, however, to leave both as they are, because they reflect two different periods of writing. In addition, there is a difference of stress and nuance between the two overlapping parts. As for the effects of the appearance of the Portuguese in the Indian Ocean on the economy of Mamlūk Egypt, I have already expressed my doubts about their magnitude long ago (*Gunpowder and Firearms, etc.*, London, 1956, p. 132, note 287). The somewhat mitigated wording of the same doubts in the present introductory note might be more correct.

sources, and even when collected at random, they may be numbered in the hundreds. There is no doubt that that sad state of things led the historians of the Circassian period to depict the earlier Turkish–Qipchāqi period in much brighter colours than it deserves. In spite of the exaggeration, however, that depiction is basically true. In the account of the history of that earlier period, there is much less of that atmosphere of gloom and despondency so characteristic of the later Mamlūk reign. It is noteworthy that students of the Mamlūk period pay little attention to the overwhelming evidence about the economic decline of the Sultanate during the greatest part of the Mamlūk reign.[9]

We shall now turn to the source–evidence.

According to the Mamlūk historians the turning point for the bad in the Mamlūk Sultanate was in the year 806/1403–1404.[10] Surely, they assert, the Sultanate suffered very heavy blows before that date, the most important of which being the great plague ("the Black Death") of 749/1348, and then the plague of 760/1359 and the great drought of 776/1375.[11] But the real decline of the Sultanate started with the attack of Tamerlane on Syria in 803/1400, an attack which brought in its wake terrible ruin and devastation,[12] and with the accession to the throne of the Sultanate in Egypt of Sultan Faraj (801–815/1398–1412), the son of Barqūq, in whose reign most bloody internal wars burst out. Since 806/1403–1404 catastrophes caused by nature were added to man-made catastrophes of which the most devastating one was low Nile stretching over a long period.[13]

In the following lines a somewhat detailed description of the destruction, as told in the Mamlūk sources, will be given.

---

9 This statement is, of course, true for the time of the writing of this article, but not for today.

10 Al-Maqrīzī, *al-Mawā'iẓ wal-I'tibār bi-Dhikr al-Khiṭaṭ wal-Āthār*, Cairo, 1270 H, vol. I, p. 5, ll. 21–24. This claim about the year 806/1403–1404 is repeated by that author very frequently in the *Khiṭaṭ*, and to a somewhat lesser extent in his chronicle *Kitāb al-Sulūk*. It is not confined, however, to him alone (see below).

11 *Idem*, I, pp. 5, ll. 1–24; 365, ll. 18–21.

12 *Idem*, I, p. 365, ll. 19–23.

13 *Idem*, I, p. 365, ll. 18–21; II, p. 131, ll. 26–27.

According to al-Maqrīzī (cited by Ibn Taghrībirdī) Sultan al-Nāṣir Faraj was the most unfortunate of all the Muslim rulers (*ash'am mulūk al-Islām*). Through his bad management he destroyed the whole of Egypt and Syria from the point of the Nile's entrance [into Egypt] and up to the bed of the Euphrates (*fa-innahu kharraba bi-sū' tadbīrihi jamī' arāḍī Miṣr wa-bilād al-Shām min ḥaythu yaṣubbu al-Nīl ilā majrā al-Furāt*). In 803/1400 Tamerlane attacked Syria and destroyed Aleppo, Hama, Baalbek and Damascus. This last-named town fell into ruins. Not even a single house was left intact in that town. A countless number of the people of Syria was killed. Since the year 806/1403–1404 onwards Egypt was afflicted by high prices. The amirs of the Mamlūk Sultanate did whatever they could to raise the prices, especially by hoarding the grains (from their feudal fiefs). They also raised the land-taxes and corrupted the currency, by substituting Frankish coins with images (*danānīr mushakhkhaṣa*) for the Muslim coins. They also raised the price of gold, so that the value of the *dīnār* rose from 20 *dirham* to 240 *dirham*. They taxed (*makasū*) everything on the one hand, and neglected the construction of dams (*jusūr*)[14] in the land of Egypt on the other. At the same time they forced the public to pay for the losses caused by the absence of dams. The Sultan's vizirs (particularly Sa'd al-Dīn Ibn Ghurāb and Jamāl al-Dīn Yūsuf) made the merchants and others buy the state's merchandise for the highest prices. They extorted whatever they could and brought it to the Sultan so that he would not dismiss them from their offices. After their death he demanded money from their successors in office, and they complied with his demands by inventing new means of extortion. Syria was destroyed because of this (*fa-kharibat al-Shām li-dhālika*). On top of all this there were the wars, revolts and insurgencies in Egypt and Syria. As a result Faraj had to head numerous military expeditions to Syria. Each such expedition cost no less than one million dinar, and he used to collect these sums by squeezing the blood and sucking the marrow of the people of Egypt (*yajbīhā min dimā' ahl Miṣr wa-muhjatihim*). Then he would go to Syria, extort its population and return to Egypt. All this could only

---

14 See also *Khiṭaṭ*, p. 101, where much important data on the Egyptian dams is collected.

increase unrest and riot. These sad circumstances brought about the destruction of Alexandria, the district of al-Buḥayra, most of the district of al-Sharqiyya, and the greatest part of the district of al-Gharbiyya, as well as the district of al-Fayyūm. Ruin also encompassed the whole of Upper Egypt, which led to the abolishment of forty *khuṭbas* there. Assuan, which had been one of the mightiest frontline towns of Islam fell into ruin (*datharat*). More than half of Cairo, its possessions (?) and its suburbs (outskirts?) (*al-Qāhira wa-amlākuhā wa-ẓawāhiruhā*) were destroyed, and about two thirds of its people died as a result of the high cost of living and the epidemics (*bil-ghalā' wal-wabā'*). In the riots and unrest of Faraj's reign people perished in countless numbers.[15]

Although Ibn Taghrībirdī, to put it mildly, does not see eye to eye with al-Maqrīzī about Faraj's personality and many of his deeds,[16] his view of the economic decline of the Mamlūk Sultanate in that Sultan's reign is quite similar to the view of that historian. The following is a typical passage:

> And in this year [806/1403–1404] was the immense drought (*sharāqī*),[17] which was followed by the terrible famine prices and then by the epidemic. This year is the first of the years of mishaps and ordeals in which the greatest part of Egypt and its provinces (*mu'ẓam al-Diyār al-Miṣriyya wa-a'mālihā*) were ruined by the *sharāqī*, by dissensions, by the frequent change of governors and by other causes.[18]

The ruin continued in full force in the reign of al-Mu'ayyad Shaykh

---

15 Ibn Taghrībirdī, *al-Nujūm al-Zāhira fī Mulūk Miṣr wal-Qāhira* (ed. Popper), Berkeley, 1920–1923, vol. VI, pp. 271, l. 19–273, l. 6; *Khiṭaṭ*, I, p. 365, ll. 18–28.

16 See e.g. the passage cited in the preceding note; and also my "The Circassians in the Mamlūk Kingdom", *JAOS*, vol. 69 (1949), pp. 141b–142a. One of the causes of Ibn Taghrībirdī's defence of Faraj was their common Rūmī origin (Faraj, the son of Circassian Barqūq, had a Rūmī mother). I am discussing this point in some detail in a study called "Baḥriyya Mamlūks; Burjiyya Mamlūks — Inadequate Names for the Two Mamlūk Reigns" (Tārīḫ, Annenberg Research Institute, Philadelphia, 1990, pp. 3–53. See especially pp. 49–53).

17 The exact meaning of *sharāqī* is: land not watered by the Nile. This happened in years when the Nile was low. Those lands which the flood waters did not reach could not be cultivated.

18 *Nujūm* (P), VI, p. 108, ll. 17–20.

(815–824/1412–1421).[19] The rural countryside (*al-aryāf*) was particularly affected because of the protection practices (*ḥimāyāt*) imposed by Sultans Faraj, Shaykh and Aynāl (857–865/1453–1460). According to our source, this was one of the main causes of the ruin.[20] In 855/1451 Egypt suffered from a very severe drought. The country was impoverished. Cairo was on the verge of ruin (*ashrafat al-Qāhira 'alā al-kharāb*). Countless numbers of its inhabitants (*khalā'iq min ahlihā lā tadkhul taḥt al-ḥaṣr*) left it for Syria. Far larger numbers of the villagers and the Bedouins entered the capital (*wa-warada 'alayhā min ahl al-qurā wa-min al-a'rāb amthāl man kharaja minhā*). Many of these poverty stricken people died in the town's streets and alleys.[21] In the same year the same author states that the land of Egypt was on the verge of destruction (*ashrafat al-Diyār al-Miṣriyya 'alā al-kharāb*) because of its being afflicted in those years by the continuous high prices and the unceasing dearth (*qaḥṭ*) and the great *sharāqī*. The inhabitants lost their property and their money and most of the villages were emptied of their people (*wa-khalat ghālib al-qurā min ahlihā*).[22] The misdeeds of the Sultan's Mamlūks (*julbān*) in the reign of Aynāl also bring Egypt to the verge of destruction (*ashrafat Miṣr fī ayyāmihim 'alā al-kharāb*). They committed against the people of that country crimes which even the *Khawārij*[23] did not dare to commit. Consequently, there were Egyptians who contemplated leaving it and moving to another country.[24] In 868/1463–1464 the district of al-Buḥayra was "on

---

19 Ibn Taghrībirdī, *al-Manhal al-Ṣāfī*, Paris MS. (de Slane No. 2068–2072), vol. III, fol. 1687, ll. 16–21; al-Sakhāwī, *al-Ḍaw' al-Lāmi'*, Cairo, 1353–1355 H, vol. III, p. 310, ll. 12–17.

20 *Khiṭaṭ*, I, p. 111, ll. 26–29; *Nujūm* (P), VII, p. 651, ll. 5–12. On the *ḥimāya* see Claude Cahen's excellent article in *EI*², vol. III, p. 394a–b, and the bibliography quoted there. See also Hassanein Rabie, *The Financial System of Egypt A.H. 564–741/A.D. 1169–1341*, London, 1972, p. 52.

21 Ibn Taghrībirdī, *Ḥawādith al-Duhūr*, ed. Popper, Leiden, 1930, pp. 108, l. 15 – 109, l. 3.

22 *Idem*, p. 110, ll. 18–20.

23 Comparison with the atrocities of the *Khawārij* is quite frequent in the Mamlūk sources.

24 *Ḥawādith*, p. 451, ll. 1–12. Stereotyped expressions which reflect the temporary -- or rather, transitory -- character of the Sultan's attempts to

the verge of destruction" because of the depredations of the Bedouins (ʿ*Urbān*) who revolted against the central government. As a result, most of the inhabitants of that district moved to the districts of al-Sharqiyya and al-Gharbiyya.[25] The weakness of the Sultan reached such a degree in that year that he opened negotiations with ʿArab Muḥārib. Their representative came to Cairo, and was received with great honour by the Sultan himself, and both sides reached an agreement in that meeting.[26] This was an extremely rare procedure in the relations between the Mamlūks and a revolting Bedouin element. In the same year a very sad picture of Egypt's plight is depicted by Ibn Taghrībirdī: most of Upper Egypt is practically ruled by the Bedouins (*li-anna ghālib bilād al-Ṣaʿīd ṣārat bi-yad al-ʿArab*). Lower Egypt is in a state of decay because of the numerous *ḥimāyāt*, the iniquity and the lack of respect and obedience to the governors (*fa-qad fasada ḥāluhu li-kathrat al-ḥimāyāt wal-ẓulm wa-qillat ḥurmat ḥukkāmihā*). Since most of the country was subjected to the practice of *ḥimāyāt*, the governors were completely unable to carry out any kind of improvement.[27] In 872/1467-1468 the author describes a most lamentable situation. The defeats suffered by the Mamlūk army from the Turcoman Shāh Siwār in the north of the realm undermined security in Egypt. The revolt by the ʿUrbān resulted ultimately in the ruin of most of the villages (*wa-ṭāla hādhā al-amr bi-aryāf Miṣr ḥattā kharaba akthar qurāhā*). This was the situation of Upper and

---

restrain the depredations of his own Mamlūks (*julbān*) which were so damaging to the Sultanate in so many respects, are: *khamadat al-fitna qalīlan; sakana al-ḥāl* (or *al-iḍṭirāb*) *qalīlan* Ibn Iyās, *Badāʾiʿ al-Zuhūr*, Cairo, 1311-12 H, vol. II, pp. 43, ll. 27-28; 54, l. 3; 57, l. 12; 60, ll. 17-18; *idem* (ed. Kahle-Mustapha), Istanbul, 1931-1936, vol. III, pp. 196, ll. 8-11; 240, l. 21; IV, pp. 8, ll. 18-19; 17, l. 20; 49, l. 23; 123, l. 12; 127, l. 21; 180, ll. 9-10; 235, ll. 20-21; 369, ll. 22-23; 430, l. 4.

25 *Ḥawādith*, p. 458. ll. 6-13.

26 *Idem*, p. 465, ll. 1-11.

27 *Idem*, pp. 458, l. 14 - 459, l. 8. Concerning the ruin of the rural countryside (*aryāf*) by the Bedouins see also *idem*, p. 643, ll. 10-12 (*wal-ḥāl ghayr mustaqīm lā siyyamā al-aryāf fa-innahu āla amruhā ilā al-kharāb min tasalluṭ al-ʿUrbān ʿalayhā*).

Lower Egypt. As for the district of al-Buḥayra,[28] it is permanently exposed to the war with the Bedouins. Therefore, most of its villages are in ruin. And, as a matter of fact, this is quite logical, for if most of the villages in the districts of al-Gharbiyya and al-Manūfiyya which are situated between two rivers [i.e. between the two branches of the delta] and are, therefore, the most flourishing in the whole of Egypt, are now in a state of ruin, how much more so is the situation in al-Buḥayra and in other areas? (*wa-ṭāla hādhā al-amr bi-aryāf Miṣr ḥattā khariba akthar qurāhā fa-hādhā mā kāna bi-Ṣaʿīd Miṣr wa-Asfalihā wa-ammā iqlīm al-Buḥayra fa-shaʾnuhum al-ḥarb wal-qitāl maʿa al-ʿArab dawāman ḥattā shamala akthar qurāhā al-kharāb wa-yaḥiqqu lahā an takhrab fa-inna iqlīm al-Gharbiyya wal-Manūfiyya jazīra bayna baḥrayn wa-humā aʿmar bilād Miṣr qad khariba al-āna akthar qurāhā fa-kayfa anta bi-iqlīm al-Buḥayra wa-ghayrihā*).[29]

According to the same author, the worst years he ever witnessed were the years 872–874/1467–1470, namely, the very last years of his life [he died in 874/1470]: (*innanī lam ara fīmā raʾaytu mundhu ʿumrī awḥash ḥālan min hādhihi al-sinīn al-thalāth sanat ithnayn wa-sabʿīn wa-allatayni baʿdahā.*)[30]

---

28 It is interesting that our author speaks about this particular district, lying to the west of the Rosetta branch of the Nile, as distinct from Lower Egypt. The reason seems to have been his desire to make a comparison between a district lying outside the Nile delta and districts lying inside it.

29 *Idem*, pp. 653–655. Most indicative is Ibn Taghrībirdī's comment on the zeal which Sultan Qāytbāy (873–901/1468–1495) showed suddenly, at the beginning of his reign, in repairing a dam in the vicinity of Cairo. He expresses his astonishment at the Sultan's concentration on that particular and not too important dam, while he neglects the whole of Upper and Lower Egypt and leaves Lower Egypt to the mercy of the destructive Bedouins. His preoccupation with the war against the Turcoman Shāh Siwār prevents him from looking after the interests of the country (*wa-taʿajjabat al-nās min ihmāl al-Sulṭān lil-bilād al-Qibliyya wal-Baḥriyya ḥattā istawlā ʿalā ghālib al-bilād al-Baḥriyya al-ʿArab wa-kharrabū ghālib bilād al-Buḥayra wal-Sulṭān mashghūl bi-amr Siwār lā yaltafit ilā maṣāliḥ al-bilād thumma innahu yahtamm bi-hādhā al-jisr alladhī lā ʿibrata lahu hādhā al-ihtimām al-ʿaẓīm*) (*idem*, p. 673, ll. 16–19).

30 *Idem*, p. 734, ll. 2–4.

Towards the end of 873/1469 our author points at the uselessness of the Sultan's making a personal appearance in the districts of al-Buḥayra, al-Gharbiyya and al-Sharqiyya, most of the villages of which had already been in complete ruin (*wa-lam yaẓhar li-safarihi ilā hādhihi al-aqālīm al-thalātha natīja bal shamala al-kharāb ghālib qurāhum* [sic!]). He is convinced that such a tour could only diminish the prestige of the central authority, for people justly argued: "If the Sultan himself cannot put an end to the Bedouins' oppression, who can?" (*fa-waqaʿa bi-dhālika ghāyat al-wahn fī al-mamlaka wa-ayisa al-nās ʿan zawāl ẓulm al-ʿArab lahum wa-qālū idhā kāna al-Sulṭān mā azāla hādhā ʿannā fa-man baqiya yuzīluhu*).[31]

The repeated military defeats which the Mamlūks suffered from the Turcoman Shāh Siwār greatly lowered the prestige of the Sultanate among the kings of the east and others, according to the explicit testimony of the late Mamlūk sources. Even the fellahs became audacious and dared to molest the Mamlūks. The Circassians almost lost their rule over the realm, and Shāh Siwār was on the verge of conquering Aleppo (*wa-qad untuhikat ḥurmat Sulṭān Miṣr ʿinda mulūk al-sharq wa-ghayrihā* [sic!] *ḥattā al-fallāḥīn* [sic!] *ṭamiʿū fī al-Turk wa-tabahdalū ʿindahum bi-sabab mā jarā ʿalayhim min Siwār wa-kādat an takhruj al-mamlaka ʿan al-Jarākisa wa-qad ashrafa Siwār ʿalā akhdh Ḥalab*).[32]

Ibn Iyās states in his account of the events of the month of Dhū al-Qaʿda 901/July 1496 that since then the economic decline of the country was accelerated. The income from the feudal fiefs was extremely diminished. Henceforward things went from bad to worse until they "surpassed all bounds" (*fa-min yawmaʾidhin talāshā amr*

---

31 *Idem*, pp. 710, l. 22 – 711, l. 18.

32 Ibn Iyās (KM) III, pp. 74–75. See also the citation from Ibn Taghrībirdī's *Ḥawādith* in note 29. The prestige of the Mamlūks reached such a low ebb among the Bedouins (*ʿUrbān*) that they dared prevent the *Mubashshir al-Ḥajj* (the messenger of the returning pilgrims' caravan announcing its safety) from arriving in Cairo. The central authority had no other way but to appoint a Bedouin to that important job, instead of the Mamlūk (*Nujūm* (P), p. 712, ll. 4–6; Ibn Iyās (E), II, pp. 47, ll. 26–27; 192, ll. 9–10; (KM) III, pp. 156, ll. 2–3; 208, l. 19; 388, ll. 14–15; IV, pp. 62, ll. 19–22; 89, ll. 16–19; 95, ll. 13–18).

al-bilād wa-inḥaṭṭa kharāj al-muqṭa'īn jiddan wa-qad tazāyada al-amr ba'da dhālika ḥattā jāwaza al-ḥadd fī al-nihāya).[33]

Bad news about the poor state of the economy follows in quick succession.[34]

In the month of Jumādā I 908/November 1502 it is stated that as a result of extortions and heavy taxation of the local and foreign merchants, the ports of Alexandria, Damietta and Jedda (which was a very important source of income in the Circassian period) as well as other harbours and frontier seaports were brought into a state of ruin which continued thenceforward (*akhraba thaghr al-Iskandariyya wa-bandar Judda wa-ghayr dhālika min al-thughūr wa-talāshā amr al-thughūr wal-banādir min yawma'idhin wa-taḍā'afat* [sic!] *amr al-mukūs jiddan ḥattā jāwazat al-ḥadd fī dhālika*).[35]

In the year 918/1512–1513 Ibn Iyās gives a most depressing picture of the economic situation in the realm.[36]

In 920/1514–1516 the same historian states that the treasuries of the main Dīwāns of the realm were completely empty. The port of Alexandria was in a state of total ruin. As for the harbour of Jedda it became desolate because of the Portuguese. No ships visited it for about six years. Damietta was in a similar state. As for al-Buḥayra, it was in complete disorder because of Bedouin depredations (*wa-kāna fī tilka al-ayyām Dīwān al-Mufrad wa-Dīwān al-Dawla wa-Dīwān al-Khāṣṣ*[37] *fī ghāyat al-inshiḥāt wal-ta'ṭīl fa-inna bandar al-Iskandariyya kharāb wa-lam tadkhul ilayhi al-qaṭā'i' fī al-sana al-khāliya wa-bandar Jadda kharāb bi-sabab ta'abbuth al-Faranj 'alā al-tujjār fī Baḥr al-Hind fa-lam tadkhul al-marākib bil-baḍā'i' ilā bandar Jadda naḥwan min sitt sinīn wa-ka-dhālika jihat Dimyāṭ wa-kānat jihat al-Buḥayra fī hādhihi al-ayyām fī ghāyat al-iḍṭirāb bi-sabab fasād al-'Urbān)*.[38]

---

33 Ibn Iyās (KM) III, p. 323, ll. 17–19.

34 See, for example, *idem*, III, pp. 360, ll. 17–21; 366, ll. 4–11; 386, ll. 6–8; 440, ll. 6–8.

35 *Idem*, IV, pp. 45, l. 19 – 46, l. 1.

36 *Idem*, pp. 262–263.

37 On these Dīwāns see my: "Studies on the Structure of the Mamlūk Army", *BSOAS*, vol. XVI (1954), pp. 61–62.

38 Ibn Iyās (KM) IV, p. 359, ll. 11–16.

A very reliable indicator for the steady decline of Alexandria under the Circassians is the following fact: The number of the town's looms dropped within less than forty-five years to almost one eighteenth! (from more than 14,000 shortly after 790/1388 to 800 in 837/1438–9) (*fa-balaghat 'iddatuhum* [sic!] *thamān mi'at nawl ba'da mā balaghat 'iddatuhā fī ayyām niyābat Ibn Maḥmūd al-Ustādār fī sanat biḍ' wa-tis'īn wa-sab'mi'a arba'at 'ashar alf nawl wa-nayyifan fa-unẓur ilā hādhā al-tafāwut fī hādhihi al-sinīn al-qalīla wa-dhālika li-ẓulm wulāt al-umūr wa-sū' sīratihim wa-'adam ma'rifatihim*).[39] As is

39 *Nujūm* (P), VI, p. 714, ll. 11–17. I have already cited that important evidence in *Gunpowder and Firearms*, p. 131, note 286. Measuring the decline of the Mamlūk Sultanate by means of the available data on the fluctuations of the numbers of its villages is absolutely unreliable for Egypt and utterly impossible for Syria. Ibn Taghrībirdī cites al-Musabbiḥī as saying that in the fourth/tenth century the number of the villages of Egypt was 10,000 as compared to only 2,170 in 837/1433–4, according to a census carried out by officials of *Dīwān al-Jaysh*. Our author finds in this decrease decisive proof of Egypt's decline (*Nujūm* (P), VI, p. 717, ll. 9–10). But this conclusion is more than doubtful for the following reasons: First, there is no evidence to corroborate it. Secondly, Ibn Taghrībirdī contradicts himself when he states elsewhere that in the time of the Fāṭimid Caliph al-Ḥākim bi-Amr Allāh (386–411/996–1020) the number of Egypt's villages was 2,390 as compared to 2,365, which were divided almost equally between Upper and Lower Egypt, in the year 863/1459–1460 (*Ḥawādith*, p. 333, ll. 14–19). Thus the number of the Egyptian villages throughout the Fāṭimid, the Ayyūbid and (almost all of) the Mamlūk periods does not seem to have undergone drastic change. This does not imply that the number of the inhabitants of each of these villages did not change substantially (see also in this connection my "Regarding Population Estimates in the Countries of Medieval Islam", *JESHO*, vol. XXVIII (1985), pp. 1–19, and especially note 34 on pp. 18–19). In Syria the situation, as far as the number of villages is concerned, is even much worse. It is stated that in 616/1219–1220 there were in *al-Bilād al-Shāmiyya* 2,000 villages, 1,600 of which were private ones (*amlāk li-ahlihā*) and the other 400 of which belonged to the state, or to the ruler (*sulṭāniyya*) (Sibṭ Ibn al-Jawzī, *Mir'āt al-Zamān*, Chicago, 1907, p. 397, ll. 6–11). This is, as far as I know, an isolated piece of evidence which might be of greater use if it could be complemented by additional data from the sources.

For further information on the decline of the Sultanate see: *Nujūm* (P), VI, pp. 463–465; 773, ll. 16–21; VII, p. 561, ll. 1–4; *Ḥawādith*, pp. 177, ll. 1–2; 222, ll. 15–18; 223, ll. 18–20; 644–645; Ibn Iyās (*KM*) III, pp. 22; 217, ll. 9–15; 366, ll. 4–11;

well known, Alexandria was a major centre of textile manufacturing.

This is a picture of continuous decline, based on evidence which can be easily multiplied indefinitely.[40]

A whole set of factors seems to have led to that decline. Some of them are obvious or traceable. Others are not so clear. Here, only one factor will be mentioned, namely *corruption*.

Cases of bribery, payment of money for getting an appointment (military, civil or religious), iniquitous extortions of money and other kinds of valuables, were quite frequent in the Turkish-Qipchāqi period.[41] This is particularly evident in the chronicles dealing with that period. But in the Circassian period corruption reached dimensions far bigger than those prevailing under the Qipchāqi Turks.

About buying commanders' offices Ibn Taghrībirdī says that it is true that this is an old scourge, but it had never reached the dimensions of his own time. In the past buying an office, etc., was an isolated phenomenon, "one out of many", whereas "in these days" it became the ordinary practice relating to every officer's rank and to every feudal estate (*hādhā shay' jadīd tajaddada fī hādhihi al-dawla a'nī bay' al-imra wa-in kāna al-balā' qadīman fa-lam yakun 'alā hādhihi al-hay'a wa-ayḍan lam yakun fī kull iqṭā' wa-innamā kāna* . . . .[42] *nādiran wāḥidan min jumla laysa mithla hādhihi al-ayyām fī kull iqṭā' wa-aẓunnu dhālika ṣāra 'ādatan wa-lā quwwata illā billāh*).[43]

The seeds of corruption on a large scale were sown already in the short reign of Sultan al-Kāmil Sha'bān (746–747/1345–1346), that is

---

383, ll. 6–8; 448, ll. 6–8; IV, pp. 93, ll. 8–16, 18; 111, l. 5; 291, 293, ll. 21–22; 302, ll. 20–23; Khalīl b. Shāhīn al-Ẓāhirī, *Zubdat Kashf al-Mamālik*, Paris, 1894, p. 98, ll. 9–12.

40 Whether, in actual fact, there were breaks in the decline, is another matter, as I have already stated in the introductory note.

41 See e.g. Ibn Kathīr, *al-Bidāya wal-Nihāya*, Cairo 1351–1358 H, vol. XIII, p. 130, ll. 9–11; al-Maqrīzī, *Kitāb al-Sulūk bi-Ma'rifat al-Duwal wal-Mulūk*, Cairo, 1934–1942, vol. I, pp. 897–899, 904, l. 4; 914, ll. 8–16; II, pp. 12; 28; 312, l. 1; 369; 381–383, 440, ll. 18–19; *Nujūm* (P), V, p. 93, ll. 3–9. On *Dīwān al-Badal* see below.

42 Here follow a number of words which are incomprehensible to me. The text is, perhaps, corrupted.

43 *Ḥawādith*, p. 339.

to say, a few decades before the Circassians came to power, with the creation of *Dīwān al-Badal* (department of exchange), through which a member of the *ḥalqa* regiment could give up his estate in exchange for a sum of money, and another person could obtain the estate in exchange for another sum.[44] Its name was purposefully distorted to *Dīwān al-Badhl* (department of wastefulness), because of the corruption and bribery which it encouraged.[45] At that time, however, corruption existed on a relatively small scale. Ibn Taghrībirdī quotes al-Maqrīzī as saying that in the reign of Sultān Barqūq (784–801/1382–1398) corruption became rampant and bribes were given openly. The Sultan himself did not appoint anybody to any post without getting paid for the appointment. This brought about deterioration in many domains. He also preferred people of lowly origin over people of respectable families (*illā annahu* [= Barqūq] *kāna muḥibban li-jam' al-māl wa-ḥadatha fī ayyāmihi tajāhur al-nās bil-ṭarābīl fa-kāna lā yakād yuwallī aḥadan waẓīfatan aw 'amalan illā bi-māl wa-fasada bi-dhālika kathīr min al-aḥwāl wa-kāna muwalla'an fī taqdīm al-asāfil wa-ḥaṭṭ dhawī al-buyūtāt*). Our author adds that in his own time things became many times worse, until they exceeded all bounds (*wa-hādhā al-balā' qad taḍā'afa al-āna ḥattā kharaja 'an al-ḥadd*).[46]

In order for corruption to be halted temporarily, the country had to be afflicted by a great epidemic, or the Sultan had to be stricken by a severe illness. Under such circumstances the sale of offices would stop for some time.[47]

These brief intervals, however, were completely insignificant, and large-scale corruption continued up to the very end of the Sultanate.[48]

---

44 On this *dīwān* see my "Studies on the Structure of the Mamlūk Army", *BSOAS*, vol. XV (1953), pp. 453–454, and on the *ḥalqa idem*, pp. 448–459, and *art.* *Ḥalqa* in *EI*[2].

45 *Nujūm* (P), V, pp. 40, l. 15; 423, ll. 8–13; Ibn Ḥajar al-'Asqalānī, *al-Durar al-Kāmina*, Hyderabad 1948–1350 H, vol. I, p. 390, ll. 9–11.

46 *Nujūm* (P), V, p. 422, ll. 4–9.

47 *Idem*, p. 763, ll. 4–6.

48 Here are just a few examples: *Nujūm* (P), VI, pp. 227, ll. 19–20; 358, ll. 12–15; 451, l. 18; 558, l. 2; 672; 804, l. 19; 832, ll. 12–14; 839, ll. 4–5; 853, l. 4; VII, pp. 150; 122,

Postscript

A. The above description does not support in any way Louis Massignon's claim, followed by that of Fernand Braudel, that corruption spread in the Ottoman Empire as a result of the conquest of Mamlūk Egypt and Syria. I discuss this matter elsewhere.

B. It should be pointed out that although corruption as a cause of the Mamlūk Sultanate's decline is singled out at the end of the initial version, some of the other causes of that decline are mentioned or clearly implied both in that version and in the introductory note.

---

ll. 14–28; 228, l. 7; 552, ll. 14–15; 568, l. 14; 572, ll. 1–2; 708, ll. 5–7; 791, l. 8; *Ḥawādith*, pp. 297, ll. 8–9; 453, ll. 21–22; 482, l. 1 - 483, l. 2; 528, ll. 13–22; 596, l. 14; 621, ll. 6–8; 622, l. 12 - 623, l. 3; Ibn al-Furāt, *Ta'rīkh al-Duwal wal-Mulūk*, Beirut, 1936–1942, IX, pp. 155–159; Ibn Iyās (C) II, p. 182, ll. 19–20; (KM) IV, pp. 190, ll. 1–2; 351, ll. 18–21; V, p. 25, ll. 16–18; al-Sakhāwī, *al-Ḍaw' al-Lāmi'*, Cairo, 1353–1355 H, vol. III, p. 276, l. 29.

IX

THE END OF THE MAMLŪK SULTANATE

(Why did the ottomans spare the mamlūks of egypt and wipe out the mamlūks of syria ?)

Introductory Remark

It is quite a long time since I have started studying, off and on, the history of Egypt (and, to a lesser extent, that of Syria) during the early Ottoman period. I intended, of course, to utilize as many of the available sources as I could. For various reasons, the chances that I shall follow up that research are not bright. I, therefore, decided to publish that part of my study which is based on the data contained in the two chronicles of Ibn Iyās (1) and Ibn Ṭūlūn (2) about the fate of the Mamluk military aristocracy in Egypt and in Syria during the first years of the Ottoman occupation.

I am well aware of the grave deficiencies of such a partial research, for which I can offer a partial justification: a) the great richness of these two chronicles (Ibn Iyās far surpassing Ibn Ṭūlūn) as compared with the poverty of the chronicles which immediately follow them; (3) b) the fact that any kind of other source material cannot replace them; c) the fact that they were not studied sufficiently. Particularly inadequate is their study against the background of the previous Mamlūk regime.

(1) Ibn Iyās, *Badā'i' al-Zuhūr fī Waqā'i' al-Duhūr*, Istanbul, 1931, vol. V.

(2) Ibn Ṭūlūn, *Mufākahat al-Khillān fī Ḥawādith al-Zamān*, Cairo, 1964, vols. I and II.

(3) See the Appendix.

I had to divide the study into two separate, but closely connected and interdependent articles: a) "Mamlūk Military Aristocracy during the First Years of the Ottoman Occupation of Egypt," to be published in the Bernard Lewis *Festschrift*; b) the present paper. A minimal degree of overlapping between the two separated parts of the same work was unavoidable.

The Background

The Ottoman conquest of Egypt (1517) constituted part of the greatest expansion in the history of that Empire into the countries of Islam, which was carried out within the period of less than three years (1514-1517). The two Muslim adversaries of the Ottomans in their big push eastwards and southwards were the Sunnite Mamlūk Empire (1250-1517), which they annihilated and the newly founded (1502) Shī'ite Ṣafawid Empire of Iran and Iraq, to which they dealt a terrible blow, but which managed to survive, recuperate and constitute for centuries a source of constant danger to the Ottomans along their eastern borders.

As a result of their drive into Islamic territory the Ottomans succeeded, in that very short period, in annexing to their Empire Syria, Egypt and the Hejaz, Iraq, as well as parts of Eastern Anatolia and North Western Iran. With additional efforts they managed to establish their mastery over the Red Sea and the Persian Gulf. These conquests had also their share in establishing the Ottomans' various and varying degrees of influence and hegemony over the countries of North Africa.

It is worthwhile to bear in mind in this connection that this expansion which transformed the map of the Islamic world took place simultaneously (or almost so) with the transformation of the whole globe by West European expansion, which established for centuries to come Christian Europe's preponderance over the rest of the world (first and foremost over the lands of Islam). Thus the end of the European medieval period witnessed at the same time vast territorial changes within the lands of Islam. These two phenomena, which are by no means isolated from each other, deserve an exhaustive examination.

To go back to the conquests of the Ottomans and to their Mamlūk policy. As already shown in the article for the Bernard Lewis *Festschrift*, Sultan Selim made a quick and total *volte-face* in his handling of the defeated Mamlūks. After having attempted to exterminate them physically, he decided to incorporate them in the Ottoman army. The obvious question which poses itself is: Why?

I believe that a combination of reasons made him change his mind so drastically and so quickly. The first of these was: The Ottomans' expansion which added to their Empire, within a few years, territories far wider than those conquered by them in Europe during centuries. The second one was their failure to annihilate the Ṣafawids. The third one was the circumnavigation of the Cape of Good Hope by the Portuguese, which took place so shortly before the Ottoman conquest of Egypt and the Fertile Crescent. The fourth reason was the Frankish threat in the Eastern Mediterranean, including the command of its most important islands.

Even without the existence of an external threat to the newly conquered vast territories, the Ottomans would have been faced with the formidable task of manning the administrative systems and the garrisons of these territories. With the presence of such mighty enemies along their borders, the drain on their manpower must have enormously increased. Of all the military elements which they subdued in their far flung drive into the Islamic countries, the Mamlūks were the most suitable for incorporation in the Ottoman army, because of their warlike ability, the common origin of the military slave systems in the two empires and the Turkish dialect spoken by those Mamlūks (even when they were not Turkish born). No wonder, therefore, that they were the first to be included in that army. The quickness with which the Ottomans sent the rehabilitated Mamlūks to the Red Sea positions, to Alexandria and, above all, to the campaign against Rhodes, is the best proof for their crying need for this kind of military manpower.

This policy was not, however, without its very grave dangers. The main problem which the Ottomans had to solve, and quite quickly, was on what a scale and within which area they can afford to reinstate the Mamlūks without endangering their own hold on that area. On the basis of the data furnished by our two sources the best way to follow the manner in which the Ottomans handled that problem is through the examination of Ottoman-Mamlūk-Ṣafawid relations.

The Case of the Ṣafawids

The magnitude of the difficulties which the Ottomans had to tackle in and around the annexed areas, and which had their direct and indirect repercussions on their attitude towards the Mamlūks, is nowhere better reflected than in their relations with the Ṣafawids, or more precisely, in the dangerous stalemate created on their Ṣafawid front.

Some of the main characteristics of the Ṣafawid dynasty and the Shī'ite movement which it represented, were its immense drive, the impact of which was felt far beyond the borders of its realm; its uncompromising hatred of the Sunna, and its amazing resilience and power of quick recovery from even the most shattering blows. In this respect the information furnished by our two sources is most revealing. From the moment of their inception as a state, the Ṣafawids are considered to be a grave threat to the Mamlūk Sultanate. The earliest reference, in a Mamlūk source, to their existence is found in Ibn Ṭūlūn's chronicle. He tells us that in Jumādā II 907/December 1501 "it became known in Damascus that a man named Ismā'īl b. Ḥaydar al-Ṣūfī (4) had conquered *the countries of Timurlank* and other countries, and he is now marching against the countries [of the Mamlūk Sultanate], and *there is no power but in God.*" (5) This short passage is a most telling proof of the dread caused by the appearance of that new power. The association with the unforgettable devastation brought about by Timurlank in his attack on both the Mamlūk and the Ottoman empires some hundred years earlier reflects the intensity of that dread.

Not until Ṣafar 908/July 1502 does Ibn Iyās mention the Ṣafawids for the first time, but from the vast preparations for a campaign to thwart their expected advance, (6) it is made clear that the Mamlūks had already been well acquainted with what they considered to be an ominous danger from the north-east. From now on, and up to the defeat of the Ṣafawids by the Ottomans in Rajab 920/August 1514, the Mamlūks lived in a state of constant nervousness and fear of a Ṣafawid attack (which never materialized), thus diverting their attention from

(4) This is the usual distortion in the Mamlūk sources of the name Ṣafawī.

(5) Ibn Ṭūlūn, I, p. 252, ll. 20-21.

(6) Ibn Iyās, V, p. 39, ll. 7-21. The preparations were not confined to Egypt, but included Syria as well (Ibn Ṭūlūn, I, p. 261, ll. 19-21).

a much more immediate threat, a fact which the Ottomans exploited to their best advantage. One Mamlūk expedition after the other, all of them of a purely defensive character, was sent to the north mainly to Aleppo, (7) in order to anticipate a Ṣafawid attack. (8)

The immense might and prestige which the Ṣafawid Empire accumulated within very few years since its establishment is reflected in our source in its defeat even more strongly than in the period which preceded it. Ibn Iyās repeatedly states that in Chaldiran the Ottomans won the greatest victory in their history, and that no victory won by Selim's forefathers could compare with it. He also gives quite numerous and detailed versions of the battle, which is a quite unusual practice. (9) More significant of all, however, is the almost immediate recovery of the Ṣafawids from their crushing defeat, and their reappearance as a major power, challenging and menacing once again both the Mamlūks and the Ottomans. As early as Ṣafar 922/March 1516, i.e. barely a year and a half after their defeat,

(7) Aleppo was the key point in the Mamlūk defensive system, both against the Ṣafawadis and against the Ottomans. See the references in the following notes. It continued to be a bastion in the Ottoman defence of Syria against the Ṣafawids. See below.

(8) Ibn Ṭūlūn, I, pp. 316, ll. 11-17, 317, ll. 1-2, 318, ll. 7-9, 328, ll. 2-3, 362, ll. 7-9. Ibn Iyās, IV, pp. 118, ll. 16-19, 121, l. 20 - 122, l. 8, 144, l. 23 - 145, l. 1, 258, ll. 4-5, 257, ll. 8-15, 262, ll. 1-6. No aggressive action on a large scale against the Ṣafawids was ever contemplated by the Mamlūks. They refused to give military assistance to the ruler of Bagdad when he was attacked and ousted by them from his capital (*ibid.*, IV, p. 146, ll. 13-6). A contributory factor to the fear of the Ṣafawids in the Mamlūk Sultanate, was that that enemy threatened it from the same direction as the Mongols (including Timurlank). A deep seated dread of the Mongols lasted a long time after their danger had been completely removed. See e.g. Ibn Ṭūlūn, I, p. 252, ll. 20-21; Ibn Iyās, IV, pp. 143, l. 11 - 144, l. 1, 227, l. 17 - 228, l. 18. It should, however, be stressed here that in spite of the anxiety and nervousness prevailing in the Mamlūk Sultanate in the last years of its existence there was no feeling that the Mamlūk regime is doomed.

(9) On the evaluation of the victory see Ibn Iyās, IV, pp. 401, ll. 4-6, 403, ll. 10-19; V, pp. 100, ll. 8-11, 350, ll. 1-3. In the last two references the victory over the Mamlūks is added to that over the Ṣafawids. On the versions of the battle see *ibid.*, pp. 393, ll. 3-11, 396, ll. 4-9, 396, ll. 4-9, 398, ll. 2-16, 400, l. 5 - 401, l. 4, 402, l. 6 - 404, l. 5. Unlike the Mamlūks, the Ṣafawids were not wiped out of existence, because, in addition to their freshness and religious zeal, they were greatly helped by the vastness of their country, its bad roads and mountainous terrain, and also by its severe winter. In the actual battles they had no answer to Ottoman firearms. Their zeal in battles of this kind could only increase their casualties.

and several months before the Ottoman-Mamlūk showdown, Ibn Iyās speaks in great detail of how the Ṣafawid army had been reorganized and replenished, and started a campaign against the Ottomans, the first fruits of which were the capture of Āmid in Northern Mesopotamia, *and how this comeback caused great concern to the Mamlūk Sultan and his advisers.* (10)

The Ottoman occupation of the Mamlūk Sultanate did not halt the Ṣafawid recovery or ambitions. Their advance in Northern Mesopotamia continued. (11) During Sultan Selim's stay in Egypt, and particularly during his passage through Syria on his way back to Istanbul, he was greatly occupied with the Ṣafawid threat, which loomed large over both countries. (12) In Syria this seems to have been the Sultan's major concern. In Muḥarran 924/January 1518 he appoints a special governor over the fringes of the District of Diyār Bakr, on the Syro-Mesopotamian border, whose sole stated object was to watch the movements of the Ṣafawids. (13) In the following month (Ṣafar/February), the *first and only* instruction which he gives Jānbirdī al-Ghazālī, his newly appointed Viceroy over *Southern* Syria, is, again, to watch the Ṣafawids and collect information about them. (14) In Rabīʿ I-Rabīʿ II/March-April of the same

(10) The information about this new revival of the Ṣafawids and their army and about their new conquests was furnished to the Mamlūk Sultan by the Viceroy of Aleppo. How great was the belief in an imminent major clash between the *recovering* Ṣafawids and the Ottomans, can be learnt from the fact that Sultan Qānṣūh al-Ghawrī expressed the desire that he himself would go to Aleppo, and await the outcome of the struggle, "*for whichever of the two will defeat his adversary, will inevitably march against our realm*" *(fa-inna kulla manintaṣara minhumā ʿalā gharīmihi lā budda an yazḥaf ʿalā bilādinā)* (*ibid.*, V, pp. 20, l. 18 - 21, l. 17). On the exchange of diplomatic envoys between the Ṣafawids and the Mamlūks, and the arrogance and haughtiness of the Ṣafawids see: Ibn Iyās, IV, pp. 123, ll. 14-18, 184, ll. 15-17, 207, ll. 18-23, 218, l. 23-220, l. 1, 220, l. 17 - 221, l. 20,265, ll. 6-18, 266, ll. 1-10, 271, ll. 7-14; V, p. 33, ll. 19-23; Ibn Ṭūlūn, I, pp. 354, ll.14-15, 257, ll. 3-12, 18-19.

(11) That the advance of the Ṣafawid army in Northern Mesopotamia was very real, can be deduced from the fact that "numerous Ottomans", including the Viceroys of Āmid and al-Ruhā, together with their retinues, arrived in Damascus in Rabīʿ I 923/March 1517, after having fled from that army (Ibn Ṭūlūn, II, p. 58, ll. 17-20).

(12) For references to the anxiety caused by the Ṣafawid threat in Egypt and Syria during Sultan Selim's stay in the area, see: Ibn Iyās, V, pp. 176, ll. 12-18, 182, ll. 2-7; Ibn Ṭūlūn, II, pp. 74, ll. 14-18, 74, l. 19 - 75, l. 2.

(13) *Ibid.*, p. 79, ll. 16-21.

(14) *Ibid.*, p. 82, ll. 8-11.

year, Selim stays in Aleppo and supervises personally the strenghtening of its fortifications (the town's wall, towers and gates) to prepare it for what he believed to be an imminent Ṣafawid attack. (15) How imminent and how dangerous this attack was considered to have been, can be learnt from the fact that in Jumādā II/June of that year prayers and recitals of the entire Koran *(khatamāt)* were performed by the graves of all the important Muslim saints in Cairo, and in the mosque of al-Azhar, wishing Sultan Selim victory over Shāh Ismāʿīl the Ṣafawid. (16) In the rest of the period under study fear of the Ṣafawids did not, in any way, subside. (17)

Had the Ṣafawid front been the only one with which the Ottomans had to cope, they would have had little reason for real concern, for they had military and technical superiority which the Ṣafawids never had a chance to context. But the Ottomans had other enemies as well, and the Ṣafawids did not content themselves in being just another enemy, but endeavoured to establish contact and coordinate their operations with the others, in spite of the fact that those others were Christians. This tendency of cooperation with the Franks against the Ottomans, which constituted a major feature of Ṣafawid policy for a long time, had its very early origins. Already in the second half of the year 916/1510 the Mamlūk Viceroy of al-Bīra (today's Birejik) on the Euphrates caught emissaries from the Ṣafawid ruler carrying letters to the Franks. These letters were addressed to the Frankish consuls in Alexandria, Damascus and Tripoli, who were asked by Shāh Ismāʿīl to write in his name to the Kings of the Franks and suggest to them a common offensive against the Mamlūks and the Ottomans. According to his plan the Ṣafawids would conduct the land offensive, while the Franks would attack the two Empires by sea. (18) A few months earlier Franks passing through Syria seem to have carried in their canes messages from the Franks to

(15) Ibn Iyās, V, pp. 243, ll. 1-20, 247, ll. 21-23, 248, l. 12 - 249, l. 9. See also Ibn Ṭūlūn, II, p. 79, ll. 2-4.

(16) Ibn Iyās, V, pp. 253, ll. 5 - 10, 253, l. 24 - 254, l. 6.

(17) *Ibid.*, pp. 254, l. 22 - 255, l. 13, 258, l. 20 - 259, l. 2, 268, ll. 9-13, 419, ll. 15-16, 452, ll. 5-8, 467, l. 18 - 468, l. 6, 470, l. 22 - 471, l. 4; Ibn Ṭūlūn, II, pp. 87, ll. 10-13, 102, ll. 14-16.

(18) Ibn Iyās, IV, pp. 191, ll. 4-9, 205, ll. 9-18.

the Ṣafawids. [19] The way was thus paved, at such an early date, for much bigger attempts of cooperation in the future. This shows that the Ottomans had to face, as a result of their unprecedented expansion, not only internal difficulties and longer hostile frontiers, but also alliances against them between those frontiers. This could only speed up their decision to reverse their initial policy towards the Mamlūks.

When the Ottomans decided to spare the Mamlūks, they could either leave them in part of their former realm or in the whole of it. They could either appoint Ottoman Viceroys over the various provinces of the defunct Mamlūk Sultanate, or Mamlūk ones. What they did was to leave the Mamlūks in the greatest part of these provinces (Egypt and Southern Syria; or, more precisely, most of the whole of Syria), and to appoint over them two Mamlūk Viceroys. This was utter folly, and the Ottomans soon paid dearly for it. When they came to realize that reviving Mamlūk power on such a large scale is too dangerous for their rule, they were confronted with the need to choose between Egypt and Syria. They chose Egypt, and rightly so.

Allowing the Mamlūks to survive in the whole or in the greatest part of their former realm would have led, as it really did, to an attempt on their part to overthrow the Ottomans and to restore their own old rule within its old boundaries. As I have already stated elsewhere: "In the course of its recorded history, including the pre-Islamic period, Syria was never ruled from Egypt for so long, or, relatively speaking, with such firmness as during the Mamlūk reign." [20] This was, indeed, an exception in the long history of Egypt, but what mattered was that for the centuries preceding the Ottoman conquest Egypt and Syria were ruled as one unit, and that, therefore, it would have been quite easy to restore that unity shortly after the separation of the two countries.

(19) Ibn Ṭūlūn, I, pp. 342, l. 23 - 343, l. 2. For Franco-Ṣafawid contacts after the Mamlūk defeat see *ibid.*, II, p. 120, ll. 12-18.

(20) Paper read in Hebrew on May 31, 1966, and published in English under the title "The Muslim City and the Mamlūk Military Aristocracy", *Proceedings of the Israel Academy of Sciences and Humanities*, vol. II, Jerusalem, 1967, p. 328. I made the same statement, in more or less the same words, in an earlier paper I read in the Colloquium on Medieval Islamic Cities in Oxford in the summer of 1965. See also my "Egypt as a Dominant Factor in Syria and Palestine", in *Egypt and Palestine, A Millenium of Association (868-1948)*, Jerusalem, 1984, pp. 33-37, and especially, p. 33.

Since preserving the Mamlūk aristocracy both in Egypt and in Syria was, from an Ottoman point of view, out of the question, there were very weighty reasons for preferring the first over the second. Egypt, being a flat and narrow country, (21) could be easily dominated from the sea and the sea-shore deep inland, (22) at least up to, and including, the capital, where the overwhelming majority of the Mamlūks resided. (23) In Syria, mastery of the sea, or of great parts of the shore, would not have had such a decisive effect on the hinterland and on the big inland cities. The mountainous character of the country, together with the fact that, in addition to the bedouins and semi-bedouins, there were in Syria the Turkmen and Kurdish tribesmen, who were practically non-existent in the Egyptian countryside, made the rule over that country far more difficult than over Egypt. The establishment of the Ṣafawid empire aggravated the situation even more: first, because of its physical proximity to Syria, and second, because of the strong Turkoman element in that country. There was a vast contiguous territory inhabited by Turkomans, which stretched deeply into Eastern Anatolia, North Western Iran and Northern Syria. (24) Now, Shāh Ismā'īl al-Ṣūfī, though the majority of his adherents were Iranians, was of a Turkoman stock, and he directed a great deal of his proselytizing propaganda towards his fellow-tribesmen. The Ottomans were particularly sensitive to what was going on in the regions of the Turkomans. There was also the problem of where to concentrate the Mamlūks. In Egypt it was quite simple, because Cairo, with the only citadel in the country, dominated all or most of the land of the Nile. In

(21) It is obvious that only the inhabited, cultivated and cultivable land of Egypt is intended in this statement.

(22) On the position of Egypt and Syria *vis-à-vis* an external naval power, see my "The Mamlūks and Naval Power", *Proceedings of the Academy of Sciences and Humanities*, vol. I, Jerusalem, 1965, pp. 10-11, and note 5 on p. 10. See also "Egypt as a Dominant Factor, etc.", *op. cit.*, pp. 35-36.

(23) During the Ottoman reign an important centre of power gradually came into being in Upper Egypt, but this belongs to a later period (see "Egypt as a Dominant Factor, etc.", pp. 40-41).

(24) In Northern Syria the Turcomans must have constituted a decisive factor over a very big region in the closing decades of the Mamlūk reign. According to an eyewitness evidence from Qā'itbāy's Sultanate the dominant language from Latakia on the Mediterranean shore to al-Bīra on the Euphrates was not Arabic, but Turkish (Abū al-Baqā' Ibn al-Jī'ān, *al-Qawl al-Mustaẓraf fī Safar al-Malik al-Ashraf*, Torino, 1978, p. 17.

Syria such a centre did not exist. Besides Damascus there were other important towns and numerous citadels. This would lead unavoidably to the establishment of several Mamlūk centres there, which would create a host of internal and external difficulties. Fortunately for the Ottomans, the Mamlūk Viceroy of Syria gave them the opportunity to put an end to their Mamlūk experiment in that country.

The Syrian Mamlūks

Now the irony of the whole matter was that it had been no other but Sultan Selim—the man who originally intended to wipe out the Mamlūks—who in actual fact not only spared them, but also made it possible for them to gather much strength within the greatest part of their former realm, thus paving the way for their attempt to overthrow the Ottomans. It was his son and successor, Suleyman the Magnificent (926-974/1520-1566), who, although he greatly improved the position of the Mamlūks of Egypt, at the same time he crushed their revolt in Syria (which was a direct result of his father's policy), eradicated them forever in that country, and contained the Mamlūk aristocracy within the boundaries of Egypt alone.

The restoration of the Mamlūks by Sultan Selim was made at the very last stage of his stay in the Mamlūk conquered territories. We have already discussed his change of policy towards the Mamlūks of Egypt, (25) but this was by no means all that he had done in this respect. When he decided to return to his capital, he had to appoint viceroys in those territories. On the 13th of Shaʿbān 923/August 31, 1517, i.e. only ten days before his departure from Egypt, he appoints amir Khāyrbak, the former Mamlūk viceroy of Aleppo, as the viceroy *(nāʾib)* of the country of the Nile. A significant feature of that appointment is, that he had already decided to appoint an Ottoman Viceroy (Yūnus Bāshā), but at the very last moment changed his mind, and appointed a Mamlūk in his stead ! (26)

(25) In the Bernard Lewis, *Festschrift*, cited above.

(26) Ibn Iyās, V, pp. 198, ll. 6-8, 199, ll. 14-16, 202, ll. 5-7, 356, ll. 20-21, 478, ll. 1-3; Ibn Ṭūlūn, II, p. 66, ll. 5-6. Selim took with him a son of Khāyrbak as a hostage. Information on the death of that son in Istanbul reached Cairo in Dhū al-Qaʿda 926/October 1520 (Ibn Iyās, V, p. 357, ll. 19-20).

Selim arrived in Damascus on the 21st of Ramaḍān 923/early October 1517, (27) where he stayed for about five months, studying the situation and making excursions into the Syrian capital's hinterland. His appointment of a viceroy was made only five days before his departure (5 Ṣafar 924/February 16, 1518), and once again his choice fell on a Mamlūk, Jānbirdī al-Ghazālī, who was Sultan Qānṣūh al-Ghawrī's viceroy of al-Ḥamā and Sultan Ṭūmān bāy's viceroy of Damascus. Of particular significance is the area upon which al-Ghazālī was given sway. According to one of our sources, he was appointed over the original Mamlūk province of Damascus, as well as over Ḥimṣ, Ḥamā, Sidon, Beirut, Jerusalem, Ramla, Lydda, Kerak "and other districts of Syria and Tripoli". (28) According to the other, he was given authority over the territory stretching from al-Maʿarra (i.e. Maʿarrat al-Nuʿmān, to the south of Aleppo) to al-ʿArīsh and the Egyptian border. (29) This was a very great and a very dangerous departure from Mamlūk policy towards Syria. Under the Mamlūks Syria was divided into seven provinces (Damascus, Aleppo, Hama, Tripoli, Safed, Gaza and Kerak), each headed by a governor or viceroy *(nā'ib)*, almost invariably responsible to Cairo. (30) There might rise, from among these governors, one who would overshadow all the rest, and exert immense influence and power; there might take place boundary changes between the various provinces; other changes might also occur. But, on the whole, the pattern was kept more or less intact, and greatly facilitated the perpetuation of Egypt's rule over Syria. Now Sultan Selim, with complete lack of knowledge of the circumstances in Syria, destroyed this well-tried pattern in one stroke, merging six of the old provinces into one, thus leaving in Syria only two provinces instead of the earlier seven, and handing over the by far bigger of the two to a Mamlūk! (the province of Aleppo was ruled from the very outset by an Ottoman Bāshā). On top of all that he put the Circassian

(27) Ibn Ṭūlūn, II, p. 67, ll. 19-21.

(28) Ibn Iyās, V, p. 378, ll. 20-26.

(29) Ibn Ṭūlūn, II, p. 82, ll. 4-7. Rumours about the appointment of al-Ghazālī as viceroy started circulating about a month before it actually took place (*ibid.*, p. 78, l. 11). Sultan Selim left Damascus on the 10th of Ṣafar/February 21, 1518 (*ibid.*, p. 82, l. 17).

(30) "The Muslims City, etc.", pp. 328-329; "Egypt as a Dominant Factor", pp. 34-35.

Mamlūks, who still remained in Syria, under the direct jurisdiction of the new Mamlūk viceroy ! *(wa-aḍāfa amr al-Jarākisa... ilayhi)*. ([31]) There might well be yet another factor which could tempt the new viceroy to raise the banner of rebellion against the Ottomans at the first opportunity. From the inadequate information at our disposal it would appear that Sultan Selim did not leave behind in Damascus as strong a contingent of Ottoman soldiers as he did in Cairo. ([32]) What might corroborate that suggestion is that even during the rebellion the existence of such a contingent is not mentioned in the sources used in this paper. But only further study will give the correct answer to this question.

Thus, within less than a year since the complete conquest of the Mamlūk Sultanate, and as a direct result of Sultan Selim's deliberate policy, almost the whole of that Sultanate was governed by Mamlūk viceroys, with quite considerable Mamlūk contingents at their disposal. This could have only one outcome.

The Revolt of al-Ghazālī

The revolt of Jānbirdī al-Ghazālī had two major characteristics of decisive importance: a) it was contemplated and prepared long before its actual outburst, so that it could take place at the very first opportunity; b) its aim was not just to free al-Ghāzālī's province from Ottoman yoke, but to restore Mamlūk rule, Mamlūk institutions and Mamlūk way of life over *all* the territories of the defeated and conquered Sultanate. At least according to one source, he abolished, during the period of his loyalty to the Ottomans, many of their institutions and innovations, in spite of the vehement opposition of the Chief Qāḍī Ibn al-Farfūr, ([33]) "for he [i.e. al-Ghazālī] was inclined to

(31) Ibn Ṭūlūn, II, p. 85, ll. 2-7. A reason for including the greatest part of Syria under one governorship might have been the great size of the Ottoman Empire, which necessitated bigger administrative units than those of Mamlūk Syria. However, this meant ignoring the particular local conditions, especially within a policy of appointing Mamlūks as viceroys of most of the area of the defunct Sultanate and of sparing the Mamlūk society.

(32) For the Ottoman contingent left by Sultan Selim in Egypt, see my article in the Bernard Lewis *Festschrift*.

(33) Ibn al-Farfūr, a Shāfi'ite under the Mamlūks, turned Ḥanafite, the *madhhab* of the new rulers, immediately after the Ottoman conquest. This was undoubtedly the reason for his excessive pro-Ottoman zeal.

leaving the old things as they were, whereas Ibn al-Farfūr wanted nothing but the establishment of the Ottoman order" *(fa innahu kāna yamīl ilā ibqā' al-qadīm 'alā qidamihi wa-kāna Ibn al-Farfūr ya'bā illā qānūn al-Arwām).* Strange as it may seem, Sultan Selim sided, according to that source, with the Viceroy, and gave him practically a free hand. ([34]) Both his policy, his personality and his good administration gained him great prestige and popularity within and without his province, ([35]) a fact which could only encourage him to revolt.

The local contemporary Arab sources are unanimous in their claim that al-Ghazālī revolted immediately after learning of Sultan Selim's death, but in none of them it is reflected so clearly and so convincingly as in Ibn Ṭūlūn's narrative. On Wednesday the 12th of Dhū al-Qa'da/October 24, 1520, two emissaries arrived in Damascus with a letter informing the Viceroy of the death of Sultan Selim. The emissaries carrying the letter were dispatched to al-Ghazālī, who was at that moment in Beirut, inspecting its fortifications. On Saturday night of the 15th (October 27) he returned *suddenly (bahtatan)* to his capital, and declared his revolt. On Monday the 17th (October 29) he besieged the Damascus citadel, which was under the command of an Ottoman officer, and captured it on the same day. As soon as he entered the citadel, he and his men put on a Circassian dress, and abolished the Ottoman dress *(wa-aẓhara libs al-Jarākisa min al-takhfīfāt wal-kalūtāt wa-abṭala libs al-Arwām min al-'amā'im wal-qafṭānāt).* ([36]) What is made so clear in the above evidence of Ibn Ṭūlūn is, that had al-Ghazālī been in Damascus on the arrival of the Ottoman emissaries, he would have started his revolt on the very same day. This evidence also proves how eager and how determined he was to return to the good old Mamlūk days.

That al-Ghazālī had always in mind the restoration of Mamlūk rule over *all* the previous territories of the Sultanate, can be learnt from the fact that already on the 26th of Dhū

(34) Najm al-Dīn al-Ghazzī, *al-Kawākib al-Sā'ira bi-A'yān al-Mi'a al-'Āshira*, Beirut, 1945, vol. I, p. 199, ll. 1-11. On al-Ghazālī's outward obedience to Selim, and his simultaneously secret preparations for revolt, see Ibn Iyās, V, p. 418, ll. 3-4. Cp. also Ibn Ṭūlūn, II, p. 85, ll. 14-18.

(35) Al-Ghazzī, I, p. 199, l. 8; Ibn Iyās, V, p. 418, l. 5.

(36) Ibn Ṭūlūn, II, pp. 123, l. 11 - 124, l. 7. On the start of the revolt see also al-Ghazzī, I, p. 199, ll. 12-15; Ibn Iyās, V, pp. 362, ll. 11-21, 418, ll. 4-6.

al-Qaʻda/November 7, namely, only eleven days after the declaration of the revolt, his emissary arrived in Cairo, carrying a letter from him to Khāyrbak and other letters to other Circassian amirs, in which he called them to join his revolt. ([37]) The mood prevailing in the ex-Mamlūk territories, the goal to which al-Ghazālī strove, and the unfounded optimism of the insurgents, are well reflected in the following passage.

"When al-Ghazālī revolted, the people of Syria *(ahl al-Shām)*, including the commanders, the army, the bedouins and the semi-nomads joined him and said to him: 'get up and proclaim yourself Sultan. For there is none in front of you whom you have to fear. As for us, we shall fight by your side to death'. He was enticed by their words, and proclaimed himself Sultan, and he became light headed and thoughtless. And how many a time haste was followed by regret! Thus he became Sultan in Syria, giving himself the title al-Malik al-Ashraf Abū al-Futūḥāt ["the father of Conquests" or "the Conqueror"]. ([38]) People kissed the ground in his presence, and his name was mentioned in the Friday sermon *(khuṭba)* in the Umayyad mosque and in the other pulpits of Damascus. When he became Sultan people told him: 'Go to Egypt, fight Khāyrbak and take possession of Egypt', to which he answered: 'Egypt is in my grasp *(fī qabḍat yadī)*. I shall [first] go to Aleppo and liberate it from the hands of the Ottomans, so that I shall not have to worry about my rear. Then I shall go to Egypt'. Had he marched on Egypt before having marched on Aleppo, it would have been better for him, for the army of the Circassian Mamlūks and the people of Egypt *(ahl Miṣr)* and all the bedouins would have risen against Khāyrbak and would have joined him [i.e. al-Ghazālī], for he was liked by the people *(fa-innahu kāna muḥabbaban lil-raʻiyya)*." ([39])

As far as Egypt was concerned, most important of all was, of course, the attitude of the army, and particularly that of the

(37) *Ibid.*, p. 362, ll. 11-21. Al-Ghazālī suggested to Khāyrbak to proclaim himself Sultan in Egypt, and thus divide between them the rule over the Mamlūk Sultanate. He even threatened him that if he refused, he had others who would readily accept his offer (*ibid.*, p. 418, ll. 18-21). This was, of course, only a tactical offer. Had the revolt succeeded, one of the two would have, undoubtedly, ousted the other, and established a unified Sultanate, with its capital in Cairo.

(38) This patronym reflects correctly al-Ghazālī's great ambitions.

(39) Ibn Iyās, V, p. 418, ll. 5-15. Al-Ghazālī failed in his attempt to capture Aleppo, and this was the beginning of his discomfiture.

Circassian Mamlūks. These received the tidings of the revolt with great rejoicing, believing that their hour of salvation *(faraj)* has arrived. [40] Numerous Circassian Mamlūks escaped from Cairo secretly and joined the insurgents. [41] Among them were some of Khāyrbak's most trusted and most favoured colleagues. [42] As for the Ottoman units stationed in Egypt, they showed no enthusiasm to fight al-Ghazālī in Syria, in spite of Khāyrbak's constant prodding and urging. They declared that they would fight him only if he attacked Egypt. [43] This declaration never had to be put to the test, because al-Ghazālī was not given the opportunity to attack the land of the Nile. In any case, the constant squabbles between these Ottoman units, and Khāyrbak's policy of discriminating some of them against the others, completely immobilized them. The army of Egypt played no part in quelling al-Ghazālī's revolt. [44]

The potentialities inherent in that revolt—which were obviously not negligible—were not given sufficient time to unfold themselves, for the revolt was very short-lived. It had been crushed by a huge Ottoman army on the 22nd of Ṣafar 927/ February 1st 1521, only three months after it had started. The army of the Ottomans was composed of units stationed in Eastern Anatolia, Aleppo and Rumelia, as well as of Turkoman cavalry. Its commander-in-chief was Farḥāt Bāshā the Third Vizir. Other commanders were the viceroy of Aleppo, and, very significantly, as we shall explain later, Ibn Siwār, the famous Turkoman chief, of the Dhū al-Qadr dynasty. [45]

(40) Ibn Iyās, V, p. 374, ll. 4-6.

(41) *Ibid.*, p. 377, ll. 17-22. See also *ibid.*, pp. 434, l. 14 - 435, l. 5.

(42) *Ibid.*, pp. 382, l. 3 - 383, l. 9. People were expecting and hoping for al-Ghazālī's conquest of Egypt.

(43) *Ibid.*, pp. 368, l. 13 - 369, l. 1, 369, l. 3 - 370, l. 3.

(44) True, Sultan Suleyman wrote to Khāyrbak shortly before the decisive battle against al-Ghazālī that there is no need for the participation of the Egyptian army in quelling the rebellion (*ibid.*, p. 371, ll. 20-21). This, however, does not alter the fact that all Khāyrbak's attempts to induce the Ottoman units to march against al-Ghazālī ended in failure. One consideration of Sultan Suleyman for not using the Ottoman units stationed in Egypt against al-Ghazālī, might have been his fear that denuding that country from those units might tempt the Circassians of Egypt to revolt. He certainly could not rely on those Circassians in his plan to crush al-Ghazālī.

(45) Ibn Iyās, V, pp. 376, l. 20 - 377, l. 10. Al-Ghazzī, I, pp. 170, l. 6 - 171, l. 8. G. W. Stripling, *The Ottoman Turks and the Arabs, 1511-1574*, The University of Illinois Press, Urbana, Illinois, 1942, pp. 75-76. Al-Ghazzī gives a slightly

The swifness with which al-Ghazālī had been overthrown, put an end to his much expected and not less publicized march on Egypt. (46) How the Circassian Mamlūks, the Ottoman units, and the various elements of the Egyptian population would have reacted, in case such invasion would have taken place, is, of course, a matter of conjecture. But that there did exist a great anti-Ottoman feeling, and an extremely great and widespread sympathy with al-Ghazālī's revolt, both in Egypt and in Syria, about this the sources leave us in no doubt whatsoever.

For the same reason the possible effects, at that time, of a Syrian revolt on the Ṣafawids, and vice versa, cannot be ascertained. There is no indication that there had ever been any contact between al-Ghazālī and the Shī'ite Empire of Iran. Our information in this respect does not go beyond a rumour, which proved to be false, that al-Ghazālī found refuge, after his defeat, with the Ṣafawids. (47) Yet the potentialities of such a revolt, from the point of view of the Ṣafawids, had it lasted longer, can be established indirectly.

In Ramaḍān 928/August 1522 it became known that the Turkoman Ibn Siwār, one of the main commanders of the army which defeated al-Ghazālī, was executed by the order of Sultan Suleyman. The reason for his execution was that the Sultan learnt that Ibn Siwār became the ally of the Ṣafawid ruler, and corresponded with him with the intent of conducting subversive activities against the Ottomans. The Sultan dispatched to Ibn Siwār his Third Vizir Farḥāt Bāshā, the above mentioned commander-in-chief of that army, under the pretext that both of them must go to Diyār Bakr, to watch the movements of the Ṣafawids. When Ibn Siwār entertained him in his camp, some of Farḥāt's Ottoman attendants pounced upon their host and finished him off. On the same occasion Farḥāt Bāshā executed three of Ibn Siwār's sons and a group of his amirs. (48)

Now the Dhū al-Qadrs, and particularly Shāh Siwār, and his son who succeeded him, were staunch allies of the Ottomans for

different information from that of Ibn Iyās. Of all the commanders of the Ottoman army Ibn Iyās mentions by name only Ibn Siwār!

(46) In addition to earlier references on this subject in the present paper, see Ibn Iyās, V, pp. 365, ll. 8-11, 369, l. 13 - 370, l. 9.

(47) *Ibid.*, p. 419, ll. 15-16.

(48) *Ibid.*, pp. 467, l. 19 - 468, l. 6.

a long time, serving as a buffer between them and the Mamlūks. In the last decades of the Mamlūk reign they fought the Mamlūks with great valour, and whether they were victorious or otherwise they always inflicted heavy losses upon them. Later they participated in Selim's campaign against the Mamlūks, and lastly played a no minor role in the defeat of al-Ghazālī. Yet all this was not sufficient to make them trustworthy in the eyes of the Ottomans, or to immune them from the contagious influence of the revived version of Shīʿism offered to them by their fellow-Turkomans. The dangerous consequences of a prolonged Mamlūk revolt on the threshold of the Turkoman area cannot, therefore, be over-estimated. This is clearly demonstrated in the attitude of Selim during his stay in Syria on his homeward journey, described above. The Ṣafawid threat was his chief preoccupation. His first and only instruction to Jānbirdī al-Ghazālī, which the contemporary Arab chronicler deems necessary to bring to the knowledge of the reader, is to keep a watchful eye on the Ṣafawids. In Aleppo he concentrated on strengthening the town's fortifications against the same enemy. Now if Syria was so important to the Ottomans as a bastion against the Ṣafawids, the revolt in that country of the very person whom they appointed as their watch-dog against the same enemy, could not have been overlooked by the new Shīʿite power. It should also be remembered, that the first objective of al-Ghazālī, after having secured Damascus, was to capture Aleppo, the very town which Selim took such care to fortify against his major enemy in the East. Furthermore, the conquest of the Aleppo province would have either established a common border between him and the Ṣafadis, or at least would have greatly shortened the distance between them.

That even relatively remote Egypt, so much removed from either Iran, Iraq, Shīʿism or the Turkomans, was not immune from the Ṣafawid impact, can be learnt from the famous unsuccessful revolt of the viceroy of Egypt, Ahmed Pasha, in the year 930/early 1524. This man was a most trusted "Mamlūk" (49) of Sultan Selim. When Suleyman became Sultan, this Ahmed coveted the office of Grand Vizir, to which the Sultan appointed somebody else. In order to compensate him,

(49) Ibn Iyās repeatedly calls the Ottoman military slaves by the name of "Mamlūks".

Suleyman gave him the Viceroyalty of Egypt, to which country he arrived in Shaʿbān 929/July 1523. Ahmed, originally a Christian Greek, soon decided to revolt, mobilizing many of the Mamlūks and other elements in the country. But he sought allies as well beyond the boundaries of Egypt. To the Franks he offered the surrender of newly conquered Rhodes. He also tried to establish contacts with the Ṣafawid ruler. According to our Arab source he became, under the influence of an Iranian religious man, named Qāḍī Zādeh al-Ardawīlī, a very devout Shīʿite, and a great believer in and propagandist for Shāh Ismāʿīl and his teachings. His persecution and extortion of the Muslim population of Egypt is attributed, by the same source, to his hatred of the Sunnites. (50)

In the early part of the sixteenth century the chances of a Mamlūk or other revolt in Egypt and Syria against the mighty Ottoman Empire were not very great, even if it had been led by less rash men than al-Ghazālī and Ahmed Pasha, and even if a real coordination could be achieved between the insurgents, the Ṣafawids and a Frankish power. Yet the possibility that such combinations would materialize in the future, and constitute a great danger, could not be ruled out. In any way, the revival of Mamlūk aristocracy both in Egypt and in Syria has already caused sufficient trouble in itself, even without the prospect of wider implications. The Ottomans learnt their lesson, and it was Suleyman who corrected his father's mistake. There was also no guarantee that in any future Mamlūk revolt in Syria the Mamlūks of Egypt would remain neutral. He, therefore, not only contained the Mamlūks within the boundaries of Egypt alone, but also decided to stop the nomination of Mamlūks as viceroys of that country. This tendency of Suleyman became evident even in the lifetime of Khāyrbak. Though he confirmed his Viceroyalty, he never sent him "the robe of the continuation of office" *(khilʿat al-istimrār)*, a fact which greatly worried Khāyrbak. Worse still, it could not be kept secret, and people started speculating about the possibility of his dismissal. (51) Yet he was not dismissed. His early death (14 Dhū al-Qaʿda 928/early October 1522), however, which, by all appearances,

(50) Al-Ghazzī, I, pp. 156, l. 13 - 159, l. 23, and particularly pp. 156, ll. 13-18, 158, ll. 5-9, 158, l. 27 - 159, l. 1. See also Stanford J. Shaw, *op. cit.*, p. 4 and index.

(51) Ibn Iyās, pp. 370, ll. 3-6, 376, ll. 1-11, 478, ll. 1-4.

had been a natural one, solved Suleyman's problem. This time he appointed as Viceroy of Egypt no lesser person than Muṣṭaphā Pasha, his Grand Vizir and brother-in-law. (52)

In the short period under study no Mamlūk contingent was sent from Egypt against the Ṣafawids. But the existence there of a strong Mamlūk element, as well as other military regiments, gave the Ottomans considerable flexibility in deploying their armed forces. (53)

Conclusions

The reinstatement of the Mamlūks so quickly after their defeat over the greatest part of their former realm is the best proof for the *urgency* of the Ottomans' need for that kind of manpower. In my view that urgency was created to no small extent (though by no means exclusively) by the Ṣafawid threat, which looms so large in the accounts of both Ibn Iyās and Ibn Ṭūlūn. It constituted the most pressing, as well as the nearest, geographical threat to the Ottomans. The danger of the Ṣafawids was so great, because of the high motivation of their movement, and because of that movement's great appeal, especially to the inhabitants on the other side of the border within the Ottoman and the ex-Mamlūk Empires (above all, the Turkomans). The fact that it could not be broken even by the absolute superiority of Ottoman firearms could only increase the fear from that danger.

That fear, however, seems to have blinded the Ottomans, and particularly Sultan Selim, to the perilous implications of the revival of the Mamlūks on such a large scale, and so shortly after their defeat. Curiously enough, the same Ṣafawids, who were a main cause in that revival on that scale, seem also to have been a great factor in reducing it to a much smaller size. The hatred and fear of the Ṣafawids during the previous reign might have misled the new rulers to believe that the Mamlūks could be relied on in the struggle against the Shīʿite enemy, or at least that they would not be a liability in that struggle. The revolt must have opened their eyes to the danger of a Mamlūk uprising

(52) *Ibid.*, pp. 485, ll. 20-22 487 ll. 16-17. Khāyrbak's appointment, on his death-bed, of Sinān Bak, the Ottoman, as his successor, was completely ignored by Sultan Suleyman.

(53) See also Shaw, *op. cit.*, p. 194.

on the threshold of the Ṣafawid realm, which might spread to Egypt as well. Therefore, the Mamlūks of Syria must be eliminated. On the other hand, leaving a low-profile Mamlūk aristocracy only in the land of the Nile, which is relatively remote from the Shīʿite territory, with tasks confined to internal security and to dealing with the Frankish enemy on two fronts, was certainly a much safer and much more manageable thing from an Ottoman point of view. Even so the Mamlūks caused much headache to their masters in the early period of the occupation.

Appendix A

A Note on

The Ottoman Conquest and Mamlūk Historiography

The Ottoman conquest, which dealt a death blow to the Mamlūk Sultanate, dealt, at the same time, almost a death blow to historiography in Egypt. As is well known, hardly any other Islamic period or region in the Middle Ages produced such an abundant and variegated amount of historiographical and related material, as did the Mamlūk Sultanate. Furthermore, the importance of that material grealy exceeds the boundaries of that Sultanate. Mamlūk historical and similar writings are a mine of precious information on many other parts of the "Abode of Islam" and on the "Abode of War", as well as on the relations between the two "Abodes". It goes without saying that these writings are the richest, as far as the history of Islamic Egypt is concerned. In Ottoman Egypt, by contrast, historiography is the poorest during the greatest part of that reign. I rather doubt whether such an abrupt decline of historiography had ever taken place in any other important part of the Muslim world.

What were the causes of that unique decline? At the present state of our knowledge I believe that only a partial answer can be given to that question.

The most important cause is the most obvious one. Egypt (and its capital Cairo), which constituted, up to the conquest, the focal part of an Empire, became just a province in a far bigger Empire. But putting it this way would reflect only part of the transformation which Egypt underwent as a result of its conquest, for the following reason. The Mamlūk Sultanate was considered, since its inception, to be the major power in the Muslim world, and it has not really relinquished that position up to its extermination, in spite of all the vicissitudes and the decline which it experienced. The unexpectedness with which that Sultanate was wiped out and the fact that up to its last years it was considered to be the Islamic power *par excellence*, must have come as a terrible shock. Few, however, could be shocked and paralyzed more than the historians who were writing the annals of that great Empire, which so suddenly ceased to exist. The incentive for writing history under the new circumstances must have disappeared. Some of the old guard might carry on their writing into the period of occupation, by the force of habit. But what prospect could historiography offer to a newcomer?

An additional important cause was the disappearance, under the Ottomans, of the offspring of the Mamlūks as a very distinct social group, for reasons which I discuss elsewhere. ([54]) A very great proportion of the historians of the Mamlūk Sultanate came from that group (the *awlād al-nās)*. Their extinction was a particularly heavy loss to Egyptian historiography, because of their scholarly training on the one hand, and their intimate knowledge of Mamlūk society on the other.

Another cause was that in the latter part of the Circassian rule (which covered the period 784-922/1382-1517), Mamlūk historiography had already passed the peak of its vitality, creativeness, diversification and output, although it still remained very powerful. To what a degree the economic decay of the Mamlūk realm caused the weakening, is a moot question. A review of the historiography of the whole Mamlūk period does not show that its ups and downs necessarily corresponded to the fluctuations of the Sultanate's economy.

Yet another cause must have been the mass transfer of historical works from Cairo to Istanbul, many of which are still found there. In view of the fact that such works, unlike so

(54) See my "Notes on the Transformation of Mamlūk Society in Egypt under the Ottomans", *JESHO,* vol. III (1960), pp. 148-174, 275-325, and "Mamlūk Aristocracy, etc." in the Bernard Lewis, *Festschrift.*

many works of a religious character, are usually available only in a very limited number of copies, the very harmful effects of their mass transfer are obvious. ([55])

Whatever the causes might be, the student of Ottoman Egypt is faced with the situation that he has at his disposal only one really important local source for the study of the beginning of the Ottoman occupation of that country, namely, the chronicle of the Mamlūk historian Ibn Iyās (852-930/1448-1524), which covers its first six years (922-928/1516-1522). Its value can hardly be overestimated, not only because it is a most detailed and a most reliable source (especially as far as the narrative of facts is concerned), but also because it is the best and most authoritative history of the last decades of Mamlūk rule, and because the last years which it covers, namely the years of the Ottoman rule, are the most detailed ones in the whole chronicle. Few other six years in Mamlūk history are dealt with in such detail by a single historian. It is, therefore, invaluable for the study of Egypt's transition period from Mamlūk into Ottoman rule, which is a decisive period, when old institutions are abolished, and new ones replace them or start taking shape (on Ibn Ṭūlūn for Syria see below).

It should be emphasized in this connection that nothing can replace the local good chronicle. Neither other kinds of historical works, nor the narratives of travellers and visitors (be they European or Ottoman), nor even the Ottoman archives. All these have, undoubtedly, their specific extremely great merits and importance. They will certainly inform us about many essential subjects, upon which a local chronicle usually passes in silence. They will help us as well in supplementing, clarifying and correcting much of the information furnished by the local chronicle. Yet they can never serve as a real substitute to it.

The part of Ibn Iyās's chronicle dedicated to Ottoman Egypt had been cited quite often in the past, and, with the growing and commendable interest in that country and that period in recent years, is being more and more utilized. Yet a systematic and exhaustive use of that part has still to be made. It has to be

(55) See also my "The Historian al-Jabartī and his Background", *BSOAS*, vol. XXIII (1960), pp. 217-218, and notes.

carried out with particular stress on comparison with the history and institutions of the Mamlūk Sultanate.

The harvest that can be gathered from the chronicle of Ibn Ṭūlūn (830-953/1476-1546) is much smaller than that of Ibn Iyās, for various reasons. First of all, because our knowledge of Mamlūk Syria, although quite impressive in itself, is very meager when compared with our knowledge of Mamlūk Egypt. Secondly, Ibn Ṭūlūn's chronicle is not very detailed, and it deals not with the whole of Syria, but mainly with Damascus and its province. Thirdly, it covers a period which is more than two years shorter than the period covered by Ibn Iyās (it ends in Dhū al-Qaʿda 926/end of October 1520). However, it begins well before the Ottoman conquest, and the information it does contain is of a high quality. In combination with the account of Ibn Iyās, which often transcends the boundaries of Egypt, we can learn from it a lot about Ottoman Syria, and about more general aspects of the Ottoman conquest and occupation.

In the articles I mentioned in the introductory remark I confined myself to the study of the policy of the Ottomans towards the Mamlūk aristocracy as reflected in the two chronicles under discussion. Needless to say, other subjects can be reconstructed with a similar degree of detail and reliability on the basis of these two sources.

Appendix B

Of all the military duties and operations in which the Mamlūks participated as part of the Ottoman army during the period under discussion by far the most important one was their share in the conquest of Rhodes, for several reasons: a) it was their first fighting under the Ottomans; b) they established a personal contact with the Ottoman Sultan, and fought under his direct command, a fact which greatly enhanced the process of their restoration in Egypt; [56] c) they proved how badly the Ottomans

(56) In addition to earlier references about Sultan Suleyman's favourable attitude towards the Mamlūks of Egypt (especially in the article in the Bernard Lewis, *Festschrift*), it should be added that the Viceroy Muṣṭafā Pasha, brought with him a special order *(marsūm)* from that Sultan, in which he demanded good treatment of the Mamlūks (Ibn Iyās, V, p. 486, l. 22).

were in need of a military element of their kind, for, though ultimately victorious, the besieging army suffered most heavy casualties, in which the Egyptian contingent had its full share. From an official letter received in Cairo it was learnt that "the number of dead among the Ottoman and Egyptian armies, from the handguns and artillery which fired on them daily, from the fortress of Rhodes, was immeasurable. Any part of the wall which the besiegers destroyed by day, was repaired by the Franks under the cover of night with a special kind of stone *(al-ḥajar al-faṣṣ)*. The besiegers were sapped and exhausted by the fortitude *(ba's)* of the Franks. The names of the dead from among the Circassian amirs and Mamlūks were kept secret." ([57])

(57) *Ibid.*, p. 483, ll. 8-15.

X

Mamlūk Military Aristocracy During the First Years of the Ottoman Occupation of Egypt

THE EXPANSION OF the Ottomans into the lands of Islam in the second decade of the sixteenth century brought about one of the most profound changes which ever took place within the boundaries of those lands. A major victim of that expansion was the Mamlūk Sultanate, which was wiped out as its territories were incorporated into the Ottoman Empire. Reconstructing the process of transition from Mamlūk to Ottoman rule is essential for various reasons, not the least of them being the fact that the Mamlūk Sultanate was the leading Muslim power until the time of its extinction.

As far as Egypt, the main country of that Sultanate, is concerned, we are lucky to have the superb chronicle of Ibn Iyās, which continues six years into the Ottoman conquest. It is a mine of first-class information on various subjects. For drawing a full picture of that process of transition, all the available sources have, of course, to be consulted. None of them, however, can match that of Ibn Iyās. Furthermore, until now that source has not been sufficiently used, while its data have not been examined and interpreted against the background of the pre-Ottoman period in Egypt.

The following lines will deal with the policy of the Ottomans toward the Mamlūks of Egypt in the period covered by our source.[1]

The Ottoman conquest of Egypt was, on the whole, quite orderly and lenient; barring a few exceptions, it was not accompanied by persecution and plundering of the civilian population. The life and property of civilians were safeguarded, so long as they did not cooperate with the Mamlūks.[2] Ottoman policy toward the Mamlūks and their collaborators was, however, completely different, particularly during the period immediately following the conquest. On the eve of the battle of al-Raydānīya, in the approaches of Cairo (Dhū 'l-Ḥijja 922/January 1517), Sultan Selīm I (918–926/1512–1520), who headed the conquering Ottoman army, declared that he would not return to his capital before having conquered Egypt and annihilated all its Circassian Mamlūks.[3] As soon as the Ottomans entered Cairo, they embarked on a large-scale search and hunt for the Mamlūks, and whenever they caught one, they immediately cut off his head.[4] At the same time, they announced that any civilian who hid a Circassian Mamlūk would be hanged over his own doorstep.[5] Most of the captured Mamlūks were transported to the Ottoman sultan's camp in al-Raydānīya, and beheaded. After having executed a very great number of Mamlūks in this way, the Ottomans erected poles, and connected them with ropes, from which they dangled the cut-off heads. The number of those executed by the Ottomans from among the Mamlūks, the bedouins (*'urbān*), and the Mamlūks' manservants (*ghilmān*)[6] in the first few days after their victory was about 4,000.[7] In the next few days, they executed another 800 Mamlūks of all ranks.[8] They also executed in the Alexandria prison[9] the former sultan al-Ẓāhir Qānṣūh (904–05/1498–99), fearing that the Mamlūks might proclaim him their king.[10] Mamlūks of all ranks who did not try to go into hiding, and who gave themselves up voluntarily, were chained and dispatched to Alexandria, and thence to Constantinople. Their number was 700 or more.[11] On Rabī' I 923/April 1517, a group of fifty-four Mamlūk commanders (emirs) of various ranks was transported to al-Raydānīya, where all of them were beheaded.[12] After the battle of Wardān[13] (Rabī' I 923/April 1517), in which the last Mamlūk sultan Ṭūmānbāy[14] was defeated and captured (and later executed), the Ottomans once again carried out a great slaughter of the Circassian Mamlūks and their allies. Eight hundred cut-off heads of these Mamlūks and bedouins were dispatched to Cairo. The rest were thrown into the Nile near the field of battle.[15] Ottoman soldiers married the wives of the executed Mamlūks, despite the explicit prohibition of the Ottoman *qāḍī*, and with the full assistance of the local *qāḍīs*.[16]

There is no way to estimate the number or proportion of the Mamlūks killed by Sultan Selīm, for we do not know the total number of the Mamlūks at that time.[17] That the proportion was very high can be learned from the fact that Ibn Iyās, in his summing up of the life of Sultan Selīm, on the occasion of the death of that monarch several years *after* the massacre, states that he killed most of the Circassian Mamlūks (*qatala ghālib 'askar Miṣr min al-mamālīk al-jarākisa*).[18] It should also be remembered, in this connection, that just before these massacres the Mamlūks must have suffered very heavy casualties at Marj Dābiq (August 1516) and al-Raydānīya (January 1517), two of the bloodiest battles in their entire history.

In this period of an all-out war of extermination and expulsion which the Ottomans waged on the Circassian Mamlūks, the sons of those Mamlūks (*awlād al-nās*) fared much better than their fathers. The Ottomans wanted at first to kill them off as well, but after having been told that these were not Mamlūks, they contented themselves with a money ransom.[19] Out of fear that they would be mistaken for Mamlūks, the *awlād al-nās* discarded the typical Mamlūk headgear of the time, the *takhfīfa* hats (pl. *takhāfīf*) and the *zamṭ* hats (pl. *zumūṭ*),[20] and wore, instead, the *'imāma*, the headgear typical of ecclesiastics, that is, the educated Muslims of nonmilitary class.[21] This practice of changing from the headgear which until very recently had been the most prestigious, to a headgear worn by a class which was lower in the social ladder was adopted not only by the sons of the simple Mamlūks, but also by the sons of the Mamlūk commanders (emirs) and even by the sons of the Mamlūk sultans. Henceforth the use of *takhāfīf* and *zumuṭ* ceased completely in Egypt.[22]

Simultaneously with the destruction of the Mamlūk army and the physical annihilation of a very substantial portion of its elite units, Sultan Selīm dismantled the country's armaments. He confiscated the arsenals of Alexandria,[23] and transferred the heavy artillery of the Cairo citadel to Istanbul.[24]

The first change for the better in the Ottoman policy toward the Circassians took place on 21 Sha'bān 923/9 September 1517, on the very eve of Sultan Selīm's departure from Egypt (23 Sha'bān/11 September), for Istanbul. Khāyrbak, the newly appointed viceroy of Egypt, released fifty-four Mamlūk emirs who had been incarcerated in the Daylam prison of Cairo.[25] At the end of the same month, immediately after the departure of Sultan Selīm (who left behind him an Ottoman garrison of 5,000 horsemen and 500 arquebusiers),[26] Khāyrbak proclaimed a general amnesty to those Circassians who were in hiding. These men emerged from their hiding places in pitiable condition, wearing tattered *fellah* clothing.[27] A greater shame and disgrace, according to their own standards, could hardly have been inflicted upon them.

In mid-Ramaḍān of the same year (early October 1517), the viceroy permitted them to ride horses and to buy arms, shortly after he himself had forbidden them to do so.[28] This far-reaching measure of reinstating the Mamlūks as a military power in Egypt was taken by Khāyrbak in spite of the stiff opposition of the Ottoman soldiers, who tried to derive advantage from this dispute with the viceroy by demanding from him feudal fiefs (*iqṭāʿāt*), and all the other kinds of payments which the Mamlūks were accustomed to receive during the Mamlūk Sultanate. Khāyrbak refused to meet their request, on the ground that only the Ottoman sultan had the authority to do so.[29] On 23 Dhū 'l-Qaʿda of the same year (7 November 1517), when pay for the Circassian Mamlūks was proclaimed, they appeared from all directions, their number exceeding 5,000![30] It would appear that the greatest, and perhaps also final, emergence of the Mamlūks from their hiding took place around this last-mentioned date. In the six weeks separating the general amnesty from the pay announcement, many of the Mamlūks seem to have remained wary and hesitant. However, their inclusion in the payroll must have removed any remaining doubts in their minds about the seriousness and durability of the amnesty. In Rabīʿ I 924/February 1518, Khāyrbak received an order from Sultan Selīm to pay a monthly salary (*jāmakīya*), "according to the old custom" (*ʿalā al-ʿāda*) to the Circassian Mamlūks and the *awlād al-nās*.[31] In the same month the viceroy appointed over every twenty Mamlūks one of their own commanders (*aghawāt*) of previous times[32] as their supervisor. A main duty of those *aghawāt* was to insure that all the Mamlūks under their supervision should report for duty when called upon to take part in military campaigns.[33] In Jumādā I of the same year (May 1518), the Circassian Mamlūks were already taking part in quelling the mutiny of the Ottoman Sipahi and Janissary regiments.[34] There is no doubt that the unruliness and quarrels of the Ottoman units stationed in Egypt greatly facilitated the task of the reestablishment of the Mamlūks. During the years 924–26/1518–20, the Circassian Mamlūks and *awlād al-nās* took part in three military campaigns: two to Red Sea destinations (Jidda;[35] Ayla and Aznam[36]), and one to a Mediterranean destination (Alexandria[37]). The purpose of all three of these expeditions was defense against the Franks.

With the death of Sultan Selīm, and the accession of his son, Sultan Suleyman the Magnificent (926–74/1520–66) to the throne,[38] the position of the Circassian Mamlūks improved greatly. Khāyrbak tried to please and conciliate them much more than he had done before. He paid them two months' *jāmakīya* all at once. The general attitude toward them had also changed completely. Whereas until then people would call them "O dogs! O [inferior type of] shoes!" (*yā kilāb yā zarābīl*) they now began to address them saying "O masters!" (*yā aghawāt*). Our source concludes: "Once the Circassian Mamlūks heard of the death of Sultan Selīm, their [fallen] crests became erect" (*wa-qad aqāmat al-mamālīk al-Jarākisa ṣudūrahā min ḥīn sami'ū bi-mawt Salīm Shāh ibn 'Uthmān*).[39] Sultan Suleyman did, indeed, firmly refuse to allow those Circassian emirs and Mamlūks who had been exiled to Istanbul to return to Egypt together with the other exiles, who were permitted to do so.[40] But on the other hand, he informed the viceroy through a personal emissary (who arrived in Cairo in Rajab 928/June 1522) that he would like to include a special contingent of Circassian Mamlūks, with their emirs, in the campaign which he was planning for the reconquest of the island of Rhodes.[41] The Egyptian expeditionary force to Rhodes numbered 1,500 men, of whom 500 or 800 were Circassians. The rest were Ottoman units of the Sipahis, Janissaries, and the Gönüllü. The Circassians had their own commander, while all the other Ottoman units were under another commander.[42] In Rhodes, Sultan Suleyman, who was personally in command of the besieging army, welcomed the Circassians warmly, and praised them highly. He deplored his father's policy toward them, describing it as unwise, and declared: "Is it possible that Mamlūks such as these would be killed?" (*istaqalla 'aql wālidihi Salīm Shāh alladhī qatala al-mamālīk al-Jarākisa wa-qāla mithla hādhihi al-mamālīk tuqtal*).[43]

Payments

One of the most reliable yardsticks for examing the attitude of the Ottoman authorities toward the defeated Mamlūks is their policy of payment to them in comparison with other units. This requires us to list these units. Our author mentions seven "bodies" or "groups" (*ṭawā'if*, sing. *ṭā'ifa*), which he gives in the following order: (a) Ottoman emirs; (b) *Sipahis* (cavalry); (c) Janissaries (infantry); (d) Gönüllü (volunteer cavalry); (e) Circassian emirs; (f) Circassian Mamlūks; (g) the Mamlūks of the viceroy.[44] The commanders of the Sipahis, Janissaries, Gönüllü (in Ibn Iyās's transcription, *Kamūlīya*) were called *aghawāt*.[45]

Whatever was left of the Mamlūk army after its defeat and decimation was divided into two categories: the Circassian Mamlūks and the *awlād al-nās*. The latter are not mentioned among the groups enumerated in the above list, and it would appear that for purposes of payment they and the Circassian Mamlūks were considered as one group,[46] even though the pay of the *awlād al-nās* was much less (see below).

According to the list provided by our author, the Circasians occupied only the fifth and sixth places among the units of the Ottoman army stationed in Egypt. The *awlād al-nās*, who were passed over in silence in that list, fared even worse. They gradually lost their feudal fiefs through a series of decrees and of arbitrary acts of injustice.[47] Once the Mamlūks had been granted amnesty and partially restored, the only thing which could befall the *awlād al-nās* was a more rapid decline. It is true that Sultan Selīm, on his return to his capital, ordered that they be paid a monthly salary (*jāmakīya*), but this was an extremely small one, ranging from two-thirds of a dinar to one dinar to two dinars.[48] This means that even the highest-paid among them received a salary three and a half times smaller than that of an ordinary Circassian Mamlūk, whereas the salary of lowest-paid among them was ten and a half times smaller.[49] As for the Circassians, the Ottomans continued to pay them exactly the same *jāmakīya* which they used to receive in the latter part of the Mamlūk Sultanate, namely, 2,000 dirhams, or seven dinars.[50] But neither they nor the other Ottoman units are said by our source to have received, in addition to the *jāmakīya*, the entire wide range of payments which they used to receive before the Ottoman conquest.[51] It is true that in Shawwāl 926/September 1520, a letter from Sultan Selīm arrived in Cairo, ordering the viceroy to pay the Circassian Mamlūks not only the *jāmakīya*, but other payments as well, such as their meat and fodder allowances "in accordance with the old usage" (*'alā al-'āda al-qadīma*).[52] Ibn Iyās, however, informs us on a later occasion that the Mamlūk's *jāmakīya* also included the pay for the meat ration,[53] which might imply that the sultan's order was not strictly observed.[54]

The monthly salaries of the Mamlūk emirs were: emir *ṭablkhāna*, forty dinars; "emir of ten," twenty-five dinars. In the case of these officers, it is specifically stated that they were granted this salary in lieu of their fiefs and their meat and fodder rations.[55] It is significant that the top rank of Mamlūk emīrs, the "emir of a hundred," completely disappears under the Ottomans in the period covered by Ibn Iyās (in the Mamlūk Sultanate the official number of emirs of that rank was twenty-four, but in fact it underwent considerable fluctuation).[56]

As for the various Ottoman units stationed in Egypt, their monthly salaries were as follows: (a) Sipahis. These were divided into several groups according to the amount of their pay. The salary of a soldier belonging to the group in the highest income bracket was sixty dinars. That of a soldier in the lowest income bracket was twenty dinars. (b) Janissaries. Most of them received fifteen dinars, and the rest only twelve dinars. (c) The *Ṣūbāshīya*, who, according to Ibn Iyās, were the heads (*aghawāt*) of the Janissaries,[57] received thirty dinars. (d) The Gönüllü. The majority of them received twelve dinars, and the rest, ten or eight dinars. (e) Circassian Mamlūks: seven dinars.[58]

The total monthly payment to each of those groups was: Sipahis, 11,000 dinars; Janissaries, 13,000 dinars; Gönüllü, 11,000 dinars; Circassian Mamlūks and *awlād al-nās*, 11,000 dinars; the Mamlūks of the viceroy and his retinue, 13,000.[59]

The above figures are very instructive in several ways. First of all, they make it abundantly clear that the Circassian Mamlūks at this stage occupied the bottom of the pay scale. Not less significant is the fact that some of the Ottoman horsemen received salaries which were 50 percent higher than the salaries of the highest-ranking Mamlūk emirs. Unfortunately, we know practically nothing about the salaries of the Ottoman commanders. It is also interesting that the total sums received by the various units were so similar in size. The above figures also indicate the already strong position of the Mamlūks of the viceroy, who received a total sum greater than that received by the rest of the Circassian Mamlūks and the *awlād al-nās*. There is no indication, however, that the monthly salary of a single Mamlūk of the viceroy was higher than that of another Mamlūk.

These payments to the army weighed very heavily on the depleted economic resources of the country, according to our source.[60] Payments were not made regularly; the accumulation of debts to the army increased steadily, and became a chronic phenomenon.[61] Under such conditions, the Mamlūks, and in particular the *awlād al-nās*, were the first to suffer. In Muḥarram 928/December 1521, during a pay parade to the Circassians, the viceroy declared that only those who intended to take part in the military expedition would be paid. He then summoned the Circassians one by one to his presence, and chose the youngest and strongest out of every ten, to join the military expedition.

In the same parade, he struck off the payroll 1,000 Circassian Mamlūks and *awlād al-nās*, among whom there were respected veteran Mamlūks of Sultan Qāytbāy (873–901/1468–95).[62] In Jumādā II of the same year (May 1522), he cut in half the salaries of numerous Circassians and *awlād al-nās*, and pensioned them off. The number of those pensioned off included young, vigorous men, capable of taking part in a campaign.[63] In Rajab (June) of the same year, he cut in half the salary of twenty emirs of *ṭablkhāna* and emirs of ten.[64]

The Ottomanization of the Mamlūk Aristocracy

The incorporation of the Mamlūks into the Ottoman army, described above, served as the basis of the Ottomanization of that aristocracy, within the framework of the Ottomanization of the entire military, administrative, and judicial apparatus. Ibn Iyās gives a detailed description of that process (especially if one takes into account the short period involved), and, on the whole, a very reliable one. But whereas one can find no reason to contest his facts, so far as they are restricted to his own time, his evaluation of those facts is quite often, though by no means always, open to criticism. There were, in my view, two principal, closely connected, reasons for Ibn Iyās's weakness in this respect. First of all, as a man who had been brought up in, and who had lived in the Mamlūk Sultanate, which was so fundamentally different from the Ottoman Empire, he, like so many of his compatriots, could not understand some of the basic, positive aspects of that empire. Second, he was a partisan of the defunct Sultanate, and a bitter antagonist of the new rulers.

Ibn Iyās was by no means a panegyrist of the Mamlūk aristocracy and of Mamlūk rule in general. Indeed, the very opposite is true. Like most of the historians of the Circassian period (784–922/1382–1517), he depicts a very gloomy picture of the Sultanate, and does not mince words in severely criticizing it.[65] However, as soon as the Mamlūks have been overpowered by the Ottomans, he almost completely forgets all the evils of the *ancien régime*, which he himself had so frequently exposed and castigated, and embarks on an idealization of that regime, turning all his fury against the newcomers. But for all Ibn Iyās's subjectiveness, one cannot say that he lacks insight into some of the fundamental differences between the two regimes.

In comparison with the pomp and the complicated ceremonial of the Mamlūk court, and the lavish way of life of the Mamlūks, the

Ottomans of that time seem still to have been lacking in polish and refinement. The urban population of Egypt, and particularly that of Cairo, which was not accustomed to such simplicity, was very adversely affected by the crudeness of its new rulers. Ibn Iyās epitomizes that prevalent feeling in the following, most revealing, short statement: "Sultan Selīm did not follow in Egypt the rules and patterns of the previous sultans of that country. Neither he, nor his high-ranking officials, nor his commanders, nor his army, had an acknowledged order. They were [all] barbarians and savages. One could not distinguish among them between the master and his servant" (*wa-lā mashā Salīm Shāh fī Miṣr 'alā qawā'id al-salāṭīn al-sālifa bi-Miṣr wa-lam yakun lahu niẓām yu'rafu lā huwa wa-lā wuzarāyihi* [sic!] *wa-lā umarāyihi* [sic!] *wa-lā 'askarihi bal kānū hamaj lā yu'rafu al-ghulām min al-ustādh*).[66] The degree of shock and aversion caused by the unfamiliar Ottoman way of government and way of life is demonstrated by Ibn Iyās's frequent repetitions of this same derogatory statement in similar words.[67]

Among the things which particularly antagonized the local population were the Ottomans' being clean-shaven (*ḥalq al-dhuqūn*), or, at most, wearing short beards; their wearing the *ṭarṭūr* headgear;[68] their habit of eating on horseback in the streets of the capital; and, above all, their public disregard of some of the basic ordinances of the Muslim religion (especially their drinking wine, their eating during the fast of Ramaḍān—both perpetrated publicly—and their refraining from participation in prayers in the mosques).[69] A longing for the splendor and stateliness of the regime which had so recently expired is reflected in almost every page of our chronicle.[70]

As far as military matters (including matters connected with military ceremony) were concerned, the population felt particular sorrow and nostalgia at the abolition of the *furūsīya* exercises and games, which had constituted the foundation of Mamlūk military training,[71] and which had included polo (*kura*), and exercises with the lance (*rumḥ*) and mace (*dabbūs*), etc.;[72] the abolition of the orchestras (*kūsāt*) which used to play in front of the gates of the Mamlūk emirs' houses;[73] and the disappearance of the sumptuous Mamlūk costume, such as the *kalafta* hat, the *qabā'* coat, the *takhfīfa* headgear, the beaver (*qundus*) fur, the red *zamṭ* hat, the robes of honor (*al-tashārīf wa'l-muthammar*), the spurs (*mihmāz*), and the *khuff* boots.[74]

As for the dress of the Circassian Mamlūks in the years under study, it was subjected to the following developments (or, more exactly, changes) in the Ottomans' attitude toward the Mamlūks. In Ramaḍān

923/September–October 1517, that is, immediately after the announcement of a general amnesty for the Circassians, they were ordered to wear *zamṭ* hats and *mallūṭa* (pl. *malālīṭ*) coats,[75] exactly as they used to do under their own sultans. The reason for this order was that numerous Circassians, like the soldiers of the Ottoman army, wore caftans (*qafṭānāt*) and turbans (*'amā'im*), and enjoyed, like them, the privilege of robbing the merchandise and snatching off the headgear of passers-by.[76] It would appear, however, that this order was not strictly observed. For as early as Dhū 'l-Qa'da of that year (November–December 1517), we are informed that the Circassian Mamlūks and emirs wore velvet (*mukhmal*) and woollen (*jūkh*) caftans, woollen *ṭarṭūrs*, round turbans (*'amā'im*) and leather *suqmān* shoes, as did the Ottomans. As a result, the Mamlūks became confused with the Ottomans to such a degree as to make it impossible to distinguish between them. They could only be distinguished by the Mamlūks' having beards and the Ottomans' being beardless (*wa-ṣārat al-mamālīk tu'rafu bi-dhuqūnihim wa'l-'Uthmānīya bi-ghayr dhuqūn*).[77] This shows how difficult it was for the Mamlūks to part with their beards, despite the great incentive they had for doing so (see also below). In Shawwāl 927/September 1521, the viceroy issued an order rescinding that of October 1517. According to this order, Mamlūks, Ottomans, and *awlād al-nās* were forbidden to wear the red *zamṭ* hat (which, as mentioned earlier in this paper, was the typical headgear of the Mamlūks in the final decades of their reign). Those who would not obey that order were warned that they would be sent to the gallows without the right of appeal. At the same time, the viceroy prohibited the Circassian emirs from wearing the Mamlūk *sarmūja* shoe, especially on their visits to the seat of government in the Citadel. Our author's comment on this order is that it was issued because of the viceroy's deep-seated hatred of all the Circassians (*wa-hādhā kulluhu 'ayn al-maqt lil-Jarākisa wa-bughḍan lahum qāṭibatan*).[78] In the following month, the Circassian amirs and *khāṣṣakīya* were forbidden to have their servant (*ghulām*) ride behind them on a mule when they rode their horses (as had been the Mamlūk custom), and ordered them to have him walk on foot in front of his master, in accordance with the Ottoman custom.[79] In Muḥarram 928/December 1521, during the same parade in which the viceroy struck 1,000 Mamlūks and *awlād al-nās* out of the payroll, he stepped toward each long-bearded Mamlūk, cut off about half his beard with his own hand, handed it over to the Mamlūk, and said to him: "Follow the Ottoman rules in cutting your beards, in making the sleeves of your dresses narrow, *and in everything which the Ottomans do*" (*imshū 'alā al-qānūn al-'uthmānī fī qaṣṣ al-liḥā wa-taḍyīq al-akmām wa-kullamā yaf'alūnahu al-'Uthmānīya*).[80]

Khāyrbak's persecution of the Circassian Mamlūks[81] and *awlād al-nās*, together with his deliberate policy of Ottomanization, should not be interpreted as an attempt on his part to exterminate the Mamlūks as such. What he really intended to do was to foster, strengthen, and increase the number of *his own* freedmen (i.e., Mamlūks purchased and manumitted by himself), at the expense of other Mamlūks who owed allegiance to other patrons. In this respect, he had only to follow the old established custom of the Mamlūk sultans, each of whom, on acceding to the throne, used to weaken the Mamlūks of his predecessor by various means, including expelling them from the barracks (*ṭibāq*, sing. *ṭabaqa*) of the Cairo citadel, and stationing his own Mamlūks in those barracks, while attempting to increase the number of his own Mamlūks by all means available to him.[82] We have already seen how strong Khāyrbak's Mamlūks and retinue had become, and how substantial was their portion of the monthly payments. On the occasion of his death we learn that he, like all the Mamlūk sultans, kept his Mamlūks near his person in the *ṭibāq* of the citadel. All of them were removed from there a fortnight after his death, even *before* the arrival of his successor Muṣṭafā Pasha. Ottoman units replaced Khāyrbak's Mamlūks in the citadel.[83] In all probability, Khāyrbak kept the citadel to himself and to his own Mamlūks throughout his viceroyalty. There is no mention of Mamlūks of other patrons, nor of any kind of Ottoman soldiery being stationed there during that period.

Khāyrbak's determination to strengthen his own and his Mamlūks' position can be gauged from the immense fortune which he accumulated, in spite of the very short period of his reign (*fī hādhihi al-mudda al-yasīra*). More than 600,000 dinars were found in his private possession, in addition to the unspecified amount found in the coffers of the Treasury (*bayt al-māl*). On top of this, he left immense quantities of movable property, which exceeded those left by his patron the great Sultan Qāytbāy, who had ruled almost thirty years (873–901/1468–95), as compared to the rule of his Mamlūk Khāyrbak, which lasted little more than five years.[84] Khāyrbak succeeded in accumulating this fabulous fortune in a time of severe economic crisis by, among other means, his refusal to pay the money due to those Mamlūks who were not his own freedmen, and to those Ottoman units which he disliked.[85]

Whereas Jānbirdī al-Ghazālī tried to obstruct and curb the Ottomanization of his Syrian province as best he could throughout the greater part of his short reign,[86] Khāyrbak went out of his way to accelerate this process in Egypt in various areas. There seems, however, to have been one focal point which he protected from radical Ottomanization, and this was the Cairo Citadel. It would appear that he wanted to have around his person as much as possible of the atmosphere and people formerly surrounding the Mamlūk sultan, and with which he had grown very familiar both as a Royal Mamlūk in the *ṭabaqa* and as Grand Emir. However, his attempt to preserve the Mamlūk character of the Citadel was crushed soon after his death, in two swift stages. In the first stage his own Mamlūks were replaced there by Ottoman units, as has just been mentioned. About a month later, as we are informed by Ibn Iyās,

> The viceroy [Muṣṭafā Pasha] took the keys of all the storehouses and depots (*ḥawāṣil*) from the doorkeepers (*bawwābūn*), and handed them over to a group of Ottomans (*Arwām*) of his own retinue, and drove away all the doormen, servants, grooms, jockeys, attendants, and others. He even dismissed the cooks of the Royal Kitchen and the water carriers, and replaced all these by Ottomans (*Arwām*). He also fired all the Qur'ān readers in the Citadel, as well as all the muezzins, and appointed just one muezzin to the mosque of al-Ḥawsh. In short, *he abolished the entire old system of the Citadel, and introduced* [in its stead] *the order of the Ottomans, which is the most evil of all orders (abṭala jamī' niẓām al-qal'a alladhī kānat 'alayhi qadīman wa-mashā 'alā al-qānūn al-'uthmānī alladhī huwa ashyam* [sic!] *qānūn*).[87]

The Ottomanization of the Cairo Citadel was thus accomplished within six weeks of Khāyrbak's death. The importance of this measure can hardly be overestimated, for the Citadel constituted the focal point of the entire Mamlūk Sultanate, as well as of the capital, from which it was dominated, and contributed much more than any other structure to the shaping of Mamlūk aristocracy. In order to uproot the old system, the Ottomans had to wipe out all its traces in the place which constituted its very heart. But the Citadel did not lose its focal position under the new rulers. The unfolding of the internal relations of the Mamlūks, as well as their relations with the Ottomans stationed in Cairo, against the background of the Citadel, will always remain one of the major subjects of the study of Ottoman Egypt.

We do not know what happened to the Mamlūks of Khāyrbak after they had been removed from the Citadel. What is absolutely certain is that this did not bring about the end of the Mamlūks in

Egypt. In the short period under discussion there is no reference, in the sources upon which this paper is based, to the importation of new Mamlūks to Egypt. Yet one cannot see how Khāyrbak could strengthen his position without such importation. The attitude of the Ottomans to the bringing over of Mamlūks to Egypt, particularly in the first decades of their rule, is another major subject which awaits systematic study.

To sum up: Mamlūk military aristocracy in Egypt, during the first years of Ottoman occupation, managed, on the one hand, to survive, but underwent a quite thorough process of Ottomanization, on the other. That process was accelerated immediately after Khāyrbak's death, especially by the transformation of the Cairo Citadel into an Ottoman bastion. It is unknown, however, how long the acceleration lasted. What is known for certain is that that aristocracy was relegated to the bottom of the Ottoman socio-military pyramid, and that it rose very little, if at all, from that level in the period covered by Ibn Iyās. In view of the scarcity and the poor quality of most of the historical sources in the period stretching between the end of the chronicle of Ibn Iyās and the beginning of the chronicle of al-Jabartī, any full reconstruction of the growth of Mamlūk power during that period will be very conjectural.[88] Under existing conditions, however, the more thoroughly the chronicle of Ibn Iyās is studied, the better are the chances for making more plausible conjectures, at least about the immediately following years.

NOTES

1. Ibn Iyās, *Badā'i' al-Zuhūr fī waqā'i' al-Duhūr*, ed. P. Kahle, M. Mostafa, and M. Sobernheim (Istanbul, 1931), vol. v. The present paper is a completely revised and enlarged version of a brief survey in Hebrew called "The Mamlūk Army at the Beginning of the Ottoman Conquest," published in *Tarbitz* (Jerusalem, 1952), pp. 221–26. My original intention was to deal with Ottoman policy toward the Mamlūks of Egypt *and* Syria simultaneously, but because of limitations of space, this could not be done. An article that compliments the present one, and which was published in *Studia Islamica*, fascicle 65 (1987), pp. 125–48 under the title "The End of the Mamlūk Sultanate," has the subtitle "Why Did the Ottomans Spare the Mamlūks of Egypt and Wipe out the Mamlūks of Syria?"

2. Upon entering Gaza the Ottoman army did not at first harm the population in any way. Only after the local garrison attacked the Ottomans,

killing 400 of their men, did a great slaughter of the townspeople take place (Ibn Iyās, v, 129, l. 15–130, l. 12). When Sultan Selīm arrived in Bilbays, on his way to Cairo from the Sinai, he issued strict orders not to molest the population. All the people of Bilbays, and the peasants of the neighborhood, welcomed him warmly (Ibn Iyās, v, 138, l. 22–139, l. 1). Upon occupying Cairo, the Ottoman army looted it for three days, but the looting was abruptly stopped by the sultan's order (ibid., v, 144, l. 20–145, l. 16). Although some of the peasants cooperated with the Mamlūks (ibid., v, 139, ll. 14–16; 140, ll. 2–4), most of them were indifferent to the change of government. On the eve of the battle of al-Raydānīya, they refused to pay the rent on cultivated lands (*kharāj*) to their Mamlūk masters, claiming that they had first to know to whom the country was going to belong, to the Mamlūks or to the Ottomans, so that they would not have to pay the rent twice (ibid., v, 130, ll. 20–22).

3. Ibid., v, 121, ll. 18–19. At that period the Ottomans are called *'Uthmānīya, Rūm* (or *Arwām*), and quite frequently *Tarākima* or *Turkmān* (see, for instance, ibid., v, 75, ll. 3–9; 184, ll. 13–17; 206, ll. 20–21; 207, l. 22; 208, l. 2; 231, l. 16; 244, l. 5; 252, ll. 13–14; 254, ll. 15–21; 298, ll. 1–10; 304, ll. 1, 9; 309, l. 13; 310, l. 5; 328, l. 2; 374, ll. 8–14; 481, ll. 20–22). The Mamlūks in this period are usually called *Jarākisa*, but the names *Atrāk* and *Turk* are by no means extinct (see, for instance, ibid., pp. 164, l. 5; 193, l. 2; 272, ll. 3–4). The name *Dawlat al-Turk* or *Dawlat al-Atrāk* is the usual name of the Mamlūk Sultanate, also in the period of Circassian predominance. The name *Turk* as designating the Ottomans or the "Turks" is extremely rare in the Mamlūk reign.

4. Ibn Iyās, v, 145, ll. 18–20; 146, ll. 9–10.

5. Ibid., v, 144, l. 22–145, l. 1.

6. Every Mamlūk usually had two servants, one white-skinned, called *ghulām* (pl. *ghilmān*), the other black, called *'abd* (pl. *'abīd*). The *ghulām* had to perform the less menial tasks.

7. Ibn Iyās, v, 146, ll. 1–16.

8. Ibid., v, 153, ll. 12–17. The executioner (*mashā'ilī*) was, according to our source, a Frank or a Jew from Anatolia (ibid., v, 153, l. 18).

9. The prison of Alexandria was the most important prison of the Mamlūk aristocracy throughout the reign of the Mamlūks.

10. Ibn Iyās, v, 160, ll. 6–17.

11. Ibid., v, 161, ll. 14–22.

12. Ibid., v, 165, l. 16–166, l. 11.

13. Wardān is situated on the western arm of the Nile, to the north of Cairo.

14. Ṭūmānbāy became sultan after Sultan Qānṣūh al-Ghawrī (906–22/1500–1516) was defeated and killed in the battle of Marj Dābiq (August 1516).

15. Ibn Iyās, v, 169, ll. 1–3.

16. Ibid., v, 180, ll. 11–20.

17. On the numbers of the Mamlūks in the Mamlūk Sultanate see my

"Studies on the Structure of the Mamlūk Army," *BSOAS*, xv (1953), pp. 222–28.

18. Ibn Iyās, v, 356, ll. 11–12. According to information arriving in Damascus in Rabīʿ ii 923/May 1517, Sultan Selīm "annihilated the Circassians" (*afnā al-Jarākisa*) (Ibn Ṭūlūn, *Mufākahat al-khillān fī ḥawādith al-zamān* [Cairo, 1964], ii, 60). Such information might, of course, be too much influenced by these still very recent and very exciting events, and would therefore tend to be exaggerated. However, together with Ibn Iyās's detailed account and his summing up in 1520 (just cited), it reflects the very great dimensions of the massacre of the Mamlūks.

19. Ibn Iyās, v, 148, ll. 4–7. The Mamlūk forces stationed in Egypt during the lifetime of the Mamlūk Sultanate were divided into three main parts:

i. The Royal Mamlūks (*al-mamālīk al-sulṭanīya*, very rarely: *mamālīk al-sulṭān*). These were of two categories:

a. The Mamlūks of the ruling sultan (*mushtarawāt, ajlāb,* or *julbān*).

b. Mamlūks who passed from the service of the ruling sultan to the service of other sultans (*mustakhdamūn*). These were divided into two:

1. Mamlūks who passed into the service of the reigning sultan from that of former sultans (*mamālīk al-salāṭin al-mutaqaddima, qarānīṣ* or *qaranisa*);

2. Mamlūks who passed into the service of the reigning sultan from that of the emirs, because of the death or dismissal of their masters (*sayfīya*).

ii. The Emirs' Mamlūks (*mamālīk al-umarā', ajnād al-umarā'*).

iii. The troops of the *ḥalqa* (*ajnād al-ḥalqa*), a corps of free, i.e., non-Mamlūk cavalry. There was within the *ḥalqa* a special unit, composed of the sons of the emirs and of the Mamlūks, called *awlād al-nās*. The commanders (*umarā'*, sing. *amīr*) of the Mamlūk army were divided into three basic ranks: (a) Emirs of a hundred; (b) Emirs of forty (also called emirs of (*ṭablkhāna*); (c) Emirs of ten. The overwhelming majority of the emirs rose to their various ranks from a special bodyguard of the sultan, called *khāṣṣakīya*, whose members were chosen mainly from among his own mamlūks. The *ḥalqa* had commanders of its own, called *muqaddamū al-ḥalqa*. For a detailed discussion of this subject, see my "Studies on the Structure of the Mamlūk Army," *BSOAS*, xv (1953), pp. 203–28, 248–76; xvi (1954), pp. 57–90.

20. L. A. Mayer, *Mamlūk Costume* (Geneva, 1952), index s.v.

21. Ibid.

22. Ibn Iyās, v, 147, ll. 6–9. This is evidence which requires further proof, considering the very short period covered by Ibn Iyās's chronicle.

23. Ibid., v, 183, ll. 13–15.

24. Ibid., v, 186, l. 23–186, l. 5.

25. Ibid., v, 200, l. 21–202, l. 1.

26. Ibid., v, 202, ll. 20–22.

27. Ibid., v, 204, ll. 15–19. According to the historian al-Isḥāqī, Sultan

Selīm allowed the inclusion of the Circassians as a separate unit in the Ottoman garrison, on the eve of his return to his capital, in response to Khāyrbak's request (*Akhbār al-Uwal*, p. 130, ll. 8–17).

28. Ibn Iyās, v, 208, l. 22–209, l. 3.

29. Ibid., v, 209, ll. 3–14.

30. Ibid., v, 220, ll. 1–8.

31. Ibid., v, 240, ll. 3–10.

32. On the *aghawāt* and *aghawāt al-ṭibāq* in the Mamlūk Sultanate, see *L'Esclavage du Mamelouk,* Oriental Notes and Studies, no. 1 (Jerusalem, 1951), index s.v.

33. Ibn Iyās, v, 240, ll. 14–17.

34. Ibid., 251, l. 3–252, l. 14.

35. Ibid., 257, ll. 17–21, 307–9.

36. Ibid., 273, ll. 2–5.

37. Ibid., 325, ll. 14–16.

38. The death of Sultan Selīm caused great rejoicing among the Circassian Mamlūks (ibid., v, 358, ll. 2–6).

39. Ibid., v, 361, l. 12–362, l. 3.

40. Ibid., 358, ll. 13–21.

41. Ibid., 458, ll. 15–17.

42. Ibid., 459, ll. 3–12.

43. Ibid., 470, ll. 7–12.

44. Ibid., 425, ll. 7–20. Cf. references in the following notes, and A. N. Poliak, *Feudalism in Egypt, Syria, Palestine and the Lebanon, 1250–1900* (London, 1939), p. 53 and notes. For information on the units of the Ottoman army see: H. A. R. Gibb and H. Bowen, *Islamic Society and the West* (London, 1950), I, i, and Stanford J. Shaw, *The Financial and Administrative Organization of Ottoman Egypt, 1517–1798* (Princeton, 1962). Khāyrbak, the viceroy (*nā'ib*) of Egypt, also held the title "King of the Emirs" (*malik al-umarā'*). This title was bestowed, in the Mamlūk Sultanate, on some important viceroys of the Syrian provinces. He already had that title as Viceroy of Aleppo under the Mamlūks, and he kept it under the Ottomans, undoubtedly in order to enhance his prestige.

45. Ibn Iyās, v, 313, l. 22; 314, ll. 4–5; 325, l. 4; 329, l. 11; 351, l. 18; 361, ll. 16–17; 427, ll. 1–2; 428, l. 23; 431, l. 22; 481, l. 12; 484, l. 24.

46. Ibid., 425, ll. 22–23.

47. Ibid., 158, l. 22–159, l. 1; 189, ll. 19–20; 249, l. 22–250, l. 3; 287, ll. 16–19.

48. Ibid., 240, ll. 4–10; 305, ll. 7–10.

49. See the immediately following lines.

50. Ibid., 240, ll. 4–10; 242, ll. 16–19; 250, ll. 19–23.

51. In the Mamlūk Sultanate, a Mamlūk who held the rank of simple soldier received, in addition to the income from his feudal fief (*iqṭā'*) the

following payments: (a) the *jāmakīya*, or monthly pay; (b) the *nafaqa*, a payment made irregularly, and especially shortly before a campaign, in order to cover its particular expenses; (c) *nafaqat al-bay'a*, a payment which the mamlūk received upon the accession of a new sultan to the throne; (d) the *kiswa*, or payment for the mamlūk's clothing (given once a year, but possibly twice a year in the early part of Mamlūk rule); (e) the *laḥm*, or meat (given in kind or in money; a daily payment); (f) *aḍḥiya* or *ḍaḥāyā*, sheep for sacrifice (given in kind or in money, once a year, in the month of Dhū al-Ḥijja, on the eve of 'Īd al-Aḍḥā, the Feast of Immolation); (g) *'alīq*, fodder (given in kind or in money, twice a week); (h) *khayl wa-jimāl*, horses and camels (given once or twice a year). The full value of the *nafaqa* (including *nafaqat al-bay'a*) was 100 dinars; that of the *jāmakīya* was seven dinars. All the other payments amounted to several tens of dinars. The income of a Mamlūk emir was, of course, much higher. For a detailed study of this subject, see my "The System of Payment in Mamlūk Military Society," *Journal of Economic and Social History of the Orient*, I (1958), pp. 37–65, 257–96.

52. Ibn Iyās, v, 348, ll. 21–23.

53. Ibid., 404, l. 22–405, l. 1.

54. See, however, ibid., v, 403, ll. 3–5, where the payment for fodder is mentioned in addition to the *jāmakīya*.

55. Ibid., v, 242, ll. 16–19; 250, ll. 9–23.

56. See "Studies on the Structure of the Mamlūk Army," pp. 468–69.

57. Ibn Iyās, v, 362, l. 10. On them see also Gibb and Bowen, op. cit., and Shaw, op. cit., indexes.

58. Ibn Iyās, v, 404, l. 15–405, l. 1. For an important piece of information on the daily pay of the Ottoman army in Egypt see ibid., 486, ll. 9–22.

59. Ibid., v, 425, l. 20–426, l. 1.

60. Ibid., v, 403–5, 424–26.

61. Ibid., v, 251, 273, ll. 13–14; 298, ll. 15–16; 305, l. 7; 448, ll. 16–17; 455, ll. 16–19. It should, however, be remembered that a quite similar situation existed during the greater part of the Circassian period in the Mamlūk Sultanate.

62. Ibid., v, 424, l. 20–425, l. 11.

63. Ibid., v, 448, ll. 17–21.

64. Ibid., v, 453, ll. 13–17.

65. Out of numerous instances, see, for instance, *Gunpowder and Firearms*, p. 107.

66. Ibn Iyās, v, 159, ll. 7–14.

67. E.g., ibid., v, 194, ll. 1–2; 204, ll. 4–5, 9–10; 488, ll. 14–15. Ibn Iyās even goes so far as to state that the reputation of the Ottomans as exceedingly just rulers, which they enjoyed before the conquest of the Mamlūk Sultanate, did not show itself at all in Egypt under the occupation (*fa-in kāna yushā' al-'adl al-zā'id 'an awlād Ibn 'Uthmān wa-hum fī bilādihim qabla an yadkhula Salīm Shāh ilā Miṣr fa-lam yaẓhar li-hādhā al-kalām natīja* [ibid., v, 159, ll. 11–12]).

This is decisive unconscious evidence for the good name which Ottoman justice enjoyed far beyond the boundaries of the Ottoman Sultanate. Such a good name cannot be earned without justification. Whether Ibn Iyās was blinded by his hatred of the new rulers, or whether the Ottomans did not observe, at that stage of their occupation, their reputed justice to the full, is beyond the scope of this paper, and should be studied separately. Whatever low opinion the people of the Mamlūk Sultanate formed of Ottoman refinement, their view of the newly established Safavid state was even lower. Commenting on the poor dress and shabby appearance of the envoys of the Safavids, who arrived in Cairo in Sha'bān 913/December 1507, our author says: "They do not have any splendor [*rawnaq*], *in contrast to the envoys of the Ottoman Sultan*[!]" (Ibn Iyās, IV, 123, ll. 14–18). At a later period such a comment could not be made, for the Safavid court developed into one of the most splendid and most refined in Muslim history.

68. Ibid., v, 194, ll. 1–2. When Sultan Selīm and his retinue went to a public bath in Damascus "they washed and shaved" (*ightasalū wa-ḥalaqū*), Ibn Ṭūlūn, II, 82, l. 12). Muṣṭafā Bāshā, who succeeded Khāyrbak as the viceroy of Egypt, is described as "clean shaven (*ḥalīq al-liḥya*) wearing only a yellow mustache" (Ibn Iyās, v, 485, ll. 11–12). For Ottoman small beards see below. For the *ṭarṭūr* headgear, see Mayer, *Mamlūk Costume*, p. 71 and Dozy's *Supplément aux dictionnaires arabes*, s.v.

69. Ibn Iyās, v, 204, ll. 5–9. It is noteworthy that even as late as the eighteenth century, the historian al-Jabartī frequently criticizes the irreligious behavior and lax morals of the Ottoman soldiers newly arriving in Egypt from other parts of the Empire.

70. In addition to references cited in other notes, see also ibid., v, 194, ll. 6–8.

71. See my "Notes on the Furūsiyya Exercises and Games in the Mamlūk Sultanate," *Studies in Islamic History and Civilization*, ed. Uriel Heyd, *Scripta Hierosolymitana*, vol. IX (Jerusalem, 1961), pp. 31–62.

72. Ibn Iyās, v, 194, ll. 9–10.

73. Ibid., 195, l. 7.

74. Ibid., 195, ll. 2, 3–5, 11. For all the terms mentioned above see Mayer, op. cit., indexes.

75. For the red *zamṭ* hats and the *mallūṭa* coats as a typical dress of the Circassians toward the end of their rule, see Mayer, op. cit., p. 24.

76. Ibn Iyās, v, 209, ll. 14–21.

77. Ibid., 216, ll. 1–12.

78. Ibid., 402, ll. 8–14.

79. Ibid., 402, l. 22–403, l. 2.

80. Ibid., 425, ll. 11–14.

81. In addition to earlier references see also: Ibn Iyās, v, 480, ll. 13–15.

82. See "Studies on the Structure of the Mamlūk Army," *BSOAS*, xv (1953), pp. 208 ff.

83. The tragic irony of the entire event was that it was Sinān Bak who ousted Khāyrbak's Mamlūks from the Citadel. The same Sinān was the person whom Khāyrbak appointed as his successor and to whom he entrusted, beside the State Treasury, his sons, his family, his retinue, and his Mamlūks (Ibn Iyās, v, 476, l. 23–477, l. 3; ll. 15–20).

84. Ibn Iyās, v, 478, ll. 14–16; 482, ll. 7–8; 487, ll. 8–12; 488, ll. 15–16.

85. See also ibid., v, 362, ll. 3–8, 8–11; 368, l. 23–369, l. 1.

86. Jānbirdī al-Ghazālī's policy is discussed in the paper mentioned in note 1.

87. Ibn Iyās, v, 488, ll. 8–15.

88. I include, of course, in this category, my article dealing with the transformation of Mamlūk society in Egypt under the Ottomans (*JESHO*, III [1960], pp. 148–74, 275–325), although I believe that some of the analogies with the Mamlūk Sultanate will prove to be correct.

Postscript

The article that complements the present one, and which was published in *Studia Islamica*, fascicle 65 (1987), pp. 125–48 under the title "The End of the Mamlūk Sultanate" has the subtitle "Why did the Ottomans spare the Mamlūks of Egypt and wipe-out the Mamlūks of Syria?" Here the "wiping out" does not mean the physical annihilation of every single Mamlūk, but the destruction of the Mamlūks as a sociomilitary and political entity.

XI

ON THE TERM *KHĀDIM* IN THE SENSE OF «EUNUCH» IN THE EARLY MUSLIM SOURCES

In a very recent article A. Cheikh Moussa studied meticulously the main passages of al-Jāḥiẓ dealing with the eunuchs in his *Kitāb al-Ḥayawān* and *Kitāb Mufākharat al-Jawārī wal-Ghilmān*[1] (later — *Ḥayawān* and *Jawārī*). This is a welcome and timely contribution. In spite of the obvious centrality of the eunuch institution in Muslim history and civilization the subject was very much neglected (with the possible partial exception of its study regarding the Ottoman empire). Any systematic research into that subject will quickly show that its importance far surpasses all previous expectations. The passages of al-Jāḥiẓ are essential for the study of certain aspects of the eunuch phenomenon in Islam, and their thorough analysis is long overdue. Their detailed scrutiny by A. Cheikh Moussa (later — M.) is certainly superior to anything written about them earlier. This does not imply the absence of certain flaws in that scrutiny, which are outside the scope of the present lines.

In an addendum to the above cited article[2], the same author expresses disagreement with a statement and a conclusion of mine included in the first installment of my study «On the Eunuchs in Islam»[3].

The statement relates to the attitude towards the black eunuchs as compared to the attitude towards unemasculated blacks in major Muslim centers. The conclusion is about the term *khādim* in the sense of «eunuch» in the Muslim Medieval (especially historical and related) sources.

Since he deals with the first of the two very briefly, and since I myself

[1] A. Cheikh Moussa, Gāḥiẓ et les Eunuques ou la confusion du même et de l'autre, *Arabica*, XXIX, 1982, pp. 184-214.

[2] *Ibid.*, pp. 212-214.

[3] *Jerusalem Studies in Arabic and Islam* (*JSAI*), Jerusalem, vol. I (1979), pp. 67-124, and especially pp. 64, 72, 83 and 85.

am discussing that subject in much greater detail in other works of mine, some of which are not yet published, I shall concentrate at this stage on replying to his arguments concerning the term *khādim*.

In a nutshell: M. disagrees with my attempt (a most tentative one, as far as the very early part of the Muslim era is concerned, a fact which I stress in my study), to establish the date of the introduction of *khādim* in the above mentioned meaning. In particular he contradicts my attributing the use of that term in that sense to al-Jāḥiẓ. From his conviction that that author never employed *khādim* as equivalent to *khaṣī* he draws much wider conclusions.

My comments on his criticism are these: From his presentation the reader cannot form a proper idea about the range and variety of the source material with which I back my conclusion on this subject, or about the reasoning and the line of argumentation which I use in order to reach it. Even if he is right about al-Jāḥiẓ and *khādim*, which I believe he is not, what he infers from it is not correct. Finally, what he attributes to me as stating is not always accurate.

These comments on M.'s criticism had been written only wih reference to two instances which I bring in my above mentioned study, where al-Jāḥiẓ uses, in my view, the term *khādim* in the sense of «eunuch»[4]. M., in opposing that identification, deals only with one instance, and overlooks the other. In both cases individual persons are involved.

Those two instances were the ones I knew (or, more precisely, remembered) when I wrote my article on the eunuchs, and in an earlier reply to M. (which I shall call «the first version») I had to confine myself only to them. It goes, of course, without saying, that in following a term and its development throughout a number of centuries, exhausting the whole data pertaining to that term is impossible. If, however, one is on the right track, there are very good chances that with further reading he will find not only additional or better proofs to support his thesis, but even such proofs which will overshadow the earlier ones. Within the context of the present difference of opinion between M. and myself, I found, after having written the first version, a proof of that category in the writings of the selfsame al-Jāḥiẓ. Furthermore, it is included in one of the two works which M. used in his research on that author and the eunuchs.

---

[4] *JSAI*, I, p. 85.

That piece of evidence is not only decisive in connection with the present difference of opinion, but is of the highest importance for the reconstruction of the history and development of our term in the early Muslim period. I shall, therefore, deal first of all with it, and in some detail. The discussion regarding the two original instances will be only somewhat abbreviated, because it contains points which are both pertinent to our subject and can be better clarified here than elsewhere.

The work of al-Jāḥiẓ which contains the evidence in question is the epistle *Jawārī*[5], mentioned in the opening lines of the present study. But before presenting and analyzing the evidence, a few remarks about the epistle have to be made, which will explain the background of the evidence.

Al-Jāḥiẓ contrasts there the qualities of the boys and the girls (mainly the slave-boys and the slave-girls), shifting very often to men and women in general, and putting special emphasis on the sexual aspect (including adultery and pederasty)[6]. He does it by means of a debate or dispute between a protagonist of the girls (*ṣāḥib al-jawārī*) and a protagonist of the boys (*ṣāḥib al-ghilmān*). A repeated argument of this second protagonist is that the lovers of the females are primitive and rude, whereas the lovers of the males are refined and sophisticated. He includes the early Arabs (and particularly their poets) in the first category and the later ones in the second.

The passage on the eunuchs occupies two full pages[7] out of a debate covering about thirty sparsely printed pages (including the scholarly apparatus)[8], and it comes at the very end of that debate. It is represented as the pronouncement of *ṣāḥib al-jawārī*, and it opens with these words.

> I. «You [i.e. *ṣāḥib al-ghilmān*] mentioned the *khiṣyān* and *the beauty of their figures* and the smoothness of their complexions, and the [practice of] having [carnal] pleasure with them. And [you also said] that that is something with which *the first ones* were not acquainted. *You thus drove me against my will* to describe the characteristics of the *khiṣyān* in spite of the fact that that is senseless in our [present] book, for we confined ourselves to speaking only about the *jawārī* and the *ghilmān*» (*wa-dhakarta al-khiṣyān wa-ḥusn qudūdihim wa-na'mat abshārihim wal-taladhdhudh bihim wa-anna dhālika lā*

---

[5] It is included in 'Abd al-Salām Muḥammad Hārūn's *Rasā'il al-Jāḥiẓ*, vol. II (1965), pp. 87-137 (it was published earlier in the form of a booklet by C. Pellat, Beirut, 1957, 94 pp.).

[6] «We liked to mention what went on between the pederasts and the adulterers» — *aḥbabnā an nadhkur mā jarā bayna al-lāṭa wal-zunāt* (*ibid.*, p. 95, ll.6-7). This statement is included in the introductory part of the epistle.

[7] *Ibid.*, pp. 123, 1.4 -125, 1.4.

[8] *Ibid.*, pp. 95, 1.12-125, 1.7.

ta'rifuhu al-awā'il fa-alja'tanā ilā[9] *an naṣif mā fī al-khiṣyān wa-in lam yakun li-dhālika ma'nan fī kitābinā idh kunnā innamā naqūl fī al-jawārī wal-ghilmān*)[10].

These opening lines are followed by the enumeration of those characteristics with the clear major aim of demonstrating that the eunuchs are neither men nor women[11] and, therefore, should be excluded from the debate.

What the protagonist of the *Jawārī* affirms in the clearest possible terms is that the whole discussion about the eunuchs had been forced upon him by his fellow-disputant, because it was *that* disputant who had been the first to refer to them. This affirmation has a sole, single and inevitable meaning: the protagonist of the boys *must* have already mentioned the eunuchs. One has only to examine the few preceding pages which contain that protagonist's statements, and he will surely discover that reference. It is most regrettable that M. did not do that obvious thing.

In looking for that reference in those preceding few pages one will not find the word *khiṣyān* (or *khaṣī*). The inescapable conclusion to be drawn from this fact is that the eunuchs *must* appear under a different name. And, indeed, they *do* appear under such name in the following circumstances.

II. According to the assertion of *ṣāḥib al-jawārī* it never happened that the love of a *ghulām* caused the death of any lover (*lam nasma' bi-'āshiq qatalahu ḥubb ghulām*). As by contrast, he names seven poets who died because of their love to a woman. Amongst them were Kuthayyir, Jamāl and 'Urwa, whose respective love to 'Azza, Buthayna and 'Afrā' had been the cause of their death[12].

The answer of *ṣāḥib al-ghilmān* to this assertion is the following one.

III. «Had Kuthayyir, Jamāl and 'Urwa, as well as their likes whom you named, seen some of the *k h a d a m of the people of our time* — [I mean] those who had been bought for huge sums of money — [and perceived] how good looking, *clean coloured*, and well balanced [they are], and how beautiful are their figures [literally: *the beauty of their figures*], they would have cast off Buthayna, 'Azza and 'Afrā' ... and discarded them

---

[9] Lane in his dictionary translates *alja'ahu ilā shay'in* thus: «He constrained, compelled, forced, drove, or necessitated, him to have recourse to or betake himself to, or to repair to, or to do a thing; he impelled him, or *drove him against his will*, to it, or to do it». I preferred the underlined.

[10] *Jawārī, etc.* p. 123, ll.4-6. To help the reader follow my line of argument I gave Roman numerals to the five major citations from al-Jāḥiẓ's epistle. For convenience sake I call all of them «passages» even when that author's words are fully or partly paraphrased.

[11] *Ibid.*, pp. 123, l.7-125, l.4.

[12] *Ibid.*, pp. 104, l.11-105, l.2.

as if they [i.e. these women] had been [mere] dogs (*law nazara Kuthayyir wa-Jumayyil wa-'Urwa wa-man sammayta min nuzarā'ihim ilā ba'd khadam ahl 'aṣrinā mimman qad ushturiya bil-māl al-'aẓīm farāhatan wa-shaṭāṭan wa-naqā' lawn wa-ḥusn i'tidāl wa-jawdat qadd wa-qawām la-nabadhū Buthayna wa-'Azza wa-'Afrā' min ḥāliq*[13] *wa-tarakūhunna bi-mazjar al-kilāb*). But your line of argument was [to bring as an evidence] against me [the view of] *rude and uncivil Beduins* (*wa-lākinnaka iḥtajajta 'alaynā bi-A'rāb ajlāf jufāt*), who were nurtured in misery and wretchedness and grew up in them. They know nothing about the luxuries of life and the worldly pleasures. They live in the deserts and shy away from [civilized] people like wild animals. They eat hedgehogs and lizards and cut open the colocynth [in order to eat its kernel]. The maximum that any one of them can reach is to cry over the remnants of the [Beduin] encampment, and liken the woman to a cow or a gazelle, when, in fact, the woman is more beautiful than both. Moreover, he [i.e. the Beduin poet] would liken her to a serpent and call her the disfigured and the scabby, alleging that he does it for fear of the evil eye»[14].

That *ṣāḥib al-jawārī* decided to speak about the *khiṣyān* only in reaction to what *ṣāḥib al-ghilmān* said about the *khadam*, there cannot be the slightest doubt. This is because another alternative simply does not exist in those few pages which contain the statements of the boys' protagonist. *This alone settles the whole matter*. Since, however, I have already decided to perform an «overkill» in connection with the term under discussion long before I came across M.'s article and comments[15], I shall do the same again.

First of all, there is complete agreement between what the protagonist of the boys says about the *khadam* and what his antagonist attributes to him as saying about the *khiṣyān*: it is their being distinguished by their beautiful features and their serving as an object of carnal pleasure. Both antagonists use also very close expressions in their respective passages (III and I): compare *jawdat qadd* with *ḥusn qudūd*, and *naqā' al-lawn* with *ṣafā' al-lawn*[16].

Secondly, the opening lines about the *khiṣyān*, which we have reproduced and translated (passage I), contain the word *al-awā'il*[17] («*the first ones*»), which is a key term in our context. The same word appears two additional times in the epistle (passages IV, V below), and once in the form of *al-awwalūn* (passage IV).

---

[13] Pellat (*op. cit.*, p. 27, l.1 and note 1) corrects حالق to حالف. I am not sure about the translation, but this has no bearing on the meaning of our passage.

[14] *Jawārī, etc.*, p. 105, ll.3-12.

[15] In the articles «From Ayyūbids to Mamlūks» (*REI*, in the press), and «Hārūn al-Rashīd and his Eunuchs» (in an advanced stage of preparation).

[16] This expression is used by *ṣāḥib al-jawārī* in connection with the *khiṣyān* a few lines after his opening words on the eunuchs, which were reproduced above (*Jawārī*, p. 123, l.10).

[17] *Ibid.*, p. 123, l.5.

IV. *Ṣāḥib al-jawārī* quotes verses of the earlier poets who wrote love songs about the women (*shabbabū bil-nisā'*) and states that those verses are far superior to the ones composed by the modern poets (about the boys)[18]. He considers Imru'u al-Qays as *shā'ir al-shu'arā' min al-awwalīn wal-ākhirīn*[19], and calls the rest of the earlier poets *al-qudamā' fī al-Jāhiliyya wal-Islām*[20] and *al-awā'il*[21]. He names the modern poets *al-muḥdathūn*[22].

The retort of *ṣāḥib al-ghilmān* to his antagonist's praise of the earlier poets is this.

> V. «You have been wrong in the debate and unjust in your argumentation. For we have not denied the merit of the *awā'il* among the poets. The only thing we said was that they had been *rude and uncivil Beduins* (*a'rāb ajlāf jufāt*). They do not know the delicacies of life and the worldly pleasures. For even if any one of them would exert himself he would [not go beyond] comparing the woman to a cow or a gazelle or a snake. And if he wanted to say that she had been well balanced and straight he would compare her to a stick and her thigh to a reed. For they grew up with wild animals and snakes, and were acquainted with nothing else. But we know that the very good looking girl is more beautiful than the cow or the gazelle, or anything else with which she had been compared»[23].

The passage just quoted (V) proves most decisively that the *awā'il* of the protagonist of the *jawārī* (passage I) and the *A'rāb ajlāf jufāt* are identical from the point of view of the protagonist of the *ghilmān*. It goes also without saying that the *a'rāb ajlāf jufāt* of this passage (V) are exactly the same as their namesakes of the *khadam* passage (III). Note also the identity of the detailed characterization of the early Arab poets (*awā'il, A'rāb ajlāf jufāt*) as primitive people by the boys' protagonist in passages III and V.

This leads to the following inescapable conclusion: When *ṣāḥib al-jawārī* quotes *ṣāḥib al-ghilmān* as saying that the *awā'il* were ignorant of the [carnal] pleasure experienced with the *khiṣyān* (passage I), he could refer to nothing else but to that selfsame person's statement about the ignorance of the *a'rāb ajlāf jufāt* (whom he identifies with the *awa'il*-passage V) of the [carnal] pleasure experienced with the *khadam* (passage III). The first line and a half of the *khiṣyān* passage (I) is purely and simply a brief summary of the *khadam* passage (III).

---

18 *Ibid.*, pp. 114, l.1-116, l.2.
19 *Ibid.*, p. 114, ll.1-2.
20 *Ibid.*, p. 115, l.10.
21 *Ibid.*, p. 115, l.13.
22 *Ibid.*, p. 115, l.12.
23 *Ibid.*, p. 116, ll.3-10.

The synonymity of *khadam* and *khiṣyān* in al-Jāḥiz's *Jawārī* has thus been determined in the most definitive way[24], and this fact has several implications. First of all, it alone demolishes the whole structure which M. built in order to disprove my argumentation about the early use of *khādim* as equivalent to «eunuch» in the Muslim historical and related sources[25]. By far his major point is that, contrary to my claim, al-Jāḥiz never employs that term in that sense in any of his writings which he (i.e. M.) or I quoted. This is how he formulates his final verdict in the very last sentence of his criticism:

> «Rien dans les passages considérés [de Ǧāḥiẓ] ne permet de relever la moindre ambiguité: *ḫādim* signifie bien serviteur mais *jamais eunuque*» (my italics — D.A.)[26].

Anything else he says becomes meaningless with the elimination of this point. Secondly, it completely vindicates my claim in my article «On the Eunuchs in Islam», that in the two instances I brought there al-Jāḥiz meant «eunuch» when he mentioned *khādim*. The proofs that I mobilized in the first version of my reply to M. thus lose their primary place. However, because of their much wider inferences I shall repeat most of them here, leaving the main implication of the evidence from *Jawārī* for a later stage in the present paper.

What I said in my article «On the Eunuchs, etc.» about al-Jāḥiz's employment of *khādim* as the synonym of *khaṣī* is this: «Jāḥiẓ also uses it, and al-Masʿūdī also attributes its use to him»[27]. What M. attempted to refute is the first part of this short passage, overlooking the second. We shall treat both of them in the same order.

Al-Jāḥiẓ, in his well known passage (or chapter) on the eunuchs in *Ḥayawān*, mentions *Ḥadīj (or Khadīj) al-khaṣī khādim al-Muthannā b. al-Zubayr*[28]. In the light of the evidence from *Jawārī*, *khādim* here can have only one meaning, especially when it is attached to *khaṣī*. This is, however, what I said in the first version of my reply.

Grammatically M. is right, of course, in separating between the two, but practically he is not so. The combination of *khādim* and *khaṣī* is most frequent in the sources, even long after the first as equivalent to the

---

[24] Needless to say that Pellat was mistaken when he stated in connection with the opening words of the *khiṣyān* passage that al-Jāḥiẓ did not mention the eunuchs in the previous pages of our epistle (*lam yadhkurhum fīmā sabaqa min naṣṣ al-kitāb*, p. 52, note 4 of his Beirut edition).

[25] See also below.

[26] *Op. cit.*, p. 214.

[27] *Op. cit.*, p. 85.

[28] *Ḥayawān*, I, p. 118.

second had already become not only well established, but absolutely dominant. The same authors, who usually use only *khādim*, revert from time to time to the combination, when the addition of *khaṣī* is utterly unneccesry[29]. Quite often one will find in one source *khādim* (or *khadam*) and in another *khādim khaṣī* (or *khadam khiṣyān*) in connection with the same person or group of persons. Of particular significance is the following instance: Hilāl al-Ṣābī, speaking of the court of Caliph al-Muqtadir, states that there were in it 11,000 *khādim*, whereas al-Khaṭīb al-Baghdādī mentions them as 11,000 *khādim khaṣī*. For him every single *khādim* of that huge group was a *khaṣī*[30], and with full justification. Incidentally, this practice of combining the two terms also helps very much in establishing their identity.

In contradiction to M.'s view, al-Jāḥiẓ's illuminating remarks about the *khaṣī*'s aptitude for «service» (*khidma*)[31], only strengthens the connection between the two terms. They give us an insight into why the euphemism *khādim* was chosen to designate *khaṣī*[32].

Thus, in each of the two works which served as the main sources for M.'s study on al-Jāḥiẓ's eunuchs, that author employed *khādim* as the equivalent of «eunuch» (once in the singular and once in the plural).

We shall now turn to the second part of my above cited statement, which M. overlooked. Since al-Jāḥiẓ had been proved to have used the term in question in the meaning under discussion, there is no wonder that other Muslim writers would attribute its use to him. That is how one of them did it.

Al-Mas'ūdī brings several anecdotes related by al-Jāḥiẓ about a Romeo and Juliet type of love affairs between slave-girls and slave-boys in the Muslim courts. The last of them starts like this: «Al-Jāḥiẓ said:

---

[29] Even in my very limited selection that combination appears quite frequently («On the Eunuchs, etc.». See e.g. passages XII (p. 78), XXXI, XXXII (p. 82)). In No. XII I put *al-khaṣī khādim* on an equal footing with *khādim khaṣī*, and this is the correct thing to do from a practical point of view. The closeness of the two is evident. After all, the development of a language and its expressions is not necessarily subject to grammatical pedantry.

[30] See «On the Eunuchs, etc.», passage VII, p. 77.

[31] Moussa, *op. cit.*, p. 214.

[32] I have already alluded briefly to the connection between *khādim* (= *khaṣī*) and *khidma* on the basis of certain data included in the published part of my study («On the Eunuchs, etc.», p. 83, note 60). In my «Hārūn al-Rashīd and his Eunuchs» I am discussing in some detail al-Jāḥiẓ's evidence on the eunuchs and the *khidma*, and my conclusions are totally different from those of M. (incidentally, this had been done long before I came across his Jāḥiẓ article). Similarly to *khādim* becoming the equivalent of *khaṣī* the reason for calling the eunuch *ustādh* was that he used to teach small children (*ibid.*, p. 90, note 91).

'I told this story to Abū 'Abdallāh Muḥammad b. Ja'far al-Anbārī in al-Baṣra'. He [al-Anbārī] said: 'I shall tell you a story similar to the one you told me. Fā'iq *al-khādim*, who was the *mawlā* of Muḥammad b. Ḥumayd al-Ṭūsī[33] told me: 'Muḥammad b. Ḥumayd was sitting once with his boon companions. A slave-girl sang behind the curtain (*sitāra*)"[34].

What should be emphasized about this quotation is that al-Jāḥiẓ speaks and cites here in the first person. This increases considerably the chances that our author preserved al-Jāḥiẓ's own words. Fā'iq is a quite frequent name among eunuchs[35].

A central aspect of M.'s interpretation of al-Jāḥiẓ's *khādim* is that he does not confine himself to that author's terminology. He has a much wider goal. By means of it he wants to question my whole attempt at tracing the earliest occurrences of that term in the sense under discussion (an attempt which he does not present with absolute accuracy). Since that interpretation had been proved to be without foundation, anything he wants to base on it belongs perforce to the same category. However, the examination of his line of argument and his conclusions contribute to the clarification of the issue of the present debate.

In the last paragraph of his *Addenda* M. states that I am completely right (*a entièrement raison*) to point out the uncertainty which dominates the employment of the term *khādim* by the authors of the second half of the third/ninth century, like al-Ṭabarī, or those of the fourth/tenth century like al-Mas'ūdī[36]. To say the least, this is not exactly my view. Here is what I say.

«It is very difficult to establish, with any degree of certainty, when the term *khādim* started to be used in the sense of eunuch. Some scholars believe it to have been in the beginning of the 4th/10th century (see below). It can be proved, however, that this had happened considerably earlier. The chronicle of al-Ṭabarī is *replete* with that term, and includes even instances pertaining to the very beginning of the 'Abbāsid period. [Jāḥiẓ (160-250/776-868) also used it, and al-Mas'ūdī also attributes its use to him.]

«Of great interest is the episode of Fākhita, Mu'āwiya's wife (passage I). The term *khādim*, mentioned in the account of that episode, might belong to the vocabulary of al-Mas'ūdī, or al-Madā'inī, or an earlier traditionalist who had been al-Madā'inī's source (even the possibility that it had been used in the reign of Mu'āwiya himself

---

[33] The commander whom al-Ma'mūn sent to fight Bābak, and whom that rebel defeated and killed in 214/929 (Ṭabarī, II, pp. 1099, lines 3-7, 1109, lines 9-11; al-Ṣafadī, *al-Wāfī bil-Wafayāt*, Wiesbaden, 1961, vol. III, p. 29, Ziriqlī, *A'lām*, VI, p. 343).

[34] *Murūj*, VII, p. 227 (Pellat's edition, V, p. 19).

[35] The famous Fā'iq, the Samanid commander (died 389/999) was a eunuch (*kāna khaṣiyyan min mawālī Nūḥ b. Asad* — Ibn al-Athīr, *al-Kāmil*, Beirut, 1966, vol. IX, p. 149, line 2). There are, of course, non-eunuch Fā'iqs, but they are not called *khādim*.

[36] *Op. cit.*, p. 214.

cannot be excluded). The same uncertainty prevails about the *khādims* mentioned by al-Ṭabarī, *and who lived in a period preceding his own time. This ambiguity, however, is not confined to the term under discussion, but extends practically to all, or most, of the terminology relating to the early period of Islam, which came down to us, in most cases, through considerably later sources.* In fact, this is the basic difficulty in dealing with early Muslim history in general since we possess for it mainly this kind of comparatively late sources. *Under these circumstances, the only thing that can be said about our term is that it appears in the sources in connection with events and occurrences which took place from the beginning of the Umayyad period* (or even earlier — see the testimony attributed to Ḥusayn b. ʿAlī, passage XVIII)»[37].

M.'s interpretation of what I say about the account regarding Muʿāwiya and his wife is included in another passage of his criticism, which will also be cited in this paper, and will be answered there. At the present moment I shall limit myself to my view of al-Ṭabarī and later historians as expressed in the just quoted passage of mine, stating beforehand that the data contained in al-Ṭabarī's chronicle about our term constitute the backbone of the study of the eunuchs in the lands of Islam during the period which it covers. What I state in that passage is precisely the contrary to what M. ascribes to me[38]. The uncertainty as I see it is not about al-Ṭabarī's own time, but about the period *preceding* it[39]. In the second half of the 3rd/9th century the term *khādim* («eunuch») becomes not only very frequent, but is the predominant one[40]. As for the beginning of the 4th/10th century and later on, there are no uncertainties whatsoever about the use of *khādim* by the historians of that period, including al-Masʿūdī, as M. believes me to think.

The greatest part of M.'s comment on my attempt at dating the earliest references to *khādim* in the sense under discussion is dedicated to the Fākhita-Muʿāwiya incident, which I mentioned in the passage quoted above in full. For that purpose he reproduces al-Masʿūdī's evidence on

---

[37] «On the Eunuchs, etc.», p. 85. All the italicized words or phrases in this passage are added. The passage in the original is also accompanied by a considerable number of notes, which are not repeated here.

[38] The extraordinary thing is that M. reproduces in the note the opening lines of the present passage (up to the word «earlier») (*op. cit.*, p. 214, note 105).

[39] In order to remove any doubt, in spite of its being self-evident, I would like to emphasize that *khādims* mentioned in al-Ṭabarī's chronicle and in writings of other authors during the periods preceding their own time, especially if they are prominent persons, are also undoubtedly eunuchs. The uncertainty is solely about whether the early lost sources call them already *khādim* (pl. *khadam*), or this represents only the terminology of later extant sources, which copied from them and changed their original wording (see also below). The insurmountable difficulty of having to reconstruct early Islamic history on the basis of later sources, which I raise so emphatically a propos the term *khādim*, will again be referred to below.

[40] This by no means implies that the term *khaṣī* became extinct (see also below).

the incident, as well as the evidence of al-Jāḥiẓ, which is almost, but not absolutely, identical.

Each of the two versions will be dealt with separately.

Al-Mas'ūdī says:

> *'Wa-dhakara al-Madā'inī anna Mu'āwiya b. Abī Sufyān dakhala dhāta yawmin 'alā imra'atihi Fākhita wa-kānat dhāt 'aql wa-ḥazm wa-ma'ahu khaṣī wa-kānat makshūfat al-ra's fa-lammā ra'at ma'ahu al-khādim ghaṭṭat ra'sahā fa-qāla Mu'āwiya innahu khaṣī fa-qālat yā amīr al-mu'minīn a-tarā al-muthla bihi aḥallat lahu mā ḥarramahu Allāh 'alayhi fa-istarja'a Mu'āwiya wa-'alima anna al-ḥaqq mā qālathu fa-lam yudkhil bā'da dhālika 'alā ḥaramihi khādiman illā kabīran fāniyan*[41].

Khādim is mentioned twice in this excerpt. According to M.'s reasoning it is more likely that in the first time it means «servant», for otherwise why should Mu'āwiya tell his wife «he is a eunuch», if she had already known it. On the other hand, M. argues, the lines from the word *istarja'a* onwards, where *khādim* appears for the second time, are not repeated in any parallel form in the earlier version of al-Jāḥiẓ. From this he concludes that this second reference to *khādim* seems to reflect only the language and connotations of the time of the later al-Mas'ūdī.

These considerations are unacceptable. First of all, because M.'s view about the meaning of that term in the vocabulary of al-Jāḥiẓ, has already been proved to be erroneous. Secondly, because they are unreasonable in themselves (we shall return to this point), and the absoluteness of that unreasonableness comes into bold relief when one considers the context in which al-Mas'ūdī brings these lines. They are part of a passage in which he comments on the murder in Damascus of Abū al-Jaysh Khumārawayhi, the son and successor of Aḥmad b. Ṭūlūn, by his eunuchs (Dhū al-Qa'da 282/December 895). He says that those who killed him were *khadam min khadamihim* («some *khadam* of their *khadam*», i.e. of himself and of Ṭughj), and he continues: «We have already exhausted the subject of *khadam* belonging to the [ethnical groups of] the Sūdān, the Ṣaqāliba, the Rūm and the Ṣīn in our book *Kitāb al-Zamān*. There we mentioned that the people of al-Ṣīn *castrate* (*yakhṣūna*) their children like the Rūm [= Byzantines] [who] do [the same] to their children. [We also spoke there] about the contradictory traits of the *khiṣyān*, resulting from the cutting of that [sexual] member. [We have also spoken about] the changes which nature brought upon them as a result of this [operation] in accordance with what people told about them and about their characteristics». The lines about

---

[41] *Murūj*, VIII, pp. 148-149.

al-Madā'inī's account on Muʿāwiya and his wife follow here uninterruptedly, and immediately after them al-Masʿūdī states that people distinguish between two kinds [of eunuchs]: the «deprived one» [of his virility] (*al-maslūb*), and the «one whose sexual organ is cut off» (*al-majbūb*). He then expresses his support to the standpoint of Muʿāwiya's wife, namely, that the fact that the eunuchs are beardless and without their male reproductive organ does not turn them into women. They remain males (*rijāl*, *dhukūr*). Al-Masʿūdī concludes his exposé in referring to the fact that the armpits of the *khadam* do not exude bad odor (repeating the word *khadam* twice in this connection), and declaring that this is one of the virtues of the *khadam*[42].

Now how on earth can *khādim* in the sense of «servant» infiltrate into such a context? Whereas M. contends that *nothing* indicates in the Masʿūdī-Madā'inī account that khādim is equivalent there to *khaṣī* (*« Rien n'indique, etc...»* — the fourth paragraph on p. 213, ll. 2-3 of that paragraph), the truth is that *everything* indicates it. Furthermore, this passage alone refutes M.'s assertion about uncertainty in the use of *khādim* by al-Masʿūdī (to say nothing about numerous other instances in his *Murūj*)[43]. The recurrence of *khādim* as equivalent to *khaṣī* in the historical and related literature of the 4th Hijra century and the centuries which follow is overwhelming in its frequency and its clarity.

Even when the account attributed to al-Madā'inī stands alone, the claim that in a passage of about four lines, *Khādim*, which is mentioned there twice in the same connexion, means «servant» in the first time and *khaṣī* in the second, does not seem to have any foundation. Furthermore, it is utterly inconceivable that Muʿāwiya would be so inconsiderate and heedless that his wife would suspect him of bringing an adult unemasculated male to her private quarters, and at a moment when she had been barefaced. If that had been the case, he would have entered first and warned her. Even with such a forewarning it is extremely doubtful that under ordinary circumstances a Muslim would allow a man to enter the

---

[42] *Muruj*, VIII, pp. 147-8 (in Pellat's edition: V, pp. 151-2). Al-Ṭabarī recounts the murder of Khumārawayhi in these words: *dhabaḥahu baʿḍ khadamihi min al-khāṣṣa ... wa-qutila min khadamihi alladhīna uttuhimū bi-qatlihi nayyif wa-ʿishrūna khādiman* (Ṭabarī, III, p. 2148, lines 15-18). Al-Ṭabarī, like on numerous other occasions in his chronicle, does not deem it necessary to explain here the meaning of our term, either in the singular or in the plural. He was absolutely certain that his readers would know that eunuchs are meant.

[43] In the Khumārawayhi-Muʿāwiya passage al-Masʿūdī employs repeatedly *khādim* (pl. *khadam*) as equivalent to *khaṣī* (pl. *khiṣyān*) in connection with *all* the ethnical groups, even before their entrance into *Dār al-Islām*. See also note 21.

secluded apartment of his wife. All this excludes the possibility that the Caliph's wife could mistake her husband's companion for an uncastrated servant. We have also to remember that we are not dealing with what crossed the mind of Muʿāwiya's wife when she saw her husband's associate but with the terminology of the transmitters of the story. And at least about the last of them, al-Masʿūdī, there cannot be the slightest doubt[44].

On top of all that, M.'s interpretation is contradictory to the very purpose of the anecdote. The Caliph's retort to his wife was not at all to dispel her fear about the masculinity of his companion. The only thing it reflects is their contrasting views about eunuchs in the *ḥarīm*; and the only reason that al-Masʿūdī calls that companion, within seven words, once *khādim* and once *khaṣī*, is to avoid repetition.

As far as *khadīm* vis-a-vis *khaṣī* is concerned, the incident just discussed, together with the whole passage in which it is included, serves as a good example for the employment of both words. Although *khādim* became more and more dominant, the original *khaṣī* by no means disappeared. It recurs in the sources quite frequently, and in passages where «eunuch» has to be mentioned repeatedly (like in the Khumārawayhi-Muʿāwiya one), they alternate the two words[45]. This greatly facilitates the task of establishing their identity.

Yet another, and very interesting, aspect of the Muʿāwiya incident is revealed by M. As already stated, he quotes another version of it which he found in al-Jāḥiẓ's writings, and which is also attributed to the same al-Madā'inī. In that version *khādim* is not mentioned at all. Since al-Jāḥiẓ was al-Madā'inī's contemporary — he argues — his citation should be considered the reliable one, and not that of the later al-Masʿūdī[46].

This piece of evidence from al-Jāḥiẓ was unknown to me. However, it still leaves insurmountable the difficulty caused by the lost early sources which I have clearly mentioned, and to which I shall return in the present paper. With the absence of the original works of al-Madā'inī, one can argue, with the same degree of credibility, that these are not identical accounts, but similar versions. Such versions of traditions grouped

---

44 The Muʿāwiya incident reflects a certain revulsion from the introduction of eunuchs into the *ḥarīm*. We know of short-lived attempts to mitigage that practice by letting into the women's quarters only over age or under age eunuchs (i.e. below or above the age of the virility of the unemasculated male).

45 See e.g. «On the Eunuchs, etc.», passage XXI, p. 80.

46 Moussa, *op. cit.*, p. 213.

together in the same source, or scattered over numerous sources, and with varying degrees of differences (including differences in wording) are very common in Muslim writings. Al-Madā'inī was a prolific writer, and both al-Jāḥiẓ and al-Mas'ūdī could pick non-identical versions either from the same or from different works of his. What supports that possibility is: a) the fundamentally different language of the two versions[47]; b) the fact that in al-Jāḥiẓ's rendition the wife in question is Maysūn, the daughter of Baḥdal, and in that of al-Mas'ūdī it is Fākhita, the daughter of Qaraẓa; c) the existence of an account about a very similar incident connected with the sister of Ḥusayn b. 'Alī[48].

The introduction of emasculated males into the *ḥarīm* must have caused hesitations and reservations, especially in the beginning; and traditions of antagonism to it connected with this or that personality is the natural thing to expect. A more thorough reading of the sources might well bring an additional crop of similar traditions. Like the three versions just referred to, they will, in all probability, differ both in language and in details of varying degrees of importance. All this serves only to diminish the chances that al-Jāḥiẓ and al-Mas'ūdī copied from al-Madā'inī exactly the same account[49]. Neither is it certain that the first of them copied more accurately than the second.

We reach now the main implication to be drawn from the *khadam* of al-Jāḥiẓ in *Jawārī*. The context of that term's appearance there shows how widespread its euphemistic use had already become in that author's time. Al-Jāḥiẓ employed *khadam* without any additional clarification, because he had no doubt that his readers would know exactly what he means. He then used *khiṣyān* without any addition. being again completely certain that those readers would know precisely to which earlier passage in his epistle he refers[50]. It is thus made absolutely certain that

---

[47] The reader can easily verify that fundamental difference, because M. reproduced the two versions.

[48] See «On the Eunuchs, etc.», passage XVIII, on pp. 79-80.

[49] As M. states (*op. cit.*, p. 213, note 103), al-Jāḥiẓ repeats the Mu'āwiya incident in *Kitāb al-Jawārī, etc.* (ed. Hārūn), II, p. 125. But there he omits the name of Mu'āwiya, as M. points out. However, he does much more than that: he replaces Mu'āwiya by «one of the kings» (*ba'ḍ al-mulūk*). He omits also the name of al-Madā'inī. Only a small part of al-Jāḥiẓ's two versions is identical in its wording. Now what is the guarantee that the version of *Kitāb al-Ḥayawān* is a verbatim copy from al-Madā'inī? The attribution of the incident to an anonymous king corroborates my view that the same anecdote had been told in connection with various personalities.

[50] There is yet another instructive aspect of the use of the term in our epistle. The one who employs the euphemism *khadam* in connection with the eunuchs is *ṣāḥib al-ghilmān*,

in our author's period *khadam* in the sense of «eunuchs» became so common and so well rooted (and consequently long in use) that there was no danger of its being confused with *khadam* in the original meaning of «servants», even when it appeared in the most general and undefined form. Thus the date of the frequent appearance of our term in its euphemistic sense can be considerably advanced. In the first version of my reply to M. I regarded the first half of the third/ninth century as a safe estimate. In view of the fact that al-Jāḥiẓ was born in 160/775 that estimate can be pushed well beyond that.

It is also worthwhile to link al-Jāḥiẓ's *khadam* with those of some contemporary, near contemporary and later authors. For the purpose of my argumentation I shall not deal with them in an exact chronological order.

The earliest author I can quote is Ibn Khurdādhbih (205 [or 211]-280 [or 300]/820 [or 825][51]-893 [or 911]) who compiled his geography in 232/846 and made a number of additions to it in 272/885[52]. I shall reproduce here two short passages.

They run as follows: a) «Jazīrat al-Dhahab [= al-Rāhib?]. The *khadam* used to be *castrated* there» (*wa-bihā kāna yukhṣā al-khadam*)[53]. b) «What is coming from the Western sea is the *khadam* belonging to the Slav, Byzantine and Frankish [ethnic groups] (*wa-*

---

who approves of pederasty with boys and eunuchs. By contrast, *ṣāḥib al-jawārī*, who disapproves of it and is particularly opposed to the inclusion of the eunuchs in the debate, calls them by the unveiled designation *khiṣyān* with all its pejorative connotations. Pederasty and sexual relations with eunuchs are discussed in considerable detail in M.'s study (*op. cit.*, pp. 206-209). One reason for al-Jāḥiẓ's rare use of *khādim* or *khadam* in his discussion of the eunuchs is that when one deals with castration and the castrated, describing the operation and the results ensuing thereof, there is little need for euphemisms. Another reason is that a major aim of that author was to show that the eunuch is the very contrary of the perfect model («modèle parfait») of the male, as M. so aptly puts it (*op. cit.*, pp. 210-211).

[51] *EI*², II, p. 839a; Ziriqlī, *A'lām*, IV, p. 343a.

[52] Miquel, *op. cit.*, I, pp. XXI, 9a. According to Brockelmann Ibn Khurdādhbih «schrieb zwischen 230-4/844-8» (*GAL*, I, p. 225 (p. 258 of the new edition). I can express no opinion about the unresolved controversy in regard to the date of the composition of the said source, and to the authenticity of the version which survived (M. Hadj-Sadok, EI², II, p. 839b). However, in view of the fact that we all treat it as a major geographical and historical source, and use it abundantly (with full justification, in the present state of our knowledge), there is no reason whatsoever to have any reservation towards these two passages (especially as long as there is no very specific and weighty cause to doubt the earliness of each one of them).

[53] *Kitāb al-Masālik wal-Mamālik*, p. 112, line 8, and also «On the Eunuchs, etc.», p. 76, passage IVa.

alladhī yajī' min al-Baḥr al-Gharbī al-khadam al-Ṣaqāliba (or: *al-Ṣaqlabiyyūn) wal-Ifranjiyyūn*)[54].

Thus the *khadam*, who are «the castrated ones» (*khisyān*) according to al-Jāḥiẓ, are the *khadam* who are castrated (*yukhṣā*) according to Ibn Khurdādhbih. Equally there cannot be the slightest doubt that the Ṣaqāliba and Frankish *khadam* of passage b from Ibn Khurdādhbih are as thoroughly castrated as the *khadam* of passage a from the same author.

Other comparatively early authors are al-Balādhurī, al-Ya'qūbī and even al-Ṭabarī. We shall skip them for the moment and go straight to the evidence of al-Mas'ūdī and al-Muqaddasī of the 4th/10th century.

Al-Mas'ūdī, in the passage we have already cited, speaks about the *khadam* belonging to the following ethnical groups: Sūdān, Ṣaqāliba, Rūm and Ṣīn. All of them undergo the process of castration (*Yakhṣūnahum*) and all of them are eunuchs (*khiṣyān*)[55].

Al-Muqaddasī speaks about the various kinds of *khadam* brought over to the lands of Islam (Barbar, Ḥabash, Ṣaqāliba, Rūm). All of them are castrated (the verb *khaṣā* in the relevant passage is mentioned four times, and *salla* once)[56].

I cannot see any difference between the *khadam* of al-Jāḥiẓ and those of the three other authors. All of them demonstrate the perseverance of that term in that meaning, and these are only very few instances out of many. Note also the all-embracing character of the term, not limited to any social group or class, and including the various races.

The evidence just quoted from Ibn Khurdādhbih and al-Muqaddasī (and corroborated by numerous other instances) is most revealing in yet another way. The eunuchs mentioned there are called *khadam* even in the process of being imported to the lands of Islam (or being the target of such importation), and, therefore, even before being assigned to any job or task. Other names for slaves represent the state in which they actually are: either their state of slavery or their youthfulness (*raqīq*, *'abīd*, *mamālīk*, *ghilmān*, *jawārī*, etc.). This can have only one meaning: these *khadam* are not «servants», because at that stage they are jobless. They must be something else. And that «something else» can be nothing but eunuchs, as proved from the evidence of Ibn Khurdādhbih and al-

---

[54] *Kitāb al-Masālik wal-Mamālik*, Leiden, 1889, p. 92, lines 4-6. Cp. also «On the Eunuchs, etc.», p. 76, passage V, no. e.

[55] *Murūj*, VIII, p. 148 (V, p. 152 in Pellat's edition).

[56] Al-Muqaddasī, pp. 242, l.2-243, l.3 (see also *JSAI*, I, pp. 75-6).

Muqaddasī and many others, as well as from the whole history of the term in the Muslim sources[57].

We shall return now to the authors whom we skipped.

Aḥmad b. Yaḥyā al-Balādhurī, who died well inside the third Hijra century (279/892 at the latest [58]), mentions Faraj *al-khādim* twice as the builder of Ṭarsūs and Adhana in the years 171/787 and 194/810[59]. Khalīfa b. Khayyāṭ calls him Faraj *al-khaṣī*[60]. The instructive thing about this piece of evidence is that al-Balādhurī did not deem it necessary to explain *khādim* in the sense under discussion to his readers. Which is a decisive proof that in his time that sense had become a matter of common knowledge[61].

The historian-geographer al-Yaʿqūbī (died 284/897) wrote his geographical book quite late in life in Egypt, in 276/889-90 or 278/891. But his chronicle, which ends with the year 259/872, is considered to have been written well before his geography, while he still had been in the East[62]. Each one of the important eunuchs of Sāmarrā he mentions in his geographical book is called *khādim*, and the whole group *al-khadam al-kibār*[63]. In al-Yaʿqūbī's earlier chronicle that term is repeatedly mentioned.

What certainly constitutes the backbone of the whole study of the eunuch institution in the early centuries of Islam, is the combination of the *chronicles* of al-Yaʿqūbī and al-Ṭabarī. Al-Ṭabarī's chronicle is, of course, much richer. But there is more than sufficient data in the first of the two, to establish that a good number of the individuals who are called *khādim* by al-Ṭabarī, are already so designated by the earlier source of al-Ya'qūbī.

That all these very numerous *khādim*s are eunuchs can be established by an argument which had not been mentioned in the published part of my study, to which M. refers. The overwhelming majority of these individuals are prominent people. In spite of the fact that most of them are repeatedly mentioned in the sources, there is no trace (or almost so),

---

[57] See also the examples in passage V, p. 76 of «On the Eunuchs in Islam», which can be multiplied.

[58] A. Miquel, *La géographie humaine du monde musulman*, Paris-La Haye vol. I (1967), p. XX. See also C. H. Becker and F. Rosenthal in *EI*[2], vol. I, p. 971b.

[59] *Futūḥ al-Buldān*, Beirut, 1957, pp. 231, lines 1-5, 232, lines 4-12 (in the Leiden, 1866, edition: pp. 168, line 19, 169, line 17, 170, line 2).

[60] *Ta'rīkh Khalīfa b. Khayyāṭ*, al-Najaf, 1967, p. 481, line 9.

[61] The same is true of other contemporaries of al-Balādhurī.

[62] Miquel, *op. cit.*, p. XXI; Brockelmann, *EI*[1], IV, pp. 1152b-1153a.

[63] See e.g. *Kitāb al-Buldān*, Leiden, 1892, p. 261, lines 10-13.

of any offspring of them[64]. Suffice it to take any small number of unemasculated dignitaries and follow their careers in the sources, and the existence of their offspring would emerge quite quickly.

The implication of this formidable fact is the following one. It is very regrettable that for the period which precedes the time of the historians whose works came down to us, we cannot establish for sure whether the term *khādim* (= *khaṣī*) had already been then in use[65]. However, any prominent person of that early period who is called *khādim* in later sources can be considered as eunuch with a very high degree (perhaps almost absolute) certainty[66]. This gives us the key for a sure and unhesitant reconstruction of the eunuch institution in the crucial Muslim period for which we possess almost no contemporary sources. This fully applies to the important reign of Hārūn al-Rashīd, on whose eunuchs I am now completing a study (see notes 15 and 32). All the prominent *khādim*s of that famous Caliph (as of other Muslim rulers) are never mentioned as having children.

A no mean factor which helped the newer meaning of *khādim* to overshadow the original one is this. With its constant spread at the expense of other synonymous terms, more and more anonymous individual, as well as groups of, eunuchs were designated by it. By repeated use, however, *khādim* lost its euphemistic character (or, at least, most of it), thus defeating the purpose for which it came into being. In spite of that it had not been replaced by another euphemism. That is what quite usually happens to euphemisms of similar character. The implication of this phenomenon is that there would be a very great reluctance to use such terms in their original (usually literal) sense, lest people would confuse them with the prevailing (or at least very common) basically offensive meaning. Consequently, there is every chance that an unemasculated man servant would be believed to have been a eunuch, if he

---

[64] There are both *khādim*s and *khaṣī*s, who are called Abū so and so. But these are non-existent sons. Some of the *khādim*s or *khaṣī*s have even wives and concubines. All this was given them in order to mitigate their mutilation.

[65] There is a reasonable possibility that it had been. It is hard to believe that later sources had been so systematic as to replace every single *khaṣī* of earlier sources by *khādim*. Thus the existence of a residue of *khādim*s from the earlier sources should not be ruled out. This supposition is considerably strengthened by al-Jāḥiẓ's use of *khādim* and *khadam* in that sense.

[66] The number of those earlier *khādim*s, who are called also *khaṣī* is not negligible. And this can serve as an excellent *Stichprobe* for verifying the identity of the two terms. The only reason for designating a prominent person with the not too flattering title of *khādim* is to avoid using a much worse designation.

had been called *khādim*. The same goes for the term «eunuch», the original meaning of which is «bed chamber attendant» (the Greek *eunoukhos*). A virile bed chamber attendant would not be called «eunuch». For the same reason «rest room», «water closet», *bayt al-rāḥa* and the numerous other euphemistic appellations of the «privy» in the various languages, would be hardly used in their literal sense.

One should not infer from the above series of arguments that every single *khādim* encountered in the historical and related sources is a eunuch beyond any shadow of doubt, especially if he is not a prominent person. Such an absolute certainty does not exist with regard to *any* term which underwent a similar process of development. I have already stressed this point several times in my study «On the Eunuchs in Islam», and I deal with a number of specific instances in «Hārūn al-Rashīd and his Eunuchs». My sole aim was to demonstrate how overwhelming are the chances that that term means «eunuchs» in this kind of sources. The absolute assertion found in a work of Ghars al-Niʿma Muḥammad, the son of Hilāl al-Ṣābī (died 480/1087), that *khādim does not have a child* (*khādim lā yakūn lahu walad*)[67] in the sense that it is *impossible* for a *khādim* to have a child, should be interpreted in this way. That is how I actually interpreted it:

> «It [*khādim* as equivalent to *khaṣī*] had become dominant to such a degree ... that it had relegated the original meaning of this common word to a very secondary place»[68].

Thus, even as late as the eleventh century, where the predominance of our return in the sense under discussion is generally accepted, there is no 100 percent certainty concerning each single case.

In concluding this reply we shall return to al-Jāḥiẓ. His employment of *khadam* as the synonym of *khiṣyān* in *Jawarī*, and the circumstances and context in which he did it, necessitated a thorough reevaluation on my part of the contribution of that author to the proper understanding of that term and its historical development[69]. The reevaluation is, however, in the very opposite direction to M.'s conclusions.

---

[67] *JSAI*, I, pp. 84-5. *Al-Hafawāt al-Nādira*, Damascus, 1967, p. 47, ll.9-110.

[68] *Ibid*., pp. 84-5. See also p. 84 above.

[69] On the basis of the data available then to M. and myself the evaluation in the first version of my reply was completely justified. See also the detailed remarks in note 50. The importance of al-Jāḥiẓ's contribution is mainly qualitative. That of al-Ṭabarī is quantitative as well. Yet al-Jāḥiẓ as a source for the study of the place and functioning of the eunuchs within the socio-military institution is of a quite marginal importance. An important aspect of the evidence of al-Jāḥiẓ, Ibn Khurdadhbih, al-Balādhuri, al-Yaʿqūbī and al-Ṭabarī is

This is as far as the reply is concerned. A remark of a much more general character has to be made. The clarification of the meaning of the term *Khādim* forms the *pivot* of the whole study of the eunuch phenomenon in Islam during the Middle Ages. Establishing its unequivocal sense is, therefore, of the highest possible importance[70].

that the lives of all these authors are overlapping. Thus we have an unbroken continuity in the study of our term.

[70] Remarks made in the present paper without the mention of sources are based partly on data scattered in the already published chapter of my study on the eunuchs and used there for a different purpose, and partly on forthcoming chapters. In those chapters the important contribution of C. Pellat to the study of the subject in his article *Khaṣī* in *EI*[2] is acknowledged.

XII

THE NUBIAN DAM

For Hayim Blanc
To whom I owe so much.

The Muslim expansion, which started outside the Arabian Peninsula in the fourth decade of the seventh century, was one of the fastest in human history. Its enduring results over such wide territories were almost unparalleled. No other religion, be it monotheistic or non-monotheistic, had a history of expansion by force of arms similar to that of Islam.

As is well known, the Muslims, in their thrust from Arabia, clashed with two great empires: the Persian–Sasanid and the Byzantine. They attacked the first through Southern Iraq and annihilated it, reaching within quite a short period of time the Caucasus, the Caspian shores and the border of Central Asia. After a certain pause, during which they absorbed and merged their conquests, they continued their advance deep into Central Asia and beyond, and into India.

The Muslims, in their war against the Byzantine empire, which they could not destroy but which they succeeded in weakening very much, tearing, moreover, great parts of its territory, after having occupied the Syro–Palestinian region, continued their thrust in two directions: to the north: towards and into Anatolia, as well as into northern Iraq; and to the southwest: into Egypt and beyond. Their advance to the north was checked in the Cilician region; but wars, raids and incursions, in between armistices and truces, were the common feature of that front. There was also the naval struggle. Both on land and on sea (including the Mediterranean islands), fortunes varied. At quite an early stage of the struggle the very heart of the Byzantine empire was threatened, when its capital was besieged by Muslim naval and land forces. At a later stage (the tenth century) the Byzantines pushed the frontier deeply into Muslim territory, threatening temporarily Bagdad and Jerusalem. Then followed, in the second half of the eleventh century, the Muslim occupation of substantial parts of Anatolia.

On the African continent two contradictory developments took place. After having occupied Egypt, the Muslims were able to march in two directions: westwards and southwards. Their advance westwards (at least in its final results) was as spectacular as their other advances, which we have just described. There were indeed checks; there were also setbacks, some of them very severe, but these occurred only after the Muslim armies had left the Egyptian western border far behind them. At the time they crossed that border the Muslim armies met with little resistance, and their initial progress deeply beyond it was quite easy (see also below). Ultimately, the whole of North Africa and much of Spain were conquered before a century had elapsed since the first outburst of the Muslim armies from Arabia. Before long, these newly occupied territories themselves began to take part in the naval struggle in the Mediterranean sea.

The only frontier along which the Muslims had no, or hardly any, advance and along which they had practically no permanent territorial gains, was that which forms the boundary between Egypt and its southern neighbour. Furthermore, that frontier remained unchanged, or almost so, up to the beginning of the Mamluk sultanate, or at least up to the Ayyūbid reign.

This is an outstanding and most instructive exception in the history of Islam's military expansion. On all the other fronts the Muslims left their points of departure hundreds and hundreds of miles behind them, whereas here they were brought to a standstill. One can offer some obvious as well as some not so obvious explanations for this phenonmenon, including such as belong to the realm of long range policy. In the present context I shall confine myself to the immediate, purely military factor, which, in my view, overshadowed and affected all the others. For this purpose I shall reproduce, in translation, some passages from the accounts of the earlier sources about the Muslim attempts to push southwards along the Nile and about the outcome of those attempts; I shall then try to elucidate what can be deduced from these accounts. At the end of my analysis I shall compare some of the elements included in the famous passage of the very late al-Maqrīzī (d. 845/1442), dealing with the evidence of the earlier sources. I would also like to state from the very outset, that I shall deal with the contents of the Muslim-Nubian agreement (*baqṭ*) only in so far as they have a bearing on the major argument of my thesis.

A. The Accounts

I. Al-Balādhurī's account (d. 274/892)

"When the Muslims conquered Egypt ʿAmr b. al-ʿĀṣ sent the [Muslim] cavalry to the countries (*qurā*)[1] around it in order to raid [and subjugate] them (*li-yaṭa'ahum*).[2] He sent ʿUqba b. Nāfiʿ al-Fihrī--Nāfiʿ was the brother of ʿAmr on his mother's side --[southwards], and their (the Muslims') calvary entered the land of the Nubians (*arḍ al-Nūba*) as it enters the Byzantine [territory] in the summer campaigns (*ka-mā tadkhul ṣawā'if al-Rūm*). The Nubians fought the Muslims back very fiercely (*fa-laqiya al-Muslimun bil-Nūba qitālan shadīdan*). When they

---

1 *Qarya* here is, of course, not a village. One of its meanings is "the whole country", or "the country as a whole" (*al-miṣr al-jāmiʿ*). See *Lisān al-ʿArab*, the Dār al-Maʿārif edition, n.d., Vol. V, p. 3617b. Particularly relevant to the present passage from al-Balādhurī is the tradition cited in the same dictionary about "the *qarya* [=al-Madīna] which will eat the [other] *qurā*". It is interpreted as being intended to denote "the towns conquered by the people of al-Madīna, and their share of the richness of those towns" (*ma yuftaḥ ʿalā aydī ahlihā min al-mudun wa-yuṣībūna min ghanā' ihā* (idem). Dozy, *Supplement*, translates the same word by *"sol, terrain"*.

2 The figurative meaning of *waṭi'a* is "to raid and kill" (*al-ghazw wal-qatl) (Lisān al-ʿArab*, VI, p. 4863b). It goes without saying that it means mainly raiding the territory of the Muslims' adversaries. *Muḥīṭ al-Muḥīṭ* says: *waṭi'a arḍ al-ʿaduww dakhalahā*. For *waṭi'a* in the sense under discussion with citations from the Muslim early sources, including al-Balāduri, see Dozy, *Supplement* s.v.

encountered them they showered them with arrows (*rashaqūhum bil-nabl*), until all of them (*'āmmatuhum*) were wounded, and they [the Muslims] withdrew (*inṣarafū*) with many wounds and gouged out eyes (*ḥadaq mafqū'a*).[3] Therefore, they [the Nubians] were called the 'marksmen of the pupil of the eye' (*rumāt al-ḥadaq*).[4] This state of things continued[5] (*fa-lam yazālū 'alā dhālika*) until 'Abdallāh b. Sa'd b. Abī Sarḥ became governor of Egypt and they [the Nubians] asked him for peace and reconcilement (*al-ṣulḥ wal-muwāda'a*), and he complied with their request, without their having to pay the poll tax (*jizya*). He made a truce (*hudna*) with them, by which they had to give the Muslims a yearly tribute of 300 heads [of slaves] in exchange for food of a corresponding value, which the Muslims would give them as a present.................A Muslim participant in the fighting on that front said: 'I took part (*shahidtu*) twice in the war against the Nubians during the reign of 'Umar b. al-Khaṭṭāb and I never saw a people fiercer in war than they are (*ashadd fī ḥarb minhum*). I saw [repeatedly] one of them saying to the Muslim: 'where would you like me to put my arrow (*an aḍa' sahmī*) into you?' and sometimes one of our [brave] youngsters (*al-fatā minnā*) would say jokingly (*'abathan*): 'in this place' and he [the Nubian] would not miss the target. They were shooting arrows (*nabl*) in great quantities, and yet hardly any arrow was seen on the ground. One day they went out against us and met us in battle array (*ṣāffūnā*). We wanted to decide the battle by launching a single [concentrated] charge with our swords, but we could not anticipate them. They shot at us until the [i.e. our] eyes were gone. A hundred and fifty gouged eyes were counted. We said, therefore, that nothing is better than making peace with these ones (*fa-qulnā mā li-hā'ulā' khayr min al-ṣulḥ*). The

---

3 For the various meaning of *faqa'a* see Lane, s.v. The different nuances in meaning do not affect the high quality of the Nubians' marksmanship.

4 For the meanings of *ḥadaq* (sing. *ḥadaqa*) see Lane, s.v. My remark in note 3 applies here as well. Lane's translation of *rumāt al-ḥadaq* is "those who hit the mark in throwing or shooting."

5 See the discussion later in this paper.

booty that one can get from them is small, whereas their harm [i.e. the harm they cause to their adversaries] is severe (*inna salabuhum la-qalīl wa-inna nikāyatahum la-shadīda*). But ʿAmr [b. al-ʿĀṣ] did not make peace with them and persisted in harassing them (*wa-lam yazal yukālibuhum*) until he had been removed from his post and ʿAbdallāh b. Saʿd b. Abī Sarḥ was appointed as governor, and he made peace with them."[6]

II. Ibn ʿAbd al-Ḥakam's account (d. 257/871)

a. " ʿAmr b. al-ʿĀṣ sent Nāfiʿ b. ʿAbd al-Qays al-Fihrī ... and their [the Muslims'] cavalvry entered the land of the Nubians (*arḍ al-Nūba*) in the form of summer campaigns like those dispatched against the Byzantines (*ṣawā'if ka-ṣawā'if al-Rūm*) and this state of things continued (*fa-lam yazal al-amr ʿalā dhālika*) until ʿAmr b. al-ʿĀṣ was dismissed from the governorship of Egypt and ʿAbdallāh b. Saʿd b. Abī Sarḥ was appointed as its governor. I shall refer to this in its proper place."[7]

b. "Then ʿAbdallāh b. Saʿd attacked (*ghazā*) the blacks, that is to say the Nubians (*al-asāwida wa-hum al-Nūba*) in the year 31/651[8]... ʿAbdallāh b. Saʿd b. Abī Sarḥ was [caliph] ʿUthmān's governor over Egypt in the year 31, and the Nubians fought him back (*fa-qātalathu al-Nūba*)[9] ... They [the Muslims and the Nubians] fought each other fiercely (*iqtatalū qitālan shadīdan*). The eyes of ... and of ... were damaged then. On that day they (the Nubians) were named 'the marksmen of the pupils of the eye' (*rumāt al-ḥadaq*). That is why ʿAbdallāh b. Saʿd made a truce with them, for he could not cope with them [or: subdue them] (*fa-hādanahum ʿAbdallāh b. Saʿd idh lam yuṭiqhum*).[10] The poet said on that occasion:

---

6 Al-Balādhurī, *Futūḥ al-Buldān*, Leiden, 1866, pp. 236, l. 14–237, l. 6.

7 *Futūḥ Miṣr wa-Akhbāruhā*, New Haven, 1921, pp. 169, l. 18–170, l. 3.

8 *Ibid.*, p. 168, ll. 2–3.

9 *Ibid.*, ll. 4–5.

10 Lane translates *lā yuṭāq* thus: "He will not, or is not to be coped with". C.C. Torrey, in his translation of Ibn ʿAbd al-Ḥakam's book, renders *lā*

'My eyes ne'er saw another fight like Damqula
With rushing horses loaded down with coats of mail.'[11]

(*lam tara 'aynī mithla yawm Dunqula wal-khayl ta'dū bil-durū' muthqala*).[12]

...'Abdallāh made peace with them which is an armistice: they [the Muslims] will not attack them [the Nubians] and the Nubians will not attack the Muslims (*ṣālaḥahum 'alā hudna baynahum 'alā annahum lā yaghzūnahum wa-lā yaqhzā al-Nūba al-Muslimīn*)[13] ... There is no treaty or pact between them and the people of Egypt. It is only an armistice, ensuring safety to one side from the other (*wa-laysa baynahum wa-bayna ahl Miṣr 'ahd wa-lā mīthāq innamā hiya hudnat amān ba'ḍinā min ba'ḍ*".[14]

III. Al-Ya'qūbī's account (d. 292/905?)[15]

" 'Amr b. al-'Āṣ conquered Cyrenaica (*Barqa*), and he made peace with them (*ṣālaḥahum*) stipulating that they would pay during that year 13,000 dinars as poll-tax (*jizya*), [a sum which would be raised] by their selling whomsoever they wanted from their male children (*min abnā'ihim*). Then he advanced (*sāra*) until he reached North African Tripoli (*Ṭarābulus Ifrīqiya*) and conquered it. He then wrote [Caliph] 'Umar asking him permission to invade (*fī ghazwi*) the rest of North Africa (*Ifrīqiya*).[16] [The Caliph] wrote him back ' [the rest

---

yuṭīquhum thus: "not being able to subdue them" (*The Mohammedan Conquest of Egypt*, Yale, 1901, p. 308).

11 Torrey's translation, *op. cit.*, p. 308.

12 Ibn 'Abd al-Ḥakam, *Futūḥ Miṣr*, p. 188, ll. 6-9.

13 *Idem*, ll. 10-11.

14 *Idem*, ll. 13-14.

15 The history of al-Ya'qūbī was compiled before his geography and well before that author's death (see e.g. A.Miquel, *La géographie humaine du monde musulman*, Paris, 1967, p. XXI).

16 On the flexibility of the term *Ifrīqiya* see the relevant article (*Ifrīḳiya*) in *EI*[2].

of North Africa] is frightening (?) (*mufarriqa*)[17] and nobody will invade it (*yaqhzūhā*) as long as I live (*mā baqītu*).' He ['Amr] sent Busr b. [Abī] Arṭāt and he made peace with the people of Fazzān. And he sent 'Uqba b. Nāfi' al-Fihrī ... to the land of the Nubians (*arḍ al-Nūba*). And the Muslims encountered severe fighting from the Nubians (*wa-laqiya al-Muslimūn min al-Nūba qitālan shadīdan*). And when the Muslims withdrew (*inṣarafū*) from the land of the Nubians (*bilād al-Nūba*), they demarcated Gizeh."[18]

IV. Al-Ṭabarī's account (d. 310/923)

"[The year 20/641] The Muslims, when they conquered Egypt, attacked the Nubians of Egypt (*ghazū Nūbat Miṣr*), and the Muslims *withdrew* with wounds and lost pupils of the eye, because of the excellence of the [Nubians'] shooting, and, therefore, they [the Nubians] were called 'the marksmen of the pupils of the eye' (*fa-qafala al-Muslimūn bil-jirāḥāt wa-dhahāb al-ḥadaq min jūdat al-ramyi fa-summū rumāt al-ḥadaq*). When 'Abdallāh b. Sa'd b. Abī Sarḥ became the governor of Egypt (he was appointed by [Caliph] 'Uthmān b. 'Affān) he made peace with them [with the Nubians], stipulating that they would hand over to the Muslims every year a gift (*hadiyya*) of a number of heads [of slaves] and the Muslims will give them as a present (*yuhdī lahum*) every year a fixed quantity of food and a corresponding number of clothes ... ... This peace was signed by [Caliph] 'Uthmān and his successors from among the governors and commanders, and it was confirmed by [Caliph] 'Umar b. 'Abd al-'Azīz, out of his care [or compassion] for the Muslims and his desire to spare [or save] their lives (*wa-amḍā dhālika al-sulḥ 'Uthmān wa-man ba'dahu min al-wulāt wal-umarā' wa-aqarrahu 'Umar b. 'Abd al-'Azīz*

17 *Farraqa* in the sense of "frighten, make fear" seems to me to be the correct one in the context of our passage.

18 Al-Ya'qūbī, *Ta'rīkh*, Leiden, 1883, vol. I, pp. 179, l. 15 - 180, l. 4.

naẓaran minhu lil-Muslimīn wa-ibqā'an 'alayhim)."[19]

V. Al-Mas'ūdī's account (d. 355/956)

a. "When 'Amr b. al-'Āṣ conquered Egypt [Caliph] 'Umar b. al-Khaṭṭāb wrote him [an order] to fight the Nubians. The Muslims attacked them, and they discovered that they [the Nubians] are 'marksmen of the pupil of the eye' (*kataba ilayhi bi-muḥārabat al-Nūba fa-ghazāhum al-Muslimūn fa-wajadūhum yarmūna al-ḥadaq*). 'Amr b. al-'Āṣ refused to make peace with them (*an yuṣāliḥahum*) until he was dismissed from Egypt. 'Abdallāh b. Sa'd was appointed its governor, and he made peace with them (*fa-ṣālaḥahum*)."[20]

b. Their [the Nubians'] king employs horses of noble stock (*al-khayl al-'itāq*) while most of the common people ride horses of mean breed (*barādhīn*). And they shoot arrows from a strange kind of bows. It was from them that the people of the Ḥijāz and the Yemen and the other Arabs learnt archery. It is they whom the Arabs call 'the marksmen of the pupil of the eye' (*wa-ramyuhum bil-nabl 'an qisī gharība wa-'anhum akhadha al-ramya ahl al-Ḥijāz wal-Yaman wa-ghayruhum min al-'Arab wa-hum alladhīna tusammīhim al-'Arab rumāt al-ḥadaq*)."[21]

---

19 Ṭabarī, *Ta'rīkh*, Leiden, 1901, vol. I, p. 2593, ll. 5-15. The meaning of *naẓara li* in al-Ṭabarī's passage is within the range of "Care, mercy, compassion," as can be seen from the following examples: a) *naẓara lahum*: "he compassioned them and aided them" (Lane, s.v.); b) *yaqūlu Ibn al-Athīr ma'nā al-naẓar hāhunā al-iḥsān wal-raḥma wal-'aṭf* (*Lisān al-'Arab*, VI, p. 4467a); c) *naẓara Allāh ilayhi*: "God chose him and compassionated him, and pitied him or regarded him with mercy" (Lane, s.v.). The expression *abqā 'alā fulān* is a particularly strong one: to spare the life of somebody who is completely at one's mercy (see the instances in Lane, s.v. and *Lisān al-'Arab*, I, p. 330 and Qur'ān, LXXIV, 28). Even when it has a somewhat milder meaning (see some of the numerous examples in Blachère's *Arabic-French-English Dictionary*, II, pp. 764a-765b) it still remains very strong.

20 *Murūj*, III, pp. 38, l. 11 - 39, l. 3.

21 *Ibid.*, II, pp. 382, l. 9 - 383, l. 2.

VI. Al-Kindī's account (d. 350/961)

"We attacked (*ghazawnā*), together with ʻAbdallāh b. Saʻd North Africa (*Ifrīqiya*) in the year 27/648. ʻAbdallāh b. Saʻd carried out his attack against the blacks (*ghazā ghazwat al-asāwid*) in the year 31/651, and he reached Dongola. The fighting against them was fierce (*qātalahum qitālan shadīdan*). The eyes of ... and of ... were hit (*uṣība*) then. The poet said ..."[22]

VII. Ibn al-Aʻtham al-Kūfī's account (d. 314/926)

"La première expédition des Musulmans en Nubie, date de l'année 20 ou 21 de l'hégire. Voici comme elle est rapportée par Ahmed al Koufy, dans l'ouvrage intitulé: *Kitab al-fotouhat* (*le livre des conquêtes*): "Amrou ben el-As étoit en Egypt, lorsqu'il reçut une lettre d'ʻOmar, qui lui ordonnoit de marcher vers la Nubie, et de faire la conquête de ce pays, ainsi que de la contrée des Berbers, de Barkah, de Tripoly du Magreb et de ses dépendances, Tandjah, Afrahenjad, jusqu'à Sous al-aksâ. A cette époque, Amrou ben el-As venoit de percevoir le tribut auquel il avoit imposé la ville d'Alexandrie, et qui s'élevoit à dix mille dinars, ou même davantage, et il se disposoit à envoyer cette somme au khalife. Mais ayant reçu l'ordre de partir pour la Nubie, il distribua les dix mille dinars à son armée, en sorte que chaque soldat en eut sa part. Ensuite ayant fait publier son expédition et achevé tous les prépartatifs nécessaires, il se mit en marche pour la Nubie, à la tête de plus de 20,000 hommes. Dès qu'il fut arrivé dans cette contrée, il lâcha la bride à ses soldats, qui se répandirent de tous côtés, et y portèrent le meutre et le pillage. Lorsque les Nubiens virent la désolation de leur pays, ils se rassemblèrent au nombre de plus de cent mille hommes, et vinrent attaquer les Musulmans avec tant de courage, que ceux-ci n'avoient jamais essuyé un choc si terrible. Il y eut dans ce combat tant de têtes abattues, de mains coupées, d'yeux

---

22 I did not translate the rest of the account, because it is identical (in spite of slight variations) with the account of Ibn ʻAbd al-Ḥakam. For the whole passage see *Kitāb al-Wulāt*, Beirut, 1908, p. 12, ll. 5-11.

crevés par les flèches, et de corps étendus sur le carreau, qu'il eût été impossible de les compter. Un des principaux Musulmans me disoit un jour: Je n'ai jamais vu d'hommes qui lancent des flèches avec autant d'adresse et de justesse que les Nubiens. Quelquefois un d'entre eux se placoit vis-à-vis un Musulman, et, posant une flèche sur son arc, il disoit: Quel membre veux-tu que je vise? Le Musulman répondoit en riant: Tel membre. Sur le champ le Nubien atteignoit la partie indiquée, sans jamais manquer son coup. Mohammed al-Wakedy a copié le récit d'un vieillard hémiarite, qui s'étoit trouvé à cette guerre. Un jour, dit-il, que nous étions en bataille dans une plaine, et aux prises avec les Nubiens, en un moment je comptai cent cinquante yeux qui tombèrent percés de leurs fléches. A notre tour nous employâmes la même méthode et dirigeâmes nos flèches vers les yeux de nos ennemis. Enfin, avec le secours de Dieu, nous les repoussâmes et remportêmes la victoire. Un grand nombre de Nubiens fut tué dans le combat; le reste se réfugia dans les déserts et les vallées, où Amrou ne jugea pas à propos de les poursuivre. Ce général, dans toute son expédition, ne put pas faire un prisonnier, et ne rapporta pas seulement un dinar ni un dirhem'."[23]

---

23 Quatremère's translation of the Persian translation of *Kitāb al-Futūḥ* in: "Mémoire sur la Nubie", *Mémoires géographiques et historiques sur l'Égypte et sur quelques contrées voisines*, Paris, 1811, vol. II, pp. 39-41. Unfortunately, in the Hyderabad edition (1968-1975), the relevant part is missing, and is filled by the editors with a Persian summary. However, the very last lines of that original were not lost, and they say: "'Amr b. al-'Āṣ did not pursue them [i.e. the retreating Nubians], and he was unable to capture even one prisoner or take a single dinar or dirham. He [al-Wāqidī] said: Then 'Amr. b. al-'Āṣ went with the Muslims against the Berbers" (*fa-lam yatba'hum 'Amr b. al-'Āṣ wa-lā qadira 'alā asīr wāḥid wa-lā 'alā dīnār wa-lā dirham qāla thumma sāra 'Amr b. al-'Āṣ bil-Muslimīn yurīd al-Barbar* (*Futūḥ*, I, p. 349, ll. 1-3). This short passage tends to prove the correctness of the Persian translation. At this stage I offer no opinion about the important question concerning the date of the compilation of Ibn al-A'tham's work. One cannot but express admiration for Quatremère's unique command and

B. Analysis of the passages

There cannot be the slightest doubt as to the cause of the Muslims' being checked and brought to a standstill in their attempt to advance southwards along the Nile. This was due to the valour and military ability of the Nubians (above all: their excellence in archery) and nothing else. Even the only source among those cited above (Ibn al-Aʿtham) which explicitly maintains that the Nubians were defeated in the last of the series of battles between the two adversaries, states that the Muslims had gained nothing as a result of their victory. The advance of the Muslims as far as Dongola (stated in VI and implied in IIb) must have been of a very brief duration. The permanent boundary between Egypt and Nubia soon became again more or less the old one. What is so significant about the unanimous evidence of our sources is that it is given by the Nubians' enemies (an evidence which is called so aptly in Arabic: *shahādat shāhid min ahlihi*). This obviously lends it much greater weight. At the same time it is also a great tribute to the objectivity of the Muslim sources and enhances considerably the chances of the reliability of their accounts in other cases. The admiration of the Muslims for the Nubians'

---

intelligent use of the Muslim Medieval sources. So much of his work, especially that connected with terminology and institutions, is still very important and useful, in spite of the fact that many of his definitions had to be corrected. For a bibliographical note updating the state of research on the *baqṭ* see M. Hinds and H. Sakbout, "A Letter from the Governor of Egypt to the King of Nubia and Muqurra Concerning Egyptian-Nubian Relations in 141/758", *Festschrift Iḥsān 'Abbās*, Beirut, 1981, p. 210, n. 5. G. Vantini's book, *Oriental Sources Concerning Nubia*, Heidelberg and Warsaw, 1975, was not available to me.

performance as archers[24] was so great, that it led to the birth of a tradition according to which those Nubians were the teachers of the Arabs in archery (passage Vb). Whether this tradition is true or false is another matter. But even if it is false, there could hardly be a more convincing way for the expression of one's admiration for an opponent, especially in a society which considered the bow and arrow to be the backbone of field warfare. It is also noteworthy that this kind of esteem was accorded to the army of a small and rather obscure people and not to the armies of the two great empires which were the main adversaries of Islam during the early stages of its expansion (at least not with such accentuation and prominence).[25] Yet another illuminating point: the saying about the Nubians: *inna salabahum la-qalīl wa-inna nikāyatahum la-shadīda* (passage I, Balādhurī) is repeatedly used, with certain variations, in extolling the military qualities of the Turks. Out of all the peoples whom the Muslims encountered on the battlefield, the Turks receive in the Muslim Medieval sources the biggest share of military praise. That praise centered first and foremost upon the Turks' superb archery. Furthermore, the Nubians were unique among the blacks of Africa to be accorded this kind of distinction, especially in connection with such crucial events as the thrust of the armies of Islam deep into the Abode of War. Finally, the clear picture of the Nubians' mettle and superb military qualities does not emerge from out of the way and marginal sources, but from two of the most important chronicles of early Islam (Ṭabarī and al-Ya'qūbī); from the two best extant books on the Muslim conquests (Balādhurī and Ibn al-A'tham); from the most central encyclopaedic work of al-Mas'ūdī; and from the two best

---

24 The great ability of the Nubians as archers was already recognized by the Pharaonic Egyptians as well as by the Meroites (P.L. Shinnie, "Christian Nubia", *The Cambridge History of Africa*, vol. II, Cambridge, 1978, pp. 564-5). See also W.Y. Adams, *Nubia, Corridor to Africa*, London, 1977, p. 451.

25 The real impact of the Persian and other archeries on that of the Muslims from the birth of Islam onwards is, of course, another matter.

early sources dedicated specifically to Egypt (Ibn ʿAbd al-Ḥakam and al-Kindī). A systematic comparative study of the evaluation by the Muslims of the wide range of peoples and ethnic groups with which they came into contact, especially during the early period of their religion, has yet to be made. I am quite certain that the Nubians will not fare badly at all within the framework of such a comparison.

All this does not tend to support the possibility that the clashes between the Muslims and the Nubians were on a minor scale, even numerically. As far as numbers are concerned, only Ibn al-Aʿtham gives them in connection with the last battle, and they are big. The sizes of the Muslim military expeditions, as well as the sizes of the armies which they met in battle, are only rarely given, and their reliability is most questionable.[26] The most common verb denoting an attack on enemy territory (mainly, but not exclusively, by a Muslim army) is *ghazā*, and the usual name for such a military operation is *ghazwa*, irrespective of the dimensions of the operation. This terminology occurs also in the above cited passages.[27] Even the great naval attack against the Byzantines, known by the name "that of the masts" (*dhū al-ṣawārī*) and commanded by our ʿAbdallāh b. Saʿd b. Abī Sarḥ, is called *ghazwa*.[28]

The importance which the Muslims attached to the Nubian front in the early years of their occupation of Egypt, both in their general strategy, and on the local level is demonstrated by the following:

a) The operations out of Egypt in both directions (southwards and westwards) were ordered by Caliph ʿUmar

---

26 The estimates of H. MacMichael and others of the size of the Arab army and the Arab population during the first years of the Muslim occupation of Egypt are without foundation. In an article named "Regarding Population Estimates in the Countries of Medieval Islam" (*JESHO*, vol. XXVIII, (1985), pp. 1-19) I am emphasizing the baselessness of this kind of estimates.

27 Passages II (twice), III, IV, V, VI (twice). See also Kindī, *op. cit.*, p. 12.

28 Kindī, *op. cit.*, p. 13, l. 3.

himself, as two parts of the same plan for the conquest of African territory. Up to the final arrest of the advance along the Nile, there is no indication of the preference of one front over the other. From Ibn al-Aʿtham's evidence (see the few surviving lines in Arabic in the Hyderabad edition, reproduced and translated in note 23) we learn how a check or only a partial success on the Nubian front spurred on a Muslim attack on the North African front.

b) The persistence of ʿAmr b. al-ʿĀṣ, one of the greatest commanders of the Muslim armies, in his attempt to break the resistance of the Nubians throughout his governorship and up to his removal from the post.

Since there is no indication whatsoever that in the very first years of Egypt's occupation any of the two fronts received more attention that the other; and since military expeditions were sent in both directions in those early years (in the reigns of ʿUmar and ʿUthmān and during the governorships of ʿAmr and ʿAbdallāh), it is most instructive to see how easily the Muslim armies advanced westwards, reaching countries and regions lying far away from the western boundaries of Egypt, and how thoroughly and absolutely those armies were checked in their thrust southwards, gaining hardly any ground in the final settlement with their adversary.

In addition to the unequivocal and unanimous evidences according to which the Muslims were forced to abandon their plan of advance southwards only as a result of the Nubians' fierce resistance, there is special significance to a statement included in the comparatively brief passage from al-Ṭabarī (passage IV) and which is not repeated in any other of the passages quoted in this paper. It is said there that Caliph ʿUmar b. ʿAbd al-ʿAzīz (99–101/717–720) ratified the agreement with the Nubians out of fear for the safety of the Muslims! This means that in the capital of Islam the memory of the military feats of the Nubians was still alive, and that the danger of an attack by them was not yet considered as a matter of the past even more than half a century after the signature of that agreement. This must have been a very important factor in its perpetuation and in its perhaps unequalled longevity (in spite of the fact that it had not been considered to be an agreement of real peace).

The contents of the *baqṭ* agreement are also very meaningful. They indicate a state of near equality between the two sides. The most relevant clause in the context of the present article is the purely military one, namely, that the two signatories will not attack one another (passage II – Ibn ʿAbd al-Ḥakam). This implies that the Muslims were also in need of a guarantee of safety from a Nubian attack. That need became all the more urgent because the Muslims do not seem to have been able to hold constantly considerable forces in the vicinity of the Nubian front. Even during the peak of the pressure on the Nubians it is explicitly stated that at the end of this or that battle the Muslims had to withdraw their forces (or more of them) away from the battle area (sometimes as far as the capital in Lower Egypt) (*inṣarafū* – Yaʿqūbī, passage III; *qafalū* – Ṭabarī, passage IV).

As already stated at the outset of this paper, the Muslims, in the period of their early conquests, were never stopped so abruptly, so thoroughly and for such a long time, in any of the directions of their thrust forward, as in the direction which is the subject of our discussion. It has also been shown in detail that the one and only cause for that unparalleled check were the Nubians. A combination of factors contributed to that spectacular result: their religious zeal; their courage and military qualities; their better acquaintance with the terrain, and the narrowness of the front which they had to defend.[29]

Given the great urge of the Muslims to advance along the Nile, and their sustained efforts to materialize that urge (as is proved by the unanimous evidence of the sources), the only obstacle to stop them being *the Nubian Dam*, it would be most

---

29 Round the middle of the sixth/twelfth century the Nubians were unable to defend themselves againt the Ayyūbid archery (Aspects, *op. cit.*, pp. 201–2). The Nubians either did not keep abreast with newer developments in that domain, or might even have regressed in comparison with their own past.

unrealistic to suppose that has the dam been inexistent, or had it been removed or broken through, the Muslims would nevertheless not have continued what they had already started so resolutely, and, for a good number of years, so unflinchingly. The close proximity to the Nile as a means of communication (in spite of the cataracts) and of abundant and constant water supply could only have stimulated their desire to push southwards.

A long thrust beyond the Egyptian–Nubian armistice line (or more precisely: area) would have created for the Muslims problems of the first magnitude. Their military manpower was very limited. Campaigns on a large scale along the Nile could not have been carried out without affecting negatively their progress in North Africa. The fact that the Muslims had to withdraw at times the main body of their expeditionary force from Upper Egypt following an unsuccessful attack on the Nubians, is a direct result of their shortage in manpower (although this might not necessarily have been the sole reason). Another factor which might have carried a great deal of weight, had there been a deep penetration southwards, was the conditions which the invading Arabs would have found in much of Northern Sudan, although not in the strip of land immediately stretching to the south of the Egyptian border. This region includes wide pasture lands very fit for nomadic life, which the Arab beduins gladly appropriated when they finally reached them at a later period. As Y.F. Ḥasan so aptly puts it: "The fall of Nubia opened the gates for the Arab nomads to reach the rich pastures beyond the Nubia desert".[30] One of the important features of the Muslim conquests, especially the early ones, which had a strong bearing on the Muslim expansion, was that a significant proportion among the conquering Arabs did not settle in the newly constructed towns, quarters and camps or in the old towns, but continued their

---

30 *The Arabs and the Sudan*, Edinburgh, 1967, p. 128. H. MacMichael was, as far as I know, the first to point out the attraction of the pasture lands of Northern Sudan to the Arab nomads.

nomadic or semi-nomadic way of life in the open country. In Egypt, for example, many of them were absorbed in the Ḥawf area in the north. Such beduins could not be controlled by the central government as thoroughly and as efficiently as those who settled in the military and other towns. For the purpose of fighting the wars of Islam they were much less reliable than their counterparts in the urban centers. The absorption of a substantial part of the conquerors in the distant Sudanese pasture expanses -- in addition to the inevitable demands of an active southern front -- would have gravely affected the already strained and depleted military reservoir of Islam in Africa, and could not but have encumbered and slowed down the conquest of North Africa and beyond, a region of much greater importance than that lying to the south of Egypt.

The process of Arabization and Islamization of the Northern Sudan can be only partly reconstructed by means of the available sources. There are many gaps which cannot be filled. However, one thing is certain. It reached very considerable dimensions only after the Arabs had ceased to be the dominant military factor in Islam, which means that this process could have had little or no effect at all on the Arab might in its heyday. Therefore, the basis which the Arabs had laid for the consolidation of Muslim rule in the already conquered territories and for its further expansion by the military elements which succeeded them, could not have been weakened by events and demands on the Nubian front.[31]

---

31 The uniqueness of the Nubian front, and even more so the implications of that uniqueness, were usually either not sufficiently stressed, or completely ignored by students of the early Muslim expansion. I was attracted by it long ago. A seminar dealing with the relations of the Abode of Islam with the Abode of War, which I have been conducting repeatedly for many years at the Hebrew University of Jerusalem was accompanied by a volume of passages from the early Muslim sources called (in Hebrew) "The Muslim World and the Peoples bordering on it" (Jerusalem, Akadamon, 1962/63). There, some passages describing the Nubians' resistance against the advance of the armies of Islam were included (*ibid*., pp. 166-178), and in the seminar the extraordinary

Within the context of our subject the long and important passage or chapter of al-Maqrīzī on the *baqṭ*[32] deserves special notice. This chapter has been frequently used and cited, and with full justification, from the beginning of the study of relations between the Muslims and the Nubians. Yet in all that long and detailed account there is not a single reference or even a hint to the prowess and highly acclaimed qualitites of the Nubians as fighters or to their excellence in archery. Neither is there the slightest mention of the account which is unanimously repeated in the earlier sources, namely, that the Muslims made peace with their southern neighbours because they failed in their repeated attempts to overcome them. And this, in spite of the fact that two of those early sources, i.e., al-Mas'ūdī and al-Balāduri, are specifically quoted by him.[33] As a matter of fact, from al-Maqrīzī's presentation one cannot understand at all why the Muslims accorded the Nubians such generous and unique terms. To my mind, the reason for al-Maqrīzī's quite peculiar omission of such a central aspect of Muslim-Nubian contacts was the result of his dislike of the Christians, and in particular of the Copts, who were monophysites like most of the Nubians, and were also their immediate neighbours. To admit the existence of such high abilities in the Nubians seems to have been too much for him.

---

included (*ibid*., pp. 166-178), and in the seminar the extraordinary character of the Nubian front was emphasized. The gist of my view about certain facets of that character and their implications was published in "Aspects of the Mamluk Phenomenon", Part I, *Der Islam*, vol. 53 (1976), pp. 200-202. The best presentation hitherto of the Nubian front vis-a-vis the other fronts of early Islam is that of P. Forand: "Early Muslim Relations with Nubia", *Der Islam*, 48 (1971), p. 111. See also W.Y. Adams, *op. cit*., p. 450.

32 *Khiṭaṭ*, I, pp. 199, l. 36 - 202, l. 23.

33 *Idem*, p. 201, ll. 33, 38.

Postscript

The Nubian Front and the Reliability of the Muslim Sources

The more I have been reading Muslim sources, including those dealing with early Islam, the more I become convinced that their evidence should be taken, on the whole, very seriously. This statement pertains also to the biased and contradictory evidence, the amount of which is by no means small. The careful study and examination of both kinds of evidence, and a great restraint in rejecting much of them, is the surest way to reach more well founded scholarly conclusions.

Regrettably, however, there is a tendency nowadays among a number of Islamists (which, I hope, has already passed its peak), to jump to hasty conclusions, based on rather questionable reasoning and proofs. This tendency of slaughtering "sacred cows" and demonstrating a not too deserved originality, should be discouraged.

As already stated in the present article, the case of the Nubian front is a striking example of a reliable account. Numerous other examples of identical or similar character are strewn in the Muslim sources. There are many other instances where those sources do not necessarily admit Muslim failures and shortcomings, yet from which the sound of truth and reality rings quite clearly.

XIII

Islam versus Christian Europe: the case of the Holy Land

The struggle for superiority between Islam and Christianity, and particularly between Islam and Christian Europe (with a greater stress on Western Europe), is one of the major factors (if not the most important) which have shaped the destiny of the human race over many centuries.

It is quite natural that the Holy Land, so sacred to all three monotheistic religions, should figure so prominently in that struggle.

In this chapter I shall try to briefly examine how this struggle was reflected on the soil of that land, attempting, at the same time, to establish the place of developments there within their wider context.

I shall start with the wider context, as I see it. In my view, the steadily growing technological preponderance of Christian Europe which began during the medieval period gave it, among other advantages, a more or less correspondingly increasing military superiority over the lands of Islam.[1] That superiority, however, became evident at sea much earlier than on land. The main reason for this was that the Muslims possessed on land a socio-military body the like of which existed neither in Christendom nor in any other civilisation, before the advent of Islam or after it. This was the Mamlūk military institution, which succeeded in delaying on land, for a good number of centuries, the inevitable outcome of Christian Europe's rising power.

These two major facets of the Muslim-Christian European contest found one of their most telling expressions on the soil of the Holy Land and its extensions during the period of the Crusades (1196–1291). What I would like to emphasise is that the implications and meaning of the final results of those Crusades went far beyond that particular trial of strength and that particular period. I shall explain what I mean by this statement later in this chapter. At this point I shall confine myself to saying that in evaluating the final outcome of the Crusades, not only what happened on land should be considered, but also what happened at sea, which was of greater importance in the long run.

But before discussing the Crusades and the Holy Land, a brief summary of the main characteristics of the Mamlūk socio-military institution should be given. This institution was, on the one hand, part and parcel of the Muslim slave-system (which was characterised, generally speaking, by its moderateness and leniency). On the other hand, it constituted a very special category within that system. In fact, it would be more appropriate to define the Mamlūks as slaves who became masters, and who formed the topmost élite layer in Muslim military society. Most of them were brought over as slaves to the lands of Islam from beyond the Muslim border,which means that they were born infidels. They were purchased only from the countries lying to the north-east and north of the Muslim territories, which means that they were fair-skinned. Blacks could not form part of the Mamlūk military élite. Within Muslim civilian society there also existed a basically negative attitude toward blacks. However, in certain ways they merged much more easily into that society than they did later into Western Christian society.

The Mamlūks imported by the slave-dealers were mainly nearing puberty or were adolescent. They were hand-picked, and only the very best could pass the scrutiny of the experienced selectors.[2] When they reached their Muslim destiny (usually the court of a ruler or important personality), they were converted to Islam. First they were taught its basic tenets, and then they were trained militarily according to the best methods available at the time. Their training was, of course, that of cavalrymen. Having terminated their period of learning and training, they were usually (though by no means always) manumitted. The important thing about this procedure was that loyalty and fidelity between the patron and his slave in Islam became effective only *after* the manumission (*al-walā' li-man a'taq*). The patron and his manumitted Mamlūks formed a kind of "big family" and strong bonds of allegiance tied the Mamlūk to his patron and to his colleagues in servitude and manumission. Those bonds developed on the basis of a very deep-rooted awareness[3] that Islam is far superior to any other religion, monotheistic or otherwise. In addition to this, there was yet another characteristic unique to the Mamlūk institution, without which all the other characteristics would have been of little value: the institution constituted a one-generation nobility. The sons of the Mamlūks were ousted from it. New Mamlūks had to be imported continuously, so that the ranks of the military élite would constantly be filled with fresh recruits from the same source of supply, thereby preserving the inborn military qualities characteristic of the people of their homelands.

One of the main reasons why the slave traffic in general, and the Mamlūk traffic in particular, could be carried out continuously on such a large scale was that the peoples of the slaves' countries of origin (whether Mamlūks or non-Mamlūks; fair skinned or blacks) usually co-operated willingly with the slave dealers. This was true of the rulers of those countries, of the heads of the tribes, and even of the close relatives of the prospective slave, including his father and mother. The scale of values of those people was different, and, consequently, family relations were different from the accepted ones in more civilised countries.

Slave traffic was extremely remunerative to all concerned. In addition, the material lot of the slave was usually better in his new country than in his original one. This was true of many of the black slaves, and particularly so of the Mamlūks who were destined from the very outset to join the military élite, and had excellent chances of rising to the highest ranks. Some of them could even hope to bring over their relatives to the countries which adopted them.

There were, however, important drawbacks to this system, the most important of which were: (a) there was little or no control over the homelands of the Mamlūks, especially to Muslim rulers whose states were distant from those homelands: (b) Muslim rulers nearer to the homelands could interfere with their passage through their territory to further destinations; (c) a Mamlūk was very expensive; (d) it took a number of years to turn a raw boy slave into a fully fledged Muslim adult warrior, and the whole process was very costly. The patron had to invest much and wait some years before reaping the benefit of his investment.

In spite of all these drawbacks and its relatively small numbers,the Mamlūk institution achieved great success,[4] both in expansion and in defence. It lasted for about 1 000 years, from the first half of the ninth century to the first half of the nineteenth. It certainly outlived its purpose for a very long time, but for a much longer time it played a decisive role in Muslim history. Nothing even remotely similar has ever existed on any appreciable scale outside the boundaries of Muslim civilisation.

We now come back to the Holy Land in the time of the Crusades. During that period the immense might of the Mamlūk system and the growing weakness of Muslim naval power were revealed in all their magnitude both in the Holy Land and its neighbouring territories. These two factors were the clearest indicators of future developments in the confrontation between Islam and European Christianity.

The Holy Land, and, above all, Jerusalem, were the obvious targets of the Crusaders. However, both the Muslims and the Franks realised that the pivot of the whole war was Egypt. The side that held Egypt would ultimately hold Palestine and Syria, and be able to drive the enemy out of them. Egypt was the ideal base for military operations against the Syro-Palestinian region or part of it.

But neither Egypt nor any of its neighbouring lands had the proper kind of armies to repel a Crusader invasion,[5] let alone oust the Crusaders from the Muslim territories which they occupied. That task could only be possible with the aid of Mamlūk forces brought over from the distant north and north-east. The great — and, as later events proved, irreversible — shrinkage of the Crusaders' hold on the Holy Land and other parts of the Syrian region began with the coming to power of the Ayyūbids (1169–1250). Contrary to the accepted view, the Mamlūks made up the core of the armies of that Kurdish dynasty, and without them the military achievements of Saladin and his successors could not have taken place. Towards the end of the Ayyūbid reign, the Mamlūk element was considerably strengthened. The Baḥriyya regiment (the Mamlūks of the Ayyūbid sultan al-Ṣāliḥ Najm al-Dīn Ayyūb), which put an end to the Ayyūbid reign and established the Mamlūk reign (1250–1517) in its stead, won, on Egyptian soil, very shortly before that (February 1250), a resounding victory over one of the biggest and strongest armies which the Franks ever sent against the Muslims during the Crusading period. Furthermore, the commander-in-chief of that army, the famous St Louis (Louis IX, king of France) was taken prisoner, together with the greatest part of his surviving army. This was the second and last time in Muslim history that a monarch of a great Christian kingdom was taken prisoner by a

Muslim army. The first was in the famous battle of Manzikert (1071), which left Anatolia wide open to the Seljuks and their Turcomans, thus paving the way to the rise of the Ottoman Empire. The decisive factor in this Muslim victory over the Byzantines was again the Mamlūk regiment of Alp Arslan (the captive king was Romanus Diogenes).

Within less than half a century after coming to power, the Mamlūks had wiped the Crusaders out of Syria and Palestine and brought an end to the Crusades. Their prestige and glory were enhanced by their stopping the advance of the Mongols at ‘Ayn Jālūt in the Plain of Esdraelon (1260), and putting an end to all their future attempts to conquer Syria or parts of it. These great victories were acknowledged and celebrated throughout the great centres of Islam.

The backbone of the might of the Ottoman Empire was its janissary corps, a direct offshoot of the Mamlūk system. Without the janissaries the Empire would never have reached its far-flung boundaries, and would never have threatened as it did the heart of Europe for centuries.

In order to complete the picture, just a few remarks about the Mamlūk institution *before* the Ayyūbids, the Mamlūks and the Ottomans. The person who made the Mamlūks the central military element of Islam was Caliph al-M‘utaṣim (833–842). His unflinching determination to bring about that far-reaching revolution in the structure and composition of the Muslim armies forced him to abandon Baghdad as the capital of the Caliphate (and, for all practical purposes, the centre of the Muslim world) and to build a new Caliphal capital, Sāmarrā, which was situated upstream on the Tigris, thus commanding Baghdad. This new capital was built, first and foremost, in order to serve the Caliph's Mamlūk corps, and perpetuate its existence as the pivot of Muslim power.

The role of Sāmarrā as the capital of Islam was short-lived. But the Mamlūks, as the core and backbone of the armies of Islam, continued to exist, as already mentioned, for about 1 000 years. Particularly worthy of note in the early centuries of Islam are the Mamlūk armies of the Sāmānids (874–999) and the Ghaznawids (962–1186) in the eastern regions of Islam. The Sāmānids penetrated deep into the lands of the Turks in central Asia and beyond, and the Ghaznawids were the major factor in widening the boundaries of Islam in India.

The Seljuks, who began penetrating the Muslim lands at the turn of the eleventh century, soon came to the conclusion that they would have to rely on Mamlūks as their élite troops. The greatest known protagonist of the Mamlūk system, both in theory and in practice, was the famous Vizir Niẓām al-Mulk. As already stated, the victory at Manzikert was won mainly because of the steadfastness of the Mamlūks of Alp Arslān. The Zangids (the Syrian branch: 1146–1181) were one of the main successors of the Seljuks. This was a Mamlūk dynasty. Its élite army consisted of Mamlūks. The Ayyūbid dynasty sprang out of the Zangid state, and the rulers of the Mamlūk sultanate came out of the Ayyūbid empire.

Only against the general and grand background ot the Mamlūk institution in Islam can the great military achievements of the Mamlūks on land against the Crusaders and the Mongols, who appeared most unexpectedly from the East, be properly understood and evaluated. It is very noteworthy that both Frankish and Muslim warriors had an extremely high regard for the military ability of their adversaries.

The situation at sea was, from a certain period onwards, completely different from that on land. During the eleventh century the Frankish navy gradually succeeded in reducing Muslim naval power to a minimum in most of the Mediterranean without a major battle. This was a vital prerequisite for the success of the Crusades, without which their efforts would have been nipped almost in the bud.

From the time the Crusaders set foot on Syro-Palestinian land, the Muslims failed to build up a naval power which would be strong enough to cut the Crusaders off from their homelands. The sea routes were almost completely open for the supply of materials and reinforcements to them throughout the Crusading period.

It took the Muslims almost 100 years to gather sufficient power on land to present, for the first time, a real threat to the whole Crusading enterprise. After the battle of Ḥaṭṭīn (1187) near Tiberias, the Muslims succeeded in reconquering Jerusalem, the focal point of the whole struggle, and vast Crusader territories, including very substantial parts of the coast, its ports and fortifications. In short, the end of the Crusades was in sight. However, at this very optimistic phase from the Muslim point of view, a growing Frankish force concentrated in Tyre was creating the conditions for the counter-offensive of the Third Crusade.

During this crucial stage in the history of the Muslim-Christian European struggle, a new Muslim military strategy was born, namely the systematic destruction of the towns, ports and fortresses on the Syro-Palestinian Coast, with particular stress on the Palestinian section of the coast, because of its proximity to Jerusalem and its suitability for landing. This was a complete departure from the strategy adopted by the Muslims during the first hundred years or so of the Crusaders' invasion, and had no real parallel in Muslim history since the advent of Islam.

After the arrival of the Crusaders, the Muslims showed no inclination whatsoever to destroy the ports which they still held, including the most important of them, although they had ample time to do so. Tripoli was captured by the Crusaders only in 1109, Tyre in 1124, and Ashkelon — the key point for an attack either on Egypt or Palestine and beyond — only in 1153.

The ease with which the Muslims conquered so much of the Crusader territories as a result of their 1187 victory, and the reverses which they suffered quite soon afterwards, pushed their military leaders, headed by Saladin, to adopt a new policy, which they carried out rapidly, albeit with much sorrow and internal antagonism. They became convinced that the only efficient way to fight the Franks was to destroy the harbours and coastal fortifications which the Muslims still held, in order to prevent their being captured intact by the formidable enemy.

Fortunately the sources, particularly *al-Fatḥ al-Qussī* by 'Imād al-Dīn al-Iṣfahānī, Saladin's close companion, enable us to follow quite systematically the development of that policy. As soon as the Muslims realised that they could not capture Tyre, and became convinced of the imminence of the Crusaders' counter-attack, their attention focused on Acre, which they succeeded in capturing from the Franks. They found its fortifications to be quite inadequate, and they were first inclined to destroy it together with Jaffa. However, they finally abondoned the idea and decided to fortify Acre as best they could in the relatively short time still available to them. The famous eunuch Qarāqū sh, the builder of the Cairo wall and citadel, was charged with this task.[6] Thus the siege of Acre became the focus of the Third Crusade.

The turning point was the fall of Acre after a very protracted siege. Saladin had to retreat southwards and when he reached Ashkelon, Richard the Lion-Heart was advancing in the same direction. He decided against stubborn opposition to raze Ashkelon to the ground, explaining that there was no alternative, and that if there had been he would rather have sacrificed his sons than remove a single stone from that town.

Parts of al-Iṣfahānī's above-cited book are very helpful in explaining the background and causes of the policy of destruction which began in Ashkelon, and which continued up to the end of the Crusading period and for some time beyond it. Here is a selection of excerpts.[7]

> The sea reinforces them [i.e. the Crusaders].[8]

> As long as the sea reinforces them and the land does not repel them, they will remain a permanent scourge upon the lands [of Islam].[9]

> This enemy is not a lone one, against whom a device can be effective, and on whom destruction can be brought. For he [i.e. that enemy] comprises everybody who is beyond the sea, and all those who are in the lands of the infidel [literally: infidelity]. There is not a single town of theirs, or a village, or an island or a province, be it big or small, which did not fit out its ships and did not alert its squadrons . . . reinforcement after reinforcement came from them continuously . . . as for their kings, who arrive by land, their countries were emptied of them, according to a steadily flowing information.[10]

Saladin, in a meeting with his commanders during his army's retreat from Acre, stated:

> You should know that this enemy of God and of ours has come with [all] its cavalry and infantry . . . and brought to combat the whole of infidelity against the whole of Islam *(qad baraza bil-kufri kullihi ilā al-Islām kullihi)* . . . and it had exhausted all that it could *(istanfada wus 'ahu)* [in the sense: mobilised all its resources] . . . As for us, there is no succour in our rear which we can expect, or a force which we can summon. Only our people was afflicted by that people. Only our army is facing the army of infidelity. There is none among the Muslims who will come to our succour and there is none in the lands of Islam who will help us.[11]

These excerpts, though written during or near the height of the Crusaders' counter-offensive at that time, reflect a deep perception of the realities of the naval balance of power between Islam and West European Christianity. What the Muslims became convinced of, with full justification, 100 years *before* the expulsion of the last Crusader from Palestine and Syria, was that under the very best circumstances (from the Muslim point of view) the Muslim coastline would remain for the foreseeable future the battle front between Islam and Christianity. This would also apply to the periods of relative peacetime between the two opponents. The fact that all the islands of the eastern

Mediterranean, including Cyprus and Rhodes, were in Christian hands, could only strengthen that very realistic conviction. After Saladin's demolition of Ashkelon and up to the end of the Crusades, the Muslims systematically destroyed the coastal fortifications and many of the port towns they captured from the Franks, together with their ports. Generally speaking, they did this with greater thoroughness on the Palestinian section of the coast than on its Syrian section, because of its proximity to Jerusalem, and because of its being more suitable for landing from the sea. To call this kind of demolition "scorched earth policy" would be most misleading, for the usual meaning of this term is an operation of destruction of a temporary character, which is carried out when the enemy attacks, or threatens to attack. As soon, however, as the enemy retreats, or the threat is removed, the act of rebuilding usually starts. In the case of the Muslims it was completely different. The operation of demolition started, habitually, as soon as the enemy had been ousted, and the demolished place was left in ruins for a long time, in most cases for centuries.

It should be emphasised and re-emphasised in this connection that this was the greatest act of destruction for defence purposes ever carried out *in the recorded history of the human race*. The permanent effects of this destruction are also unparalleled. The uniqueness of that operation in human history, or even in a more limited history, have never been pointed out by any scholar other than the present writer; certainly not its import and implications in the wider context of the struggle for supremacy between Islam and European Christianity.

Perhaps the best proof of the Muslims' admission of their naval inferiority and their disbelief in their ability to rectify that situation within a definite period is the following fact. From the middle of the thirteenth century onwards, and up until the total expulsion of the Franks in 1291, the Crusaders' power declined steadily. For no less than 40 years the Muslims were able to play a cat-and-mouse game with them and capture their strongholds one after the other at their convenience. Yet they continued methodically to destroy the coastal strongholds, and in many cases blocked the destroyed ports by the debris which they threw into the water, thus demonstrating their intention to put those ports out of use for a very long time. Even the fact that the same areas which had been the target of the Crusaders' invasion had now been defended by the extremely powerful Mamlūk army, which was far stronger than anything the Muslims had since the beginning of the Crusades, was not sufficient to dissuade them from their consistent policy of destruction.

Finally, the hindsight we possess today was obviously not available to the Muslims at that time. As is well known, the Crusading spirit did not die out in 1291. Plans and schemes to revive the Crusades did exist, and some of them did not look impractical at all. The full scale of the divisions within the Frankish camp was unknown to the Muslims; but even if they had known about them, they would have had no guarantee that those divisions would continue indefinitely.[12]

As a matter of fact the Franks had, on paper, the means of defeating the strongest Muslim military power in the later Middle Ages through a naval blockade, which would have deprived it of vital raw materials like wood and metals, and, no less important, of a very substantial part of its Mamlūks, because many (perhaps most) of them were brought over to Egypt and Syria on board Frankish ships. This was, of course, a theoretical possibility, because the chances of a Frankish united front against Islam were very meagre indeed. What I wish to point out, however, is that even a divided Christian Europe, beset by internal problems and antagonisms, could have reduced, without difficulty, the Muslim naval power in the Mediterranean sea to near insignificance.

Islamic naval inferiority came about at a much earlier date than military inferiority on land. A major cause of this delay, as I have already stated, was the Mamlūk socio-military institution, the like of which neither Europe nor any other civilisation possessed. But it *had* to take place because that institution was bound to become outdated sooner or later, both as a result of the grinding process of the relatively slow-growing European technological superiority, and as a result of technological breakthroughs.

One of these breakthroughs was the invention and introduction of firearms. Although the adoption of that weapon was very slow and painful, it was a breakthrough all the same. Particularly important is the fact that in Europe, generally speaking, it was adopted more efficiently than in the Muslim armies. Even more important: in Europe there existed the proper industrial foundations for its manufacture and development in the future.

One of the main obstacles for the efficient employment of firearms in most of the Muslim armies, above all the Mamlūk armies (with the exception of the janissary offshoot), was that the élite units of those armies consisted of cavalrymen. This was particularly decisive when the handgun, the personal weapon of the soldier, was introduced on a grand scale. It meant, for quite a long period, dismounting from the horse.

There is no doubt that the Ottomans defeated the Mamlūks and wiped out their empire mainly because of their superiority in firearms, and their correct handling of the weapons. The Ottomans were much more open than any other great Muslim state to technological innovations, and to adapting their military machine to them. They had a superb infantry, and developed a very impressive naval power. However, since the production of weapons went hand in hand with industrial development, and since the Ottomans did not have a strongly developed industrial sector, they were faced with two equally bad alternatives: either to produce weapons of their own, which could not be of the highest quality, or to import weapons from European industrial centres, which had their own interests in mind and quite often preferred to sell obsolete or obsolescent types of armament to their less industrially developed clients.

The temporary dominance of the Ottoman navy in the Mediterranean sea, or, more precisely, in parts of it, might create a misleading impression. At that time the naval struggle moved gradually but steadily to the great oceans, and it was a purely Western European struggle in which the Muslims could not take part, in spite of the fact that it changed the face of the globe in a way which proved to be very detrimental to Islam.[13]

As already stated, Muslim military inferiority on land was bound to come, and it did, at a steady pace. After a long and almost uninterrupted series of defeats, Muslim rulers came one after the other, with great reluctance and against a very strong internal antagonism, to the conclusion that they would have to build their armed forces, *from top to bottom,* according to the European model. The first to do so in the vast area which includes the whole of Africa and the whole of Asia, together with the islands of the Pacific Ocean, was Egypt's ruler Muḥammad 'Alī, in the first half of the nineteenth century. In order to achieve that aim, he had to remove the older military elements (mainly cavalrymen), particularly the Mamlūks, whom he wiped out, and the Bedouins, whom he settled. The main element from which he built his new navy was Egypt's *fellahin.* The fruits of his military revolution were reaped quickly. Under his rule Egypt expanded over most of the Arabian peninsula, conquered the Sudan,[14] the whole of the Syro-Palestinian region and penetrated deeply into Anatolia, to be stopped only by the European powers' intervention. *Never in its recorded history had Egypt expanded so far beyond its borders.*

Today all the Muslim armies are based on the European model and have hardly any connection with the older armies of Islam. This is also true of the non-Muslim armies in the vast area mentioned above, which are likewise modelled on the European pattern.

To sum up: the Crusading phase in the struggle between Islam and Christian Europe, which centred on the Holy Land and on Jerusalem, had implications in history which went far beyond that particular period and geographical area. These implications are reflected in the temporary occupation of some Middle Eastern countries — including all the areas which the Crusaders ruled — by European powers in the first half of the twentieth century. These powers had to leave those countries for reasons other than the local military might.

The wrong impression may be created by ending this discussion here. European society was certainly more open to innovations and changes in the military and in other fields than Muslim society, but it was also beset by prejudices and conservatisms which continued well into the twentieth century. In 1925, Field Marshal Earl Haig, the commander of the British Expeditionary Force in the Western Front in the First World War, asserted emphatically that the aeroplane and the tank could only be accessories to man and the horse. Other British personalities in key military positions continued in the mid-thirties to praise the horse as an essential element in modern warfare, and demonstrated great reluctance to accelerate the process of mechanisation of the British army.[15] The Soviet marshal Semion Budenny was still sure in 1967 that in a third world war the horse would play a decisive role.[16] Not less significant was the attitude of the American naval command after the First World War to William Mitchell, who strove to provide air cover to the American naval units.[17]

NOTES

1 This increasing military superiority had, of course, its ups and downs. In this chapter only existing situations and their impact are discussed. In my view, it is too early to pinpoint the whole set of underlying causes which created those situations. Although I put here the stress on the technological and military aspects, it should be remembered that these aspects are only part of a much wider background. Another thing that should be borne in mind is that it is, of course, very important to establish where a certain invention or innovation came into being. But what is far more important is how it merged into the general stream of creativeness and

activity (or the lack of them) and what was the follow up resulting from its appearance and adoption (in those cases where it *was* adopted).

2 These were the ideal stipulations, which were ignored from time to time, but not to a degree that could endanger the system.

3 The word "fanaticism" would be completely misleading within the conceptions of those times.

4 The Mamlūks always constituted a small part of the whole body of armed forces of any state, including the Mamlūk sultanate.

5 Of course, the expression "proper kind of armies" applies to the ideas and conceptions of those times.

6 See especially *al-Fatḥ al-Qussī fī al-Fatḥ al-Qudsī*, Leiden, 1888, pp. 117–19.

7 These excerpts were cited in Arabic transcription, without translation, in my "The Great Yāsa of Chingiz Khān — A Reexamination", part C_2, *Studia Islamica*, Paris, 1973, pp. 153–4. Here only the translations are given.

8 Al-Iṣfahānī, op. cit., p. 233, l.6.

9 Ibid., p. 204, ll.20–21.

10 Ibid., pp. 222, l. 14–223, l. 13.

11 Ibid., p. 109, ll. 4–11.

12 I dealt with the destruction of the Syro-Palestinian coastal fortifications and towns in "The Mamlūks and Naval Power — A Phase in the Struggle between Islam and Christian Europe", *Proceedings of the Israel Academy of Sciences and Humanities*, Vol. I, Jerusalem, 1965, pp. 1–2; in Baḥriyya (the Navy), *EI*[2], and in other studies. The detailed description of the demolishing of each of those strongholds is contained in a chapter on the naval power of the Mamlūks, which had not yet been published.

13 Besides firearms, the most important technological innovation in the later Middle Ages was the printing press. In Europe it spread very quickly and its tremendous impact was felt in many major fields. In Islam its introduction and spread were incomparably slower, as a result of a deliberate policy of the Muslim authorities, who allowed (in the Ottoman Empire) the Jews, the Greek Orthodox and the Armenians to have printing presses at quite early dates, but forbade them to print anything for the Muslims. Printing in Arabic characters started in Europe long before it started in any Muslim country. This is an important example of the difference in attitude towards change between Islam and European Christianity.

14 In fact, the Arabian Peninsula and the Sudan were conquered at a very early stage of Muḥammad ʻAlī's military reformation, and before the recruitment of the Egyptian *fellah* to the new army.

15 B.H. Liddell Hart, "Horse, Foot and Tank", *Spectator*, 28 September 1956, pp. 412–13.

16 Harrison G. Salisbury, "Budenny Recalls Soviet Setbacks", *New York Times*, 10 October 1967.

17 Part of what is said in this chapter is based on a much more detailed examination in other studies of mine.

XIV

THE IMPACT OF FIREARMS ON THE MUSLIM WORLD

Few inventions have influenced the course of history so greatly as the invention of firearms. We, who live in a time of transition from the period of firearms to that of atomic and nuclear weapons, are perhaps better able than past generations to understand the impact of this revolutionary invention on that civilization and society in which the Muslim peoples held a central place.

Before we discuss the influence of firearms on Islam, two questions have to be answered:

(1) Is there any ground to suppose that the Muslims first invented them?

(2) If not, under what influence did the Muslims adopt and use them?

On the basis of our present state of knowledge, we must answer "no" to the first question. The earliest reliable information about the use of firearms in any part of the Muslim world dates from the sixties of the fourteenth century, although there are signs of their use even before that. Parallel information from Europe dates from the twenties of the same century and for China eminent scholars claim an even earlier date. Gunpowder was known some time before the invention of firearms (second half of the thirteenth century), but was employed only as an incendiary.

The answer to the second question is that, even though we cannot completely exclude the possibility that gunpowder or firearms or both reached the Muslims directly from China, regular and continuous Muslim contact for their use was chiefly with Europe. The development of firearms in the Muslim world was, therefore, primarily linked with their development in Europe. Categorical proof of this – and by no means the only proof – is to be found in the fact that the Muslim countries situated on the sea and land routes from China into the heart of the Muslim world, such as North India, the countries bordering on the Indian Ocean, Central Asia, Afghanistan, Persia and Iraq, adopted firearms at a much later date and on a much more limited scale than those near Europe and on the Mediterranean, such as Egypt, North Africa, Syria, Anatolia and the European parts of the Ottoman Empire. As for South Arabia and other regions on the Indian Ocean, the explicit testimony of contemporary Arab historians is that firearms were unknown there before the beginning of the sixteenth century. The Portuguese, who reached the Indian Ocean by way of the Cape of Good Hope, and the Mamluks and Ottomans, their adversaries, introduced firearms to South Arabia. As for the use of firearms in the Muslim countries on the Mediterranean, it should be noted that North Africa lagged behind Anatolia and European Turkey until the overthrow of the Mamluk Sultanate by the Ottomans in 1516-1517. It is true that the Mamluks adopted firearms some fifty to sixty years before the Ottomans, but they did not keep pace with the Ottomans in their efficient use.

It follows, therefore, that only in the northwestern regions of Islam, which formed a relatively small part of the far-reaching Muslim world, were firearms used from the very beginning on any large or growing scale. This basic fact had wideranging consequences in different directions, the most important being the helplessness of the Muslims in their attempts to withstand expanding European domination in South Asia and the Far East.

Western Europe extended its hegemony across the seas thanks to its constantly growing technical superiority. The two main instruments which facilitated and hastened the pace of that extension were their superior naval and gun power and more and better firearms. Nothing in the world could resist that powerful combination.

In their conquest of the Western Hemisphere, the Europeans did not encounter any opposition on the seas, and on land had to subdue only populations armed with most primitive weapons. Conditions were less favorable in their drive towards the Far East, but even there their technical superiority enabled them to establish their rule with comparative ease. After the Portuguese had circumnavigated the Cape of Good Hope at the end of the fifteenth century, the only local power in the vast area stretching from the coasts of East Africa to the Pacific Ocean that had any chance of halting or containing the European intruder, was a Muslim one: the Mamluk Sultanate. The Mamluks did, in fact, send out several fleets to fight the Portuguese, but they were easily defeated and the majority of their ships were sunk along with the heavy loads of firearms on their decks. By the time the Ottomans, who were far ahead of the Mamluks in naval strength and firearms, had conquered the Mamluk Sultanate, the Europeans were already firmly entrenched in the countries round the Indian Ocean, and Ottoman efforts to expel them ended, on the whole, in failure. Thus, a small number of European ocean-going ships of a new kind, armed with a new kind of weapon, succeeded in robbing the Muslims, almost overnight, of the absolute hegemony which they had exercised for hundreds of years over the most important international trade route of those days. The way was now paved for the building of the large empires of modern times, which drew their might from their dominions overseas, and within the confines of each of which were included millions of Muslims.

Moreover, for centuries after Muslim supremacy over the Indian Ocean was destroyed by the Portuguese, no local power of similar strength to that of the Mamluks was able to rise against the Europeans.

The decisive role of firearms in the establishment of European mastery overseas may be deduced from the following facts.

By the end of the fifteenth and the beginning of the sixteenth centuries, the period during which the great European advance to the extreme limits of the earth began, firearms had become decisive weapons both in siege and in field warfare, though they had not yet wholly replaced other kinds of weapons. In Europe and in the northwestern part of the Muslim world, victory in major campaigns went to the side that had an advantage in firearms, especially when they were aimed against cavalry units having no past experience with them. The armies which the Europeans encountered east of Suez, if one may be permitted to use a modern expression, were markedly inferior not only to those European and Muslim armies, which were already in possession of firearms, but also to the Muslim armies which had not yet adopted them, and which, for this very reason, were defeated in battle, as we shall see. Moreover, from the end of the fifteenth century onwards, firearms were developed and improved at a much quicker pace than formerly, and this fact increased the initial advantage which the Europeans possessed at the moment when they appeared east of Suez. It is impossible to imagine that a handful of Europeans could have dominated such vast and populous areas, armed only with navies and weapons that *preceded* the use of firearms.

Some incidents from Muslim history make this clear. One South Arabian ruler who had adopted firearms in the first half of the sixteenth century destroyed his local enemies though they outnumbered him by far, and completely scattered them in a single battle. If such was the success of a primitive local army, how much more triumphant that of an European army!

Extant official Ottoman documents tell us that during the years 1520-1540 Muslim and non-Muslim rulers from India and Sumatra implored the Ottoman Sultan to supply them with firearms against the Christian enemy. The non-Muslim rulers of Sumatra even undertook to embrace Islam in exchange for such help. The Sultan answered that he could help, but there is little doubt that he was over-optimistic. The European naval preponderance was so over-whelming, that any decisive help from the Ottomans was out of the question. In any event the Ottomans were the only Power, to which the population, Muslim and non-Muslim, of this great region could turn for help. For the Chinese, who were perhaps the inventors of firearms, did not develop them to the same extent and efficiency as the Europeans.

The military helplessness of the Muslims and their non-Muslim neighbors before the European armies had far-reaching consequences for Islam, because the overwhelming majority of Muslims was concentrated in India and in the islands of the Dutch Indies (today's Indonesia). Thus, once the Europeans began their conquests in the East, they incorporated a large Muslim element into every one of the modern European empires from the very start.

Firearms were decisive not only in the subjection of Muslim and other non-European countries, but also in another way: countries not directly governed by the Europeans faced two equally unwelcome alternatives, either to import obsolete or obsolescent firearms from Europe, or to manufacture firearms of inferior quality themselves. Before the invention and development of firearms, the gap between European weapons and those of other parts of the world had not been so wide. Since that invention, however, those other parts became much more dependent on Europe for the supply of weapons than ever before.

The consequences of European superiority in firearms might have been even more deadly for Islam, had not the Ottomans been there to withstand it. The powerful Ottoman Empire used firearms on a large scale in the conquest of its enemies, whether Christians in Europe or Muslims in Asia and Africa. Without them it would have been unable to become the world power, that for centuries threatened the heart of Christian Europe. It is indeed true that Ottoman military strength was founded on the spirit of conquering the Christian infidel and on what is usually called the slave armies of that Empire. But this strength would not have achieved as much without help from the newest weapons of those times.

The Ottomans, however, were unable to go on providing their armies with the most modern weapons for very long. They were unable to do so because of the economic decline of the Empire, the decay of their peculiar military institutions, the lack of financial means, and also because from the very beginning the Ottoman Empire lagged behind most European countries in technical and industrial development. For the manufacture of firearms the Ottomans tried to bridge the gap by employing European craftsmen, many of them brought from outside the Empire. This expedient worked only so long as the processes in the manufacture of firearms were still relatively uncomplicated. Later, it became more and more difficult to manufacture modern firearms in a country whose industry as a whole was undeveloped. For that reason, firearms produced by the Ottomans gradually worsened in quality in comparison with those produced by their European enemies, and the Ottomans accordingly became more and more dependent on European sources of supply.

So much for the influence of firearms on the Muslim world from the point of view of relations between the Muslims and outside powers, mainly Christian Europe. We shall now discuss the attitude toward firearms within the Muslim world itself.

We have already noted that firearms did not play an important role in the Muslim world save in two of its northwestern states bordering on the Mediterranean: the Mamluk Sultanate and the Ottoman Empire. But the attitude towards firearms was fundamentally different in each one of them. The Mamluks, perhaps the first in Islam to adopt firearms and use them extensively, were filled with contempt for this kind of arms and did not promote them to be the main weapons of their soldiery. *They employed firearms only in sieges, never in field battle.* Enjoying, as they did, a privileged and exclusive status, the Mamluks were not willing to demean themselves by using firearms; instead, they entrusted their use to non-Mamluk units, of lower social standing, or to the black slaves who constituted the lowest rung in the military and social ladder. Let us consider two instances which exemplify the Mamluk attitude.

1. In 1495, there came to the throne a fourteen year old youth who was fascinated by firearms. With them he equipped a large unit of black slaves, who would march with them in front of him on official parades. This sight was deemed (and I quote the sources) "frivolous", "foolish", "criminal", and "a shame for the state" by the old and sophisticated Mamluk commanders. The young Sultan's habit of coming into social contact with his black slaves, and with other socially inferior and contemptible folk of the population of Cairo, shocked the Mamluks. The climax was reached when, in 1497, the Sultan decided to bestow the dress of a Mamluk Amir on the commander of his unit of black slaves and let him marry a white-skinned Circassian slave girl. (The Circassians were then the ruling race among the Mamluks.) The Mamluks could not endure this state of affairs any longer. They rebelled, killed the Negro commander and a number of his officers, and compelled the Sultan to disband the unit. Less than a year later, they assassinated the Sultan himself for his contempt of the throne.

The episode is most instructive, for it demonstrates clearly the social and psychological attitudes of the Mamluks. Less than twenty years before their own overthrow by firearms, nobody except a lightminded youth could seriously envisage the adoption of firearms as the chief weapon of the Sultanate.

2. The second incident concerns Sultan Qansuh al-Ghawri, one of the great and respected Sultans in Mamluk history. In 1510, he formed a unit of arquebusiers in addition to the several artillery units already in existence, as part of his plan of defense against the double danger of the Ottomans and the Portuguese, who threatened the existence of his Sultanate. The new unit was drawn from the lowest social elements among the sons of Mamluks (they did not belong to the upper class, since Mamluk society was a non-hereditary aristocracy). In addition to Mamluk's sons, the unit had Cairene tailors, cobblers and food vendors. The salary of these semi-soldiers was much less than that of the Mamluks and they got it on a different payday, at the end and not in the middle of the month, to emphasize their lowly status in comparison to that of the select Mamluk regiments. They were called al-'askar al-mulaffaq, i.e. the "false army" or "the patched up army". The pure Mamluks were contemptuous of the unit and considered it a worthless parasite on their own backs. But their attempts to disband it succeeded only in part.

Firearms won appreciation and admiration in the Mamluk Sultanate only during the last five months of its existence: after the first defeat of the Mamluk army by Ottoman firearms in North Syria (August 1516), and before its second defeat at the gates of Cairo (January 1517).

The last Mamluk Sultan, Tuman Bay, who ascended the throne after the defeat of August 1516, and who, by the way, had been a Mamluk of that young Sultan who had paid with his life for his interest in firearms, made every effort to equip the army of the Sultanate with firearms to be used in the *open field.* His efforts came too late, however, and could not avert disaster.

Tuman Bay's desperate endeavor clearly illustrates the great aversion for firearms felt by the Mamluks. Even at this critical moment, when their existence was at stake, the Mamluks themselves did not use these weapons but entrusted them to units composed of semi-civilians and black slaves, exactly as in the past.

The use of firearms by non-Mamluks alone prevented them from becoming the main weapon of the Mamluk Sultanate, not only because of the low social status of the units using them, but also because of the Mamluk's understandable apprehension that, should these units grow and become stronger, they might displace them from their ruling position by the force of superior arms.

It is not difficult to single out the causes for the Mamluk dislike of firearms. The Mamluks, who became the rulers of Egypt and Syria from the middle of the 13th century onwards, were a military society of horsemen, and horsemanship (in Arabic furūsiyya), with all that it involved, formed the central axis around which the whole way of life of the Mamluk ruling class revolved, and from which it drew its pride and sense of superiority. Horse, horsemen and horsemanship are terms which the reader encounters on almost every page in Mamluk historiography, and these were indeed the truly important matters from the point of view of a Mamluk; without them his life was barren and purposeless. As a matter of fact, the beginnings of the powerful link between the Mamluk and his horse and bow had much deeper roots than those existing in the Cairo military schools. These beginnings were associated with his early childhood, when he still lived on the steppe or in the savage mountainous area of his native country. There, the horsemen constituted the backbone of society and its elite, in both war and peace.

Firearms, and in particular handguns, which are individual weapons and, therefore, mass weapons, would have deprived the Mamluk of his bow and, what is more important, of his horse because at that time firearms could not yet be handled from horseback. This would have meant the end of his world.

Opposition to firearms on the basis of their allegedly immoral and anti-Muslim character is also found in Mamluk sources where it is attributed to the Mamluks themselves. This kind of opposition, however, was much weaker than the one deriving from the equestrian character of Mamluk society, and is mentioned only very rarely, mostly in sources of the period following the defeat of the Mamluks by the Ottomans.

A contemporary Mamluk chronicle, which deals with the conquest of Syria and Egypt by the Ottomans, contains a number of reasons against the use of firearms. According to this chronicle, a meeting took place between the Ottoman Sultan Selim I, conqueror of Egypt, and the captive Amir Kurt Bay, one of the leading Mamluk commanders. The discussion soon became heated, and the chronicler continues:

> "... Then, when Kurt Bāy saw treachery in the eyes of Sultan Selim and realized that the latter would kill him anyway, he threw politeness and good manners to the wind, and spoke the words of a man who despaired of life. He fixed his eyes on the Sultan's eye, and raised his right hand in the Sultan's face and said to him: "Hear my words and listen to them, so that you and others will know that amongst us are the horsemen of destiny and red death. A single one of us can defeat your whole army. If you do not believe it, you may try, only please order your army to stop shooting with firearms. You have here with you two hundred thousand soldiers of all races. Remain in your place and array your army in battle order. Only three of us will come out against you: I, the servant of God; the charging horseman Sultan Tuman Bay and Amir Allān, and you will see with your own eyes the feats performed by these three. Moreover, you will then know your own self and you will learn whether you are a king or deserve to be king because kingship befits only him who is an experienced, gallant man, for such were our upright predecessors. Study the books of history, and there you will learn of the bravery of Caliphs 'Umar b. al-Lhattāb and 'Ali b. Abi Talib. As for you (you are totally different from them); you have patched up (laffaqta) an army from all parts of the world: Christians, Greeks and others, and you have brought with you this contrivance artfully devised by the Christians of Europe when they were incapable of meeting the Muslim armies on the battlefield. The contrivance is that bullet (bunduq) which, even if a woman were to fire it, would hold up such and such number of men. Had we chosen to employ this weapon, you would not have preceded us in its use. But we are the people who do not discard the sunna of our prophet Muhammed which is the *jihād* for the sake of Allah, with sword and lance. And woe to thee! How darest thou shoot with firearms at Muslims. A Maghribine brought this arquebus to Sultan al-Malik al-Ashraf Qansuh al Ghari and informed him that this arquebus had come from Venice and that all the armies of the Ottomans and the West have already made use of it. The Mamluk Sultan ordered the Maghribine to train some of his Mamluks in the use of the arquebus, and that is what he did. Then these Mamluks were brought before the Sultan, and they fired their arquebuses in his presence. The Sultan was displeased with their firing and said to the Maghribine: "We shall not abandon the *sunna* of our Prophet and follow the *sunna* of the Christians, for Allah had already said

> that if Allah helps you nobody will defeat you! So the Maghribine went back to his country saying "Those now living will live to see the conquest of this Kingdom by this arquebus and that is what really happened. The Sultan Selim asked Kurt Bay: "If bravery and brave men and horsemen had been amongst you and you had followed the Koran and the *sunna*, then why have we defeated you and expelled you from your country and enslaved your children and annihilated most of you, and why are you yourself my prisoner?! Kurt Bay answered: "By Allah, you have not conquered my country by your power and by your horsemanship (furūsiyya). This was ordained and predestined by Allah from eternity, for God has made a beginning and an end to everything, and he has allotted and fixed a period of existence to every kingdom. . . You yourself will die, and your kingdom will come to an end." (Ibn Zunbul, pp. 37-39).

The Mamluks and the Turkoman horsemen of Safawid Persia as well as the Ottoman Sipahis were not the only ones to find firearms distasteful. A similar attitude is encountered also in other places during the Middle Ages. The opposition of the European knights to firearms is well known, and it is a pity that until now no thorough research has been done into the role played by firearms in the process of the disintegration of European feudal society. I shall only quote here a passage from a lecture delivered on the BBC's Third Programme in April 1956: "The cruel art: this was Ariosto's name for the use of gunpowder in warfare. His voice was only one in a chorus of protest against the use of the new weapon. It was challenged on humanitarian grounds, attacked because it was un-Christian, reviled because it threatened to shatter the dream-castles of chivalry by enabling a base born gunner to blast a knight out of his saddle from afar. The use of gunpowder ran directly counter to the teaching of the Church and to the social code to which the vast majority of influential men subscribed." (*The Listener*, April 19, 1956.)

It is doubtful, however, that in any other military society there existed such an intense dislike of firearms as amongst the Mamluks. The European knights finally yielded to and adopted firearms, and the Ottomans, it seems, received them from the beginning without much difficulty. The Mamluks, on the other hand, persisted in their opposition to the very end and preferred destruction to the handling of these hateful arms. During the last days of their Sultanate, they had to fight almost simultaneously on two separate fronts, far removed from each other (against the Portuguese in the southeast and against the Ottomans in the north). They sent the majority of the units which employed firearms to the secondary, the Portuguese front, whereas they themselves fought on the main one, against the Ottomans. The Mamluks were armed mainly with bows, swords and lances, and, with these had to fight an enemy equipped with firearms! A battle of this kind could have only one outcome.

During the whole of Muslim history, there was never a large-scale battle between the armies of important Muslim states, in which the weapons employed by the opposing armies were so fundamentally different as in the battle fought by the Mamluks against the Ottomans in the years 1516 and 1517 and by the Persians against the same enemy in 1514. By these three victories the Ottomans succeeded, within two or three years and with only relatively few losses, in conquering huge areas in Asia and Africa, areas much larger than those they could occupy in Europe after numerous battles and much bloodshed over centuries. The Ottoman Empire could not have become so powerful in the Muslim world without its overwhelming superiority in firearms over its Muslim enemies.

Firearms were forced on the Mamluks after the Ottoman conquest, when they became incorporated into the Ottoman army, the best units of which were equipped with firearms. It should, however, be noted that now the Mamluks were not compelled to forsake their horses, since in the meantime new types of guns had been invented that could be easily fired from horseback. So the Mamluks never turned into infantrymen during the whole course of their long history in Egypt, from the middle of the thirteenth century to the beginning of the nineteenth. Not only did they not relinquish their horses, but they did not substantially change their ways of fighting as a result of their adoption of firearms.

A similar phenomenon occurred among the nomads of the Middle East. They, too, were not forced to abandon their horses, for they adopted firearms only after it was possible to handle them from horse or camel back. They, too, did not appreciably have to change their mode of combat as a result of the change of weapons. Their use of firearms was considerably facilitated because the gun was a simple weapon, easy to handle, which even a primitive man could fire without trouble. As a matter of fact, the handgun was the only firearm used by the nomads, and artillery gave the regular Muslim armies a considerable advantage over them.

One question which requires a somewhat detailed answer is why the attitude of the Ottomans towards firearms was so fundamentally different from that of the Mamluks. Although the history of firearms in the Ottoman Empire is still to be written, it is possible, nevertheless, to point out some of the reasons for the difference.

One decisive factor is found in the respective structures of the Ottoman and Mamluk military societies. Both systems were based on the following principle. Non-Muslim youths belonging to races well-known for their high military talent were brought to the capital. There they were taught the basic tenets of Islam, had the best military training and became excellent soldiers, faithful to Islam and loyal to their masters. So far the similarity, in an oversimplified presentation! Along with this, however, there were wide differences. The Ottoman Sultan himself was not an infidel converted to Islam. He was Muslim by birth, and was an hereditary heir of his office, the Ottoman Sultanate. The fact that a single dynasty ruled over the Ottoman

Empire from its birth around the year 1300 until its downfall in 1918, was of primary importance. The Mamluk Sultan, on the other hand, was a Mamluk like all the others. His juridical position was identical with that of any other Mamluk. The Sultanate, especially during the Circassian period, which was also the period of firearms, was not hereditary, and the Mamluks were loyal only to that particular Sultan who had bought and freed them. Whilst obedience and loyalty to one dynasty and to the ruling Sultan were the mark of the Ottoman Empire, in the Mamluk Sultanate military society was divided into rival factions, each loyal to a different Sultan, and this loyalty survived even after that Sultan's death or dethronement. Thus, the Ottoman Sultan could, in general, impose his will on his army, whereas the most that a Mamluk Sultan could hope for was to maintain a precarious balance between the contending Mamluk factions.

Only against this background, of a society torn from within by rival and contending groups, is it possible to understand the insurmountable difficulties that faced any Mamluk Sultan who wanted to compel these unruly horsemen to use firearms, weapons which they abhorred and whose use they considered degrading and shameful.

But difference in social structure was by no means the only reason for the great divergence of attitude towards firearms. Another reason was that firearms were introduced in the Mamluk Sultanate after it had already passed the peak of its power and was on the verge of a period of economic decline, whereas the Ottoman Empire adopted firearms during a period of rise, growth and expansion. Another factor: the Mamluks, until the last decades of their dominion, did not fight any external enemies who were equipped with firearms; the Europeans, who were the principal enemies of the Ottomans, used firearms on an ever increasing scale.

Yet another factor: the Mamluks did not have any real infantry units before the introduction of firearms; the Ottomans already possessed the Janissary corps d'élite which was composed mainly of such units, many years before the adoption of firearms.

And again, the Ottoman Empire possessed within its political confines the metals used for casting guns: the Mamluks had to import the bulk of these metals.

Let us conclude with two concrete examples, from contemporary history, which might help us to understand the full impact of a conservatism associated with ideas of horsemanship. Our own world of concepts is so completely different from that of the Middle Ages that we may tend to be skeptical about the influence of the psychological and social factors described in this paper.

In June 1956, I met the famous British military historian, Captain Liddell Hart, in England. He told me that he had himself encountered in the British Army of the twentieth century an attitude towards mechanization which was very similar to that of the Mamluks towards the use of firearms. As is known, Captain Liddell Hart occupied a central place in the fight for reforms in the British Army between the two World Wars; he was the advisor on military matters to the Secretary of State for War, Hoare Belisha, on the eve of the Second World War.

In the *Spectator* of 28 September 1956 he published an article on the occasion of the fourtieth anniversary of the introduction of the tank into warfare, for the first time in history, by the British. In this, he criticized the accepted view, that the reason why the British did not fully exploit the possibilities of the tank, since it had been invented by them, was that they regarded it as merely an auxiliary to infantry. In his view, there was a more decisive factor for the failure to develop and use the tank. He contended that whoever fought for greater armoured mobility in the British Army between the two World Wars, found to his regret that the persistent attachment of the British officers to the horse, an attachment which is particularly strong and widespread in England, was a basic obstacle in the way of military progress. Even during the years of financial stress, it would have been possible to do much more towards the modernization of the British Army, had there not existed a persistent reluctance to reduce the numbers of horsed cavalry.

Liddell Hart supported his thesis with quotations from the speeches of important personalities between the two World Wars. Despite the spectacular failure of the cavalry during the First World War, Field Marshal Earl Haig, who had been the British Commander-in-Chief on the Western Front, said in the summer of 1925: "Some enthusiasts today talk about the probability of horses becoming extinct and prophesy that the aeroplane, the tank and the motor car will supersede the horse in future wars. I believe that the value of the horse and the opportunity of the horse in the future are likely to be as great as ever. . . I am all for using aeroplanes and tanks, but they are only accessories to the man and the horse, and I feel that, as time goes on, you will find just as much use for the horse – the well-bred horse – as you have ever done in the past."

About a decade later, the Secretary of State for War, Duff Cooper, introduced the Army Estimates for 1934-35 under the new rearmament programme that followed Hitler's rise to power; he was warmly applauded by the Government benches when he declared: "I have had occasion during the past year to study military affairs . . . and the more I study them the more impressed I become by the importance of cavalry in modern warfare." In the following autumn, the Chief of the Imperial General Staff, General Sir Archibald Montgomery-Massingberd, emphatically declared that "we should go slow" with mechanization.

The source and support of this attitude were epitomized in a letter received by Liddell Hart at the time from a person unnamed: "An enormous number of influential people in the House and in the Counties are intensely pro-cavalry, without having any reasons for their convictions. A love of the horse and of hunting seems to blunt all their reasoning faculties."

Liddell Hart gave some examples from the past which testify to a similar attitude and he pointed out that, throughout a large part of British history, attachment to the horse was, more than in continental history, a cardinal bar to the full exploitation of firearms. Cromwell's army was able to defeat the Royalist army because it was free from this extravagant affection. At the end of his article he found in the Mamluks a parallel and striking precedent for the immense damage wrought by the military conservatism of a society of horsemen.

The other example, of an even more recent history, is the following one. In the summer of 1967, Harrison G. Salisbury, of the *New York Times*, visited the Soviet Union, where he met a most famous Soviet commander of the older Guard, and this is what he has to tell us about that meeting: "Budenny Recalls Soviet Setbacks."

> One bright July day last summer, Marshal Semyon M. Budenny, veteran of six wars and long an intimate of Stalin, was asked about the Soviet disasters in World War II. At 84, Marshal Budenny, his broad chest covered with eight rows of military medals, the first won in the Russo-Japanese war of 1905, is proud that he is still on active service in the cavalry. When asked whether cavalry would still play a role if World War III should come, Marshal Budenny was appalled. "A role?" he said indignantly, "The decisive role!" (The *New York Times*, October 10, 1967.)

Now, nobody in a key position in the Soviet Union from the end of World War II onwards would have paid the slightest attention to Budenny's views of how future wars, in which Russia might be involved, should be conducted. But things were different before that. In the years immediately preceding Hitler's attack on Russia, Budenny was First Deputy Commissar of Defense, and was thus personally responsible for the inadequate preparedness of the Soviet Army. During the early stages of the Nazi offensive he was entrusted with the command of the Southwestern front, which crumbled under the Nazi onslaught. He was removed from his post, and never was given a responsible command thereafter. The damage which he had caused, however, before his removal, must have been incalculable. He, personally, seems to have learnt nothing from his own bitter experience.

It seems to me that the conclusion is almost self-evident: if, in the twentieth century, amongst military circles in countries like Britain, the Soviet Union, and, undoubtedly, other important countries as well, deep-seated notions of horsemanship and cavalry were responsible for incalculable calamity in two World Wars, how much more so amongst the Mamluks of the Middle Ages? The Mamluks' defeat and downfall as the outcome of sociopsychological factors seems, therefore, to be logical and understandable.

INDEX